Collins
gem

Hockey Facts & Stats
2007–08

Andrew Podnieks

HarperCollins*PublishersLtd*

Collins Gem Hockey Facts & Stats 2007-08
Copyright © 2007 by Andrew Podnieks.
All rights reserved.

First edition

Published by Collins, an imprint of HarperCollins Publishers Ltd.

HarperCollins books may be purchased for educational, business, or sales
promotional use through our Special Markets Department.

HarperCollins Publishers Ltd
2 Bloor Street East, 20th Floor
Toronto, Ontario, Canada
M4W 1A8

www.harpercollins.ca

Library and Archives Canada Cataloguing in Publication

Podnieks, Andrew
Collins Gem hockey facts & stats 2007–08/ Andrew Podnieks—1st ed.

ISBN-13: 978-0-00-638513-4
ISBN-10: 0-00-638513-3

1. National Hockey League-Miscellanea. 2. Hockey-Miscellanea.
I. Title. II. Title: Collins Gem hockey facts and stats.

GV847.8.N3P573 2006 796.962´64 C2006-903985-2

WEBCOM 9 8 7 6 5 4 3 2 1

Contents

Introduction

When the Anaheim Ducks skated off with the Stanley Cup to end the 2006–07 season, they continued the trend of first-time champions begun by the Tampa Bay Lightning in 2004 and continued by the Carolina Hurricanes in 2006. The Ducks were also the sixth different team in as many finals to lay claim to hockey's most prized possession. The win capped a whirlwind season for Anaheim, one that began with two key acquisitions: defencemen Chris Pronger and Rob Niedermayer. The Ducks also benefited from the emergence of several young stars, notably Ryan Getzlaf, Corey Perry, Travis Moen, Dustin Penner and Samuel Pahlsson.

Their opponents in the finals were the Ottawa Senators, who were making their first appearance in the championship series. The Sens had so often provided fans with a great regular season, only to disappoint with an early playoff exit, but this year they found the ambition and determination to go all the way, as it were.

Over and above that final showdown, the 2006–2007 season provided fans with plenty of drama and entertainment. Evgeni Malkin and Jordan Staal emerged as two sensational rookies who played alongside 19-year-old Sidney Crosby, turning the Pittsburgh Penguins into the most talented young team in the league. At season's end, Crosby won the three most prestigious individual awards—the Hart, Lester B. Pearson and Art Ross. The Pens were the centre of more attention early in the year when Jim Balsillie agreed to buy the team, only to withdraw his offer at the last minute after limitations on moving the team were imposed on him.

Balsillie returned to the spotlight in April 2007 when he agreed to buy the Nashville Predators, then made a series of moves designed to transfer the team to Hamilton as quickly as possible.

For the first time since 1970, both Toronto and Montreal failed to make the playoffs. The Maple Leafs eliminated the Canadiens on the final Saturday of the schedule, only to suffer the same fate the next afternoon. The New York Islanders claimed the final Eastern Conference playoff berth in dramatic fashion, beating New Jersey in a shootout after the Devils tied the game with two seconds left in regulation time.

Two other notable teams missed the playoffs: Edmonton and Carolina. For the first time in NHL history, both Stanley Cup finalists from the previous year failed to qualify.

In international hockey, Canada asserted itself as the dominant power once again, as its representatives won gold medals in the World Junior Championship (for the third straight year), the World Women's Championship and the World Championship. In the latter tournament, the Canadian squad, led by Rick Nash and Shane Doan, defeated Finland 4–2 in Moscow in the gold-medal game. These wins paved the way for this coming year when, for the first time, Canada will host the World Championship. In May 2008, sixteen teams from around the world will meet in Quebec City and Halifax to contest the world hockey crown. The event is doubly significant because the International Ice Hockey Federation (IIHF) is celebrating its 100th anniversary in 2008.

Of course, this second edition of Collins *GEM: Hockey Facts and Stats* reflects the world of hockey, taking a look back at the past year as well as looking forward to the 2007–08 season. The statistical coverage is bigger and better this year and, in anticipation of the IIHF's centennial, the international section is more detailed.

Finally, there are several new sections which are intended to edify and enlighten both the die-hard and casual fan of the game. Enjoy!

Andrew Podnieks
August 2007

GLOSSARY OF ABBREVIATIONS

NHL Teams

ANA= Anaheim Ducks, ATL=Atlanta Thrashers, BOS=Boston Bruins, BUF=Buffalo Sabres, CAL=Calgary Flames, CAR=Carolina Hurricanes, CHI=Chicago Blackhawks, COL=Colorado Avalanche, CBJ=Columbus Blue Jackets, DAL=Dallas Stars, DET=Detroit Red Wings, EDM=Edmonton Oilers, FLO=Florida Panthers, LA=Los Angeles Kings, MIN=Minnesota Wild, MON=Montreal Canadiens, NAS=Nashville Predators, NJ=New Jersey Devils, NYI=New York Islanders, NYR=New York Rangers, OTT=Ottawa Senators, PHI=Philadelphia Flyers, PHO=Phoenix Coyotes, PIT=Pittsburgh Penguins, STL=St. Louis Blues, SJ=San Jose Sharks, TB=Tampa Bay Lightning, TOR=Toronto Maple Leafs, VAN=Vancouver Canucks, WAS=Washington Capitals

International

AUT	Austria	LTU	Lithuania
BLR	Belarus	NIG	Nigeria
CAN	Canada	NOR	Norway
CZE	Czech Republic	POL	Poland
FIN	Finland	RUS	Russia
FRA	France	SLO	Slovenia
GBR	Great Britain	SUI	Switzerland
GER	Germany	SVK	Slovakia
IRL	Ireland	SWE	Sweden
KAZ	Kazakhstan	UKR	Ukraine
LAT	Latvia	USA	United States

ANAHEIM DUCKS

(name changed from Mighty Ducks of Anaheim on June 22, 2006)
First Game Played: October 8, 1993
Detroit Red Wings 7 at Mighty Ducks of Anaheim 2
Nickname Provenance: Owners, Disney, named team after a popular kids' movie, *The Mighty Ducks* (1992)
Mascot: Wild Thing
Arena History: Arrowhead Pond, 1993–2006; Honda Centre 2006–present (capacity 17,174)
Retired Numbers: none
Hall of Famers: Players (1): Jari Kurri
Website: www.anaheimducks.com
Minor League Affiliate(s): Portland Pirates (AHL), Augusta Lynx (ECHL)
Stanley Cups: (1) 2006–07
Hosted All-Star Game: none
1st Overall Draft Choices: none

ATLANTA THRASHERS

First Game Played: October 2, 1999
New Jersey Devils 4 at Atlanta Thrashers 1
Nickname Provenance: The Brown Thrasher is the state bird of Georgia
Mascot: Thrash (b. September 4, 1999)
Arena History: Philips Arena, 1999–present (capacity 18,545)
Retired Numbers: Dan Snyder (43, unofficial)
Hall of Famers: none
Website: www. atlantathrashers.com
Minor League Affiliate(s): Chicago Wolves (AHL), Gwinnett Gladiators (ECHL)
Stanley Cups: none

Hosted All-Star Game: Will host 2008 game on January 16, 2008
1st Overall Draft Choices: 1999 (Patrik Stefan), 2001 (Ilya Kovalchuk)

BOSTON BRUINS

First Game Played: December 1, 1924
Montreal Maroons 1 at Boston Bruins 2
Nickname Provenance: Named by owner Art Ross for the brown bear
Mascot: Blades (b. October 9, 2000)
Arena History: Boston Arena, 1924–28; Boston Garden, 1928–95; FleetCenter, 1995–2003; TD Banknorth Garden (formerly known as the FleetCenter), 2005–present (capacity 17,565)
Retired Numbers: Eddie Shore (2), Lionel Hitchman (3), Bobby Orr (4), Dit Clapper (5), Phil Esposito (7), Cam Neely (8), Johnny Bucyk (9), Milt Schmidt (15), Terry O'Reilly (24), Ray Bourque (77)
Hall of Famers: Players (45): Marty Barry, Bobby Bauer, Leo Boivin, Ray Bourque, Frank Brimsek, Johnny Bucyk, Billy Burch, Gerry Cheevers, Dit Clapper, Sprague Cleghorn, Paul Coffey, Roy Conacher, Bun Cook, Bill Cowley, Cy Denneny, Woody Dumart, Phil Esposito, Fern Flaman, Frank Fredrickson, Harvey Jackson, Tom Johnson, Duke Keats, Guy Lapointe, Harry Lumley, Mickey MacKay, Sylvio Mantha, Joe Mullen, Cam Neely, Harry Oilver, Bobby Orr, Bernie Parent, Brad Park, Jacques Plante, Babe Pratt, Bill Quackenbush, Jean Ratelle, Art Ross (inducted as Player, associated with Boston as Builder), Terry Sawchuk, Milt Schmidt, Eddie Shore, Babe Siebert, Hooley Smith, Allan Stanley, Nels Stewart, Tiny Thompson, Cooney Weiland; Builders (5): Charles Adams, Weston Adams, Walter Brown, Bud Poile (played with Boston, inducted as Builder), Glen Sather (played with Boston, inducted as Builder), Harry Sinden
Website: www.bostonbruins.com
Minor League Affiliate(s): Providence Bruins (AHL)

Stanley Cups: (5) 1928–29, 1938–39, 1940–41, 1969–70, 1971–72
Hosted All-Star Game: (2) 1971, 1996
1st Overall Draft Choices: 1982 (Gord Kluzak),
1997 (Joe Thornton)

BUFFALO SABRES

First Game Played: October 10, 1970
Buffalo Sabres 2 at Pittsburgh Penguins 1
Nickname Provenance: a contest determined the name Sabres
Mascot: Sabre-Tooth
Arena History: Memorial Auditorium ("The Aud"), 1970–96;
Marine Midland Bank Arena, 1996–2000; HSBC Arena (formerly
known as the Marine Midland Bank Arena), 2000–present
(capacity 18,690)
Retired Numbers: Tim Horton (2), Rick Martin (7), Gilbert Perreault
(11), Rene Robert (14), Pat LaFontaine (16), Danny Gare (18)
Hall of Famers: Players (8): Dick Duff, Tim Horton, Gilbert
Perreault, Dale Hawerchuk, Clark Gillies, Grant Fuhr, Pat
LaFontaine, Marcel Pronovost (inducted as Player, associated
with Buffalo as Builder); Builders (4): Scotty Bowman, Punch
Imlach, Seymour Knox III, Roger Neilson
Website: www.sabres.com
Minor League Affiliate(s): Rochester Americans (AHL—shared
with Florida)
Stanley Cups: none
Hosted All-Star Game: 1978
1st Overall Draft Choices: 1970 (Gilbert Perreault),
1987 (PierreTurgeon)

CALGARY FLAMES

First Game Played:
As Atlanta Flames: October 7, 1972
Atlanta Flames 3 at New York Islanders 2

As Calgary Flames: October 9, 1980
Quebec Nordiques 5 at Calgary Flames 5
Nickname Provenance: Flames was chosen by contest, representative of Atlanta during the Civil War when much of it was burned to the ground
Mascot: Harvey the Hound
Arena History: The Omni (Atlanta), 1972–80; Stampede Corral, 1980–83; Olympic Saddledome, 1983–95; Canadian Airlines Saddledome, 1995–2001; Pengrowth Saddledome (same building as previous two Saddledomes), 2001–present (capacity 19,289)
Retired Numbers: Lanny McDonald (9), Mike Vernon (30)
Hall of Famers: Players (4): Lanny McDonald, Joe Mullen, Grant Fuhr, Al MacInnis; Builders (2): Cliff Fletcher, Harley Hotchkiss
Website: www.calgaryflames.com
Minor League Affiliate(s): Omaha Ak-Sar-Ben Knights (AHL), Las Vegas Wranglers (ECHL)
Stanley Cups: (1) 1988–89
Hosted All-Star Game: 1985
1st Overall Draft Choices: none

CAROLINA HURRICANES

First Game Played:
As Hartford Whalers: October 11, 1979
Hartford Whalers 1 at Minnesota North Stars 4
As Carolina Hurricanes: October 1, 1997
Carolina Hurricanes 2 at Tampa Bay Lightning 4
Nickname Provenance: Whalers adopted because it contained the letters of the WHA and it was emblematic of the region
Mascot: Stormy
Arena History: Springfield Civic Center (Hartford), 1979–80; Hartford Civic Center (Hartford), 1980–97; Greensboro Coliseum, 1997–99; Raleigh Entertainment & Sports Arena, 1999–2003; RBC Center, 2003–present (capacity 18,730)

Retired Numbers: Ron Francis (10)
Hall of Famers: Players (5): Paul Coffey (Hartford/Carolina),
Gordie Howe (Hartford), Bobby Hull (Hartford), Dave Keon
(Hartford), Ron Francis (Hartford/Carolina)
Website: www.carolinahcanes.com
Minor League Affiliate(s): Albany River Rats (AHL—shared with
Colorado), Florida Everblades (ECHL—shared with Florida)
Stanley Cups: 2005–06
Hosted All-Star Game: 1986 (as Hartford Whalers)
1st Overall Draft Choices: none

CHICAGO BLACKHAWKS

First Game Played: November 17, 1926
Toronto St. Pats 1 at Chicago Blackhawks 4
Nickname Provenance: (spelling changed from "Black Hawks" to
"Blackhawks" in 1986)
Mascot: none
Arena History: Chicago Coliseum, 1926–32; Chicago Stadium,
1932–94; United Center, 1995–present (opening of United Center
delayed by disruption of 1994–95 NHL season, capacity 20,500)
Retired Numbers: Glenn Hall (1), Bobby Hull (9), Denis Savard
(18), Stan Mikita (21), Tony Esposito (35)
Hall of Famers: Players (37): Sid Abel, Doug Bentley, Max Bentley,
Georges Boucher, Frank Brimsek, Billy Burch, Paul Coffey, Lionel
Conacher, Roy Conacher, Art Coulter, Babe Dye, Phil Esposito,
Tony Esposito, Bill Gadsby, Charlie Gardiner, Herb Gardiner,
Michel Goulet, Glenn Hall, George Hay, Bobby Hull, Duke Keats,
Hugh Lehman, Ted Lindsay, Harry Lumley, Mickey MacKay, Stan
Mikita, Howie Morenz, Bill Mosienko, Bert Olmstead, Bobby Orr,
Pierre Pilote, Denis Savard, Earl Seibert, Clint Smith, Allan Stanley,
Barney Stanley, Jack Stewart, Carl Voss (played for Chicago,
inducted as Builder), Harry Watson; Builders (10): Al Arbour, Emile
Francis (played for Chicago, inducted as Builder), Dick Irvin

(played for Chicago, inducted as Builder), Tommy Ivan, John
Mariucci (also played for Chicago), Major Frederic McLaughlin,
James Norris, James Norris, Jr., Rudy Pilous, Bud Poile (played for
Chicago, inducted as Builder), Arthur Wirtz, William Wirtz
Website: www.chicagoblackhawks.com
Minor League Affiliate(s): Norfolk Admirals (AHL), Greenville
Grrrowl (ECHL)
Stanley Cups: (3) 1933–34, 1937–38, 1960–61
Hosted All-Star Game: (4) 1948, 1961, 1974, 1991
1st Overall Draft Choices: Pat Kane

COLORADO AVALANCHE

First Game Played:
As Quebec Nordiques: October 10, 1979
Atlanta Flames 5 at Quebec Nordiques 3
As Colorado Avalanche: October 6, 1995
Detroit Red Wings 2 at Colorado Avalanche 3
Nickname Provenance: Team owners polled fans. Out of 8 names
offered, Avalanche was the most popular.
Mascot: Howler
Arena History: McNichols Sports Arena, 1995–99; Pepsi Center,
1999–present (capacity 18,007)
Retired Numbers: J-C Tremblay (3), Marc Tardif (8), Michel
Goulet (16), Peter Stastny (26), Patrick Roy (33), Ray Bourque (77)
Hall of Famers: Players (6): Ray Bourque, Patrick Roy, Michel Goulet
(Quebec), Jari Kurri, Guy Lafleur (Quebec), Peter Stastny (Quebec)
Website: www.coloradoavalanche.com
Minor League Affiliate(s): Albany River Rats (AHL—shared with
Carolina), Arizona Sun Dogs (CHL)
Stanley Cups: (2) 1995–96, 2000–01
Hosted All-Star Game: 2001
1st Overall Draft Choices: 1989 (Mats Sundin—Quebec Nordiques),
1990 (Owen Nolan—Quebec), 1991 (Eric Lindros—Quebec)

COLUMBUS BLUE JACKETS

First Game Played: October 7, 2000
Chicago Blackhawks 5 at Columbus Blue Jackets 3
Nickname Provenance: reflects patriotism and history of the Civil War
Mascot: Stinger
Arena History: Nationwide Arena, 2000–present (capacity 18,136)
Retired Numbers: none
Hall of Famers: none
Website: www. bluejackets.com
Minor League Affiliate(s): Syracuse Crunch (AHL), Dayton
Bombers (ECHL)
Stanley Cups: none
Hosted All-Star Game: none
1st Overall Draft Choices: 2002 (Rick Nash)

DALLAS STARS

First Game Played:
As Minnesota North Stars: October 11, 1967
Minnesota North Stars 2 at St. Louis Blues 2
As Dallas Stars: October 5, 1993
Detroit Red Wings 4 at Dallas Stars 6
Nickname Provenance: shortening of North Stars, consistent
with Texas as the Lone Star state
Mascot: none
Arena History: Metropolitan Sports Center (also known as the Met
Center), 1967–93; Reunion Arena, 1993–2001; American Airlines
Center, 2001–present (capacity 18,532)
Retired Numbers: Neal Broten (7), Bill Goldsworthy (8), Bill
Masterton (19)
Hall of Famers: Players (5): Mike Gartner (Minnesota), Harry
Howell (Minnesota), Larry Murphy (Minnesota), Gump Worsley
(Minnesota), Leo Boivin (Minnesota); Builders (3): Herb Brooks
(coached Minnesota), Glen Sather (played for University of
Minnesota), John Mariucci

Website: www.dallasstars.com
Minor League Affiliate(s): Iowa Stars (AHL), Idaho Steelheads (ECHL)
Stanley Cups: 1998–99
Hosted All-Star Game: 1972 (as North Stars); 2007
1st Overall Draft Choices: 1978 (Bobby Smith—Minnesota North Stars), 1983 (Brian Lawton—Minnesota), 1988 (Mike Modano—Minnesota)

DETROIT RED WINGS

First Game Played:
As Detroit Cougars: November 18, 1926
Boston Bruins 2 at Detroit Cougars 0
As Detroit Falcons: November 13, 1930
New York Rangers 0 at Detroit Falcons 1
As Detroit Red Wings: November 10, 1932
Chicago Blackhawks 1 at Detroit Red Wings 3
Nickname Provenance: Owner James Norris, a Montreal native, used the Winged Wheel from his hometown and combined it with Detroit's place in America as a car-making centre
Mascot: none
Arena History: Windsor Arena (Border Cities Arena), 1926–27; Olympia, 1929–79; Joe Louis Arena, 1979–present (capacity 20,066)
Retired Numbers: Terry Sawchuk (1), Ted Lindsay (7), Gordie Howe (9), Alex Delvecchio (10), Sid Abel (12), Steve Yzerman (19)
Hall of Famers: Players (45): Sid Abel, Jack Adams (inducted as Player, associated with Detroit as builder), Marty Barry, Andy Bathgate, Johnny Bucyk, Paul Coffey, Charlie Conacher, Roy Conacher, Alec Connell, Alex Delvecchio, Marcel Dionne, Bernie Federko, Slava Fetisov, Frank Foyston, Frank Fredrickson, Bill Gadsby, Ed Giacomin, Ebbie Goodfellow, Glenn Hall, Doug Harvey, George Hay, Harry Holmes, Gordie Howe, Syd Howe, Duke Keats, Red Kelly, Brian Kilrea (played for Detroit, inducted as Builder), Herbie Lewis, Ted Lindsay, Harry Lumley, Frank

Mahovlich, Larry Murphy, Reg Noble, Brad Park, Bud Poile (played for Detroit, inducted as Builder), Marcel Pronovost, Bill Quackenbush, Borje Salming, Terry Sawchuk, Earl Seibert, Darryl Sittler, Jack Stewart, Tiny Thompson, Norm Ullman, Jack Walker, Harry Watson, Cooney Weiland; Builders (9): Al Arbour (played for Detroit, inducted as Builder), Leo Boivin (played for Detroit, inducted as Builder), Scotty Bowman, Tommy Ivan, Bruce Norris, James Norris, James Norris, Jr., Carl Voss (played for Detroit, inducted as Builder)
Website: www.detroitredwings.com
Minor League Affiliate(s): Grand Rapids Griffins (AHL), Toledo Storm (ECHL)
Stanley Cups: (10) 1935–36, 1936–37, 1942–43, 1949–50, 1951–52, 1953–54, 1054–55, 1996–97, 1997–98, 2002–02
Hosted All-Star Game: (5) 1950, 1952, 1954, 1955, 1980
1st Overall Draft Choices: 1977 (Dale McCourt), 1986 (Joe Murphy)

EDMONTON OILERS

First Game Played: October 10, 1979
Edmonton Oilers 2 at Chicago Black Hawks 4
Nickname Provenance: from Alberta Oilers and later Edmonton Oilers of WHA, to refer to Alberta's place as an oil capital in Canada
Mascot: none
Arena History: Northlands Coliseum, 1979–99; Skyreach Centre, 1999–2003; Rexall Place, 2005–present (all three are the same building, capacity 16,839)
Retired Numbers: Al Hamilton (3), Mark Messier (11), Paul Coffey (7), Jari Kurri (17), Grant Fuhr (31), Wayne Gretzky (99—leaguewide recognition)
Hall of Famers: Players (5): Paul Coffey, Grant Fuhr, Wayne Gretzky, Jari Kurri, Mark Messier; Builders (1): Glen Sather
Website: www.edmontonoilers.com
Minor League Affiliate(s): Stockton Thunder (ECHL)
Stanley Cups: (5) 1983–84, 1984–85, 1986–87, 1987–88, 1989–90

Hosted All-Star Game: 1989
1st Overall Draft Choices: none

FLORIDA PANTHERS

First Game Played: October 6, 1993
Florida Panthers 4 at Chicago Blackhawks 4
Nickname Provenance: named for the animal, which is common in Florida
Mascot: Stanley C. Panther
Arena History: Miami Arena, 1993–99; National Car Rental Center, 1999–2002; Office Depot Center, 2002–03; BankAtlantic Center, 2005–present (previous three are the same building, capacity 19,250)
Retired Numbers: none
Hall of Famers: none
Website: www.floridapanthers.com
Minor League Affiliate(s): Rochester Americans (AHL—shared with Buffalo), Florida Everblades (ECHL—shared with Carolina)
Stanley Cups: none
Hosted All-Star Game: 2003
1st Overall Draft Choices: 1994 (Ed Jovanovski)

LOS ANGELES KINGS

First Game Played: October 14, 1967
Philadelphia Flyers 2 at Los Angeles Kings 4
Nickname Provenance: named by owner Jack Kent Cooke to give the team a royal (i.e., important) sound to it
Mascot: none
Arena History: Long Beach Arena, October 1967; Los Angeles Sports Arena, November–December 1967; The Forum, 1967–88; Great Western Forum, 1988–99 (same building as The Forum); Staples Center, 1999–present (capacity 18,118)
Retired Numbers: Marcel Dionne (16), Dave Taylor (18), Luc

Robitaille (20), Rogie Vachon (30), Wayne Gretzky (99—leaguewide recognition)
Hall of Famers: Players (13): Paul Coffey, Marcel Dionne, Dick Duff, Grant Fuhr, Wayne Gretzky, Harry Howell, Jari Kurri, Larry Murphy, Bob Pulford, Larry Robinson, Terry Sawchuk, Steve Shutt, Billy Smith; Builders (1): Brian Kilrea (played for Los Angeles, inducted as Builder)
Website: www.lakings.com
Minor League Affiliate(s): Manchester Monarchs (AHL), Reading Royals (ECHL)
Stanley Cups: none
Hosted All-Star Game: (2) 1981, 2002
1st Overall Draft Choices: none

MINNESOTA WILD

First Game Played: October 6, 2000
Minnesota Wild 1 at Mighty Ducks of Anaheim 3
Nickname Provenance: selected by fan contest
Mascot: none
Arena History: Xcel Energy Center, 2000–present (capacity 18,064)
Retired Numbers: none
Hall of Famers: none
Website: www.wild.com
Minor League Affiliate(s): Houston Aeros (AHL), Texas Wildcatters (ECHL), Austin Ice Bats (CHL)
Stanley Cups: none
Hosted All-Star Game: (1) 2004
1st Overall Draft Choices: none

MONTREAL CANADIENS

First Game Played:
In NHA: January 19, 1910
Montreal Canadiens 4 at Renfrew Millionaires 9
In NHL: December 19, 1917
Ottawa Senators 4 at Montreal Canadiens 7

Nickname Provenance: as a Canadian team based in Quebec, simply called Canadians in French (they are also known as "the Habs," short for "*les habitants*," a name given to the early settlers of the province)

Mascot: Youppi

Arena History: Westmount Arena, 1909–1918; Jubilee Arena, 1918–20; Mount Royal Arena, 1920–24; Montreal Forum, 1924–96 (refurbished in 1968); Molson Centre, 1996–2002; Bell Centre, 2002–present (same building as Molson Centre, capacity 21,273)

Retired Numbers: Jacques Plante (1), Doug Harvey (2), Jean Beliveau (4), Bernie Geoffrion (5), Howie Morenz (7), Maurice Richard (9), Guy Lafleur (10), Yvan Cournoyer (12), Dickie Moore (12), Henri Richard (16), Serge Savard (18), Ken Dryden (29)

Hall of Famers: Players (43): Marty Barry, Harry Cameron, Gord Drillon, Dick Duff, Tony Esposito, Rod Langway, Roy Worters, Dick Irvin (inducted as Player, associated with Montreal as Builder); Howie Morenz, Georges Vezina, Aurel Joliat, Newsy Lalonde, Joe Malone, Sprague Cleghorn, Herb Gardiner, Sylvio Mantha, Joe Hall, George Hainsworth, Maurice Richard, Jack Laviolette, Didier Pitre, Bill Durnan, Babe Siebert, Toe Blake, Emile Bouchard, Elmer Lach, Ken Reardon, Tom Johnson, Jean Beliveau, Bernie Geoffrion, Doug Harvey, Dickie Moore, Jacques Plante, Henri Richard, Patrick Roy, Gump Worsley, Frank Mahovlich, Yvan Cournoyer, Ken Dryden, Jacques Lemaire, Bert Olmstead, Serge Savard, Jacques Laperriere, Guy Lafleur, Buddy O'Connor, Bob Gainey, Guy Lapointe, Steve Shutt, Larry Robinson, Denis Savard; Builders (11): Cliff Fletcher, William Northey, Hon. Donat

Raymond, Frank Selke, Ambrose O'Brien, Leo Dandurand,
Tommy Gorman, Hon. Hartland de Montarville Molson, Joseph
Cattarinich, Sam Pollock, Scotty Bowman, Glen Sather (played
with Montreal, inducted as Builder)
Website: www.canadiens.com
Minor League Affiliate(s): Hamilton Bulldogs (AHL), Cincinnati
Cyclones (ECHL), Long Beach Ice Dogs (ECHL)
Stanley Cups: (23) 1923–24, 1929–30, 1930–31, 1943–44, 1945–46,
1952–53, 1955–56, 1956–57, 1957–58, 1958–59, 1959–60, 1964–65,
1065–66, 1967–68, 1968–69, 1970–71, 1972–73, 1975–76, 1976–77,
1977–78, 1978–79, 1985–86, 1992–93
Hosted All-Star Game: (11) 1953, 1956, 1957, 1958, 1959, 1960, 1965,
1967, 1969, 1975, 1993
1st Overall Draft Choices: 1969 (Rejean Houle), 1971 (Guy Lafleur),
1980 (Doug Wickenheiser)

NASHVILLE PREDATORS

First Game Played: October 10, 1998
Florida Panthers 1 at Nashville Predators 0
Nickname Provenance: selected by fans
Mascot: Gnash
Arena History: Gaylord Entertainment Center, 1998–2006;
Sommet Centre, 2007–present (capacity 17,113)
Retired Numbers: none
Hall of Famers: none
Website: www.nashvillepredators.com
Minor League Affiliate(s): Milwaukee Admirals (AHL)
Stanley Cups: none
Hosted All-Star Game: none
1st Overall Draft Choices: none

NEW JERSEY DEVILS

First Game Played:
As Kansas City Scouts: October 9, 1974
Kansas City Scouts 2 at Toronto Maple Leafs 6
As Colorado Rockies: October 5, 1976
Toronto Maple Leafs 2 at Colorado Rockies 4
As New Jersey Devils: October 5, 1982
Pittsburgh Penguins 3 at New Jersey Devils 3
Nickname Provenance: selected by fans in reference to legend of a demonic baby produced by one Mrs. Leeds in 1735, her 13th child
Mascot: The Devil
Arena History: Kemper Arena (Kansas City), 1974–76; McNichols Sports Arena (Colorado), 1976–82; Brendan Byrne Arena, 1982–83; Byrne Meadowlands Arena, 1983–92 (same building as Brendan Byrne Arena); Meadowlands Arena (same building as Byrne Meadowlands Arena), 1992–96; Continental Airlines Arena (same building as Meadowlands Arena), 1996–present (capacity 19,040)
Retired Numbers: Ken Daneyko (3), Scott Stevens (4)
Hall of Famers: Players (4): Slava Fetisov, Lanny McDonald (Colorado Rockies), Peter Stastny, Scott Stevens; Builders (1): Herb Brooks
Website: www.newjerseydevils.com
Minor League Affiliate(s): Lowell Devils (AHL)
Stanley Cups: (3) 1994–95, 1999–2000, 2002–03
Hosted All-Star Game: 1984
1st Overall Draft Choices: 1979 (Rob Ramage—Colorado Rockies)

NEW YORK ISLANDERS

First Game Played: October 7, 1972
Atlanta Flames 3 at New York Islanders 2
Nickname Provenance: named, simply, because the team is located on Long Island, New York
Mascot: none

Arena History: Nassau Veterans' Memorial Coliseum, 1972–present (capacity 16,234)
Retired Numbers: Denis Potvin (5), Clark Gillies (9), Bryan Trottier (19), Mike Bossy (22), Bob Nystrom (23), Billy Smith (31)
Hall of Famers: Players (6): Mike Bossy, Pat LaFontaine, Denis Potvin, Billy Smith, Bryan Trottier, Clark Gillies; Builders (2): Al Arbour, Bill Torrey
Website: www.newyorkislanders.com
Minor League Affiliate(s): Bridgeport Sound Tigers (AHL)
Stanley Cups: (4) 1979–80, 1980–81, 1981–82, 1982–83
Hosted All-Star Game: 1983
1st Overall Draft Choices: 1972 (Billy Harris), 1973 (Denis Potvin), 2000 (Rick DiPietro)

NEW YORK RANGERS

First Game Played: November 16, 1926
Montreal Maroons 0 at New York Rangers 1
Nickname Provenance: Emerged when sportswriters in New York called the new franchise Tex's Rangers, in reference to Tex Rickard, the president of Madison Square Garden and the man who assembled the executive for the team in 1926
Mascot: none
Arena History: Madison Square Garden, 1926–68; Madison Square Garden, 1968–present (newly built, capacity 18,200)
Retired Numbers: Ed Giacomin (1), Rod Gilbert (7), Mark Messier (11), Mike Richter (35)
Hall of Famers: Players (42): Dick Duff, Howie Morenz, Lester Patrick, Bill Cook, Frank Boucher, Ching Johnson, Babe Siebert, Earl Seibert, Doug Bentley, Max Bentley, Babe Pratt, Neil Colville, Bryan Hextall, Bill Gadsby, Terry Sawchuk, Bernie Geoffrion, Doug Harvey, Charlie Rayner, Art Coulter, Johnny Bower, Tim Horton, Andy Bathgate, Jacques Plante, Harry Howell, Lynn Patrick, Pat LaFontaine, Harry Lumley, Gump Worsley, Allan Stanley, Rod Gilbert, Phil Esposito, Jean Ratelle, Ed Giacomin, Guy Lafleur,

Buddy O'Connor, Brad Park, Clint Smith, Marcel Dionne, Edgar Laprade, Bun Cook, Wayne Gretzky, Mike Gartner, Jari Kurri, Mark Messier; Builders (7): Herb Brooks, Bud Poile (played with Rangers, inducted as Builder), Emile Francis (also played for Rangers), William Jennings, John Kilpatrick, Roger Neilson, Craig Patrick, Glen Sather (played with Rangers, inducted as Builder), Carl Voss (played with Rangers, inducted as Builder)
Website: www.newyorkrangers.com
Minor League Affiliate(s): Hartford Wolf Pack (AHL), Charlotte Checkers (ECHL—shared with Ottawa)
Stanley Cups: (4) 1927–28, 1932–33, 1939–40, 1993–94
Hosted All-Star Game: (2) 1973, 1994
1st Overall Draft Choices: none

OTTAWA SENATORS

First Game Played: October 8, 1992
Montreal Canadiens 3 at Ottawa Senators 5
Nickname Provenance: from original team of same name from 1917–34
Mascot: Spartacat
Arena History: Civic Centre, 1992–96; Palladium, 1996; Corel Centre, 1996–2006; Scotiabank Place, 2006–present (same building as Palladium and Corel Centre, capacity 19,153)
Retired Numbers: Frank Finnigan (8)
Hall of Famers: none
Website: www.ottawasenators.com
Minor League Affiliate(s): Binghamton Senators (AHL), Charlotte Checkers (ECHL—shared with NY Rangers)
Stanley Cups: none
Hosted All-Star Game: none
1st Overall Draft Choices: 1993 (Alexandre Daigle), 1995 (Bryan Berard), 1996 (Chris Phillips)

PHILADELPHIA FLYERS

First Game Played: October 11, 1967
Philadelphia Flyers 1 at Oakland Seals 5
Nickname Provenance: named by a nine-year-old in a fan contest
Mascot: none
Arena History: The Spectrum, 1967–96; CoreStates Center, 1996–98; First Union Center, 1998–2003 (same building as CoreStates Center); Wachovia Center, 2003–present (same building as First Union Center, capacity 19,523)
Retired Numbers: Bernie Parent (1), Barry Ashbee (4), Bill Barber (7), Bobby Clarke (16)
Hall of Famers: Players (4): Paul Coffey, Bernie Parent, Bobby Clarke, Bill Barber, Dale Hawerchuk, Darryl Sittler, Allan Stanley; Builders (2): Ed Snider, Keith Allen
Website: www.philadelphiaflyers.com
Minor League Affiliate(s): Philadelphia Phantoms (AHL), Trenton Titans (ECHL)
Stanley Cups: (2) 1973–74, 1974–75
Hosted All-Star Game: (2) 1976, 1992
1st Overall Draft Choices: 1975 (Mel Bridgman)

PHOENIX COYOTES

First Game Played:
As Winnipeg Jets: October 10, 1979
Winnipeg Jets 2 at Pittsburgh Penguins 4
As Phoenix Coyotes: October 5, 1996
Phoenix Coyotes 0 at Hartford Whalers 1
Nickname Provenance: the logo depicts a Kachina coyote, indigenous to the region
Mascot: none
Arena History: Winnipeg Arena (Winnipeg), 1979–96; America West Arena, 1996–98; Cellular One Ice Den (same building as America West Arena), 1998–99; America West Arena, 1999–2000; Alltel Ice Den, 2000–03; Glendale Arena, 2003–present (capacity 17,799)

Retired Numbers: Bobby Hull (9), Thomas Steen (25)
Hall of Famers: Players (3): Mike Gartner, Bobby Hull (Winnipeg), Dale Hawerchuk (Winnipeg), Serge Savard (Winnipeg)
Website: www.phoenixcoyotes.com
Minor League Affiliate(s): San Antonio Rampage (AHL), Phoenix RoadRunners (ECHL), Laredo Bucks (CHL)
Stanley Cups: none
Hosted All-Star Game: none
1st Overall Draft Choices: 1981 (Dale Hawerchuk—Winnipeg Jets)

PITTSBURGH PENGUINS

First Game Played: October 11, 1967
Montreal Canadiens 2 at Pittsburgh Penguins 1
Mascot: Iceburgh
Arena History: Civic Arena ("The Igloo"), 1967–2000; Mellon Arena, 2000–present (same building as Civic Arena, capacity 16,940)
Retired Numbers: Michel Briere (21), Mario Lemieux (66)
Hall of Famers: Players (9): Leo Boivin, Paul Coffey, Tim Horton, Red Kelly (inducted as Player, associated with Pittsburgh as Builder), Andy Bathgate, Mario Lemieux, Larry Murphy, Bryan Trottier, Joe Mullen, Ron Francis; Builders (4): Scotty Bowman, Bob Johnson, Craig Patrick, Glen Sather (played for Pittsburgh, inducted as Builder)
Website: www.pittsburghpenguins.com
Minor League Affiliate(s): Wilkes-Barre/Scranton Penguins (AHL), Wheeling Nailers (ECHL)
Stanley Cups: (2) 1990–91, 1991–92
Hosted All-Star Game: 1990
1st Overall Draft Choices: 1984 (Mario Lemieux), 2003 (Marc-Andre Fleury), 2005 (Sidney Crosby)

ST. LOUIS BLUES

First Game Played: October 11, 1967
Minnesota North Stars 2 at St. Louis Blues 2
Nickname Provenance: named to remember the city's place in the history of music
Mascot: none
Arena History: St. Louis Arena, 1967–94; Kiel Center, 1994–2000; Savvis Center, 2000–present (same building as Kiel Center, capacity 19,022)
Retired Numbers: Al MacInnis (2), Bob Gassoff (3), Barclay Plager (8), Brian Sutter (11), Brett Hull (16), Bernie Federko (24)
Hall of Famers: Players (11): Grant Fuhr, Bernie Federko, Dale Hawerchuk, Joe Mullen, Wayne Gretzky, Peter Stastny, Guy Lapointe, Jacques Plante, Glenn Hall, Dickie Moore, Doug Harvey, Al MacInnis, Scott Stevens; Builders (5): Roger Neilson, Al Arbour, Scotty Bowman, Emile Francis, Craig Patrick (played for St. Louis, inducted as Builder), Lynn Patrick, Glen Sather (played for St. Louis, inducted as Builder)
Website: www.stlouisblues.com
Minor League Affiliate(s): Peoria Rivermen (AHL), Alaska Aces (ECHL)
Stanley Cups: none
Hosted All-Star Game: (2) 1970, 1988
1st Overall Draft Choices: none

SAN JOSE SHARKS

First Game Played: October 4, 1991
San Jose Sharks 3 at Vancouver Canucks 4
Nickname Provenance: named by team owners after a fan contest
Mascot: S.J. Sharkie (b. January 1992)
Arena History: Cow Palace, 1991–93; San Jose Arena, 1993–2001; Compaq Center, 2001–03; HP Pavilion, 2003–present (same building as Compaq Center and San Jose Arena, capacity 17,496)
Retired Numbers: none

Hall of Famers: none
Website: www.sjsharks.com
Minor League Affiliate(s): Worcester Sharks (AHL), Fresno
Falcons (ECHL), Toledo Storm (ECHL)
Stanley Cups: none
Hosted All-Star Game: 1997
1st Overall Draft Choices: none

TAMPA BAY LIGHTNING

First Game Played: October 7, 1992
Chicago Blackhawks 3 at Tampa Bay Lightning 7
Mascot: Thunder Bug
Arena History: Expo Hall, 1992–93; ThunderDome, 1993–96
(five home games played at Orlando Arena); Ice Palace,
1998–2003; *St. Petersburg Times* Forum, 2003–present (same build-
ing as Ice Palace, capacity 19,758)
Retired Numbers: none
Hall of Famers: Players (1): Denis Savard
Website: www.tampabaylightning.com
Minor League Affiliate(s): Springfield Falcons (AHL), Johnstown
Chiefs (ECHL)
Stanley Cups: 2003–04
Hosted All-Star Game: 1999
1st Overall Draft Choices: 1992 (Roman Hamrlik), 1998 (Vincent
Lecavalier)

TORONTO MAPLE LEAFS

First Game Played:
As Toronto Arenas: December 19, 1917
Toronto Arenas 9 at Montreal Wanderers 10
As Toronto St. Pats: December 23, 1919
Toronto St. Pats 0 at Ottawa Senators 3
As Toronto Maple Leafs: February 17, 1927
New York Americans 1 at Toronto Maple Leafs 4

Nickname Provenance: named by owner Conn Smythe after a World War I regiment

Mascot: Carlton the Bear

Arena History: Arena Gardens (Mutual Street Arena), 1917–31; Maple Leaf Gardens, 1931–99; Air Canada Centre, 1999–present (capacity 18,819)

Retired Numbers: Bill Barilko (5), Ace Bailey (6)

Honoured Numbers: Turk Broda (1), Johnny Bower (1), Red Kelly (4), King Clancy (7), Tim Horton (7), Charlie Conacher (9), Ted Kennedy (9), Syl Apps (10), George Armstrong (10), Borje Salming (21), Frank Mahovlich (27), Darryl Sittler (27)

Hall of Famers: Players (59): Jack Adams, Syl Apps, Al Arbour, George Armstrong, Ace Bailey, Andy Bathgate, Max Bentley, Leo Boivin, Johnny Bower, Turk Broda, Harry Cameron, Gerry Cheevers, King Clancy, Sprague Cleghorn, Charlie Conacher, Rusty Crawford, Hap Day, Gord Drillon, Dick Duff, Babe Dye, Fern Flaman, Grant Fuhr, Mike Gartner, Eddie Gerard, George Hainsworth, Harry Holmes, Red Horner, Tim Horton, Syd Howe, Harvey Jackson, Red Kelly, Ted Kennedy, Dave Keon, Harry Lumley, Frank Mahovlich, Lanny McDonald, Dickie Moore, Larry Murphy, Frank Nighbor, Reg Noble, Bert Olmstead, Bernie Parent, Pierre Pilote, Jacques Plante, Babe Pratt, Joe Primeau, Marcel Pronovost, Bob Pulford, Borje Salming, Terry Sawchuk, Sweeney Schriner, Darryl Sittler, Allan Stanley, Norm Ullman, Carl Voss, Harry Watson, Ron Francis; Builders (9): Harold Ballard, J.P. Bickell, Cliff Fletcher, Foster Hewitt, William Hewitt, Punch Imlach, Dick Irvin (played for Toronto, inducted as Builder), Frank Mathers (played for Toronto, inducted as Builder), Rudy Pilous, Bud Poile (played for Toronto, inducted as Builder), Frank Selke, Conn Smythe

Website: www.torontomapleleafs.com

Minor League Affiliate(s): Toronto Marlies (AHL), Columbia Inferno (ECHL)

Stanley Cups: (13) 1917–18, 1921–22, 1931–32, 1941–42, 1944–45, 1946–47, 1947–48, 1948–49, 1950–51, 1961–62, 1962–63, 1963–64, 1966–67

Hosted All-Star Game: (8) 1947, 1949, 1951, 1962, 1963, 1964, 1968, 2000
1st Overall Draft Choices: 1985 (Wendel Clark)

VANCOUVER CANUCKS

First Game Played: October 9, 1970
Los Angeles Kings 3 at Vancouver Canucks 1
Nickname Provenance: continuation of WHL franchise nickname
Mascot: none
Arena History: Pacific Coliseum, 1970–95; General Motors (GM) Place, 1995–present (capacity 18,630)
Retired Numbers: Wayne Maki (11, unofficial, later worn by Mark Messier but not before or since), Stan Smyl (12)
Hall of Famers (2): Cam Neely, Mark Messier
Website: www.canucks.com
Minor League Affiliate(s): Manitoba Moose (AHL), Victoria Salmon Kings (ECHL)
Stanley Cups: none
Hosted All-Star Game: (2) 1977, 1998
1st Overall Draft Choices: none

WASHINGTON CAPITALS

First Game Played: October 9, 1974
Washington Capitals 3 at New York Rangers 6
Nickname Provenance: so called because the team plays in the capital city of the USA
Mascot: Slapshot
Arena History: Capital Center, 1974–93; US Air Arena, 1993–95; (same building as Capital Center); MCI Center, 1995–present, Verizon Center (same building as MCI Center—capacity 18,277)
Retired Numbers: Rod Langway (5), Yvon Labre (7), Dale Hunter (32)
Hall of Famers: Players (4): Mike Gartner, Rod Langway, Larry Murphy, Scott Stevens; Builders (1): Craig Patrick (played for Washington, inducted as Builder)

Website: www.washingtoncaps.com
Minor League Affiliate(s): Hershey Bears (AHL), South Carolina Stingrays (ECHL)
Stanley Cups: none
Hosted All-Star Game: 1982
1st Overall Draft Choices: 1974 (Greg Joly), 1976 (Rick Green), (2005) Alexander Ovechkin

FINAL STANDINGS, REGULAR SEASON, 2006–07

EASTERN CONFERENCE

Atlantic Division	GP	W	L	OT	GF	GA	P
New Jersey	82	49	24	9	216	201	107
Pittsburgh	82	47	24	11	277	246	105
NY Rangers	82	42	30	10	242	216	94
NY Islanders	82	40	30	12	248	240	92
Philadelphia	82	22	48	12	214	303	56

Northeast Division							
Buffalo	82	53	22	7	308	242	113
Ottawa	82	48	25	9	288	222	105
Toronto	82	40	31	11	258	269	91
Montreal	82	42	34	6	245	256	90
Boston	82	35	41	6	219	289	76

Southeast Division							
Atlanta	82	43	28	11	246	245	97
Tampa Bay	82	44	33	5	253	261	93
Carolina	82	40	34	8	241	253	88
Florida	82	35	31	16	247	257	86
Washington	82	28	40	14	235	286	70

WESTERN CONFERENCE

Central Division							
Detroit	82	50	19	13	254	199	113
Nashville	82	51	23	8	272	212	110
St. Louis	82	34	35	13	214	254	81
Columbus	82	33	42	7	201	249	73
Chicago	82	31	42	9	201	258	71

Northwest Division

Vancouver	82	49	26	7	222	201	105
Minnesota	82	48	26	8	235	191	104
Calgary	82	43	29	10	258	226	96
Colorado	82	44	31	7	272	251	95
Edmonton	82	32	43	7	195	248	71

Pacific Division

Anaheim	82	48	20	14	258	208	110
San Jose	82	51	26	5	258	199	107
Dallas	82	50	25	7	226	197	107
Los Angeles	82	27	41	14	227	283	68
Phoenix	82	31	46	5	216	284	67

Carolina won Stanley Cup best-of-seven 4–3.

NUMBERS RETIRED & OTHER CAREER HONOURS, 2006–07

Boston—Johnny Bucyk, February 13, 2007 (honoured for his 50 years with the Bruins)

Buffalo—Phil Housley, February 7, 2007 (inducted into Sabres' hall of fame in pre-game ceremony)

Calgary—Mike Vernon, February 6, 2007 (retired #30)

Detroit—Steve Yzerman, January 2, 2007 (retired #19)

Edmonton—Mark Messier, February 27, 2007 (retired #11)

Los Angeles—Luc Robitaille, January 20, 2007 (retired #20)

Montreal—Serge Savard, November 18, 2006 (retired #18); Ken Dryden, January 29, 2007 (retired #29)

Philadelphia—Keith Primeau, February 12, 2007 (night in his honour)

Pittsburgh—Mario Lemieux, October 5, 2006 (#66 raised to the rafters again after his final retirement; it had been taken down when he returned to the game after his first retirement in 1996)

St. Louis—Brett Hull, December 5, 2006 (retired #16)

Tampa Bay—Dave Andreychuk, December 5, 2006 (night in his honour)

Toronto—Red Kelly, October 4, 2006 (honoured #4); Borje Salming, October 4, 2006 (honoured #21)

SCORING LEADERS & GOALIE LEADERS, 2006–07

(Nationality and NHL affiliation appear in parentheses)

Points	GP	G	A	P	PIM
Sidney Crosby (CAN–PIT)	79	36	84	120	60
Joe Thornton (CAN–SJ)	82	22	92	114	44
Vincent Lecavalier (CAN–TB)	82	52	56	108	44
Dany Heatley (CAN–OTT)	82	50	55	105	74
Martin St. Louis (CAN–TB)	82	43	59	102	28
Marian Hossa (SVK–ATL)	82	43	57	100	49
Joe Sakic (CAN–COL)	82	36	64	100	46
Jaromir Jagr (CZE–NYR)	82	30	66	96	78
Marc Savard (CAN–BOS)	82	22	74	96	96
Daniel Briere (CAN–BUF)	81	32	63	95	89

Goals

Vincent Lecavalier (CAN–TB)	52
Dany Heatley (CAN–OTT)	50
Teemu Selanne (FIN–ANA)	48
Alexander Ovechkin (RUS–WAS)	46
Martin St. Louis (CAN–TB)	43
Marian Hossa (SVK–ATL)	43
Thomas Vanek (AUT–BUF)	43
Ilya Kovalchuk (RUS–ATL)	42
Simon Gagne (CAN–PHI)	41
Jason Blake (USA–NYI)	40

Assists

Joe Thornton (CAN–SJ)	92
Sidney Crosby (CAN–PIT)	84
Marc Savard (CAN–BOS)	74
Henrik Sedin (SWE–VAN)	71

Jaromir Jagr (CZE–NYR)   66
Joe Sakic (CAN–COL)   64
Daniel Briere (CAN–BUF)   63
Pavel Datsyuk (RUS–DET)   60
Martin St. Louis (CAN–TB)   59
Alex Tanguay (CAN–CAL)   59

Penalty Minutes

Ben Eager (CAN–PHI)   233
Josh Gratton (CAN–PHO)   188
Chris Neil (CAN–OTT)   177
Shane O'Brien (CAN–TB)   176
Sean Avery (CAN–NYR)   174
Donald Brashear (USA–WAS)   156
Alexander Svitov (RUS–CBJ)   145
Raitis Ivanins (LAT–LA)   140
Nick Boynton (CAN–PHO)   138
Sheldon Souray (CAN–MON)   135

Most Wins, Goalie

Martin Brodeur (CAN–NJ)   48
Roberto Luongo (CAN–VAN)   47
Marc–Andre Fleury (CAN–PIT)   40
Ryan Miller (USA–BUF)   40
Miikka Kiprusoff (FIN–CAL)   40
Dominik Hasek (CZE–DET)   38
Marty Turco (CAN–DAL)   38
Henrik Lundqvist (SWE–NYR)   37
Andrew Raycroft (CAN–TOR)   37
J–S Giguere (CAN–ANA)   36

Most Losses, Goalie

Dwayne Roloson (CAN–EDM)   34
Curtis Joseph (CAN–PHO)   31

Tim Thomas (USA–BOS)	29
Antero Niittymaki (FIN–PHI)	29
Nikolai Khabibulin (RUS–CHI)	26
Andrew Raycroft (CAN–TOR)	25
Miikka Kiprusoff (FIN–CAL)	24
Kari Lehtonen (FIN–ATL)	24
Olaf Kolzig (GER–WAS)	24
Martin Brodeur (CAN–NJ)	23
Fredrik Norrena (FIN–CBJ)	23

Best GAA

Niklas Backstrom (FIN–MIN)	1.97
Dominik Hasek (CZE–DET)	2.05
Martin Brodeur (CAN–NJ)	2.18
Marty Turco (CAN–DAL)	2.23
J–S Giguere (CAN–ANA)	2.26
Roberto Luongo (CAN–VAN)	2.29
Evgeni Nabokov (RUS–SJ)	2.29
Henrik Lundqvist (SWE–NYR)	2.34
Vesa Toskala (FIN–SJ)	2.35
Chris Mason (CAN–NAS)	2.38

GOALIE SCORING STATISTICS, 2006–07

Goalie	G	A	P	Pim
David Aebischer	0	0	0	2
Craig Anderson	0	0	0	0
J-S Aubin	0	0	0	0
Alexander Auld	0	1	1	2
Jason Bacashihua	0	0	0	2
Niklas Backstrom	0	1	1	2
Ed Belfour	0	2	2	10
Martin Biron	0	0	0	25
Brian Boucher	0	0	0	0
Martin Brodeur	0	1	1	12
Barry Brust	0	0	0	0
Ilya Bryzgalov	0	0	0	0
Peter Budaj	0	2	2	0
Sean Burke	0	1	1	4
Sebastien Caron	0	0	0	0
Frederic Cassivi	0	0	0	0
Scott Clemmensen	0	0	0	0
Dan Cloutier	0	1	1	21
Ty Conklin	0	0	0	2
Marc Denis	0	0	0	2
Rick DiPietro	0	2	2	24
Wade Dubielewicz	0	0	0	0
Mike Dunham	0	1	1	0
Ray Emery	0	1	1	30
Robert Esche	0	2	2	2
Manny Fernandez	0	0	0	12
Brian Finley	0	0	0	0
Marc-Andre Fleury	0	3	3	4
Yutaka Fukufuji	0	0	0	0
Mathieu Garon	0	1	1	6

Goalie	G	A	P	Pim
Martin Gerber	0	0	0	0
J-S Giguere	0	2	2	0
John Grahame	0	3	3	2
Jaroslav Halak	0	1	1	2
Josh Harding	0	0	0	0
Dominik Hasek	0	2	2	20
Johan Hedberg	0	1	1	6
Johan Holmqvist	0	3	3	4
Martin Houle	0	0	0	0
Cristobal Huet	0	1	1	0
Brent Johnson	0	1	1	4
Curtis Joseph	0	0	0	10
Nikolai Khabibulin	0	0	0	8
Miikka Kiprusoff	0	0	0	2
Olaf Kolzig	0	3	3	10
Patrick Lalime	0	0	0	0
Pascal Leclaire	0	0	0	2
Manny Legace	0	0	0	2
Kari Lehtonen	0	1	1	6
Michael Leighton	0	0	0	0
David LeNeveu	0	0	0	0
Henrik Lundqvist	0	0	0	0
Roberto Luongo	0	2	2	10
Joey MacDonald	0	0	0	0
Jussi Markkanen	0	0	0	0
Chris Mason	0	1	1	4
Jamie McLennan	0	0	0	16
Ryan Miller	0	2	2	2
Michael Morrison	0	0	0	0
Evgeni Nabokov	0	0	0	6
Antero Niittymaki	0	0	0	2
Fredrik Norrena	0	0	0	6
Chris Osgood	0	1	1	6

Goalie	G	A	P	Pim
Tomas Popperle	0	0	0	0
Karri Ramo	0	0	0	0
Andrew Raycroft	0	1	1	8
Dwayne Roloson	0	3	3	12
Dany Sabourin	0	0	0	0
Curtis Sanford	0	0	0	0
Philippe Sauve	0	0	0	0
Marek Schwarz	0	0	0	0
Mike Smith	0	0	0	2
Mikael Tellqvist	0	1	1	0
Jose Theodore	0	1	1	6
Jocelyn Thibault	0	0	0	0
Tim Thomas	0	0	0	6
Hannu Toivonen	0	0	0	2
Vesa Toskala	0	3	3	0
Marty Turco	0	4	4	18
Stephen Valiquette	0	0	0	0
Tomas Vokoun	0	2	2	4
Michael Wall	0	1	1	0
Cam Ward	0	1	1	6
Kevin Weekes	0	0	0	0

GAMES PLAYED, 2006–07

(arranged by most games, team, alphabetical)

Player	GP
Sean Avery (LA-NYR)	84
Ryan Getzlaf (ANA)	82
Andy McDonald (ANA)	82
Travis Moen (ANA)	82
Rob Niedermayer (ANA)	82
Samuel Pahlsson (ANA)	82
Dustin Penner (ANA)	82
Corey Perry (ANA)	82
Teemu Selanne (ANA)	82
Bobby Holik (ATL)	82
Marian Hossa (ATL)	82
Ilya Kovalchuk (ATL)	82
Greg de Vries (ATL)	82
Marc Savard (BOS)	82
Brian Campbell (BUF)	82
Dmitri Kalinin (BUF)	82
Adam Mair (BUF)	82
Jason Pominville (BUF)	82
Thomas Vanek (BUF)	82
Craig Adams (CAR)	82
Mike Commodore (CAR)	82
Eric Staal (CAR)	82
Justin Williams (CAR)	82

Player	GP
Duncan Keith (CHI)	82
Martin Lapointe (CHI)	82
Tyler Arnason (COL)	82
Andrew Brunette (COL)	82
Brett Clark (COL)	82
Joe Sakic (COL)	82
Paul Stastny (COL)	82
Jason Chimera (CBJ)	82
Manny Malhotra (CBJ)	82
David Vyborny (CBJ)	82
Stu Barnes (DAL)	82
Niklas Hagman (DAL)	82
Jussi Jokinen (DAL)	82
Kirk Maltby (DET)	82
Jason Smith (EDM)	82
Petr Sykora (EDM)	82
Raffi Torres (EDM)	82
Bryan Allen (FLO)	82
Jay Bouwmeester (FLO)	82
Martin Gelinas (FLO)	82
Nathan Horton (FLO)	82
Olli Jokinen (FLO)	82
Ruslan Salei (FLO)	82
Alexander Frolov (LA)	82
Aaron Miller (LA)	82

Player	GP
P-M Bouchard (MIN)	82
Mikko Koivu (MIN)	82
Branko Radivojevic (MIN)	82
Nick Schultz (MIN)	82
Mike Komisarek (MON)	82
Michael Ryder (MON)	82
J-P Dumont (NAS)	82
Paul Kariya (NAS)	82
Ryan Suter (NAS)	82
Sergei Brylin (NJ)	82
Jamie Langenbrunner (NJ)	82
Paul Martin (NJ)	82
Jay Pandolfo (NJ)	82
Zach Parise (NJ)	82
Brian Rafalski (NJ)	82
Jason Blake (NYI)	82
Richard Park (NYI)	82
Mike Sillinger (NYI)	82
Blair Betts (NYR)	82
Jaromir Jagr (NYR)	82
Dany Heatley (OTT)	82
Chris Kelly (OTT)	82
Andrej Meszaros (OTT)	82
Chris Neil (OTT)	82
Chris Phillips (OTT)	82

Player	GP
Derian Hatcher (PHI)	82
Zbynek Michalek (PHO)	82
Derek Morris (PHO)	82
Sergei Gonchar (PIT)	82
Mark Recchi (PIT)	82
Christian Ehrhoff (SJ)	82
Joe Thornton (SJ)	82
Eric Brewer (STL)	82
Radek Dvorak (STL)	82
Lee Stempniak (STL)	82
Doug Weight (STL)	82
Dan Boyle (TB)	82
Vincent Lecavalier (TB)	82
Eric Perrin (TB)	82
Vaclav Prospal (TB)	82
Brad Richards (TB)	82
Cory Sarich (TB)	82
Martin St. Louis (TB)	82
Bates Battaglia (TOR)	82
Hal Gill (TOR)	82
Bryan McCabe (TOR)	82
Matt Stajan (TOR)	82
Alex Steen (TOR)	82
Markus Naslund (VAN)	82
Henrik Sedin (VAN)	82

Player	GP
Brendan Morrison (VAN)	82
Bryan Smolinski (VAN)	82
Alexander Ovechkin (WAS)	82

PLAYERS WHO PLAYED IN 2005–06, BUT NOT IN 2006–07

PLAYER	2006–07 STATUS
Albelin, Tommy	retired
Allison, Jamie	played in AHL (Binghamton)
Allison, Jason	retired
Andreychuk, Dave	retired
Artyukhin, Evgeni	played in Russia (Yaroslavl)
Aubin, Serge	played in Switzerland (Geneva)
Balej, Josef	played in Switzerland (Fribourg)
Barinka, Michal	played in Czech Republic (Vitkovice)
Barney, Scott	played mostly in AHL (Hershey)
Bartovic, Milan	played in Switzerland (Zurich)
Belanger, Ken	retired
Berg, Aki	played in Finland (TPS Turku)
Bergenheim, Sean	played in Sweden (Frolunda)
Berkhoel, Adam	played mostly in ECHL (Dayton)
Biron, Mathieu	played in AHL (mostly Hamilton)
Blatny, Zdenek	played in AHL (Springfield) and Sweden (MoDo)
Bouchard, Joel	played briefly in AHL
Boughner, Bob	retired
Boulerice, Jesse	played in AHL (Albany)
Brendl, Pavel	played in Sweden (Mora)
Brennan, Kip	played mostly in AHL (Hershey)
Brown, Mike	retired
Brown, Sean	played in Germany (DEG)
Butenschon, Sven	played in Germany (Mannheim)
Caldwell, Ryan	played in AHL (Syracuse)
Campbell, Jim	played in Switzerland (Basel)
Carkner, Matt	played in AHL (Wilkes-Barre/Scranton)
Cassels, Andrew	retired
Chouinard, Eric	played in Germany (Straubing)

Cibak, Martin	played in Sweden (Frolunda)
Coleman, Gerald	played in AHL & ECHL
Colley, Kevin	retired
Collins, Rob	played in Germany (DEG)
Cote, Jean-Philippe	played in AHL (Hamilton)
Crawford, Corey	played in AHL (Norfolk)
Cross, Cory	played in Germany (Hamburg)
Czerkawski, Mariusz	played in Switzerland (Rapperswil)
Dagenais, Pierre	played in Austria & Finland
Daigle, Alexandre	played in Switzerland (Davos)
Danis, Jann	unknown
Daze, Eric	retired
Delmore, Andy	played in AHL (Springfield & Chicago)
Desjardins, Eric	retired
DiMaio, Rob	retired
Dingman, Chris	retired
DiSalvatore, Jon	played in AHL (Peoria)
Divis, Reinhard	played in Austria (Salzburg)
Domi, Tie	retired
Doull, Doug	retired
Eklund, Brian	retired
Endicott, Shane	played in AHL (Iowa)
Fedorov, Fedor	played in Russia & Sweden
Ferguson, Scott	played in AHL (Worcester)
Ferland, Jonathan	played in AHL (Hamilton)
Fischer, Jiri	retired
Fitzgerald, Tom	retired
Flinn, Ryan	played in AHL (San Antonio)
Forbes, Colin	played in Germany (Mannheim)
Gainey, Steve	retired
Gamache, Simon	played in Switzerland (Bern)
Garnett, Michael	played in AHL (Chicago)
Gavey, Aaron	played in Germany (Cologne)

Gillies, Trevor	played in AHL & ECHL
Giuliano, Jeff	played in AHL (Manchester)
Grebeshkov, Denis	played in Russia (Yaroslavl)
Harvey, Todd	retired
Hauser, Adam	played in Germany (Cologne)
Healey, Eric	played in AHL (Springfield)
Healey, Paul	played in Sweden & Finland
Hedstrom, Jonathan	played in Sweden (Timra)
Hemingway, Colin	played in ECHL & Germany Div. 2
Henry, Alex	played in AHL (Milwaukee)
Holt, Chris	played primarily in ECHL (Charlotte)
Howard, James	unknown
Hrdina, Jan	played in Sweden & Finland
Hull, Brett	retired
Hulse, Cale	retired
James, Connor	played in AHL (Wilkes-Barre/Scranton)
Jancevski, Dan	played in AHL (Hamilton)
Jarrett, Cole	played in Germany (Berlin)
Jillson, Jeff	played in Germany (Berlin)
Johansson, Jonas	played in AHL (Hershey & Grand Rapids)
Johnson, Greg	retired
Kanko, Petr	played in AHL (Manchester)
Karpovtsev, Alexander	played in Russia (Novosibirsk)
Kavanagh, Pat	played in Sweden & Finland
Khavanov, Alexander	played in Switzerland (Davos)
Kloucek, Tomas	played in AHL (Syracuse)
Koalska, Matt	played in AHL (mostly Binghamton)
Kolanos, Krys	played in AHL & Switzerland
Kolesnik, Vitaly	played in Russia (Mytischi)
Koltsov, Konstantin	played in Russia (Ufa Salavat)
Kondratiev, Maxim	played in Russia (Togliatti)
Konowalchuk, Steve	retired

Kronwall, Staffan	played in AHL (Toronto)
Kvasha, Oleg	played in Russia (Chekhov)
LaBarbera, Jason	played in AHL (Manchester)
Langdon, Darren	retired
Leach, Jay	played in AHL (Providence)
Leclerc, Mike	retired
Leetch, Brian	did not play—retired May 24, 2007
Lefebvre, Guillaume	played in NAHL (St. Jean)
Lemieux, Mario	retired
Lessard, Francis	played in AHL (Hartford)
Loyns, Lynn	played in Germany (Krefeld)
Majesky, Ivan	played in Sweden & Finland
Marchment, Bryan	did not play
Marjamaki, Masi	played in AHL (Bridgeport)
Marshall, Grant	played in AHL (Lowell)
Marshall, Jason	played in Germany (Cologne)
Martins, Steve	played in AHL (Chicago)
McEachern, Shawn	retired
McGillis, Dan	played in AHL (Lowell)
McVicar, Rob	played in ECHL (Utah)
Milley, Norm	played in AHL (Springfield)
Mink, Graham	played in AHL (Worcester)
Mogilny, Alexander	retired
Munro, Adam	played in Switzerland (Fribourg)
Murley, Matt	played in AHL (Albany)
Murray, Rem	played in Finland (HIFK Helsinki)
Nash, Tyson	played in AHL (Toronto & San Antonio)
Nazarov, Andrei	retired
Nickulas, Eric	played in Germany (Hanover)
Nokelainen, Petteri	played in AHL (Bridgeport)
Nordgren, Niklas	played in Switzerland (Rapperswil)
Noronen, Mika	played in Russia (Ak-bars Kazan)
Nystrom, Eric	played in AHL (Omaha)
O'Brien, Doug	played in AHL (Springfield & Portland)

Odelein, Lyle	retired
Oliver, David	retired
Oliwa, Krzysztof	retired
Orszagh, Vladimir	retired
Ouellet, Maxime	retired
Palffy, Ziggy	retired
Peat, Stephen	played in AHL (Albany)
Perrott, Nathan	played briefly in AHL (Toronto)
Petiot, Richard	played in AHL (Manchester)
Pettinen, Tomi	played in Sweden (Frolunda)
Pirjeta, Lasse	played in Sweden (Malmo)
Poapst, Steve	retired
Primeau, Keith	retired
Prusek, Martin	played in Russia (St. Petersburg)
Pushor, Jamie	played in AHL (Syracuse)
Ready, Ryan	played in Germany (Iserlohn)
Rheaume, Pascal	played in AHL (San Antonio)
Rinne, Pekka	played in AHL (Milwaukee)
Rita, Jani	played in Finland (Jokerit)
Roach, Andy	played in Germany (Berlin)
Robinson, Nathan	played in Germany (Mannheim)
Robitaille, Louis	played in AHL (Hershey)
Robitaille, Luc	retired
Ryan, Matt	played in AHL (Manchester)
Ryan, Prestin	played in AHL (Manitoba)
Ryznar, Jason	played in AHL (Lowell)
St. Jacques, Bruno	played in AHL (Portland & Norfolk)
Sarno, Peter	played in Switzerland (Fribourg)
Savage, Brian	retired
Schaefer, Nolan	played in AHL (mostly Worcester)
Severson, Cam	played in Germany (Straubing)
Shields, Steve	retired
Shishkanov, Timofei	played in Russia (Chekhov)
Sigalet, Jordan	played in AHL (Providence)

Simon, Ben	played in AHL (Syracuse & Grand Rapids)
Simpson, Todd	played in Germany (Hanover)
Skolney, Wade	played in AHL (Wilkes-Barre/Scranton)
Slegr, Jiri	played in Czech Republic (Litvinov)
Smith, Dan	played in AHL (Grand Rapids)
Snow, Garth	retired
Spiller, Matthew	played in AHL (San Antonio)
Stevenson, Grant	played in AHL (Worcester)
Stevenson, Jeremy	played in NAHL (Thetford Mines)
Stevenson, Turner	retired
Stuart, Mike	played in AHL (Peoria)
Suchy, Radoslav	played in Switzerland (Zurich)
Sundstrom, Niklas	played in Sweden (MoDo)
Surovy, Tomas	played in Sweden (Lulea)
Svoboda, Jaroslav	played in Czech Republic (Znojemsti)
Sykora, Petr	played in Czech Republic (Pardubice)
Tarnstrom, Dick	played in Switzerland (Lugano)
Taticek, Petr	played in Switzerland & Czech Republic
Tenute, Joey	played in AHL (Hershey)
Therien, Chris	retired
Traverse, Patrick	played in AHL (Worcester & Hamilton)
Ulanov, Igor	played in Russia (Yaroslavl)
Vandenbussche, Ryan	played in CHL & Finland (Jokerit)
Varada, Vaclav	played in Switzerland (Davos)
Vorobiev, Pavel	played in Russia (Mytischi)
Weinrich, Eric	played in AHL (Portland)
Whitfield, Trent	played in AHL (Peoria)
Wiemer, Jason	retired

Wilm, Clarke	played in Finland (Jokerit)
Wiseman, Chad	played in AHL (Hershey)
Woolley, Jason	played in Sweden (Malmo)
Wright, Tyler	played in Switzerland (Basel)
Yakubov, Mikhail	played in Russia (Cherepovets)
Yonkman, Nolan	played in AHL (Milwaukee)
Young, Scott	retired
Yzerman, Steve	retired
Zhamnov, Alexei	retired

2007 PLAYOFF RESULTS

Eastern Conference Quarterfinals

New York Islanders vs. Buffalo Sabres
April 12   NY Islanders 1 at Buffalo 4
April 14   NY Islanders 3 at Buffalo 2
April 16   Buffalo 3 at NY Islanders 2
April 18   Buffalo 4 at NY Islanders 2
April 20   NY Islanders 3 at Buffalo 4
Buffalo wins best-of-seven 4–1

Tampa Bay Lightning vs. New Jersey Devils
April 12   Tampa Bay 3 at New Jersey 5
April 14   Tampa Bay 3 at New Jersey 2
April 16   New Jersey 2 at Tampa Bay 3
April 18   New Jersey 4 at Tampa Bay 3 (Gomez 12:54 OT)
April 20   Tampa Bay 0 at New Jersey 3 [Brodeur]
April 22   New Jersey 3 at Tampa Bay 2
New Jersey wins best-of-seven 4–2

New York Rangers vs. Atlanta Thrashers
April 12   NY Rangers 4 at Atlanta 3
April 14   NY Rangers 2 at Atlanta 1
April 17   Atlanta 0 at NY Rangers 7 [Lundqvist]
April 18   Atlanta 2 at NY Rangers 4
NY Rangers win best-of-seven 4-0

Pittsburgh Penguins vs. Ottawa Senators
April 11   Pittsburgh 3 at Ottawa 6
April 14   Pittsburgh 4 at Ottawa 3
April 15   Ottawa 4 at Pittsburgh 2
April 17   Ottawa 2 at Pittsburgh 1

April 19   Pittsburgh 0 at Ottawa 3 [Emery]
Ottawa wins best-of-seven 4–1

Western Conference Quarterfinals

Calgary Flames vs. Detroit Red Wings

April 12   Calgary 1 at Detroit 4
April 15   Calgary 1 at Detroit 3
April 17   Detroit 2 at Calgary 3
April 19   Detroit 2 at Calgary 3
April 21   Calgary 1 at Detroit 5
April 22   Detroit 2 at Calgary 1 (Franzen 24:23 OT)
Detroit wins best-of-seven 4–2

Minnesota Wild vs. Anaheim Ducks

April 11   Minnesota 1 at Anaheim 2
April 13   Minnesota 2 at Anaheim 3
April 15   Anaheim 2 at Minnesota 1
April 17   Anaheim 1 at Minnesota 4
April 19   Minnesota 1 at Anaheim 4
Anaheim wins best-of-seven 4–1

Dallas Stars vs. Vancouver Canucks

April 11   Dallas 4 at Vancouver 5 (H. Sedin 78:06 OT)
April 13   Dallas 2 at Vancouver 0 [Turco]
April 15   Vancouver 2 at Dallas 1 (Pyatt 7:47 OT)
April 17   Vancouver 4 at Dallas 1
April 19   Dallas 1 at Vancouver 0 (Morrow 6:22 pp OT)[Turco]
April 21   Vancouver 0 at Dallas 2 [Turco]
April 23   Dallas 1 at Vancouver 4
Vancouver wins best-of-seven 4–3

San Jose Sharks vs. Nashville Predators

April 11   San Jose 5 at Nashville 4 (Rissmiller 28:14 OT)

April 13	San Jose 2 at Nashville 5
April 16	Nashville 1 at San Jose 3
April 18	Nashville 2 at San Jose 3
April 20	San Jose 3 at Nashville 2

San Jose wins best-of-seven 4–1

Eastern Conference Semifinals

Ottawa Senators vs. New Jersey Devils

April 26	Ottawa 5 at New Jersey 4
April 28	Ottawa 2 at New Jersey 3 (Langenbrunner 21:55 OT)
April 30	New Jersey 0 at Ottawa 2 [Emery]
May 2	New Jersey 2 at Ottawa 3
May 5	Ottawa 3 at New Jersey 2

Ottawa wins best-of-seven 4–1

New York Rangers vs. Buffalo Sabres

April 25	NY Rangers 2 at Buffalo 5
April 27	NY Rangers 2 at Buffalo 3
April 29	Buffalo 1 at NY Rangers 2 (Rozsival 36:43 OT)
May 1	Buffalo 1 at NY Rangers 2
May 4	NY Rangers 1 at Buffalo 2 (Afinogenov 4:39 OT)
May 6	Buffalo 5 at NY Rangers 4

Buffalo wins best-of-seven 4–2

Western Conference Semifinals

Vancouver Canucks at Anaheim Ducks

April 25	Vancouver 1 at Anaheim 5
April 27	Vancouver 2 at Anaheim 1 (Cowan 27:49 OT)
April 29	Anaheim 3 at Vancouver 2
May 1	Anaheim 3 at Vancouver 2 (Moen 2:07 OT)
May 3	Vancouver 1 at Anaheim 2 (S. Niedermayer 24:30 OT)

Anaheim wins best-of-seven 4–1

San Jose Sharks at Detroit Red Wings

April 26	San Jose 2 at Detroit 0 [Nabokov]
April 28	San Jose 2 at Detroit 3
April 30	Detroit 1 at San Jose 2
May 2	Detroit 3 at San Jose 2 (Schneider 16:04 OT)
May 5	San Jose 1 at Detroit 4
May 7	Detroit 2 at San Jose 0 [Hasek]

Detroit wins best-of-seven 4–2

Eastern Conference Finals

Ottawa Senators vs. Buffalo Sabres

May 10	Ottawa 5 at Buffalo 2
May 12	Ottawa 4 at Buffalo 3 (Corvo 24:58 OT)
May 14	Buffalo 0 at Ottawa 1 (Alfredsson 13:40 2nd) [Emery]
May 16	Buffalo 3 at Ottawa 2
May 19	Ottawa 3 at Buffalo 2

Ottawa wins best-of-seven 4–1

Western Conference Finals

Anaheim Ducks vs. Detroit Red Wings

May 11	Anaheim 1 at Detroit 2
May 13	Anaheim 4 at Detroit 3 (S. Niedermayer 14:17 OT)
May 15	Detroit 5 at Anaheim 0 [Hasek]
May 17	Detroit 3 at Anaheim 5
May 20	Anaheim 2 at Detroit 1 (Selanne 11:57 OT)
May 22	Detroit 3 at Anaheim 4

Anaheim wins best-of-seven 4–2

Stanley Cup Finals

Ottawa Senators vs. Anaheim Ducks

May 28   Ottawa 2 at Anaheim 3
May 30   Ottawa 0 at Anaheim 1 (Pahlsson 14:15 3rd) [Giguere]
June 2   Anaheim 3 at Ottawa 5
June 4   Anaheim 3 at Ottawa 2
June 6   Ottawa 2 at Anaheim 6
Anaheim wins best-of-seven 4–1

PLAYER STATISTICS BY TEAM, 2007 PLAYOFFS

Anaheim

	GP	G	A	P	Pim
Ryan Getzlaf	21	7	10	17	32
Corey Perry	21	6	9	15	37
Teemu Selanne	19	5	10	15	10
Chris Pronger	21	3	12	15	26
Andy McDonald	21	10	4	14	10
Travis Moen	21	7	5	12	22
Samuel Pahlsson	21	3	9	12	20
Scott Niedermayer	21	3	8	11	26
Rob Niedermayer	21	5	5	10	39
Francois Beauchemin	20	4	4	8	16
Dustin Penner	21	3	5	8	2
Chris Kunitz	13	1	5	6	19
Todd Marchant	11	0	3	3	12
Ric Jackman	7	1	1	2	2
Sean O'Donnell	21	0	2	2	10
Brad May	18	0	1	1	28
Kent Huskins	21	0	1	1	11
Shawn Thornton	15	0	0	0	19
George Parros	5	0	0	0	10
Ryan Shannon	11	0	0	0	6
Joe DiPenta	16	0	0	0	4
Andrew Miller	3	0	0	0	2
Joe Motzko	3	0	0	0	2
J-S Giguere	18	0	0	0	0
Ilya Bryzgalov	5	0	0	0	0
Ryan Carter	4	0	0	0	0
Mark Hartigan	1	0	0	0	0
Aaron Rome	1	0	0	0	0

Goalies	GP	W-L	Mins	GA	SO	GAA
J-S Giguere	18	13–4	1,067:04	35	1	1.97
Ilya Bryzgalov	5	3–1	266:51	10	0	2.25

Atlanta

	GP	G	A	P	Pim
Keith Tkachuk	4	1	2	3	12
Pascal Dupuis	4	1	2	3	4
Ilya Kovalchuk	4	1	1	2	19
Niclas Havelid	4	0	2	2	0
Brad Larsen	4	0	2	2	0
Eric Belanger	4	1	0	1	12
Greg de Vries	4	1	0	1	4
Shane Hnidy	4	1	0	1	0
Marian Hossa	4	0	1	1	6
Bobby Holik	4	0	1	1	0
Eric Boulton	4	0	0	0	24
Andy Sutton	4	0	0	0	10
Garnet Exelby	4	0	0	0	6
Slava Kozlov	4	0	0	0	6
Scott Mellanby	4	0	0	0	4
Alexei Zhitnik	4	0	0	0	4
Jim Slater	4	0	0	0	2
Jonathan Sim	4	0	0	0	0
Johan Hedberg	2	0	0	0	0
Kari Lehtonen	2	0	0	0	0

Goalies	GP	W-L	Mins	GA	SO	GAA
Johan Hedberg	2	0–2	117:29	5	0	2.56
Kari Lehtonen	2	0–2	118:04	11	0	5.59

Buffalo

	GP	G	A	P	Pim
Daniel Briere	16	3	12	15	16
Chris Drury	16	8	5	13	2
Thomas Vanek	16	6	4	10	10
Jason Pominville	16	4	6	10	0
Maxim Afinogenov	15	5	4	9	6
Tim Connolly	16	0	9	9	4
Dainius Zubrus	15	0	8	8	8
Brian Campbell	16	3	4	7	14
Derek Roy	16	2	5	7	14
Jochen Hecht	16	4	1	5	10
Dmitri Kalinin	16	2	3	5	14
Adam Mair	16	1	4	5	10
Toni Lydman	16	2	2	4	14
Ales Kotalik	16	2	2	4	8
Drew Stafford	10	2	2	4	4
Teppo Numminen	16	0	4	4	4
Henrik Tallinder	16	0	2	2	10
Paul Gaustad	7	0	1	1	2
Jaroslav Spacek	16	0	0	0	10
Ryan Miller	16	0	0	0	2
Daniel Paille	1	0	0	0	0

Goalie	**GP**	**W-L**	**Mins**	**GA**	**SO**	**GAA**
Ryan Miller	16	9–7	1,029:03	38	0	2.22

Calgary

	GP	G	A	P	Pim
Jarome Iginla	6	2	2	4	12
Daymond Langkow	6	2	2	4	4
Alex Tanguay	6	1	3	4	8
Craig Conroy	6	1	1	2	8
Matt Lombardi	6	1	1	2	0
Wayne Primeau	6	0	2	2	14
Kristian Huselius	6	0	2	2	4
Dion Phaneuf	6	1	0	1	7
Andrei Zyuzin	5	1	0	1	2
Mark Giordano	4	1	0	1	0
Roman Hamrlik	6	0	1	1	8
Brad Stuart	6	0	1	1	6
Tony Amonte	6	0	1	1	0
David Moss	6	0	1	1	0
Jamie McLennan	1	0	0	0	12
Rhett Warrener	6	0	0	0	10
Byron Richie	1	0	0	0	10
David Hale	2	0	0	0	6
Marcus Nilson	6	0	0	0	2
Stephane Yelle	6	0	0	0	2
Jeff Friesen	5	0	0	0	2
Miikka Kiprusoff	6	0	0	0	0
Robyn Regehr	1	0	0	0	0

Goalies	GP	W-L	Mins	GA	SO	GAA
Miikka Kiprusoff	6	2–4	383:35	18	0	2.81
Jamie McLennan	1	0–0	00:18	0	0	0.00

Dallas

	GP	G	A	P	Pim
Stu Barnes	7	1	3	4	4
Sergei Zubov	6	0	4	4	2
Brenden Morrow	7	2	1	3	18
Jeff Halpern	7	2	1	3	4
Mike Ribeiro	7	0	3	3	4
Joel Lundqvist	7	2	0	2	6
Ladislav Nagy	7	1	1	2	2
Antti Miettinen	4	1	1	2	2
Mike Modano	7	1	1	2	4
Darryl Sydor	7	1	1	2	4
Trevor Daley	7	1	0	1	4
Niklas Hagman	7	0	1	1	10
Philippe Boucher	7	0	1	1	6
Stephane Robidas	7	0	1	1	2
Loui Eriksson	4	0	1	1	0
Jussi Jokinen	4	0	1	1	0
Mattias Norstrom	7	0	0	0	8
Steve Ott	6	0	0	0	8
Marty Turco	7	0	0	0	4
Eric Lindros	3	0	0	0	4
Jon Klemm	1	0	0	0	2
Jere Lehtinen	7	0	0	0	2

Goalie	GP	W-L	Mins	GA	SO	GAA
Marty Turco	7	3-4	509:13	11	3	1.30

Detroit

	GP	G	A	P	Pim
Nicklas Lidstrom	18	4	14	18	6
Pavel Datsyuk	18	8	8	16	8
Henrik Zetterberg	18	6	8	14	12
Daniel Cleary	18	4	8	12	30
Mikael Samuelsson	18	3	8	11	14
Tomas Holmstrom	15	5	3	8	14
Robert Lang	18	2	6	8	8
Todd Bertuzzi	16	3	4	7	15
Johan Franzen	18	3	4	7	10
Chris Chelios	18	1	6	7	12
Mathieu Schneider	11	2	4	6	16
Valtteri Filppula	18	3	2	5	2
Kris Draper	18	2	0	2	24
Kirk Maltby	18	1	1	2	10
Brett Lebda	12	0	2	2	8
Jiri Hudler	6	0	2	2	4
Andreas Lilja	18	1	0	1	10
Kyle Calder	13	0	1	1	8
Danny Markov	18	0	0	0	13
Tomas Kopecky	4	0	0	0	6
Dominik Hasek	18	0	0	0	2
Kyle Quincey	13	0	0	0	2

Goalie	GP	W-L	Mins	GA	SO	GAA
Dominik Hasek	18	10–8	1,139:49	34	2	1.79

Minnesota

	GP	G	A	P	Pim
Marian Gaborik	5	3	1	4	8
Pavol Demitra	5	1	3	4	0
Brian Rolston	5	1	1	2	4
P-M Bouchard	5	1	1	2	0
Petteri Nummelin	3	1	1	2	0
Kurtis Foster	3	0	2	2	0
Mikko Koivu	5	1	0	1	4
Mark Parrish	5	1	0	1	0
Derek Boogaard	4	0	1	1	20
Brent Burns	5	0	1	1	14
Wes Walz	5	0	1	1	4
Niklas Backstrom	5	0	1	1	2
Nick Schultz	5	0	1	1	0
Adam Hall	3	0	0	0	7
Keith Carney	5	0	0	0	4
Martin Skoula	5	0	0	0	4
Stephane Veilleux	5	0	0	0	4
Branko Radivojevic	5	0	0	0	2
Kim Johnsson	4	0	0	0	2
Wyatt Smith	4	0	0	0	0
Todd White	4	0	0	0	0

Goalie	GP	W-L	Mins	GA	SO	GAA
Niklas Backstrom	5	1–4	296:39	11	0	2.22

Nashville

	GP	G	A	P	Pim
J-P Dumont	5	4	2	6	0
Alexander Radulov	4	3	1	4	19
Peter Forsberg	5	2	2	4	12
Jason Arnott	5	2	1	3	2
David Legwand	5	0	3	3	2
Shea Weber	5	0	3	3	2
Scott Hartnell	5	1	1	2	28
Vernon Fiddler	5	1	1	2	4
Kimmo Timonen	5	0	2	2	4
Marek Zidlicky	5	0	2	2	4
Paul Kariya	5	0	2	2	2
Greg Zanon	5	0	2	2	2
Ryan Suter	5	1	0	1	8
Jordin Tootoo	4	0	1	1	21
Dan Hamhuis	5	0	1	1	2
Martin Erat	3	0	1	1	0
Scott Nichol	5	0	0	0	17
Jerred Smithson	5	0	0	0	17
Tomas Vokoun	5	0	0	0	2
Ramzi Abid	2	0	0	0	0
Darcy Hordichuk	2	0	0	0	0

Goalie	GP	W-L	Mins	GA	SO	GAA
Tomas Vokoun	5	1-4	323:38	16	0	2.96

New Jersey

	GP	G	A	P	Pim
Scott Gomez	11	4	10	14	14
Zach Parise	11	7	3	10	8
Patrik Elias	10	1	9	10	4
Brian Gionta	11	8	1	9	4
Brian Rafalski	11	2	6	8	8
Jamie Langenbrunner	11	2	6	8	7
Travis Zajac	11	1	4	5	4
Paul Martin	11	0	4	4	6
Andy Greene	11	2	1	3	2
Sergei Brylin	11	1	2	3	6
John Madden	11	1	1	2	2
Jay Pandolfo	11	1	0	1	4
Michael Rupp	9	0	1	1	7
John Oduya	6	0	1	1	6
Martin Brodeur	11	0	1	1	2
Brad Lukowich	11	0	1	1	2
Erik Rasmussen	11	0	0	0	14
Richard Matvichuk	9	0	0	0	10
Colin White	7	0	0	0	6
Jim Dowd	11	0	0	0	4
David Clarkson	3	0	0	0	2

Goalie	GP	W-L	Mins	GA	SO	GAA
Martin Brodeur	11	5–6	688:06	28	1	2.44

New York Islanders

	GP	G	A	P	Pim
Ryan Smyth	5	1	3	4	4
Trent Hunter	5	3	0	3	0
Jason Blake	5	1	2	3	2
Miroslav Satan	5	1	2	3	0
Tom Poti	5	0	3	3	6
Marc-Andre Bergeron	5	1	1	2	6
Chris Campoli	5	1	1	2	2
Bruno Gervais	5	1	1	2	2
Mike Sillinger	5	1	1	2	2
Randy Robitaille	5	0	2	2	8
Viktor Kozlov	5	0	2	2	2
Arron Asham	5	1	0	1	0
Brendan Witt	5	0	1	1	6
Richard Park	5	0	1	1	2
Richard Zednik	5	0	0	0	8
Andy Hilbert	5	0	0	0	2
Alexei Yashin	5	0	0	0	0
Rick DiPietro	4	0	0	0	0
Sean Hill	4	0	0	0	0
Wade Dubielewicz	1	0	0	0	0
Drew Fata	1	0	0	0	0

Goalies	GP	W-L	Mins	GA	SO	GAA
Rick DiPietro	4	1–3	236:19	13	0	3.31
Wade Dubielewicz	1	0–1	59:03	4	0	4.07

New York Rangers

	GP	G	A	P	Pim
Michael Nylander	10	6	7	13	0
Jaromir Jagr	10	5	6	11	12
Martin Straka	10	2	8	10	2
Brendan Shanahan	10	5	2	7	12
Michal Rozsival	10	3	4	7	10
Sean Avery	10	1	4	5	27
Fedor Tyutin	10	0	5	5	8
Paul Mara	10	2	2	4	18
Marcel Hossa	10	2	2	4	4
Marek Malik	10	1	3	4	10
Matt Cullen	10	1	3	4	6
Karel Rachunek	6	0	4	4	2
Ryan Callahan	10	2	1	3	6
Thomas Pock	4	0	3	3	4
Petr Prucha	10	0	1	1	4
Colton Orr	4	0	0	0	12
Blair Betts	10	0	0	0	4
Daniel Girardi	10	0	0	0	4
Jed Ortmeyer	9	0	0	0	2
Brad Isbister	4	0	0	0	2
Ryan Hollweg	2	0	0	0	2
Henrik Lundqvist	10	0	0	0	0
Nigel Dawes	1	0	0	0	0

Goalie	GP	W-L	Mins	GA	SO	GAA
Henrik Lundqvist	10	6–4	637:25	22	1	2.07

Ottawa

	GP	G	A	P	Pim
Daniel Alfredsson	20	14	8	22	10
Dany Heatley	20	7	15	22	14
Jason Spezza	20	7	15	22	10
Mike Fisher	20	5	5	10	24
Wade Redden	20	3	7	10	10
Joe Corvo	20	2	7	9	6
Dean McAmmond	18	5	3	8	11
Chris Kelly	20	3	4	7	4
Tom Preissing	20	2	5	7	10
Andrej Meszaros	20	1	6	7	12
Anton Volchenkov	20	2	4	6	24
Mike Comrie	20	2	4	6	17
Peter Schaefer	20	1	5	6	10
Antoine Vermette	20	2	3	5	6
Chris Neil	20	2	2	4	20
Oleg Saprykin	15	1	1	2	4
Patrick Eaves	7	0	2	2	2
Ray Emery	20	0	2	2	0
Christoph Schubert	20	0	1	1	22
Chris Phillips	20	0	0	0	24

Goalie	GP	W-L	Mins	GA	SO	GAA
Ray Emery	20	13–7	1,248:37	47	3	2.26

Pittsburgh

	GP	G	A	P	Pim
Sidney Crosby	5	3	2	5	4
Gary Roberts	5	2	2	4	2
Sergei Gonchar	5	1	3	4	2
Evgeni Malkin	5	0	4	4	8
Mark Recchi	5	0	4	4	0
Jordan Staal	5	3	0	3	2
Ryan Whitney	5	1	1	2	6
Michel Ouellet	5	0	2	2	6
Colby Armstrong	5	0	1	1	11
Maxime Talbot	5	0	1	1	7
Jarkko Ruutu	5	0	0	0	10
Brooks Orpik	5	0	0	0	8
Erik Christensen	4	0	0	0	6
Josef Melichar	5	0	0	0	2
Rob Scuderi	5	0	0	0	2
Ronald Petrovicky	3	0	0	0	2
Mark Eaton	5	0	0	0	0
Marc-Andre Fleury	5	0	0	0	0
Ryan Malone	5	0	0	0	0
Georges Laraque	2	0	0	0	0
Nils Ekman	1	0	0	0	0
Jocelyn Thibault	1	0	0	0	0

Goalies	GP	W-L	Mins	GA	SO	GAA
Marc-Andre Fleury	5	1–4	286:42	18	0	3.76
Jocelyn Thibault	1	0–0	8:02	0	0	0.00

San Jose

	GP	G	A	P	Pim
Joe Thornton	11	1	10	11	10
Ryane Clowe	11	4	2	6	17
Milan Michalek	11	4	2	6	4
Jonathan Cheechoo	11	3	3	6	6
Patrick Marleau	11	3	3	6	2
Craig Rivet	11	2	3	5	18
Matt Carle	11	2	3	5	0
Mike Grier	11	2	2	4	27
Pat Rissmiller	11	1	3	4	0
Kyle McLaren	11	0	4	4	10
Marcel Goc	11	2	1	3	4
Scott Hannan	11	0	2	2	33
Bill Guerin	9	0	2	2	12
Christian Ehrhoff	11	0	2	2	6
Curtis Brown	11	0	2	2	2
Joe Pavelski	6	1	0	1	0
Steve Bernier	11	0	1	1	2
Marc-Edouard Vlasic	11	0	1	1	2
Mark Smith	3	0	0	0	4
Mark Bell	4	0	0	0	2
Evgeni Nabokov	11	0	0	0	0

Goalie	GP	W-L	Mins	GA	SO	GAA
Evgeni Nabokov	11	6–5	700:50	26	1	2.23

Tampa Bay

	GP	G	A	P	Pim
Martin St. Louis	6	3	5	8	8
Brad Richards	6	3	5	8	6
Vincent Lecavalier	6	5	2	7	10
Filip Kuba	6	1	4	5	4
Vaclav Prospal	6	1	4	5	4
Eric Perrin	6	1	1	2	2
Jason Ward	6	0	1	1	6
Paul Ranger	6	0	1	1	4
Dan Boyle	6	0	1	1	2
Andre Roy	6	0	0	0	17
Ryan Craig	6	0	0	0	12
Shane O'Brien	6	0	0	0	12
Nick Tarnasky	6	0	0	0	10
Nolan Pratt	6	0	0	0	5
Ruslan Fedotenko	4	0	0	0	4
Cory Sarich	6	0	0	0	2
Johan Holmqvist	6	0	0	0	0
Andreas Karlsson	6	0	0	0	0
Tim Taylor	6	0	0	0	0
Doug Janik	1	0	0	0	0

Goalie	GP	W-L	Mins	GA	SO	GAA
Johan Holmqvist	6	2–4	369:56	18	0	2.92

Vancouver

	GP	G	A	P	Pim
Mattias Ohlund	12	2	5	7	12
Trevor Linden	12	2	5	7	6
Taylor Pyatt	12	2	4	6	6
Markus Naslund	12	4	1	5	16
Daniel Sedin	12	2	3	5	4
Henrik Sedin	12	2	2	4	14
Bryan Smolinski	12	2	2	4	8
Brendan Morrison	12	1	3	4	6
Jeff Cowan	10	2	0	2	22
Jan Bulis	12	1	1	2	2
Lukas Krajicek	12	0	2	2	12
Alexandre Burrows	11	1	0	1	14
Willie Mitchell	12	0	1	1	12
Josh Green	9	0	1	1	12
Jannik Hansen	10	0	1	1	4
Sami Salo	10	0	1	1	4
Brandon Reid	1	0	1	1	0
Kevin Bieksa	9	0	0	0	20
Rory Fitzpatrick	3	0	0	0	6
Brent Sopel	11	0	0	0	2
Alexander Edler	3	0	0	0	2
Matt Cooke	1	0	0	0	2
Nathan Smith	4	0	0	0	0
Ryan Kesler	1	0	0	0	0
Tommi Santala	1	0	0	0	0

Goalies	GP	W-L	Mins	GA	SO	GAA
Roberto Luongo	12	5–7	847:26	25	0	1.77
Dany Sabourin	2	0–0	14:29	1	0	4.29

GAME SUMMARIES, 2006–07

(SO: game was decided in a shootout. Shootout information: names in CAPS=goal; lower case=miss; names in brackets after team name refer to opposing goalie)

October 4, 2006

Buffalo 3 at Carolina 2 (SO)
BUF (vs. Ward)—BRIERE, Vanek/CAR (vs. Miller)—Whitney, Staal, Cole
Ottawa 4 at Toronto 1
Dallas 3 at Colorado 2 (Sydor 2:07 OT)

October 5, 2006

Toronto 6 at Ottawa 0
Washington 2 at NY Rangers 5
Tampa Bay 3 at Atlanta 6
TB (vs. Denis)—LECAVALIER, Richards/ATL (vs. Lehtonen)—Kozlov, Sim, Kovalchuk
Vancouver 3 at Detroit 1
Philadelphia 0 at Pittsburgh 4
Chicago 8 at Nashville 6
Colorado 2 at Minnesota 3 (T. White 1:03 OT)
NY Islanders 3 at Phoenix 6
Calgary 1 at Edmonton 3
St. Louis 4 at San Jose 5 (C. Brown 2:12 OT)

October 6, 2006

New Jersey 4 at Carolina 0
Vancouver 3 at Columbus 2 (D. Sedin 0:31 OT)
Boston 3 at Florida 8
Montreal 4 at Buffalo 5 (SO)

MON (vs. Miller)—Ryder, Kovalev/BUF (vs. Huet)—Briere,
    AFINOGENOV, VANEK
Los Angeles 3 at Anaheim 4

October 7, 2006

Montreal 3 at Toronto 2 (SO)
MON (vs. Raycroft)—HIGGINS, Koivu, Kovalev, RYDER/TOR (vs.
    Aebischer)—SUNDIN, Wellwood, Tucker, Ponikarovsky
Buffalo 4 at Ottawa 3
NY Rangers 5 at Philadelphia 4 (SO)
NYR (vs. Niittymaki)—Jagr, Nylander, Prucha, Shanahan, Cullen,
    Hall, Straka, Dawes, Betts, Rozsival, Hollweg, Ward,
    HOSSA/PHI (vs. Lundqvist)—Gagne, Richards, Sanderson,
    Nedved, Calder, Forsberg, Carter, Pitkanen, Robitaille,
    Knuble, Kapanen, Umberger, Meyer
Carolina 2 at Washington 5
Florida 0 at Atlanta 6
Detroit 2 at Pittsburgh 0
Boston 3 at Tampa Bay 2
Nashville 5 at Minnesota 6
New Jersey 1 at Dallas 3
Columbus 5 at Chicago 4
Anaheim 2 at Phoenix 1
Edmonton 1 at Calgary 2
St. Louis 1 at Los Angeles 4
NY Islanders 0 at San Jose 2

October 8, 2006

Vancouver 2 at Colorado 3

October 9, 2006

Phoenix 1 at Columbus 5
Florida 1 at Toronto 2 (SO)

FLO (vs. Raycroft)—Horton, Bertuzzi/TOR (vs. Auld)—O'Neill,
    SUNDIN, TUCKER
Atlanta 1 at Tampa Bay 0
San Jose 4 at Calgary 1
St. Louis 0 at Anaheim 2

October 10, 2006

Philadelphia 4 at NY Rangers 2
Vancouver 1 at Minnesota 2 (SO)
VAN (vs. Fernandez)—NASLUND, D. Sedin, MORRISON,
    Bulis/MIN (vs. Luongo)—DEMITRA, KOIVU, Rolston,
    NUMMELIN
NY Islanders 2 at Los Angeles 4

October 11, 2006

Boston 1 at Atlanta 4
Montreal 3 at Philadelphia 1
Carolina 3 at Florida 6
Phoenix 2 at Detroit 9
NY Islanders 5 at Anaheim 4 (SO)
NYI (vs. Giguere)—Satan, KOZLOV, Hunter, Blake, Yashin,
    YORK/ANA (vs. Dunham)—SHANNON, Pronger, McDonald,
    Selanne, Kunitz, R. Niedermayer

October 12, 2006

Pittsburgh 6 at NY Rangers 5
Calgary 1 at Ottawa 0
Toronto 6 at New Jersey 7 (SO)
TOR (vs. Brodeur)—STAJAN, Sundin, Tucker, Ponikarovsky/NJ
    (vs. Aubin)—Elias, GIONTA, Brylin, MADDEN
Boston 2 at St. Louis 3
BOS (vs. Legace)—Bergeron, Boyes, Sturm, Savard/STL (vs.
    Thomas)—Wideman, Weight, TKACHUK, STEMPNIAK
Washington 2 at Minnesota 3 (SO)

WAS (vs. Fernandez)—Ovechkin, Semin, Zednik/MIN (vs.
    Johnson)—Demitra, KOIVU
Nashville 1 at Chicago 3
San Jose 4 at Edmonton 6
Dallas 4 at Los Angeles 1

October 13, 2006

Buffalo 3 at Detroit 2 (SO)
BUF (vs. Hasek)—BRIERE, Afinogenov, Vanek, KOTALIK/DET
    (vs. Miller)—Williams, DATSYUK, Zetterberg, Holmstrom
Carolina 4 at Atlanta 3
Tampa Bay 2 at Florida 3
San Jose 6 at Vancouver 4

October 14, 2006

NY Rangers 4 at Buffalo 7
Calgary 4 at Toronto 5 (Sundin 0:50 OT)
Ottawa 3 at Montreal 2 (SO)
OTT (vs. Huet)—VERMETTE, McAmmond, FISHER/MON (vs.
    Emery)—Higgins, Koivu
Boston 1 at NY Islanders 4
Atlanta 4 at Washington 3 (Kovalchuk 3:02 OT)
Philadelphia 2 at New Jersey 3
Carolina 5 at Pittsburgh 1
Florida 1 at Tampa Bay 4
Chicago 3 at St. Louis 4
Phoenix 1 at Nashville 4
Columbus 0 at Minnesota 5
Edmonton 4 at Colorado 3
Dallas 4 at Los Angeles 1

October 15, 2006

Dallas 4 at Anaheim 3 (SO)

DAL (vs. Giguere)—ZUBOV, JOKINEN/ANA (vs. Turco)—
    Shannon, McDONALD, Pahlsson

October 16, 2006

New Jersey 2 at NY Rangers 4
Carolina 5 at Tampa Bay 1
Nashville 2 at NY Islanders 1 (SO)
NAS (vs. Dunham)—SULLIVAN, KARIYA/NYI (vs. Vokoun)—
    Satan, Kozlov
Chicago 5 at Colorado 3
Edmonton 1 at Vancouver 2
Detroit 3 at Los Angeles 1

October 17, 2006

Philadelphia 1 at Buffalo 9
Calgary 4 at Montreal 5
Phoenix 5 at St. Louis 2
Vancouver 1 at Edmonton 2
Dallas 0 at San Jose 2

October 18, 2006

Nashville 3 at NY Rangers 0
Florida 2 at Washington 5
Colorado 4 at Toronto 1
New Jersey 2 at Pittsburgh 1
Montreal 1 at Chicago 2
Detroit 1 at Anaheim 4
Minnesota 2 at Los Angeles 1 (Gaborik 0:25 OT)

October 19, 2006

Calgary 2 at Boston 3
Washington 3 at Atlanta 4 (SO)
WAS (vs. Lehtonen)—Semin, Ovechkin/ATL (vs. Johnson)—
    KOZLOV, HOSSA

Colorado 2 at Ottawa 1
Nashville 4 at New Jersey 3 (SO)
NAS (vs. Clemmensen)—Zidlicky, Kariya, ERAT/NJ (vs.
    Mason)—Parise, Gionta, Elias
Pittsburgh 4 at NY Islanders 3 (Gonchar 3:33 OT)
Philadelphia 1 at Tampa Bay 4
Los Angeles 4 at Phoenix 0
Detroit 1 at San Jose 5

October 20, 2006

Toronto 4 at Columbus 2
Philadelphia 2 at Florida 3
Vancouver 3 at St. Louis 2 (Salo 4:59 OT)
Carolina 4 at Buffalo 5
Chicago 4 at Dallas 5
Minnesota 1 at Anaheim 2

October 21, 2006

Buffalo 6 at Boston 2
NY Rangers 5 at Toronto 4 (SO)
NYR (vs. Raycroft)—Jagr, Nylander, SHANAHAN/TOR (vs.
    Lundqvist)—Sundin, Ponikarovsky, Tucker
Colorado 5 at Montreal 8
New Jersey 1 at Ottawa 8
Carolina 3 at NY Islanders 4 (Poti 0:23 OT)
Tampa Bay 6 at Washington 4
Florida 2 at Atlanta 4
Columbus 3 at Pittsburgh 5
Vancouver 4 at Nashville 3 (Krajicek 2:32 OT)
St. Louis 4 at Chicago 3
Dallas 4 at Phoenix 0
Detroit 1 at Edmonton 3
Minnesota 4 at San Jose 1

October 22, 2006

Anaheim 3 at Los Angeles 2 (SO)
ANA (vs. Garon)—Shannon, SELANNE, McDonald, Kunitz,
    GETZLAF/LA (vs. Giguere)—Cammalleri, Kopitar, FROLOV,
    O'Sullivan, Armstrong

October 23, 2006

San Jose 3 at Columbus 0
Buffalo 4 at Montreal 1
Atlanta 6 at Florida 3
Los Angeles 1 at Colorado 6
Vancouver 1 at Dallas 2
Phoenix 2 at Edmonton 5

October 24, 2006

New Jersey 2 at Pittsburgh 4
Ottawa 6 at Toronto 2
Phoenix 1 at Calgary 6

October 25, 2006

Florida 4 at NY Rangers 2
Atlanta 4 at Carolina 5 (Babchuk 1:11 OT)
San Jose 1 at Detroit 2
Los Angeles 1 at Minnesota 3
Vancouver 5 at Chicago 0
Washington 5 at Colorado 3
Edmonton 2 at Anaheim 6

October 26, 2006

Montreal 3 at Boston 2
Atlanta 2 at Philadelphia 3 (SO)
ATL (vs. Niittymaki)—KOZLOV, Hossa, Kovalchuk/PHI (vs.
    Lehtonen)—GAGNE, FORSBERG, Richards
Toronto 2 at Ottawa 7

Florida 0 at New Jersey 2
Buffalo 3 at NY Islanders 0
Carolina 1 at Tampa Bay 5
San Jose 3 at Nashville 4
Edmonton 2 at Phoenix 6

October 27, 2006

Los Angeles 0 at Columbus 2
Anaheim 2 at Minnesota 3 (SO)
ANA (vs. Fernandez)—Shannon, Getzlaf, Selanne/MIN (vs.
    Giguere)—Demitra, KOIVU
Detroit 4 at Dallas 3
Washington 2 at Vancouver 3 (SO)
WAS (vs. Luongo)—Pettinger, Ovechkin/VAN (vs. Kolzig)—D.
    Sedin, NASLUND, MORRISON

October 28, 2006

Ottawa 1 at Boston 2
Atlanta 5 at Buffalo 4 (SO)
ATL (vs. Miller)—KOZLOV, Hossa/BUF (vs. Lehtonen)—Briere,
    Afinogenov, Vanek
Toronto 5 at Montreal 4 (SO)
TOR (vs. Aebischer)—KABERLE, Sundin, Tucker, Steen, Stajan,
    Ponikarovsky, WELLWOOD/MON (vs. Aubin)—SAMSONOV,
    Kovalev, Ryder, Streit, Koivu, Higgins, Perezhogin
Florida 3 at NY Islanders 4 (SO)
FLO (vs. DiPietro)—Horton, Kolnik, JOKINEN, Stumpel, Olesz,
    Bouwmeester, Weiss, Gelinas, Roberts, KWIATKOWSKI/NYI
    (vs. Belfour)—SATAN, Kozlov, York, Hunter, Blake, Yashin,
    Bates, Sillinger, Poti, HILBERT
Pittsburgh 8 at Philadelphia 2
Tampa Bay 4 at Carolina 6
Columbus 0 at New Jersey 1
Detroit 3 at St. Louis 2

Los Angeles 2 at Dallas 3
Anaheim 3 at Chicago 0
NY Rangers 7 at Phoenix 3
Washington 0 at Edmonton 4
Nashville 3 at Calgary 2

October 29, 2006

San Jose 4 at Tampa Bay 2
Minnesota 1 at Colorado 4

October 30, 2006

Chicago 0 at Philadelphia 3
Atlanta 2 at Toronto 4
Anaheim 6 at St. Louis 5 (SO)
ANA (vs. Sanford)—GETZLAF, SELANNE/STL (vs. Giguere)—
    Stempniak, Tkachuk
Washington 4 at Calgary 2
NY Rangers 1 at Los Angeles 4

October 31, 2006

Chicago 2 at NY Islanders 5
Ottawa 2 at Montreal 4
San Jose 2 at Florida 1
Nashville 3 at Vancouver 2

November 1, 2006

Carolina 5 at Atlanta 2
Colorado 5 at Columbus 3
Toronto 4 at Tampa Bay 2
Calgary 2 at Detroit 3
St. Louis 1 at Dallas 4
NY Rangers 4 at Anaheim 3 (Jagr 3:09 OT)
Nashville 5 at Edmonton 3
Pittsburgh 4 at Los Angeles 3 (Malkin 2:45 OT)

November 2, 2006

Buffalo 5 at Boston 4 (SO)
BUF (vs. Thomas)—BRIERE, Afinogenov, KOTALIK/BOS (vs.
    Miller)—Murray, Axelsson, MURRAY
Tampa Bay 5 at Philadelphia 2
Montreal 4 at Carolina 0
NY Islanders 5 at New Jersey 2
Toronto 2 at Florida 4
Colorado 1 at St. Louis 4
Vancouver 2 at Minnesota 5
Detroit 2 at Chicago 1
NY Rangers 3 at San Jose 1

November 3, 2006

Atlanta 4 at Washington 3
Calgary 4 at Columbus 5 (SO)
CAL (vs. Leclaire)—Lombardi, Iginla, Amonte, TANGUAY,
    HUSELIUS, Boyd, RITCHIE, Langkow, Phaneuf, Friesen,
    Kobasew/CBJ (vs. McLennan)—Modin, Nash, Zherdev,
    VYBORNY, FEDOROV, Brule, CARTER, Chimera, Svitov,
    Eriksson, MALHOTRA
Dallas 3 at Edmonton 2
Phoenix 2 at Anaheim 6

November 4, 2006

Tampa Bay 5 at Boston 6 (Murray 0:17 OT)
Toronto 4 at Buffalo 1
New Jersey 2 at Montreal 1
Carolina 3 at Ottawa 2
Atlanta 4 at NY Islanders 1
Washington 5 at Philadelphia 3
Columbus 1 at Detroit 4
Calgary 3 at St. Louis 2
Nashville 4 at Minnesota 3

Los Angeles 4 at Phoenix 6
Vancouver 2 at Colorado 3
Pittsburgh 2 at San Jose 3

November 5, 2006

Buffalo 4 at NY Rangers 3 (Briere 3:57 OT)

November 6, 2006

Ottawa 3 at Washington 4 (Clark 1:33 OT)
Boston 3 at Atlanta 5
Philadelphia 1 at Toronto 4
Tampa Bay 5 at NY Islanders 1
Dallas 1 at Vancouver 2
Pittsburgh 2 at Anaheim 3 (Selanne 0:44 OT)

November 7, 2006

Carolina 2 at New Jersey 3 (SO)
CAR (vs. Brodeur)—Williams, Whitney, BRIND'AMOUR, Staal,
    Cole, Walker/NJ (vs. Ward)—Elias, GIONTA, Parise, Zajac,
    Brylin, MADDEN
Edmonton 2 at Montreal 3 (SO)
EDM (vs. Aebischer)—Sykora, HEMSKY, Pisani, Stoll/MON(vs.
    Roloson)—KOIVU, Latendresse, Samsonov, KOVALEV
Los Angeles 6 at Colorado 5
Dallas 1 at Calgary 3
Minnesota 1 at San Jose 3

November 8, 2006

Ottawa 4 at Atlanta 5
Tampa Bay 4 at Pittsburgh 3 (Lecavalier (2:41 OT)
NY Rangers 4 at Florida 3 (SO)
NYR (vs. Belfour)—NYLANDER, Shanahan/FLO (vs.
    Lundqvist)—Jokinen, Horton
Edmonton 0 at Detroit 3

November 9, 2006

Toronto 6 at Boston 4
NY Islanders 3 at Philadelphia 1
Washington 0 at Carolina 5
Chicago 1 at New Jersey 2 (SO)
CHI (vs. Brodeur)—Bourque, Holmqvist/NJ (vs. Boucher)—
    PARISE, GIONTA
Columbus 4 at St. Louis 2
Dallas 1 at Phoenix 0
Anaheim 6 at Vancouver 0
San Jose 7 at Los Angeles 3

November 10, 2006

Edmonton 4 at Columbus 1
Ottawa 6 at Pittsburgh 3
NY Rangers 5 at Atlanta 2
Nashville 0 at Detroit 3
Florida 4 at Buffalo 5 (Vanek 0:19 OT)
St. Louis 1 at Chicago 3
Anaheim 0 at Calgary 3

November 11, 2006

Ottawa 3 at Boston 4
Montreal 1 at Toronto 5
Buffalo 5 at Philadelphia 4 (Briere 0:21 OT)
NY Rangers 1 at Washington 3
Pittsburgh 2 at Carolina 6
Florida 2 at New Jersey 4
Atlanta 3 at Tampa Bay 5
Colorado 0 at Nashville 1
San Jose 2 at Phoenix 1
Calgary 3 at Vancouver 2
Minnesota 3 at Los Angeles 2 (SO)
MIN (vs. Garon)—Demitra, Koivu, ROLSTON, Bouchard,

NUMMELIN, WHITE/LA (vs. Fernandez)—Frolov, KOPITAR, Cammalleri, Willsie, BROWN, Avery

November 12, 2006

Edmonton 3 at St. Louis 5
Columbus 0 at Chicago 1
Minnesota 2 at Anaheim 3

November 13, 2006

Buffalo 7 at Carolina 4
Montreal 6 at Ottawa 3
Philadelphia 2 at Pittsburgh 3
Washington 4 at Florida 1
Edmonton 2 at Colorado 1
San Jose 2 at Los Angeles 4

November 14, 2006

New Jersey 2 at NY Rangers 3
Minnesota 3 at Phoenix 4
St. Louis 0 at Calgary 3
Detroit 3 at Vancouver 2

November 15, 2006

Ottawa 4 at Buffalo 2
Boston 3 at Washington 2 (SO)
BOS (vs. Kolzig)—Sturm, BERGERON/WAS (vs. Thomas)—
    Semin, Ovechkin, Pettinger
NY Rangers 1 at Carolina 2
Nashville 5 at Columbus 4
Montreal 3 at Tampa Bay 1
NY Islanders 3 at Dallas 0
San Jose 4 at Colorado 3
Philadelphia 7 at Anaheim 4

November 16, 2006

Toronto 1 at Boston 2 (Bergeron 0:34 OT)
Montreal 1 at Florida 5
Minnesota 7 at Nashville 6 (SO)
MIN (vs. Mason)—DEMITRA, Koivu, NUMMELIN,
    ROLSTON/NAS (vs. Backstrom)—SULLIVAN, KARIYA, Erat,
    Vasicek
St. Louis 2 at Edmonton 6
Chicago 2 at Phoenix 3 (SO)
CHI (vs. Joseph)—Vrbata, HAMILTON, Holmqvist/PHO (vs.
    Boucher)—PERREAULT, NAGY
Philadelphia 4 at Los Angeles 3

November 17, 2006

Carolina 4 at Washington 1
Colorado 3 at Columbus 0
Ottawa 2 at New Jersey 3
Dallas 5 at Atlanta 3
Pittsburgh 2 at Buffalo 4
NY Islanders 2 at Tampa Bay 3 (SO)
NYI (vs. Holmqvist)—Satan, Kozlov, York, Hunter, Blake, Yashin,
    Hilbert/TB (vs. DiPietro)—Lecavalier, Richards, St. Louis,
    Prospal, Perrin, Kuba, AFANASENKOV
Detroit 1 at Calgary 4
St. Louis 2 at Vancouver 4
Chicago 4 at Anaheim 3 (SO)
CHI (vs. Bryzgalov)—Hamilton, Vrbata, RUUTU/ANA (vs.
    Khabibulin)—Selanne, Getzlaf, McDonald

November 18, 2006

Phoenix 3 at Los Angeles 5
Washington 2 at Boston 3 (Murray 2:06 OT)
New Jersey 2 at Toronto 1
Atlanta 1 at Montreal 3

Buffalo 1 at Ottawa 4
Dallas 4 at Carolina 5
NY Rangers 1 at Pittsburgh 3
NY Islanders 4 at Florida 1
Columbus 2 at Nashville 4
Colorado 2 at Minnesota 1 (SO)
COL (vs. Backstrom)—WOLSKI, Svatos, SAKIC/MIN (vs.
    Budaj)—Demitra, KOIVU, Rolston
Detroit 3 at Edmonton 4 (SO)
DET (vs. Roloson)—Hudler, WILLIAMS, Datsyuk, Zetterberg,
    CLEARY, Samuelsson, Lang/EDM (vs. MacDonald)—
    Hemsky, SYKORA, Smyth, Lupul, PISANI, Thoresen, TORRES
Philadelphia 1 at San Jose 6

November 19, 2006

Tampa Bay 1 at NY Rangers 4
Phoenix 4 at Anaheim 6
Chicago 1 at Vancouver 2

November 20, 2006

Florida 3 at Boston 2
Tampa Bay 2 at Buffalo 7
Pittsburgh 5 at Philadelphia 3
Nashville 3 at Columbus 1
NY Islanders 2 at Toronto 4
Minnesota 3 at Ottawa 5
Colorado 4 at Dallas 5

November 21, 2006

Carolina 0 at NY Rangers 4
Calgary 1 at Edmonton 2
San Jose 0 at Anaheim 5

November 22, 2006

Toronto 4 at Buffalo 7
Ottawa 3 at Philadelphia 2 (Redden 4:39 OT)
Atlanta 4 at Washington 2
St. Louis 4 at Columbus 3 (SO)
STL (vs. Leclaire)—Rucinsky, Weight, Tkachuk, GUERIN/CBJ (vs. Legace)—Zherdev, Modin, Vyborny, Malhotra
Vancouver 4 at Detroit 3 (Morrison 3:01 OT)
Minnesota 2 at Montreal 4
Carolina 2 at NY Islanders 4
Boston 4 at Pittsburgh 3 (SO)
BOS (vs. Fleury)—STURM, Bergeron/PIT (vs. Thomas)—Ouellet, Malkin, Gonchar
Tampa Bay 6 at Florida 4
Nashville 0 at Dallas 1
Anaheim 2 at Colorado 3 (SO)
ANA (vs. Theodore)—Selanne, Shannon, Getzlaf/COL (vs. Giguere)—Stastny, Svatos, SAKIC
New Jersey 1 at Phoenix 3
Chicago 1 at Calgary 4
Los Angeles 3 at San Jose 6

November 23, 2006

Vancouver 0 at Nashville 6

November 24, 2006

Carolina 5 at Boston 1
Columbus 2 at Philadelphia 3
Phoenix 0 at Minnesota 4
Pittsburgh 1 at NY Islanders 3
New Jersey 2 at Anaheim 4
Toronto 7 at Washington 1
Ottawa 6 at Florida 4
St. Louis 3 at Detroit 2 (SO)

STL (vs. Hasek)—RUCINSKY, WEIGHT/DET (vs. Legace)—
    Williams, Datsyuk
Montreal 2 at Buffalo 1 (Souray 4:59 OT)
Atlanta 2 at Tampa Bay 3 (St. Louis 2:25 OT)
Los Angeles 3 at Dallas 5
Chicago 1 at Edmonton 5

November 25, 2006

Boston 3 at Toronto 1
Philadelphia 4 at Montreal 2
Washington 1 at NY Islanders 4
Florida 0 at Atlanta 1
Minnesota 3 at Columbus 5
NY Rangers 2 at Pittsburgh 1 (Straka 4:57 OT)
Phoenix 2 at St. Louis 1
Detroit 2 at Nashville 6
Vancouver 1 at Colorado 4
Calgary 1 at Los Angeles 3
New Jersey 0 at San Jose 2

November 26, 2006

Ottawa 1 at Tampa Bay 3
Buffalo 3 at NY Rangers 2 (Drury 1:36 OT)
Calgary 3 at Anaheim 5

November 27, 2006

Dallas 1 at Detroit 2
New Jersey 2 at Los Angeles 3 (SO)
NJ (vs. Garon)—Elias, Gionta/LA (vs. Brodeur)—KOPITAR,
    Brown, FROLOV

November 28, 2006

Atlanta 5 at NY Rangers 4 (Holik 2:55 OT)
NY Islanders 2 at Pittsburgh 3

Ottawa 4 at Carolina 1
Boston 4 at Toronto 1
Florida 0 at Montreal 1 (SO)
FLO (vs. Huet)—PELTONEN, Jokinen, Nieuwendyk/MON (vs.
    Auld)—KOVALEV, KOIVU, Ryder
Washington 5 at Tampa Bay 2
San Jose 2 at St. Louis 0
Colorado 2 at Calgary 5
Anaheim 3 at Edmonton 2 (Getzlaf 2:19 OT)
Columbus 0 at Vancouver 1

November 29, 2006

Nashville 3 at Philadelphia 2
San Jose 2 at Minnesota 1
Dallas 1 at Chicago 2

November 30, 2006

Tampa Bay 3 at Boston 4 (SO)
TB (vs. Thomas)—Lecavalier, Richards, St. Louis, Perrin, Prospal,
    Afanasenkov, Fedotenko/BOS (vs. Denis)—Sturm, Bergeron,
    Murray, Savard, Boyes, Tenkrat, KESSEL
Dallas 3 at Washington 4
Montreal 2 at Carolina 4
Toronto 0 at Atlanta 5
Florida 0 at Ottawa 6
Philadelphia 3 at Islanders 2
Nashville 5 at St. Louis 4
Colorado 7 at Edmonton 3
Los Angeles 4 at Phoenix 7
Anaheim 2 at Vancouver 1

December 1, 2006

Pittsburgh 2 at New Jersey 5
Detroit 3 at Minnesota 0

NY Rangers 3 at Buffalo 4 (SO)
NYR (vs. Miller)—Nylander, Shanahan, Prucha/BUF (vs.
Weekes)—BRIERE, Kotalik, Afinogenov
St. Louis 2 at Chicago 5
Columbus 1 at Calgary 2

December 2, 2006

Anaheim 4 at Los Angeles 3
Toronto 3 at Montreal 4 (SO)
TOR (vs. Huet)—Kaberle, SUNDIN, Wellwood/MON (vs.
Raycroft)—Kovalev, KOIVU, SOURAY
Tampa Bay 2 at Ottawa 5
Boston 2 at Carolina 5
San Jose 3 at Detroit 2
New Jersey 4 at Philadelphia 3 (SO)
NJ (vs. Niittymaki)—PARISE, GIONTA/PHI (vs. Brodeur)—
Gagne, Nedved
NY Islanders 5 at Pittsburgh 3
Atlanta 3 at Florida 1
Columbus 4 at Edmonton 0
Chicago 4 at Nashville 3 (Hamilton 0:59 OT)
Minnesota 3 at Dallas 4 (SO)
MIN (vs. Turco)—Koivu, ROLSTON/DAL (vs. Backstrom)—
ZUBOV, JOKINEN, RIBEIRO
Buffalo 4 at Washington 7
Colorado 1 at Vancouver 2

December 3, 2006

NY Islanders 7 at NY Rangers 4
Los Angeles 3 at Anaheim 2

December 4, 2006

Boston 6 at Montreal 5

San Jose 0 at Dallas 1
Nashville 2 at Phoenix 3
Edmonton 4 at Vancouver 0

December 5, 2006

Atlanta 5 at Toronto 2
Ottawa 4 at NY Islanders 2
Florida 3 at Pittsburgh 2
Buffalo 4 at Tampa Bay 1
Detroit 5 at St. Louis 1
Chicago 2 at Minnesota 3 (SO)
CHI (vs. Fernandez—HAMILTON, T. Ruutu, Vrbata, SMOLINSKI,
    Bochenski, Sharp/MIN (vs. Khabibulin—T. White., M.
    KOIVU, Rolston, NUMMELIN, Parrish, BOUCHARD)
Columbus 0 at Colorado 0
Carolina 0 at Calgary 3

December 6, 2006

Ottawa 2 at Washington 6
Montreal 1 at New Jersey 2 (Elias 4:52 OT)
Phoenix 0 at Dallas 3
Carolina 1 at Edmonton 3
Nashville 0 at Anaheim 4

December 7, 2006

Toronto 1 at Boston 3
Pittsburgh 2 at NY Rangers 3 (SO)
PIT (vs. Lundqvist)—Malkin, Ekman, Crosby/NYR (vs. Fleury)—
    SHANAHAN, Cullen
Montreal 4 at NY Islanders 2
Atlanta 0 at Tampa Bay 8
Buffalo 1 at Florida 3
St. Louis 3 at Detroit 4 (Datsyuk 3:23 OT)
Calgary 2 at Minnesota 3 (SO)

CAL (vs. Fernandez)—Tanguay, RITCHIE, Huselius/MIN (vs. Kiprusoff)—ROLSTON, KOIVU
Phoenix 2 at Chicago 1 (SO)
PHO (vs. Khabibulin)—Fischer, Nagy, Perreault, Nolan, ZIGO-MANIS, DOAN/CHI (vs. Tellqvist)—Hamilton, Smolinski, Holmqvist, Salmelainen, RUUTU, Vrbata
Nashville 4 at Los Angeles 1
Colorado 5 at San Jose 2

December 8, 2006

Anaheim 6 at Washington 1
Philadelphia 0 at New Jersey 2
Edmonton 2 at Dallas 0
Carolina 3 at Vancouver 4 (D. Sedin 3:04 OT)

December 9, 2006

NY Rangers 3 at Ottawa 1
New Jersey 5 at Boston 1
Buffalo 3 at Montreal 2 (SO)
BUF (vs. Huet)—BRIERE, VANEK/MON (vs. Miller)—KOVALEV, Koivu, Samsonov
Florida 4 at NY Islanders 5 (SO)
FLO (vs. DiPietro)—Peltonen, Olesz/NYI (vs. Auld)—SATAN, KOZLOV
Washington 5 at Philadelphia 3
Pittsburgh 4 at Atlanta 3 (Armstrong 3:51 OT)
Toronto 1 at Detroit 5
Anaheim 4 at Tampa Bay 3
Columbus 5 at St. Louis 1
Chicago 4 at Minnesota 5 (Parrish 3:18 OT)
Dallas 4 at Phoenix 3 (Lehtinen 4:55 OT)
Vancouver 3 at Calgary 5
Colorado 4 at Los Angeles 5
Nashville 1 at San Jose 3

December 10, 2006

Ottawa 2 at Columbus 6
Edmonton 1 at Chicago 4
Florida 1 at NY Rangers 2

December 11, 2006

Pittsburgh 5 at Washington 4 (SO)
PIT (vs. Kolzig)—CHRISTENSEN, Crosby, MALKIN/WAS (vs.
    Fleury)—Green, OVECHKIN, Clark
Carolina 2 at Colorado 5
Phoenix 0 at San Jose 4

December 12, 2006

Buffalo 3 at New Jersey 2
NY Rangers 3 at Philadelphia 1
Tampa Bay 4 at Toronto 5
Boston 3 at Montreal 4
Anaheim 5 at Florida 4
Ottawa 3 at Detroit 2
Chicago 3 at St. Louis 2
Edmonton 2 at Nashville 3
Columbus 3 at Dallas 1
Minnesota 2 at Calgary 5
Phoenix 2 at Vancouver 5
San Jose 3 at Los Angeles 1

December 13, 2006

Anaheim 2 at Atlanta 1
Philadelphia 4 at Pittsburgh 8
St. Louis 1 at Colorado 4

December 14, 2006

New Jersey 3 at Boston 5
Florida 1 at Buffalo 2

Tampa Bay 2 at Montreal 4
Ottawa 0 at Nashville 6
Detroit 3 at Chicago 2
NY Rangers 5 at Dallas 2
Minnesota 1 at Edmonton 3
Columbus 4 at Phoenix 5 (SO)
CBJ (vs. Tellqvist)—Vyborny, Nash, Fedorov/PHO (vs.
    Norrena)—Perreault, Zigomanis, COMRIE
Calgary 1 at Vancouver 3
Los Angeles 4 at San Jose 2

December 15, 2006

Toronto 4 at Carolina 3
NY Islanders 4 at Pittsburgh 7
Washington 3 at Atlanta 2 (Ovechkin 0:06 OT)
Edmonton 1 at Colorado 4

December 16, 2006

Detroit 2 at New Jersey 1
Dallas 4 at Los Angeles 3 (SO)
DAL (vs. Brust)—Zubov, Jokinen, RIBEIRO/LA (vs. Turco)—
    Brown, Kopitar, Frolov
Florida 6 at Boston 3
Ottawa 3 at Buffalo 1
NY Rangers 2 at Toronto 9
Pittsburgh 3 at Montreal 6
Atlanta 0 at NY Islanders 6
Philadelphia 1 at Washington 4
Chicago 6 at Columbus 4
Carolina 3 at Tampa Bay 2
St. Louis 2 at Nashville 3 (SO)
STL (vs. Mason)—Rucinsky, Tkachuk, Weight/NAS (vs. Legace)—
    Sullivan, KARIYA
Calgary 6 at Phoenix 3

Minnesota 1 at Vancouver 2
Anaheim 3 at San Jose 4

December 17, 2006

Nashville 2 at St. Louis 1 (Timonen 3:11 OT)
Colorado 1 at Chicago 2
New Jersey 6 at NY Rangers 1

December 18, 2006

Detroit 3 at Columbus 4
Calgary 1 at Anaheim 4

December 19, 2006

Montreal 5 at Buffalo 2
NY Islanders 4 at NY Rangers 3
Carolina 2 at Philadelphia 1
St. Louis 4 at Pittsburgh 1
Tampa Bay 5 at Washington 4
Florida 7 at Toronto 3
Boston 7 at Ottawa 2
Atlanta 4 at New Jersey 3 (SO)
ATL (vs. Brodeur)—KOZLOV, HOSSA/NJ (vs. Lehtonen)—Parise,
   Gionta
Vancouver 2 at Minnesota 5
Colorado 7 at Edmonton 6
Calgary 5 at Los Angeles 3

December 20, 2006

Columbus 0 at Detroit 5
Nashville 2 at Chicago 1
Dallas 1 at Anaheim 4

December 21, 2006

Vancouver 0 at Boston 2
Pittsburgh 3 at Atlanta 4 (SO)
PIT (vs. Lehtonen)—Christensen, Crosby/ATL (vs. Thibault)—
    KOZLOV, HOSSA
Philadelphia 2 at Montreal 4
Tampa Bay 4 at Ottawa 2
NY Rangers 2 at Florida 3
Los Angeles 2 at St. Louis 5
Buffalo 7 at Nashville 2
Edmonton 3 at Phoenix 2
Dallas 3 at San Jose 0

December 22, 2006

New Jersey 4 at Washington 1
NY Islanders 1 at Carolina 5
Vancouver 2 at Columbus 3
Minnesota 1 at Detroit 3
Toronto 1 at Chicago 3

December 23, 2006

Ottawa 6 at Philadelphia 3
Montreal 2 at Boston 4
Washington 3 at Toronto 2
Columbus 0 at NY Islanders 4
New Jersey 2 at Atlanta 5
NY Rangers 3 at Tampa Bay 4
Carolina 3 at Florida 2 (Cole 1:59 OT)
Buffalo 2 at St. Louis 3
Los Angeles 0 at Nashville 7
Detroit 2 at Minnesota 3 (Bouchard 0:45 OT)
Edmonton 2 at Dallas 3
Chicago 2 at Colorado 3

Anaheim 0 at Phoenix 2
Calgary 1 at San Jose 4

December 26, 2006

Dallas 1 at Chicago 2
Washington 3 at Buffalo 6
Florida 2 at Carolina 4
Tampa Bay 1 at Atlanta 2
Boston 4 at Columbus 5 (Vyborny 3:06 OT)
Minnesota 3 at Toronto 4
Pittsburgh 0 at New Jersey 3
NY Rangers 0 at NY Islanders 2
St. Louis 2 at Nashville 3 (SO)
STL (vs. Mason)—Guerin, Rucinsky, Tkachuk, Weight/NAS (vs.
    Legace)—Sullivan, Kariya, Erat, RADULOV
Vancouver 3 at Calgary 1
Phoenix 3 at Los Angeles 4 (SO)
PHO (vs. Brust)—Zigomanis, Comrie/LA (vs. Tellqvist)—Frolov,
    KOPITAR, BROWN
Anaheim 4 at San Jose 3

December 27, 2006

Montreal 4 at Washington 1
NY Islanders 0 at Ottawa 2
Atlanta 4 at Pittsburgh 2
Philadelphia 1 at Florida 3
Minnesota 1 at Detroit 3
Dallas 5 at Colorado 4
Calgary 5 at Vancouver 6 (Salo 2:46 OT)

December 28, 2006

Carolina 1 at Buffalo 4
Detroit 7 at Columbus 4
Philadelphia 4 at Tampa Bay 3

Los Angeles 7 at Edmonton 4
Phoenix 3 at San Jose 2

December 29, 2006

Anaheim 2 at Carolina 4
NY Rangers 0 at Ottawa 1
Washington 3 at New Jersey 4
Toronto 1 at Pittsburgh 4
Montreal 1 at Florida 3
Columbus 3 at Minnesota 4 (Walz 1:29 OT)
Boston 5 at Chicago 3
Nashville 1 at Dallas 4
St. Louis 4 at Colorado 2
Los Angeles 4 at Calgary 6

December 30, 2006

Atlanta 1 at Buffalo 4
Ottawa 3 at Toronto 2 (Phillips 2:39 OT)
New Jersey 2 at NY Islanders 0
Washington 1 at NY Rangers 4
Montreal 1 at Tampa Bay 3
Colorado 0 at St. Louis 2
Boston 0 at Nashville 5
San Jose 0 at Phoenix 8
Vancouver 6 at Edmonton 2

December 31, 2006

Anaheim 3 at Minnesota 4
Los Angeles 2 at Detroit 6
Chicago 1 at Columbus 3
Edmonton 2 at Calgary 4
San Jose 4 at Dallas 2
Philadelphia 5 at Carolina 2

January 1, 2007

Phoenix 3 at Washington 2
Colorado 5 at Nashville 3
Atlanta 3 at Ottawa 2 (Kozlov 1:48 OT)
NY Islanders 1 at Buffalo 3
Boston 1 at Toronto 5

January 2, 2007

Tampa Bay 2 at Montreal 5
NY Rangers 3 at New Jersey 2 (SO)
NYR (vs. Lundqvist)—NYLANDER, SHANAHAN, Jagr, Prucha,
    CULLEN, Straka, Hall, HOSSA/NJ (vs. Brodeur)—PARISE,
    Gionta, ELIAS, Brylin, MADDEN, Gomez, Langenbrunner,
    Zajac
Philadelphia 3 at NY Islanders 2
Carolina 0 at Pittsburgh 3
Anaheim 1 at Detroit 2
Chicago 4 at St. Louis 1
Atlanta 1 at Minnesota 5
Vancouver 3 at Calgary 2
Florida 1 at Edmonton 4

January 3, 2007

Buffalo 3 at Ottawa 6
Dallas 1 at Vancouver 2 (SO)
DAL (vs. Luongo)—JOKINEN, Ribeiro, Eriksson, Miettinen,
    Barnes, Zubov/VAN (vs. Turco)—Naslund, MORRISON,
    D. Sedin, Pyatt, Bieksa, KESLER
Columbus 0 at Los Angeles 3

January 4, 2007

Toronto 10 at Boston 2
Philadelphia 2 at NY Rangers 3
Montreal 1 at Washington 5

Phoenix 2 at Carolina 0
NY Islanders 3 at New Jersey 4
Chicago 0 at St. Louis 2
Tampa Bay 3 at Minnesota 2
Florida 4 at Calgary 5 (Giordano 4:30 OT)
Dallas 6 at Edmonton 5 (SO)
DAL (vs. Roloson)—ZUBOV, JOKINEN/EDM (vs. Turco)—
    Hemsky, Sykora
Detroit 4 at San Jose 9

January 5, 2007

Phoenix 5 at Atlanta 4 (Perreault 2:31 OT)
Pittsburgh 4 at Buffalo 2
Nashville 8 at Chicago 3
Tampa Bay 2 at Colorado 4
Edmonton 2 at Vancouver 3 (Cooke 1:24 OT)
Columbus 4 at Anaheim 3

January 6, 2007

Philadelphia 3 at Boston 4
New Jersey 3 at Ottawa 2
NY Rangers 4 at Montreal 3
Buffalo 4 at Toronto 3
Atlanta 2 at Washington 3 (Semin 4:42 OT)
NY Islanders 2 at Carolina 4
St. Louis 2 at Nashville 3
Colorado 2 at Minnesota 1 (SO)
COL (vs. Fernandez)—WOLSKI, Stastny, Sakic, HEJDUK/MIN
    (vs. Budaj)—DEMITRA, Koivu, Rolston, Bouchard
Dallas 2 at Calgary 4
Detroit 2 at Los Angeles 4
Columbus 2 at San Jose 5

January 7, 2007

Phoenix 4 at Chicago 2

Philadelphia 1 at Ottawa 6

New Jersey 3 at Montreal 0

Tampa Bay 3 at Pittsburgh 2 (SO)

TB (vs. Fleury)—Lecavalier, Richards, ST. LOUIS/PIT (vs.
   Holmqvist)—Christensen, Malkin, Crosby

Detroit 2 at Anaheim 4

Florida 3 at Vancouver 4 (SO)

FLO (vs. Luongo)—Peltonen, MONTADOR, Jokinen, Olesz,
   Horton, Stumpel/VAN (vs. Belfour)—Morrison, KESLER,
   Naslund, D. Sedin. H. Sedin, GREEN

January 8, 2007

Edmonton 2 at Los Angeles 1 (Hejda 1:14 OT)

January 9, 2007

NY Islanders 5 at NY Rangers 3

Philadelphia 2 at Washington 6

St. Louis 4 at Columbus 3 (SO)

STL (vs. Norrena)—RUCINSKY, WEIGHT, STEMPNIAK/CBJ (vs.
   Legace)—VYBORNY, ZHERDEV, Modin

Carolina 4 at Toronto 1

Atlanta 2 at Montreal 4

Boston 2 at Ottawa 5

Pittsburgh 2 at Tampa Bay 3

Anaheim 4 at Nashville 5 (Sullivan 3:12 OT)

Phoenix 5 at Dallas 2

Detroit 4 at Colorado 3 (SO)

DET (vs. Budaj)—Williams, DATSYUK, ZETTERBERG/COL (vs.
   Hasek)—Wolski, Hejduk, SAKIC

Minnesota 0 at Calgary 3

January 10, 2007

St. Louis 3 at New Jersey 2
Pittsburgh 2 at Florida 5
Buffalo 2 at Chicago 1
Edmonton 3 at San Jose 2

January 11, 2007

NY Islanders 5 at Boston 4 (SO)
NYI (vs. Toivonen)—SATAN, Kozlov, Hunter, BLAKE/BOS (vs.
    DiPietro)—Sturm, Bergeron, SAVARD, Boyes
Toronto 4 at Buffalo 2
Ottawa 6 at NY Rangers 4
Montreal 4 at Philadelphia 2
Florida 4 at Carolina 6
Washington 4 at Tampa Bay 5
Anaheim 5 at Dallas 1
Calgary 7 at Colorado 3
Detroit 5 at Phoenix 1
Minnesota 5 at Vancouver 2
San Jose 5 at Los Angeles 2

January 12, 2007

Atlanta 1 at New Jersey 2
Columbus 0 at Nashville 2
Minnesota 4 at Edmonton 2

January 13, 2007

Los Angeles 5 at St. Louis 6
Montreal 3 at Ottawa 8
Boston 1 at NY Rangers 3
Pittsburgh 5 at Philadelphia 3
Tampa Bay 3 at Buffalo 2
Vancouver 6 at Toronto 1
New Jersey 2 at NY Islanders 1 (Gomez 3:40 OT)

Atlanta 4 at Carolina 3 (SO)
ATL (vs. Ward)—KOZLOV, HOSSA/CAR (vs. Lehtonen)—Whitney,
  Williams
Chicago 3 at Detroit 6
Nashville 4 at Columbus 1
Washington 3 at Florida 7
San Jose 4 at Phoenix 1
Colorado 3 at Anaheim 2 (SO)
COL (vs. Bryzgalov)—WOLSKI, Svatos, Sakic, HEJDUK/ANA (vs.
  Budaj)—KUNITZ, Getzlaf, Perry, McDonald
Edmonton 1 at Calgary 3

January 14, 2007

Minnesota 4 at Chicago 3 (SO)
MIN (vs. Khabibulin)—DEMITRA, Koivu/CHI (vs. Fernandez)—
  Hamilton, Havlat, Arkhipov

January 15, 2007

Tampa Bay 4 at NY Islanders 3
Buffalo 2 at Boston 3 (SO)
BUF (vs. Thomas)—Briere, Kotalik, Vanek/BOS (vs. Miller)—
  STURM, Murray
St. Louis 4 at Phoenix 5 (SO)
STL (vs. Tellqvist)—Rucinsky, Stempniak, WEIGHT, Sejna/PHO
  (vs. Legace)—Roenick, Perreault, DOAN, NAGY
Los Angeles 1 at Dallas 3
Calgary 3 at Nashville 5
Montreal 0 at Detroit 2
Colorado 1 at San Jose 3

January 16, 2007

NY Islanders 2 at Pittsburgh 5
Los Angeles 2 at Atlanta 6
Columbus 5 at Chicago 4 (Chimera 2:31 OT)

Vancouver 4 at Montreal 0
Washington 2 at Ottawa 5
NY Rangers 0 at New Jersey 1
Toronto 4 at Tampa Bay 2
Carolina 3 at Florida 2 (Williams 1:47 OT)
Edmonton 2 at Minnesota 1
St. Louis 6 at Anaheim 2

January 17, 2007

Boston 3 at Buffalo 6
Nashville 3 at Detroit 5
Calgary 2 at Dallas 4
Phoenix 3 at Colorado 4

January 18, 2007

Pittsburgh 4 at Boston 5 (SO)
PIT (vs. Toivonen)—CHRISTENSEN, Malkin, Crosby, Gonchar/BOS
   (vs. Fleury)—STURM, Bergeron, Savard, KESSEL
NY Islanders 4 at Philadelphia 2
Washington 5 at Carolina 2
Montreal 4 at Atlanta 1
Vancouver 2 at Ottawa 1
Tampa Bay 3 at New Jersey 2 (SO)
TB (vs. Brodeur)—Lecavalier, RICHARDS, St. Louis/NJ (vs.
   Holmqvist)—Parise, Gionta, Elias
Toronto 3 at Florida 2
Columbus 0 at Nashville 4
Anaheim 1 at Edmonton 4
St. Louis 3 at Los Angeles 1
Phoenix 2 at San Jose 5

January 19, 2007

Detroit 1 at Columbus 3
Vancouver 3 at Buffalo 4 (SO)

VAN (vs. Miller)—Kesler, MORRISON, Naslund, Green/BUF (vs.
    Sabourin)—Briere, AFINOGENOV, Vanek, KOTALIK
Minnesota 3 at Chicago 0
Anaheim 2 at Calgary 3

January 20, 2007

Philadelphia 3 at New Jersey 4 (SO)
PHI (vs. Brodeur)—Gagne, Forsberg, Richards/NJ (vs.
    Niittymaki)—GIONTA, Elias
Atlanta 3 at NY Rangers 1
Florida 4 at Washington 1
Ottawa 3 at Boston 0
Buffalo 3 at Montreal 4
Toronto 2 at Pittsburgh 8
Chicago 3 at Nashville 6
Tampa Bay 6 at Carolina 5 (SO)
TB (vs. Ward)—Lecavalier, Richards, St. Louis, PROSPAL/CAR
    (vs. Denis)—Whitney, Brind'Amour, Williams, Staal
Detroit 1 at Colorado 3
Dallas 2 at Minnesota 1 (SO)
DAL (vs. Backstrom)—RIBEIRO, Jokinen, Stefan, Eriksson,
    Miettinen, LINDROS, Lehtonen, Hagman, BARNES/MIN (vs.
    Turco)—Demitra, Gaborik, NUMMELIN, Bouchard, Rolston,
    KOIVU, Parrish, Walz, Dupuis
Calgary 4 at Edmonton 0
Phoenix 3 at Los Angeles 2
St. Louis 1 at San Jose 0

January 26, 2007

Washington 2 at Carolina 6
Buffalo 2 at Columbus 3
NY Islanders 4 at Atlanta 5 (Kovalchuk 2:59 OT)
Detroit 1 at St. Louis 2 (Guerin 1:09 OT)
Calgary 1 at Minnesota 2 (SO)

CAL (vs. Backstrom)—Tanguay, Ritchie/MIN (vs. Kiprusoff)—
    DEMITRA, NUMMELIN
New Jersey 2 at Tampa Bay 0
Nashville 3 at Chicago 1
Pittsburgh 4 at Dallas 3 (SO)
PIT (vs. Turco)—CHRISTENSEN, Crosby/DAL (vs. Fleury)—
    Zubov, Jokinen, Ribeiro
Phoenix 5 at Colorado 4 (SO)
PHO (vs. Budaj)—Reinprecht, NAGY/COL (vs. Joseph)—Wolski,
    Hejduk, Sakic
San Jose 5 at Edmonton 1
Los Angeles 3 at Vancouver 2 (Frolov 1:48 OT)

January 27, 2007

NY Rangers 2 at Philadelphia 1
Boston 1 at Ottawa 3
Montreal 1 at Toronto 4
Buffalo 3 at NY Islanders 5
Carolina 3 at Washington 7
Minnesota 2 at Columbus 3
New Jersey 2 at Florida 4
Nashville 6 at St. Louis 3
Pittsburgh 7 at Phoenix 2

January 28, 2007

Calgary 3 at Chicago 4 (Arkhipov 2:53 OT)
Dallas 1 at Anaheim 4
Philadelphia 2 at Atlanta 1
Colorado 1 at Detroit 3
San Jose 1 at Vancouver 3

January 29, 2007

NY Rangers 6 at Boston 1
Ottawa 1 at Montreal 3

January 30, 2007

Boston 1 at Buffalo 7
Tampa Bay 4 at Philadelphia 3 (SO)
TB (vs. Esche)—LECAVALIER, RICHARDS/PHI (vs. Holmqvist)—
    Gagne, Forsberg
Toronto 4 at Carolina 1
New Jersey 4 at Atlanta 5 (SO)
NJ (vs. Lehtonen)—GIONTA, Parise, Madden/ATL (vs.
    Brodeur)—KOZLOV, HOSSA, Kovalchuk
Washington 2 at Ottawa 3
Detroit 4 at NY Islanders 3 (Zetterberg 2:57 OT)
Florida 0 at Pittsburgh 3
Nashville 3 at Colorado 4
Minnesota 5 at St. Louis 2
Los Angeles 1 at Calgary 4
Columbus 3 at Vancouver 2 (SO)
CBJ (vs. Luongo)—VYBORNY, Nash, ZHERDEV/VAN (vs.
    Conklin)—Naslund, MORRISON, Green
Dallas 3 at San Jose 2 (SO)
DAL (vs. Toskala)—ZUBOV, JOKINEN, RIBEIRO/SJ (vs. Turco)—
    CLOWE, PAVELSKI, Marleau

January 31, 2007

Toronto 2 at NY Rangers 1
Phoenix 1 at Anaheim 2
Columbus 2 at Edmonton 5

February 1, 2007

Buffalo 3 at Boston 1
New Jersey 6 at Philadelphia 5 (Lukowich 4:10 OT)
Tampa Bay 4 at Carolina 0
NY Islanders 5 at Atlanta 2
Montreal 4 at Pittsburgh 5 (SO)

MON (vs. Fleury)—KOVALEV, Higgins, Plekanec PIT (vs. Aebischer)—CHRISTENSEN, Crosby, MALKIN

Washington 3 at Florida 6

Minnesota 5 at Colorado 3

Nashville 2 at Phoenix 3

Edmonton 3 at Vancouver 5

Chicago 3 at Los Angeles 2 (Kukkonen 0:57 OT)

Dallas 4 at San Jose 2

February 2, 2007

St. Louis 3 at Detroit 5

Columbus 2 at Calgary 6

February 3, 2007

Washington 0 at Pittsburgh 2

NY Islanders 4 at Montreal 2

Edmonton 3 at Colorado 2

Chicago 2 at San Jose 4

Toronto 3 at Ottawa 2 (SO)

TOR (vs. Emery)—Antropov, SUNDIN, Kaberle, Ponikarovsky, POHL/OTT (vs. Raycroft)—VERMETTE, Comrie, Fisher, Heatley, Spezza

Philadelphia 5 at Atlanta 2

Buffalo 2 at New Jersey 3

NY Rangers 2 at Tampa Bay 3

Los Angeles 7 at Florida 0

Dallas 0 at St. Louis 2

Anaheim 0 at Nashville 3

Boston 4 at Carolina 3 (Chara 1:49 OT)

Minnesota 1 at Phoenix 0

Vancouver 3 at Calgary 4

February 4, 2007

NY Islanders 1 at Washington 2 (SO)
NYI (vs. Kolzig)—Satan, Kozlov, Blake/WAS (vs. DiPietro)—
    SEMIN, Ovechkin, Zubrus
Pittsburgh 3 at Montreal 4 (Souray 2:01 OT)

February 5, 2007

Detroit 4 at NY Rangers 3

February 6, 2007

Boston 3 at Washington 2 (SO)
BOS (vs. Kolzig)—Bochenski, BERGERON, KESSEL/WAS (vs.
    Thomas)—SEMIN, Ovechkin, Fehr
Buffalo 4 at Atlanta 3 (SO)
BUF (vs. Lehtonen)—BRIERE, KOTALIK/ATL (vs. Miller)—
    Kozlov, Hossa
Phoenix 3 at Columbus 0
Carolina 2 at Montreal 1
NY Rangers 2 at New Jersey 3 (SO)
NYR (vs. Brodeur)—Nylander, Shanahan, Cullen/NJ (vs.
    Lundqvist)—GIONTA, Brylin
Nashville 1 at Pittsburgh 4
Los Angeles 2 at Tampa Bay 3 (SO)
LA (vs. Holmqvist)—Frolov, KOPITAR/TB (vs. Burke)—LECAVA-
    LIER, RICHARDS, ST. LOUIS
Toronto 2 at St. Louis 1
Minnesota 2 at Dallas 4
Florida 4 at Colorado 5 (Sakic 0:25 OT)
Chicago 3 at Calgary 2 (SO)
CHI (vs. Kiprusoff)—HAVLAT, HAMILTON/CAL (vs.
    Khabibulin)—Huselius, Tanguay
Vancouver 5 at Edmonton 2
Anaheim 7 at San Jose 4

February 7, 2007

Ottawa 2 at Buffalo 3
Philadelphia 0 at NY Islanders 2
Phoenix 2 at Detroit 4
Chicago 3 at Vancouver 0
San Jose 3 at Anaheim 2

February 8, 2007

Carolina 5 at Boston 2
Pittsburgh 5 at Philadelphia 4 (SO)
PIT (vs. Niittymaki)—Christensen, Malkin, CROSBY/PHI (vs. Fleury)—Carter, Forsberg, Gagne
Los Angeles 3 at Washington 4 (Zubrus 2:28 OT)
Calgary 1 at Columbus 2
Montreal 1 at Ottawa 4
NY Islanders 0 at New Jersey 2
Detroit 0 at St. Louis 1
Toronto 2 at Nashville 4
Florida 2 at Minnesota 4
Atlanta 6 at Colorado 3

February 9, 2007

Tampa Bay 0 at NY Rangers 5
Chicago 1 at Edmonton 2

February 10, 2007

Anaheim 0 at Dallas 1
NY Islanders 3 at Boston 4 (SO)
NYI (vs. Thomas)—Satan, KOZLOV, Hilbert, Hunter, Blake, Sillinger, ROBITAILLE, Tambellini, Poti/BOS (vs. DiPietro)—Sturm, BERGERON, Kessel, Bochenski, Savard, Boyes, TENKRAT, Axelsson, CHARA
Calgary 2 at Buffalo 3 (SO)

CAL (vs. Miller)—Phaneuf, Lombardi, Huselius / BUF (vs.
Kiprusoff)—Briere, KOTALIK, Vanek
Pittsburgh 6 at Toronto 5 (J. Staal 3:54 OT)
Ottawa 5 at Montreal 3
St. Louis 3 at Philadelphia 4 (Gagne 0:27 OT)
NY Rangers 5 at Washington 2
Phoenix 2 at Florida 5
Los Angeles 4 at Nashville 1
Carolina 4 at Minnesota 5
Atlanta 2 at Vancouver 3

February 11, 2007

Colorado 5 at Dallas 7
Tampa Bay 4 at New Jersey 1
Chicago 5 at Columbus 4
Calgary 4 at Detroit 7
Atlanta 1 at Edmonton 5

February 12, 2007

Detroit 1 at Philadelphia 6

February 13, 2007

Edmonton 0 at Boston 3
Los Angeles 1 at Carolina 2
NY Islanders 3 at Toronto 2 (SO)
NYI (vs. Raycroft)—NIELSEN, Satan, KOZLOV / TOR (vs.
DiPietro)—Ponikarovsky, SUNDIN, Antropov
Florida 1 at Montreal 0
Phoenix 3 at Tampa Bay 5
San Jose 6 at St. Louis 5
Anaheim 0 at Colorado 2
Atlanta 1 at Calgary 4

February 14, 2007

St. Louis 4 at Columbus 2
Florida 0 at Ottawa 4
Montreal 2 at New Jersey 5
Chicago 4 at Pittsburgh 5 (SO)
CHI (vs. Fleury)—Havlat, Smolinski/PIT (vs. Khabibulin)—
    CHRISTENSEN, Crosby, MALKIN
San Jose 0 at Nashville 5
Detroit 3 at Dallas 1
Vancouver 3 at Minnesota 2 (Salo 4:20 OT)

February 15, 2007

Edmonton 1 at Buffalo 2 (Briere 1:02 OT)
Toronto 4 at Philadelphia 2
NY Rangers 4 at Carolina 1
Boston 1 at NY Islanders 4
Washington 2 at Tampa Bay 3 (SO)
WAS (vs. Denis)—Semin, Ovechkin, Pettinger/TB (vs.
    Johnson)—Lecavalier, Richards, ST. LOUIS
Anaheim 5 at Phoenix 4 (Selanne 1:53 OT)
Colorado 7 at Calgary 5

February 16, 2007

San Jose 0 at Columbus 3
Pittsburgh 5 at New Jersey 4
Nashville 0 at St. Louis 1
Vancouver 2 at Chicago 1 (SO)
VAN (vs. Lalime)—LINDEN, MORRISON/CHI (vs. Luongo)—
    Havlat, St. Pierre

February 17, 2007

Philadelphia 5 at NY Rangers 3
Atlanta 3 at Ottawa 5

Boston 4 at Buffalo 3 (SO)
BOS (vs. Miller)—Sturm, Murray, Kessel, Bochenski, Savard,
    Chara, Boyes, TENKRAT/BUF (vs. Thomas)—Briere,
    Stafford, Vanek, Pominville, Drury, Roy, MacArthur, Hecht
Edmonton 3 at Toronto 4
Carolina 5 at Montreal 3
New Jersey 2 at NY Islanders 0
Tampa Bay 4 at Florida 5 (Horton 0:29 OT)
Minnesota 4 at Nashville 1
Detroit 4 at Phoenix 1
Colorado 2 at Calgary 5
Anaheim 3 at Los Angeles 2 (SO)
ANA (vs. Garon)—Getzlaf, SELANNE, McDonald, Kunitz,
    PERRY/LA (vs. Giguere)—Kopitar, CAMMALLERI,
    Kostopoulos, Brown, Frolov

February 18, 2007

San Jose 2 at Dallas 5
Chicago 1 at NY Rangers 2
Washington 2 at Pittsburgh 3
Minnesota 3 at St. Louis 5
Montreal 3 at Columbus 2
Los Angeles 4 at Anaheim 3 (SO)
LA (vs. Giguere)—Cammalleri, KOPITAR, O'Sullivan, LUND-
    MARK, Brown, VISNOVSKY/ANA (vs. Burke)—GETZLAF,
    Selanne, Perry, KUNITZ, McDonald, R. Niedermayer
Colorado 4 at Vancouver 5

February 19, 2007

Pittsburgh 5 at NY Islanders 6
Phoenix 1 at Nashville 4
Boston 6 at Philadelphia 3

February 20, 2007

Philadelphia 3 at Buffalo 6
Boston 3 at Toronto 0
Atlanta 3 at Carolina 1
Washington 3 at Montreal 5
Edmonton 3 at Ottawa 4 (SO)
EDM (vs. Gerber)—Hemsky, Sykora/OTT (vs. Markkanen)—
    Vermette, MCAMMOND, COMRIE
NY Rangers 1 at New Jersey 2
Florida 2 at Tampa Bay 3 (SO)
FLO (vs. Denis)—HORTON, Peltonen, Montador/TB (vs.
    Belfour)—Lecavalier, RICHARDS, ST. LOUIS
Columbus 4 at St. Louis 5 (SO)
CBJ (vs. Legace)—Zherdev, Vyborny/STL (vs. Norrena)—STEMP-
    NIAK, WEIGHT
Dallas 1 at Minnesota 2 (SO)
DAL (vs. Backstrom)—Zubov, Jokinen, Ribeiro/MIN (vs.
    Turco)—Demitra, Rolston, KOIVU
Calgary 3 at Colorado 4
Vancouver 3 at Anaheim 2 (D. Sedin 2:19 OT)

February 21, 2007

San Jose 3 at Washington 2 (SO)
SJ (vs. Johnson)—Clowe, PAVELSKI, CHEECHOO/WAS (vs.
    Nabokov)—PETTINGER, Ovechkin, Semin
Chicago 2 at Detroit 4

February 22, 2007

Ottawa 5 at Buffalo 6 (SO)
OTT (vs. Miller)—Vermette, McAmmond, Comrie, Fisher/BUF
    (vs. Gerber)—Briere, Vanek, Pominville, STAFFORD
New Jersey 3 at NY Rangers 2 (SO)
NJ (vs. Lundqvist)—PARISE, Elias, Brylin, LANGENBRUNNER/NYR
    (vs. Brodeur)—NYLANDER, Hossa, Cullen, Prucha

Philadelphia 2 at Carolina 3 (Wesley 0:16 OT)
Tampa Bay 5 at Atlanta 4 (St. Louis 3:44 OT)
Edmonton 4 at Columbus 0
Toronto 2 at NY Islanders 3 (SO)
TOR (vs. DiPietro)—Pohl, Sundin, Ponikarovsky/NYI (vs.
    Raycroft)—Satan, Kozlov, ROBITAILLE
Pittsburgh 2 at Florida 1 (Armstrong 2:39 OT)
Montreal 6 at Nashville 5 (SO)
MON (vs. Vokoun)—Kostitsyn, Perezhogin, PLEKANEC, KOIVU/
    NAS (vs. Halak)—Dumont, KARIYA, Erat, Forsberg
San Jose 2 at Chicago 0
Minnesota 4 at Colorado 3
Calgary 2 at Phoenix 3 (Doan 0:54 OT)
Vancouver 3 at Los Angeles 2

February 23, 2007

Edmonton 4 at Detroit 3 (SO)
EDM (vs. Hasek)—SMYTH, Hemsky/DET (vs. Roloson)—
    Zetterberg, Datsyuk, Williams
Boston 6 at Tampa Bay 2
Anaheim 1 at Dallas 4

February 24, 2007

Washington 4 at New Jersey 2
Montreal 2 at NY Islanders 3
Buffalo 5 at Ottawa 6
Columbus 3 at NY Rangers 2
Toronto 5 at Philadelphia 2
Carolina 4 at Atlanta 1
Boston 2 at Florida 7
Detroit 3 at Nashville 4 (Forsberg 2:11 OT)
San Jose 4 at Calgary 7
Colorado 5 at Los Angeles 6 (SO)
COL (vs. Burke)—SVATOS, Hejduk, SAKIC, Stastny, McLEAN,

Brunette/LA(vs. Budaj)—Kopitar, CAMMALLERI, FROLOV, Visnovsky, LUNDMARK, BROWN

February 25, 2007

New Jersey 3 at Washington 2
Edmonton 1 at Minnesota 4
St. Louis 1 at Chicago 5
Vancouver 1 at Dallas 2 (Lehtinen 4:17 OT)
Pittsburgh 1 at Tampa Bay 5
Nashville 4 at Columbus 3 (SO)
NAS (vs. Conklin)—RADULOV, Kariya/CBJ (vs. Mason)—
    Vyborny, Zherdev, Nash
Colorado 3 at Anaheim 5

February 26, 2007

Atlanta 3 at Boston 2
Toronto 4 at Montreal 5
Phoenix 2 at Calgary 5
Anaheim 3 at San Jose 2

February 27, 2007

Montreal 0 at NY Rangers 4
Florida 6 at Washington 5 (SO)
FLO (vs. Cassivi)—Jokinen, STUMPEL, PELTONEN/WAS (vs.
    Belfour)—Semin, Ovechkin
Ottawa 4 at Carolina 2
Buffalo 6 at Toronto 1
Philadelphia 5 at NY Islanders 6 (Hunter 4:29 OT)
New Jersey 1 at Pittsburgh 0
Dallas 2 at Tampa Bay 1 (Nagy 1:35 OT)
Vancouver 1 at St. Louis 3
Detroit 4 at Chicago 1
Columbus 3 at Colorado 2
Phoenix 3 at Edmonton 0

February 28, 2007

Carolina 0 at Ottawa 2
Minnesota 1 at Calgary 2 (SO)
MIN (vs. Kiprusoff)—Demitra, Koivu, Bouchard/CAL (vs.
    Harding)—Tanguay, Amonte, IGINLA
Nashville 4 at San Jose 3 (SO)
NAS (vs. Nabokov)—RADULOV, Kariya, Erat, DUMONT/SJ (vs.
    Vokoun)—Clowe, PAVELSKI, Thornton, Cheechoo

March 1, 2007

Philadelphia 4 at Boston 3 (Upshall 4:50 OT)
Pittsburgh 4 at NY Rangers 3 (SO)
PIT (vs. Lundqvist)—Christensen, Malkin, CROSBY/NYR (vs.
    Fleury)—Nylander, Jagr, Prucha
Tampa Bay 5 at Washington 4 (SO
TB (vs. Johnson)—Lecavalier, Richards, St. Louis, Prospal, Kuba,
    Fedotenko, Perrin, Craig, Boyle, TARNASKY/WAS (vs.
    Holmqvist)—Laich, Fleischmann, Semin, Ovechkin,
    Novotny, Beech, Clymer, Pothier, Brashear, Bradley
St. Louis 3 at NY Islanders 2 (Stempniak 0:25 OT)
Dallas 1 at Florida 2 (O. Jokinen 2:11 OT)
Colorado 6 at Chicago 1
Minnesota 5 at Edmonton 0
Phoenix 3 at Vancouver 4
Anaheim 3 at Los Angeles 4 (Cammalleri 3:17 OT)

March 2, 2007

Pittsburgh 2 at Carolina 3
Toronto 4 at New Jersey 3 (SO))
TOR (vs. Brodeur)—Stajan, Sundin, PERREAULT, STEEN,
    O'NEILL/NJ (vs. Raycroft)—PARISE, Elias, Madden,
    LANGENBRUNNER, Brylin
Ottawa 2 at Atlanta 4
Chicago 2 at Detroit 6

Montreal 5 at Buffalo 8
Columbus 3 at Dallas 2 (SO)
CBJ (vs. Turco)—CHIMERA, Konopka/DAL (vs. Norrena)—
    Zubov, Modano, Jokinen
San Jose 1 at Anaheim 3

March 3, 2007

St. Louis 2 at NY Rangers 3 (SO)
STL (vs. Valiquette)—STEMPNIAK, WEIGHT, Boyes,
    Metropolit/NYR (vs. Sanford)—NYLANDER, Prucha, JAGR,
    HOSSA
Nashville 6 at Los Angeles 3
Montreal 1 at Boston 3
Buffalo 3 at Toronto 1
NY Islanders 6 at Washington 2
Tampa Bay 2 at Florida 6
Columbus 4 at Phoenix 3
Calgary 4 at Edmonton 2

March 4, 2007

Philadelphia 3 at Pittsburgh 4 (SO)
PHI (vs. Fleury)—Ruzicka, Upshall/PIT (vs. Biron)—CHRIS-
    TENSEN, Malkin, CROSBY
Colorado 4 at Detroit 3 (Richardson 2:41 OT)
Carolina 1 at Atlanta 3
Ottawa 3 at Chicago 4 (SO)
OTT (vs. Lalime)—Spezza, Alfredsson, HEATLEY, Vermette/CHI
    (vs. Gerber)—Williams, Havlat, HAMILTON, VRBATA
San Jose 4 at Dallas 0
Boston 4 at New Jersey 1
Nashville 2 at Anaheim 3 (SO)
NAS (vs. Giguere)—Radulov, KARIYA, Erat/ANA (vs. Vokoun)—
    GETZLAF, SELANNE, Perry
Minnesota 3 at Vancouver 4 (SO)

MIN (vs. Luongo)—DEMITRA, Nummelin, Koivu, ROLSTON, Gaborik, Bouchard/VAN (vs. Backstrom)—SMOLINSKI, Morrison, Naslund, LINDEN, Pyatt, D. SEDIN

March 5, 2007

NY Islanders 1 at NY Rangers 2 (SO)
NYI (vs. Lundqvist)—Satan, Kozlov, Robitaille/NYR (vs. DiPietro)—Nylander, CULLEN, Jagr

March 6, 2007

Colorado 2 at Boston 0
New Jersey 4 at Philadelphia 5 (Gagne 1:47 OT)
Florida 2 at Atlanta 4
Washington 0 at Toronto 3
Pittsburgh 5 at Ottawa 4 (SO)
PIT (vs. Emery)—CHRISTENSEN, Malkin, CROSBY/OTT (vs. Thibault)—Heatley, Vermette, MCAMMOND
Nashville 3 at Detroit 4 (SO)
NAS (vs. Osgood)—Radulov, KARIYA, Dumont, Erat/DET (vs. Vokoun)—DATSYUK, Hudler, Filppula, FRANZEN
Calgary 4 at St. Louis 2
San Jose 3 at Minnesota 0
Los Angeles 0 at Chicago 3
Tampa Bay 1 at Vancouver 5

March 7, 2007

Colorado 3 at Buffalo 2
Los Angeles 2 at Columbus 3 (Vyborny 4:38 OT)
Phoenix 1 at Anaheim 2
Tampa Bay 3 at Edmonton 1

March 8, 2007

Minnesota 2 at Boston 1
Florida 2 at Philadelphia 1

Montreal 2 at Atlanta 6
Toronto 1 at Ottawa 5
NY Rangers 2 at NY Islanders 1
New Jersey 4 at Pittsburgh 3 (SO)
NJ (vs. Fleury)—Parise, Langenbrunner, ELIAS/PIT (vs.
    Brodeur)—Christensen, Malkin, Crosby
Dallas 3 at St. Louis 5
Calgary 3 at Nashville 6
Vancouver 4 at Phoenix 2

March 9, 2007

Carolina 3 at Washington 0
Dallas 3 at Columbus 0
Los Angeles 2 at Detroit 3 (Samuelsson 3:26 OT)
Minnesota 5 at Buffalo 1
Edmonton 1 at Anaheim 5
Vancouver 2 at San Jose 1 (H. Sedin 3:30 OT)

March 10, 2007

Boston 1 at Philadelphia 4
NY Rangers 2 at Pittsburgh 3 (Armstrong 1:19 OT)
New Jersey 3 at Buffalo 2
Ottawa 3 at Toronto 4 (Tucker 3:11 OT)
Washington 2 at NY Islanders 5
Atlanta 2 at Florida 3
Montreal 4 at St. Louis 3
Columbus 1 at Nashville 2
Chicago 7 at Phoenix 5
Tampa Bay 3 at Calgary 2 (Boyle 2:59 OT)

March 11, 2007

Carolina 1 at NY Rangers 2 (SO)
CAR (vs. Lundqvist)—Williams, Whitney/NYR (vs. Grahame)—
    Nylander, CULLEN, JAGR

Boston 6 at Detroit 3
Colorado 2 at Minnesota 3 (Burns 4:41 OT)
Los Angeles 3 at Dallas 4 (Modano 0:35 OT)
Vancouver 2 at Anaheim 4
Edmonton 0 at San Jose 3

March 12, 2007

Washington 2 at Atlanta 4
St. Louis 4 at Calgary 5 (SO)
STL (vs. Kiprusoff)—Stempniak, Weight/CAL (vs. Bacashihua)—
    Huselius, TANGUAY, IGINLA
Philadelphia 0 at Phoenix 4
Edmonton 1 at Los Angeles 5

March 13, 2007

Ottawa 3 at NY Rangers 2
Florida 1 at Carolina 3
Tampa Bay 2 at Toronto 3
NY Islanders 3 at Montreal 5
Buffalo 4 at Pittsburgh 5 (SO)
BUF (vs. Fleury)—Briere, STAFFORD, Vanek/PIT (vs. Miller)—
    CHRISTENSEN, Ruutu, CROSBY
Detroit 5 at Nashville 2
Philadelphia 2 at Dallas 3
Minnesota 3 at Vancouver 2 (Burns 4:24 OT)
Chicago 1 at San Jose 7

March 14, 2007

Pittsburgh 3 at New Jersey 0
Nashville 2 at Detroit 4
Calgary 2 at Colorado 3
Columbus 5 at Anaheim 4 (SO)
CBJ (vs. Giguere)—Hainsey, Chimera, Picard, Zherdev, VYBORNY/
    ANA (vs. Norrena)—Getzlaf, Selanne, McDonald, Kunitz, Perry

March 15, 2007

Washington 3 at Boston 4 (SO)
WAS (vs. Thomas)—Semin, Laich, OVECHKIN/BOS (vs.
    Kolzig)—Sturm, BERGERON, KESSEL
Atlanta 2 at Philadelphia 3
New Jersey 3 at Carolina 2
NY Islanders 2 at Ottawa 5
Buffalo 5 at Florida 3
Calgary 2 at Dallas 4
Minnesota 2 at Edmonton 1
San Jose 5 at Phoenix 1
St. Louis 2 at Vancouver 3 (D. Sedin 1:09 OT)
Chicago 4 at Los Angeles 3 (SO)
CHI (vs. Burke)—Williams, HAVLAT, Hamilton, Arkhipov, Ruutu,
    SHARP, ALEXEEV/LA (vs. Khabibulin)—BROWN,
    Cammalleri, Lundmark, Clarke, Visnovsky, FROLOV, Willsie

March 16, 2007

Toronto 1 at Washington 5
Montreal 3 at Pittsburgh 6
NY Rangers 1 at Atlanta 2 (Zhitnik 2:18 OT)
Buffalo 3 at Tampa Bay 2
Chicago 2 at Anaheim 5
Columbus 0 at San Jose 3

March 17, 2007

Carolina 7 at New Jersey 2
Toronto 2 at Montreal 3 (SO)
TOR (vs. Halak)—Wellwood, SUNDIN, Perreault, Tucker/MON
    (vs. Raycroft)—Kovalev, Plekanec, KOIVU, KOSTITSYN
Philadelphia 2 at Ottawa 3
Boston 0 at NY Rangers 7
NY Islanders 5 at Florida 8
St. Louis 3 at Edmonton 2 (Brewer 2:04 OT)

Dallas 2 at Nashville 3
Minnesota 4 at Calgary 2
Colorado 6 at Phoenix 3
Detroit 1 at Vancouver 4
Columbus 3 at Los Angeles 5

March 18, 2007

Tampa Bay 1 at Washington 7
Buffalo 3 at Atlanta 4 (Tkachuk 4:22 OT)
Ottawa 3 at Pittsburgh 4 (SO)
OTT (vs. Fleury)—Comrie, McAmmond, Vermette/PIT (vs.
    Emery)—Christensen, RUUTU, Crosby
Los Angeles 5 at Anaheim 3
San Jose 3 at Colorado 4 (Hejduk 0:19 OT)
Phoenix 4 at Dallas 5 (Ribeiro 4:19 OT)

March 19, 2007

Pittsburgh 1 at NY Rangers 2
Vancouver 2 at Edmonton 1

March 20, 2007

Boston 0 at Montreal 1
Florida 4 at Philadelphia 1
Chicago 2 at Columbus 5
New Jersey 1 at Toronto 2
NY Islanders 3 at Tampa Bay 4 (Kuba 0:55 OT)
Ottawa 4 at St. Louis 2
Phoenix 2 at Minnesota 3
Detroit 1 at Calgary 2

March 21, 2007

Washington 2 at Buffalo 5
Philadelphia 0 at NY Rangers 5
San Jose 4 at Chicago 1

Colorado 5 at Edmonton 1
Nashville 0 at Vancouver 2
Dallas 4 at Los Angeles 2

March 22, 2007

Washington 3 at Carolina 4
San Jose 5 at Atlanta 1
Montreal 6 at Boston 3
Pittsburgh 1 at NY Islanders 3
New Jersey 1 at Tampa Bay 3
Ottawa 4 at Florida 2
Columbus 2 at Detroit 1 (SO)
CBJ (vs. Osgood)—VYBORNY, Platt, Zherdev, NASH, Chimera,
    FEDOROV/DET (vs. Norrena)— DATSYUK, Bertuzzi,
    Franzen, CLEARY, Filppula, Samuelsson
St. Louis 1 at Minnesota 5
Nashville 2 at Calgary 3 (Warrener 1:27 OT)
Anaheim 1 at Phoenix 2

March 23, 2007

Toronto 4 at Buffalo 5
Los Angeles 2 at Chicago 1
Colorado 4 at Edmonton 4 (SO)
COL (vs. Roloson)—Svatos, Hejduk, Sakic, McLean, Wolski/EDM
    (vs. Budaj)—Hemsky, Sykora, Pisani, Lupul, REASONER
Dallas 2 at Anaheim 3 (S. Niedermayer 2:28 OT)

March 24, 2007

NY Rangers 2 at Boston 1 (SO)
NYR (vs. MacDonald)—NYLANDER, Cullen, JAGR/BOS (vs.
    Lundqvist)—BERGERON, Sturm, Kessel
NY Islanders 4 at Philadelphia 3
Atlanta 1 at Pittsburgh 2
St. Louis 3 at Detroit 2 (SO)

STL (vs. Hasek)—Stempniak, WEIGHT/DET (vs. Bacashihua)—
   Datsyuk, Bertuzzi, Cleary
Buffalo 1 at Toronto 4
Washington 1 at Montreal 4
San Jose 4 at Carolina 6
Ottawa 7 at Tampa Bay 2
New Jersey 4 at Florida 3 (SO)
NJ (vs. Belfour)—PARISE, ZAJAC/FLO (vs. Brodeur)—PELTO-
   NEN, Horton, Jokinen
Los Angeles 1 at Minnesota 4
Dallas 4 at Phoenix 3 (SO)
DAL (vs. Joseph)—Zubov, Jokinen, Ribeiro, Modano, Nagy,
   Miettinen, LEHTONEN/PHO (vs. Turco)—Kapanen, Adams,
   Doan, Carcillo, Reinprecht, Taffe, Zigomanis
Nashville 4 at Edmonton 0

March 25, 2007

NY Rangers 2 at NY Islanders 1 (Nylander 4:11 OT)
Boston 0 at Pittsburgh 5
Calgary 3 at Chicago 2
St. Louis 1 at Columbus 4
Colorado 5 at Vancouver 4 (SO)
COL (vs. Luongo)—MCLEAN, Hejduk/VAN (vs. Theodore)—
   Linden, Morrison, D. Sedin

March 26, 2007

Anaheim 0 at Detroit 1

March 27, 2007

Pittsburgh 4 at Washington 3
Florida 5 at Tampa Bay 2
Carolina 1 at Toronto 6
NY Rangers 4 at Montreal 6
Boston 3 at Ottawa 2

New Jersey 3 at NY Islanders 2
Columbus 4 at St. Louis 1
Edmonton 3 at Nashville 4
Calgary 1 at Minnesota 0 (SO)
CAL (vs. Backstrom)—TANGUAY, IGINLA/MIN (vs. Kiprusoff)—
    Demitra, Rolston
Phoenix 0 at Dallas 6
Vancouver 3 at Colorado 0
Los Angeles 1 at San Jose 3

March 28, 2007

New Jersey 3 at Buffalo 4
Carolina 1 at Philadelphia 5
Atlanta 2 at Florida 3 (SO)
ATL (vs. Anderson)—Kozlov, Hossa/FLO (vs. Lehtonen)—
    Peltonen, HORTON, STUMPEL
Anaheim 3 at Chicago 1

March 29, 2007

Pittsburgh 4 at Boston 2
Toronto 2 at Atlanta 3 (Kozlov 4:13 OT)
Anaheim 5 at Columbus 2
Edmonton 2 at St. Louis 5
Detroit 2 at Nashville 1
Calgary 4 at Minnesota 2
Colorado 4 at Phoenix 3
Vancouver 4 at Los Angeles 2

March 30, 2007

Tampa Bay 4 at Carolina 2
Montreal 2 at Ottawa 5
Philadelphia 1 at New Jersey 3
Washington 2 at Florida 3 (Gelinas 2:01 OT)
Dallas 4 at Detroit 3 (SO)

DAL (vs. Hasek)—Lehtonen, ZUBOV, Ribeiro/DET (vs. Smith)—
    Datsyuk, Cleary, Bertuzzi
NY Islanders 4 at Buffalo 6
Columbus 1 at Chicago 3
Phoenix 2 at San Jose 4

March 31, 2007

Atlanta 3 at Boston 2
Minnesota 1 at Colorado 2
Pittsburgh 4 at Toronto 5 (Kaberle 3:55 OT)
Buffalo 3 at Montreal 4
Ottawa 5 at NY Islanders 2
NY Rangers 6 at Philadelphia 4
Washington 2 at Tampa Bay 5
Anaheim 3 at St. Louis 2 (McDonald 0:25 OT)
Dallas 4 at Nashville 2
Calgary 3 at Vancouver 2

April 1, 2007

Detroit 4 at Columbus 1
Edmonton 1 at Chicago 2
Boston 1 at New Jersey 3
Carolina 4 at Florida 3 (Whitney 1:30 OT)
Los Angeles 2 at San Jose 6
Toronto 2 at NY Rangers 7

April 2, 2007

St. Louis 4 at Dallas 2

April 3, 2007

Buffalo 4 at Pittsburgh 1
Florida 0 at Washington 1
Philadelphia 2 at Toronto 3 (McCabe 2:18 OT)
Boston 0 at Montreal 2

Ottawa 1 at New Jersey 2 (SO)
OTT (vs. Brodeur)—Alfredsson, Heatley, Spezza, VERMETTE,
    COMRIE, Fisher/NJ (vs. Emery)—Parise, Zajac, Elias,
    LANGENBRUNNER, BRYLIN, MADDEN
NY Rangers 2 at NY Islanders 3 (SO)
NYR (vs. Dubielewicz)—Nylander, Shanahan, Jagr/NYI (vs.
    Lundqvist)—SATAN, Kozlov, Smyth
Carolina 2 at Tampa Bay 3
Columbus 0 at Detroit 3
Chicago 3 at Nashville 2 (SO)
CHI (vs. Mason)—WILLIAMS, VRBATA, HAMILTON/NAS (vs.
    Lalime)—Radulov, KARIYA
Edmonton 0 at Minnesota 3
Colorado 4 at Calgary 3
Los Angeles 2 at Vancouver 4
St. Louis 5 at Phoenix 2

April 4, 2007

Washington 3 at Atlanta 2
San Jose 3 at Anaheim 2 (SO)
SJ (vs. Bryzgalov)—CHEECHOO, CLOWE/ANA (vs. Nabokov)—
    GETZLAF, Selanne, McDonald

April 5, 2007

Boston 2 at Buffalo 4
Montreal 1 at NY Rangers 3
New Jersey 3 at Philadelphia 2
Dallas 1 at Columbus 2 (Nash 1:04 OT)
Pittsburgh 3 at Ottawa 2
Toronto 2 at NY Islanders 5
St. Louis 1 at Nashville 4
Edmonton 0 at Minnesota 3
Detroit 2 at Chicago 3 (SO)

DET (vs. Khabibulin)—DATSYUK, Lang, Holmstrom,
    Hudler/CHI (vs. Osgood)—WILLIAMS, Vrbata, Hamilton,
    SHARP
Colorado 3 at Vancouver 1
Los Angeles 2 at Phoenix 3
Calgary 3 at San Jose 4

April 6, 2007

Atlanta 4 at Carolina 1
Florida 7 at Tampa Bay 2
Anaheim 1 at Dallas 2 (SO)
ANA (vs. Turco)—McDonald, Getzlaf, Selanne, Perry/DAL (vs.
    Bryzgalov)—Jokinen, Zubov, Modano, NAGY

April 7, 2007

NY Islanders 4 at Philadelphia 2
Buffalo 2 at Washington 0
Chicago 2 at Detroit 7
Phoenix 2 at Los Angeles 3
Vancouver 4 at San Jose 3 (Ohlund 0:34 OT)
Ottawa 6 at Boston 3
Montreal 5 at Toronto 6
Florida 4 at Carolina 5 (Brind'Amour 4:36 OT)
Tampa Bay 2 at Atlanta 3 (SO)
TB (vs. Lehtonen)—Lecavalier, RICHARDS, St. Louis, PROSPAL,
    Ward, Perrin/ATL (vs. Holmqvist)—Kozlov, Hossa,
    KOVALCHUK, TKACHUK, Belanger, SIM
Anaheim 4 at Columbus 3
NY Rangers 1 at Pittsburgh 2
St. Louis 1 at Minnesota 5
Nashville 4 at Colorado 2
Edmonton 3 at Calgary 2

April 8, 2007

Chicago 2 at Dallas 3
Buffalo 3 at Philadelphia 4
NY Islanders 3 at New Jersey 2 (SO)
NYI (vs. Clemmensen)—SATAN, KOZLOV, Smyth/NJ (vs. Dubielewicz)—PARISE, Gionta, Brylin
Vancouver 1 at Phoenix 3
Calgary 3 at Colorado 6

SHOOTOUT LEADERS, 2006–07

Goals

Erik Christensen (PIT)	8
Mikko Koivu (MIN)	8
Vyacheslav Kozlov (ATL)	7
Paul Kariya (NAS)	7
Brian Gionta (NJ)	7
Zach Parise (NJ)	7
Petteri Nummelin (MIN)	6
Brendan Morrison (VAN)	6
Doug Weight (STL)	6
Mats Sundin (TOR)	6
Patrice Bergeron (BOS)	6
Daniel Briere (BUF)	6
Pavol Demitra (MIN)	6

Game-Winning Goals

Vyacheslav Kozlov (ATL)	5
Mikko Koivu (MIN)	4
Sidney Crosby (PIT)	4
Ales Kotalik (BUF)	4
Ladislav Nagy (DAL)	4
Phil Kessel (BOS)	4
Erik Christensen (PIT)	3
Daniel Briere (BUF)	3
Martin St. Louis (TB)	3
John Madden (NJ)	3
Lee Stempniak (STL)	3
Marcel Hossa (NYR)	3

Most Shots

Mikko Koivu (MIN)	15
Sidney Crosby (PIT)	15

Erik Christensen (PIT)	14
Zach Parise (NJ)	14
Daniel Briere (BUF)	14
Pavol Demitra (MIN)	14
Brian Gionta (NJ)	13
Michael Nylander (NYR)	13
Miroslav Satan (NYI)	13
Viktor Kozlov (NYI)	13

Shooting Percentage

(minimum 5 attempts)

	Shots	Goals	Pct.
Petteri Nummelin (MIN)	7	6	85.7
Ales Kotalik (BUF)	7	5	71.4
Brendan Morrison (VAN)	9	6	66.7
John Madden (NJ)	6	4	66.7
Ladislav Nagy (DAL)	6	4	66.7
Vyacheslav Kozlov (ATL)	11	7	63.6
Paul Kariya (NAS)	11	7	63.6
Jamie Langenbrunner (NJ)	5	3	60.0
Erik Christensen (PIT)	14	8	57.1
Phil Kessel (BOS)	7	4	57.1

Most Wins, Goalie

Ryan Miller (BUF)	10
Martin Brodeur (NJ)	10
Marc-Andre Fleury (PIT)	9
Tim Thomas (BOS)	8
Henrik Lundqvist (NYR)	8
Marty Turco (DAL)	8
Manny Fernandez (MIN)	7
Kari Lehtonen (ATL)	7

Johan Holmqvist (TB)	6
Manny Legace (STL)	5
Roberto Luongo (VAN)	5
Rick DiPietro (NYI)	5

Most Losses, Goalie

Martin Brodeur (NJ)	6
J-S Giguere (ANA)	6
Andrew Raycroft (TOR)	6
Marc-Andre Fleury (PIT)	5
Niklas Backstrom (MIN)	5
Olaf Kolzig (WAS)	5
Dominik Hasek (DET)	5
Ed Belfour (FLO)	5
Brent Johnson (WAS)	5

Most Shots Faced, Goalie

Martin Brodeur (NJ)	60
Henrik Lundqvist (NYR)	50
Ryan Miller (BUF)	46
Tim Thomas (BOS)	46
Marty Turco (DAL)	46
Rick DiPietro (NYI)	44
Marc-Andre Fleury (PIT)	39
J-S Giguere (ANA)	39
Johan Holmqvist (TB)	33
Nikolai Khabibulin (CHI)	33

Save Percentage, Goalie

(minimum 20 shots faced)

	Shots	Goals	Save %
Marc Denis (TB)	20	2	.900
Johan Holmqvist (TB)	33	4	.879
Tim Thomas (BOS)	46	8	.826
Henrik Lundqvist (NYR)	50	9	.820
Ryan Miller (BUF)	46	9	.804
Rick DiPietro (NYI)	44	9	.796
Marc-Andre Fleury (PIT)	39	9	.769
Marty Turco (DAL)	46	11	.761
Antero Niittymaki (PHI)	23	6	.739
Manny Legace (STL)	25	7	.720

NATIONALITY OF ALL PLAYERS, 2006–07

SUMMARY
(figures in parentheses show leaguewide representation as a percentage)

TOTAL	**945**
CANADA	496 (52.4%)
Alberta	88
British Columbia	48
Manitoba	26
New Brunswick	2
Newfoundland	4
Northwest Territories	1
Nova Scotia	10
Ontario	190
Prince Edward Island	3
Quebec	80
Saskatchewan	44
USA	183 (19.4%)
CZECH REPUBLIC	65 (6.9%)
SWEDEN	49 (5.2%)
FINLAND	42 (4.4%)
RUSSIA	37 (3.9%)
SLOVAKIA	25 (2.6%)
GERMANY	8 (0.8%)
UKRAINE	8 (0.8%)
SWITZERLAND	5 (0.5%)
KAZAKHSTAN	4 (0.4%)
LATVIA	4 (0.4%)
AUSTRIA	2 (0.2%)
BELARUS	2 (0.2%)
DENMARK	2 (0.2%)

LITHUANIA	2 (0.2%)
NORWAY	2 (0.2%)
BRAZIL	1 (0.1%)
FRANCE	1 (0.1%)
JAPAN	1 (0.1%)
MALAYSIA	1 (0.1%)
POLAND	1 (0.1%)
SLOVENIA	1 (0.1%)
SOUTH AFRICA	1 (0.1%)
SOUTH KOREA	1 (0.1%)
UNITED KINGDOM	1 (0.1%)

NATIONALITY BREAKDOWN

CANADA	**496**	
Alberta	**88**	
Airdrie	1	Darcy Campbell
Banff	1	Ryan Smyth
Beaverlodge	1	Matt Walker
Blackie	1	Jeremy Colliton
Calgary	16	Nolan Baumgartner, Braydon Coburn, Micki Dupont, Patrick Eaves, Brad Ference, Mike Green, Jameson Hunt, Robert Nilsson, Lawrence Nycholat, Chris Phillips, Jeff Schultz, Jason Smith, Brent Sopel, Jeff Tambellini, Wes Walz, Kyle Wanvig
Camrose	2	Tyler Bouck, Josh Green
Caroline	1	Jim Vandermeer
Castor	1	Darcy Tucker
Cold Lake	1	Alexander Auld
Coleman	1	Rick Rypien

Edmonton	31	Shawn Belle, Blair Betts, Jay Bouwmeester, Gilbert Brule, Jason Chimera, Erik Christensen, Mike Comrie, Andrew Ference, Vernon Fiddler, Jarome Iginla, Brad Isbister, Matt Keith, Daymond Langkow, Jamie Lundmark, Joffrey Lupul, Richard Matvichuk, Jamie McLennan, Duncan Milroy, Derek Morris, Scott Nichol, Scott Niedermayer, Matt Pettinger, Dion Phaneuf, Fernando Pisani, Steve Regier, Steve Reinprecht, Mark Smith, Nathan Smith, Jason Strudwick, Brian Sutherby, Darryl Sydor
Elk Point	1	Sheldon Souray
Fort McMurray	2	Nolan Pratt, Scottie Upshall
Fort Saskatchewan	2	Mike Commodore, Ray Whitney
Grand Cache	2	Dean McAmmond, Travis Roche
Halkirk	1	Shane Doan
Hinton	1	Dave Scatchard
Lac La Biche	2	Rene Bourque, Darren Reid
Lloydminster	1	Clarke MacArthur
Mannville	2	Kyle Calder, Mike Rathje
Medicine Hat	2	Brooks Laich, Trevor Linden
Peace River	1	Chris Osgood
Red Deer	3	Trent Hunter, Chris Mason, Glen Wesley
Redwater	1	Todd Fedoruk
Rocky Mountain House	2	Brad Stuart, Nick Tarnasky
St. Paul	1	Kyle Brodziak
Sherwood Park	2	Ben Ondrus, Cam Ward
Spruce Grove	3	Stu Barnes, Nathan Dempsey
Stony Plain	1	Steve Goertzen
Vermilion	1	Jeff Woywitka

British Columbia	**48**	
Abbotsford	4	Ryan Craig, Kyle Cumiskey, Michael Funk, Brad Moran
Burnaby	4	Darren McCarty, Byron Ritchie, Joe Sakic, Greg Zanon
Campbell River	1	Carsen Germyn
Cassiar	1	Rob Niedermayer
Castlegar	1	Travis Green
Comox	1	Brett McLean
Cranbrook	2	Jon Klemm, Brad Lukowich
Duncan	1	Matt Ellison
Fernie	2	Jason Krog, David Leneveu
Fort St. John	1	Mark Hartigan
Hope	1	Jeff Hoggan
Invermere	1	Wade Dubielewicz
Kamloops	1	Mark Recchi
Kelowna	1	Josh Gorges
Kitimat	1	Rodney Pelley
Maple Ridge	1	Andrew Ladd
Nakusp	1	Brad Larsen
Osoyoos	1	Chuck Kobasew
Penticton	1	Mark Rycroft
Pitt Meadows	1	Brendan Morrison
Port McNeill	1	Willie Mitchell
Richmond	2	Scott Hannan, Brent Seabrook
Salmon Arm	1	Kris Beech
Sicamous	2	Colin Fraser, Shea Weber
Smithers	1	Dan Hamhuis
Telkwa	1	Michael Wall
Trail	4	Dallas Drake, Shawn Horcoff, Barret Jackman, Steve McCarthy
Vancouver	5	Troy Brouwer, Paul Kariya, Steve Montador, Shaone Morrisonn, Jonathan Sigalet

Vernon	3	Eric Brewer, Eric Godard, Jerred Smithson

Manitoba	**26**	
Brandon	2	Triston Grant, Bryce Salvador
Carman	1	Ed Belfour
Churchill	1	Jordin Tootoo
Lyleton	1	Marty Murray
Neepawa	1	Shane Hnidy
Nesbitt	1	Aaron Rome
Notre Dame de Lourdes	1	J.P. Vigier
Portage La Prairie	1	Arron Asham
Swan River	1	Barry Brust
Thompson	1	Jody Shelley
Winkler	2	Eric Fehr, Dustin Penner
Winnipeg	13	Cam Barker, Dustin Boyd, Riley Cote, Nigel Dawes, Lee Goren, Duncan Keith, Derek Meech, Bryan Muir, Colton Orr, Alexander Steen, Duvie Westcott, Ian White, Travis Zajac

Ontario	**190**	
Ajax	1	Brent Burns
Alfred	1	Benoit Pouliot
Almonte	1	Kent Huskins
Barrie	2	Joe DiPenta, John Madden
Beaconsfield	1	Ben Walter
Belleville	3	Matt Cooke, Andrew Raycroft, Brad Richardson
Bowmanville	1	Bryan Bickell
Bramalea	1	Mike Weaver
Brampton	2	Rick Nash, Kris Newbury
Brantford	1	Chris Gratton
Brockville	1	Alyn McCauley

Cambridge	2	Tim Brent, Scott Walker
Carp	1	Kurtis Foster
Cayuga	1	Ray Emery
Chapleau	1	Jason Ward
Cobourg	1	Justin Williams
Collingwood	1	Jason Arnott
Cornwall	1	Chad Kilger
Dryden	1	Chris Pronger
Elliott Lake	1	Zachery Stortini
Grimsby	1	Kevin Bieksa
Guelph	4	Krys Barch, Greg Jacina, Kirk Maltby, Rich Peverley
Hamilton	3	Adam Mair, Brian McGratton, Steve Staios
Huntsville	1	Ethan Moreau
Kanata	1	Todd White
Kenora	1	Mike Richards
Keswick	1	Curtis Joseph
King City	1	Daniel Carcillo
Kingston	6	Bryan Allen, John Erskine, Jay McClement, Jay McKee, Mike Smith, Andy Sutton
Kirtland Hills	1	Peter Harrold
Kitchener	5	Mike Card, Kevin Klein, Kyle Quincey, Dennis Wideman, Bryan Young
London	11	Gregory Campbell, Jeff Carter, Eric Lindros, Mark Mancari, Cody McCormick, Brandon Prust, Joe Thornton, Scott Thornton, Mike Van Ryn, Jason Williams, Brian Willsie
Markdale	1	Chris Neil
Millgrove	1	Danny Syvret
Mimico	1	Brendan Shanahan

Mississauga	6	Brad Boyes, Tom Kostopoulos, Manny Malhotra, Allan Rourke, Jason Spezza, Matt Stajan
Moose Factory	1	Jonathan Cheechoo
Nepean	1	Jason York
Niagara Falls	2	Kevin Dallman, Mike Glumac
Niagara-on-the-Lake	1	Zenon Konopka
Nobleton	1	Nick Boynton
North Bay	1	Craig Rivet
Oakville	2	Eric Cairns, Matt Foy
Oshawa	3	Jay Harrison, Joe Nieuwendyk, Shawn Thornton
Ottawa	17	Derek Armstrong, Adrian Aucoin, Matthew Barnaby, Brendan Bell, Dan Boyle, Rod Brind'Amour, Ben Eager, Mark Fraser, Marc Methot, Sean O'Donnell, Luke Richardson, Jamie Rivers, Randy Robitaille, Derek Roy, Marc Savard, Martin St. Pierre, Stephane Yelle
Owen Sound	1	Curtis Sanford
Peterborough	3	Mike Fisher, Corey Perry, Cory Stillman
Petrolia	1	Michael Leighton
Pickering	1	Sean Avery
Port Hope	1	Shane O'Brien
Richmond Hill	2	Mike Cammalleri, Jeff O'Neill
Rockland	1	Serge Payer
Sault Ste. Marie	5	Drew Fata, Rico Fata, Brian Finley, Chris Thorburn, Marty Turco
Seaforth	1	Boyd Devereaux
Shelburne	1	Aaron Downey
Simcoe	3	Rob Blake, Jassen Cullimore, Dwayne Roloson

St. Catharines	3	Rob Davison, Bryan McCabe, Andrew Peters
Stittsville	1	Matt Bradley
Stoney Creek	1	Mark Popovic
St. Paul's	1	Mark Bell
Stratford	1	Tim Taylor
Strathroy	2	Brian Campbell, Andy McDonald
Sudbury	3	Todd Bertuzzi, Andrew Brunette, Derek MacKenzie
Sundridge	1	Greg de Vries
Thornhill	1	Dominic Moore
Thunder Bay	8	Danny Bois, Ryan Johnson, Trevor Letowski, Taylor Pyatt, Steve Rucchin, Patrick Sharp, Eric Staal, Jordan Staal
Timmins	2	Shean Donovan, Steve Sullivan
Toronto	35	Michael Blunden, Dave Bolland, Darryl Bootland, Chris Campoli, Anson Carter, David Clarkson, Carlo Colaiacovo, Jeff Cowan, Trevor Daley, Kris Draper, Manny Fernandez, Adam Foote, Mark Giordano, Josh Gratton, Darren Haydar, Ric Jackman, Mike Johnson, Chris Kelly, Mike Knuble, Manny Legace, Brad May, Jamal Mayers, Glen Metropolit, Michael Peca, Geoff Platt, Wayne Primeau, Mike Ricci, Gary Roberts, Karl Stewart, Raffi Torres, Stephen Valiquette, Joel Ward, Kevin Weekes, Stephen Weiss, Mike Zigomanis
Wawa	1	Chris Simon
Welland	4	Matt Ellis, Daniel Girardi, Nathan Horton, Daniel Paille
Whitby	1	Paul Ranger

Windsor	5	Sean Burke, Ed Jovanovski, David Liffiton, Aaron Ward, Kyle Wellwood
Woodbridge	1	Steve Eminger
Quebec	**80**	
Amqui	1	Sebastien Caron
Ancienne-Lorette	1	Patrice Bergeron
Beauceville	1	Stephane Veilleux
Chandler	1	Mathieu Garon
Charlesbourg	1	Marc Chouinard
Gatineau	2	Daniel Briere, Alexandre Picard (b. Jul '85)
Hull	1	Pierre Parenteau
Ile Bizard	1	Vincent Lecavalier
Kirkland	1	Brandon Reid
Lac St. Charles	1	Martin Biron
Lachute	1	Denis Hamel
La Salle	1	Anthony Stewart
Laval	4	Pascal Dupuis, Martin Grenier, Martin St. Louis, Jose Theodore
Lemoyne	1	Maxime Talbot
Les Saules	1	Alexandre Picard (b. Oct '85)
Longueuil	1	Bruno Gervais
Mont Laurier	2	Sebastien Bisaillon, Dan Cloutier
Montreal	23	Ramzi Abid, J-S Aubin, Patrice Brisebois, Martin Brodeur, Mathieu Darche, Marc Denis, J-P Dumont, Denis Gauthier, J-S Giguere, Ben Guite, Martin Houle, Ian Laperriere, Georges Laraque, Yanick Lehoux, Kris Letang, Matt Lombardi, Roberto Luongo, Scott Mellanby, Alain Nasreddine, Joel Perrault, Mike Ribeiro, Jocelyn Thibault, Marc-Edouard Vlasic

Pointe aux Trembles	1	Yannick Tremblay
Pointe Claire	1	Alexandre Burrows
Quebec City	5	Steve Bernier, Alexandre Giroux, Marc-Antoine Pouliot, Paul Stastny, Yan Stastny
Repentigny	2	Pascal Leclaire, Jason Pominville
Rimouski	1	Michel Ouellet
Rouyn	1	Pierre Turgeon
Shawinigan	1	Martin Gelinas
Sherbrooke	5	Eric Belanger, Pierre-Marc Bouchard, Mathieu Dandenault, Yanic Perreault, Stephane Robidas
Sorel	3	Francois Beauchemin, Frederic Cassivi, Marc-Andre Fleury
St. Agapit	1	Antoine Vermette
St. Bonaventure	1	Patrick Lalime
Ste. Apollinaire	1	Philippe Boucher
Ste. Catherine	1	Guillaume Latendresse
St. Fabien	1	Patrick Coulombe
Ste. Foy	1	Simon Gagne
Ste. Justine	1	Alex Tanguay
St. Georges	1	Mathieu Roy
St. Joseph de Beauce	1	Junior Lessard
St. Leonard	1	Maxim Lapierre
St. Louis de France	1	Marc-Andre Bergeron
Terrebonne	1	J-F Jacques
Trois-Rivieres	1	Steve Begin
Val d'Or	1	Dany Sabourin
Ville St. Pierre	1	Martin Lapointe
New Brunswick	**2**	
Quispamsis	1	Randy Jones
Shippagan	1	Luc Bourdon

Newfoundland	4	
Carbonear	1	Daniel Cleary
St. John's	3	Ryane Clowe, Jason Morgan, Michael Ryder
Northwest Territories	1	
Hay River	1	Geoff Sanderson
Nova Scotia	10	
Antigonish	1	Craig MacDonald
Halifax	3	Eric Boulton, Sidney Crosby, Glen Murray
New Glasgow	3	Jon Sim, Derrick Walser, Colin White
Pictou	1	Joey MacDonald
Port Hawkesbury	1	Aaron Johnson
Sydney	1	Don MacLean
Prince Edward Island	3	
Kinkora	1	Nathan McIver
Murray Harbour	1	Brad Richards
Summerside	1	Steve Ott
Saskatchewan	44	
Aneroid	1	Patrick Marleau
Carlyle	1	Brenden Morrow
Central Butte	1	Blair Jones
Craik	2	Garnet Exelby, Jeremy Reich
Humboldt	2	Kyle McLaren, Brendan Witt
Kamsack	1	Darcy Hordichuk
Kindersley	2	Curtis Glencross, Joel Kwiatkowski
Lanigan	2	Sheldon Brookbank, Wade Brookbank
Leroy	1	Nathan Paetsch
Lloydminster	2	Colby Armstrong, Wade Redden
Meadow Lake	3	Blake Comeau, Jeff Friesen, D.J.King

Melville	1	Jarret Stoll
Moose Jaw	1	Reed Low
Outlook	1	Shay Stephenson
Prince Albert	1	Ryan Parent
Regina	8	Ryan Getzlaf, Josh Harding, Scott Hartnell, Jamie Heward, Chris Kunitz, Garth Murray, Mike Sillinger, Jeremy Williams
Rosthern	1	Richie Regehr
Saskatoon	4	Ryan Bayda, Wade Belak, Derek Boogaard, Cory Sarich
Shaunavon	1	Rhett Warrener
Stewart Valley	1	Travis Moen
Strasbourg	2	Jesse Schultz, Nick Schultz
Swift Current	1	Boyd Kane
Unity	2	Curtis Brown, Boyd Gordon
Wapella	1	Brett Clark
Yellow Grass	1	Peter Schaefer

USA 179

Alaska	5	Matt Carle, Ty Conklin, Brandon Dubinsky, Scott Gomez, Nate Thompson
California	5	Noah Clarke, Gabe Gauthier, Ryan Hollweg, Brooks Orpik, Scott Parker
Colorado	2	John Grahame, David Hale
Connecticut	6	Eric Boguniecki, Chris Clark, Chris Drury, Ron Hainsey, Matt Hussey, Ryan Shannon
Delaware	1	Mark Eaton
Florida	1	Dan Hinote
Georgia	1	Mark Mowers
Illinois	9	Craig Anderson, Bates Battaglia, Chris Chelios, Joe Corvo, Andrew

		Hutchinson, Matt Jones, Brett Lebda, Danny Richmond, Andy Wosniewski
Indiana	4	Donald Brashear, Jack Johnson, Ken Klee, John-Michael Liles
Iowa	1	Scott Clemmensen
Maine	1	Mike Morrison
Maryland	2	Kevyn Adams, Jeff Halpern
Massachusetts	26	Bobby Allen, Tony Amonte, Keith Aucoin, Shawn Bates, Carl Corazzini, Niko Dimitrakos, Rick DiPietro, Jim Fahey, Hal Gill, David Gove, Bill Guerin, Joshua Hennessy, Doug Janik, Dan LaCouture, Pat Leahy, Brad Norton, Jay Pandolfo, Brian Pothier, Tom Poti, Pat Rismiller, Jeremy Roenick, Michael Ryan, Keith Tkachuk, Noah Welch, Ryan Whitney, Keith Yandle
Michigan	28	Jason Bacashihua, David Booth, Chris Conner, Jeff Finger, Tim Gleason, Rob Globke, Andy Greene, Matt Greene, Mike Grier, Adam Hall, Derian Hatcher, Andy Hilbert, Brent Johnson, Ryan Kesler, Drew Larman, Chad LaRose, David Legwand, Ryan Miller, Mike Modano, David Moss, Brian Rafalski, Eric Reitz, Brian Rolston, Jim Slater, Tim Thomas, Doug Weight, James Wisniewski, Mike York
Minnesota	31	Andrew Alberts, David Backes, Keith Ballard, Jason Blake, Brandon Bochenski, Dustin Byfuglien, Ryan Carter, Ben Clymer, Mark Cullen, Matt Cullen, Tom Gilbert, Bret Hedican,

		Sean Hill, Bryce Lampman, Jamie Langenbrunner, Josh Langfeld, Jordan Leopold, Paul Martin, Joe Motzko, Zach Parise, Mark Parrish, Toby Petersen, John Pohl, Tom Preissing, Erik Rasmussen, Kurt Sauer, Wyatt Smith, Mark Stuart, Jeff Taffe, David Tanabe, Erik Westrum
Missouri	1	Cam Janssen
Nebraska	1	Jed Ortmeyer
New Hampshire	2	Freddy Meyer, Deron Quint
New Jersey	3	Jim Dowd, Paul Mara, Andrew Miller
New York	23	Francis Bouillon, Dustin Brown, Ryan Callahan, Erik Cole, Tim Connolly, Craig Conroy, Mike Dunham, Robert Esche, Rory Fitzpatrick, Brian Gionta, Chris Higgins, Patrick Kaleta, Mike Komisarek, Matt Lashoff, Todd Marchant, Aaron Miller, Marty Reasoner, Andre Roy, Philippe Sauve, Mathieu Schneider, Rob Schremp, Rob Scuderi, Lee Stempniak
North Carolina	1	Patrick O'Sullivan
North Dakota	4	Paul Gaustad, Tim Jackman, Ryan Potulny, Barry Tallackson
Ohio	5	Dan Fritsche, Jeff Hamilton, Ian Moran, Mike Rupp, Brian Smolinski
Oklahoma	1	Tyler Arnason
Pennsylvania	6	Nathan Guenin, Ryan Malone, George Parros, Bill Thomas, R.J. Umberger, John Zeiler
Rhode Island	3	Bryan Berard, Brian Boucher, Keith Carney
Vermont	1	John LeClair

Wisconsin	9	Alexander Brooks, Adam Burish, Phil Kessel, Joe Pavelski, Joe Piskula, Drew Stafford, David Steckel, Ryan Suter, Brad Winchester
CZECH REPUBLIC	65	Jaroslav Balastik, Radek Bonk, Jan Bulis, Petr Cajanek, Radek Dvorak, Patrik Elias, Martin Erat, Tomas Fleischmann, Roman Hamrlik, Dominik Hasek, Martin Havlat, Jan Hejda, Milan Hejduk, Ales Hemsky, Bobby Holik, Jiri Hudler, Jaromir Jagr, Frantisek Kaberle, Tomas Kaberle, Petr Kalus, Jakub Klepis, Rostislav Klesla, David Koci, Ales Kotalik, Lukas Krajicek, David Krejci, Kamil Kreps, Filip Kuba, Pavel Kubina, Robert Lang, Martin Lojek, Marek Malik, Radek Martinek, Josef Melichar, Milan Michalek, Zbynek Michalek, Jaroslav Modry, Tomas Mojzis, Petr Nedved, Filip Novak, Jiri Novotny, Rostislav Olesz, Tomas Plekanec, Tomas Plihal, Roman Polak, Vojtech Polak, Tomas Popperle, Vaclav Prospal, Petr Prucha, Karel Rachunek, Michal Rozsival, Martin Rucinsky, Marek Schwarz, Martin Skoula, Ladislav Smid, Jaroslav Spacek, Patrik Stefan, Martin Straka, Petr Sykora, Petr Tenkrat, Josef Vasicek, Tomas Vokoun, Radim Vrbata, David Vyborny, Marek Zidlicky

SWEDEN 49 Daniel Alfredsson, P-J Axelsson, Christian Backman, Alexander Edler, Nils Ekman, Anders Eriksson, Loui Eriksson, Peter Forsberg, Johan Franzen, Nicklas Grossman, Niclas Havelid, Johan Hedberg, Johan Holmqvist, Mikael Holmqvist, Tomas Holmstrom, Kristian Huselius, Kim Johnsson, Lars Jonsson, Andreas Karlsson, Niklas Kronwall, Nicklas Lidstrom, Andreas Lilja, Joakim Lindstrom, Henrik Lundqvist, Joel Lundqvist, Bjorn Melin, Fredrik Modin, Doug Murray, Markus Naslund, Marcus Nilson, Jonas Nordqvist, Mattias Norstrom, Michael Nylander, John Oduya, Mattias Ohlund, Samuel Pahlsson, David Printz, Mikael Samuelsson, Daniel Sedin, Henrik Sedin, Fredrik Sjostrom, Mats Sundin, Henrik Tallinder, Mikael Tellqvist, Daniel Tjarnqvist, Mathias Tjarnqvist, Niclas Wallin, Mattias Weinhandl, Henrik Zetterberg

FINLAND 42 Niklas Backstrom, Valtteri Filppula, Niklas Hagman, Jarkko Immonen, Jussi Jokinen, Olli Jokinen, Niko Kapanen, Sami Kapanen, Miikka Kiprusoff, Mikko Koivu, Saku Koivu, Lasse Kukkonen, Antti Laaksonen, Jere Lehtinen, Kari Lehtonen, Mikko Lehtonen, Toni Lydman, Tomi Maki, Jussi Markkanen, Antti Miettinen, Ville

Nieminen, Janne Niinimaa, Antero
Niittymaki, Fredrik Norrena, Petteri
Nummelin, Teppo Numminen, Ville
Peltonen, Thomas Pihlman, Joni
Pitkanen, Karri Ramo, Jarkko Ruutu,
Tuomo Ruutu, Tony Salmelainen,
Sami Salo, Tommi Santala, Teemu
Selanne, Jussi Timonen, Kimmo
Timonen, Hannu Toivonen, Vesa
Toskala, Lauri Tukonen, Ossi
Vaananen

RUSSIA   37   Dmitry Afanasenkov, Maxim
Afinogenov, Nikita Alexeev, Denis
Arkhipov, Sergei Brylin, Ilya Bryzgalov,
Stanislav Chistov, Pavel Datsyuk,
Sergei Fedorov, Alexander Frolov,
Sergei Gonchar, Alexei Kaigorodov,
Dmitri Kalinin, Nikolai Khabibulin,
Ilya Kovalchuk, Alexei Kovalev, Viktor
Kozlov, Vyacheslav Kozlov, Enver Lisin,
Vladimir Malakhov, Evgeni Malkin,
Andrei Markov, Danny Markov,
Alexander Ovechkin, Alexander
Radulov, Sergei Samsonov, Oleg
Saprykin, Alexei Semenov, Alexander
Semin, Aleksander Suglobov,
Alexander Svitov, Fedor Tyutin, Anton
Volchenkov, Alexei Yashin, Alexei
Zhitnik, Sergei Zubov, Andrei Zyuzin

SLOVAKIA   25   Peter Budaj, Zdeno Chara, Pavol
Demitra, Marian Gaborik, Jaroslav
Halak, Michal Handzus, Marcel Hossa,

Marian Hossa, Milan Jurcina, Juraj Kolnik, Tomas Kopecky, Tomas Malec, Andrej Meszaros, Branislav Mezei, Ladislav Nagy, Ronald Petrovicky, Branko Radivojevic, Stefan Ruzicka, Miroslav Satan, Peter Sejna, Andrej Sekera, Jozef Stumpel, Marek Svatos, Lubomir Visnovsky, Richard Zednik

GERMANY 8 Christian Ehrhoff, Marcel Goc, Mikhail Grabovski, Dany Heatley, Jochen Hecht, Christoph Schubert, Dennis Seidenberg, Marco Sturm

UKRAINE 8 Anton Babchuk, Peter Bondra, Ruslan Fedotenko, Alexei Mikhnov, Alexei Ponikarovsky, Oleg Tverdovsky, Vitali Vishnevsky, Nikolai Zherdev

SWITZERLAND 5 David Aebischer, Patrick Fischer, Martin Gerber, Timo Helbling, Mark Streit

KAZAKHSTAN 4 Nik Antropov, Evgeny Nabokov, Alexander Perezhogin, Konstantin Pushkarev

LATVIA 4 Raitis Ivanins, Sandis Ozolinsh, Karlis Skrastins, Janis Sprukts

AUSTRIA 2 Thomas Pock, Thomas Vanek

BELARUS 2 Andrei Kostitsyn, Ruslan Salei

DENMARK	2	Jannik Hansen, Frans Nielsen
LITHUANIA	2	Darius Kasparaitis, Dainius Zubrus
NORWAY	2	Patrick Thoresen, Ole-Kristian Tollefsen
BRAZIL	1	Robyn Regehr
FRANCE	1	Cristobal Huet
JAPAN	1	Yutaka Fukufuji
MALAYSIA	1	Craig Adams
POLAND	1	Wojtek Wolski
SLOVENIA	1	Anze Kopitar
SOUTH AFRICA	1	Olaf Kolzig
SOUTH KOREA	1	Richard Park
UNITED KINGDOM	1	Owen Nolan

FIRST GAMES PLAYED, 2006–07

SKATERS (Nationality) NHL TEAM (first game) GOALIES (Nationality) NHL TEAM (first game)	**G** **Mins**	**A** **GA**	**P** **W-L**	**Pim**

* indicates player traded later in season

Regular Season

ND indicates No Decision

David Backes (USA)	STL (Dec. 19)	0	1	1	0
Niklas Backstrom (FIN)	MIN (Oct. 7)	39:53	2	W	
Krys Barch (CAN)	DAL (Jan. 15)	0	0	0	0
Shawn Belle (CAN)	MIN (Dec. 1)	0	0	0	0
Bryan Bickell (CAN)	CHI (Apr. 5)	1	0	1	0
Sebastien Bisaillon (CAN)	EDM (Mar. 19)	0	0	0	0
Michael Blunden (CAN)	CHI (Oct. 25)	0	0	0	0
Danny Bois (CAN)	OTT (Dec. 6)	0	0	0	7
Dave Bolland (CAN)	CHI (Oct. 25)	0	0	0	0
David Booth (USA)	FLO (Nov. 20)	0	0	0	0
Luc Bourdon (CAN)	VAN (Oct. 10)	0	0	0	0
Dustin Boyd (CAN)	CAL (Nov. 1)	0	0	0	0
Tim Brent (CAN)	ANA (Jan. 5)	0	0	0	0
Sheldon Brookbank (CAN)	NAS (Feb. 6)	0	1	1	2
Alexander Brooks (USA)	NJ (Oct. 16)	0	1	1	0
Troy Brouwer (CAN)	CHI (Dec. 23)	0	0	0	0
Barry Brust (CAN)	LA (Nov. 30)	50:23	4	L	
Adam Burish (USA)	CHI (Oct. 14)	0	0	0	0
Ryan Callahan (USA)	NYR (Dec. 1)	0	0	0	0
Darcy Campbell (CAN)	CBJ (Mar. 30)	0	0	0	0
Daniel Carcillo (CAN)	CBJ (Mar. 3)	0	0	0	0

Mike Card (CAN)	BUF (Nov. 11)	0	0	0	0
Ryan Carter (USA)	ANA (May 17)	0	0	0	0
David Clarkson (CAN)	NJ (Mar. 15)	0	0	0	0
Blake Comeau (CAN)	NYI (Dec. 7)	0	0	0	0
Chris Conner (USA)	DAL (Dec. 8)	0	0	0	0
Riley Cote (CAN)	PHI (Mar. 24)	0	0	0	4
Patrick Coulombe (CAN)	VAN (Nov. 9)	0	0	0	0
Kyle Cumiskey (CAN)	COL (Jan. 1)	0	0	0	0
Nigel Dawes (CAN)	NYR (Oct. 5)	0	0	0	0
Brandon Dubinsky (USA)	NYR (Mar. 8)	0	0	0	0
Alexander Edler (SWE)	VAN (Nov. 4)	0	0	0	0
Matt Ellis (CAN)	DET (Dec. 18)	0	0	0	0
Loui Eriksson (SWE)	DAL (Oct. 4)	1	0	1	0
Drew Fata (CAN)	NYI (Feb. 4)	0	0	0	0
Jeff Finger (USA)	COL (Feb. 20)	0	0	0	0
Patrick Fischer (SUI)	PHO (Oct. 5)	0	0	0	2
Colin Fraser (CAN)	CHI (Jan. 7)	0	0	0	2
Mark Fraser (CAN)	NJ (Jan. 6)	0	0	0	0
Yutaka Fukufuji (JPN)	LA (Jan. 13)	19:17	1	L	
Michael Funk (CAN)	BUF (Nov. 18)	0	0	0	0
Gabe Gauthier (USA)	LA (Mar. 11)	0	0	0	0
Tom Gilbert (USA)	EDM (Jan. 10)	0	0	0	0
Daniel Girardi (CAN)	NYR (Jan. 27)	0	0	0	2
Curtis Glencross (CAN)	ANA (Jan. 13)	1	0	1	2
Mikhail Grabovski (GER)	MON (Jan. 6)	0	0	0	0
Triston Grant (CAN)	PHI (Oct. 26)	0	0	0	0
Andy Greene (USA)	NJ (Jan. 12)	0	0	0	0
Niklas Grossman (SWE)	DAL (Dec. 2)	0	0	0	4
Nathan Guenin (USA)	PHI (Jan. 18)	0	0	0	0
Jaroslav Halak (SVK)	MON (Feb. 18)	59:51	2	W	
Jannik Hansen (DEN)	VAN (Apr. 13)	0	0	0	0
Peter Harrold (USA)	LA (Nov. 22)	0	1	1	0
Jan Hejda (CZE)	EDM (Nov. 3)	0	0	0	0

Joshua Hennessy (USA)	OTT (Dec. 12)	0	0	0	0
Martin Houle (CAN)	PHI (Dec. 13)	2:12	1	ND	
Jameson Hunt (CAN)	WAS (Dec. 29)	0	0	0	0
Kent Huskins (CAN)	ANA (Dec. 23)	0	0	0	0
Jack Johnson (USA)	LA (Mar. 29)	0	0	0	0
Blair Jones (CAN)	TB (Nov. 20)	0	0	0	0
Lars Jonsson (SWE)	PHI (Oct. 26)	0	1	1	0
Alexei Kaigorodov (RUS)	OTT (Oct. 14)	0	1	1	0
Patrick Kaleta (USA)	BUF (Feb. 22)	0	1	1	10
Petr Kalus (CZE)	BOS (Mar. 24)	0	0	0	0
Phil Kessel (USA)	BOS (Oct. 6)	0	0	0	0
D.J. King (CAN)	STL (Oct. 5)	0	0	0	0
David Koci (CZE)	CHI (Mar. 10)	0	0	0	42
Anze Kopitar (SLO)	LA (Oct. 6)	2	0	2	0
David Krejci (CZE)	BOS (Jan. 30)	0	0	0	0
Kamil Kreps (CZE)	FLO (Jan. 7)	0	0	0	2
Drew Larman (USA)	FLO (Nov. 13)	0	0	0	0
Matt Lashoff (USA)	BOS (Oct. 26)	0	0	0	2
Guillaume Latendresse (CAN)	MON (Oct. 6)	0	0	0	0
Mikko Lehtonen (FIN)	BUF (Oct. 7)	1	0	1	0
Kris Letang (CAN)	PIT (Oct. 5)	0	0	0	0
Enver Lisin (RUS)	PHO (Oct. 14)	0	0	0	0
Martin Lojek (CZE)	FLO (Feb. 3)	0	0	0	0
Joel Lundqvist (SWE)	DAL (Dec. 4)	0	0	0	0
Clarke MacArthur (CAN)	BUF (Dec. 19)	0	0	0	0
Joey MacDonald (CAN)	BOS (Oct. 19)	45:28	2	ND	
Tomi Maki (FIN)	CAL (Dec. 12)	0	0	0	0
Evgeni Malkin (RUS)	PIT (Oct. 18)	1	0	1	0
Mark Mancari (CAN)	BUF (Feb. 24)	0	0	0	2
Nathan McIver (CAN)	VAN (Nov. 9)	0	0	0	7
Derek Meech (CAN)	DET (Dec. 7)	0	0	0	0
Bjorn Melin (SWE)	ANA (Jan. 7)	1	0	1	0
Marc Methot (CAN)	CBJ (Feb. 25)	0	0	0	0

Alexei Mikhnov (UKR)	EDM (Oct. 23)	0	0	0	0
Andrew Miller (USA)	ANA (Apr. 19)	0	0	0	0
Duncan Milroy (CAN)	MON (Feb. 17)	0	0	0	0
David Moss (USA)	CAL (Dec. 19)	1	0	1	0
Kris Newbury (CAN)	TOR (Dec. 23)	0	0	0	0
Frans Nielsen (DEN)	NYI (Jan. 6)	0	0	0	0
Jonas Nordqvist (SWE)	CHI (Apr. 5)	0	1	1	0
Fredrik Norrena (FIN)	CBJ (Oct. 14)	25:57	1	ND	
Shane O'Brien (CAN)	ANA (Oct. 6)	0	0	0	0
John Oduya (SWE)	NJ (Oct. 6)	0	0	0	0
Patrick O'Sullivan (USA)	LA (Oct. 6)	0	0	0	0
Ryan Parent (CAN)	PHI (Apr. 5)	0	0	0	0
Pierre Parenteau (CAN)	CHI (Feb. 7)	0	0	0	0
Joe Pavelski (USA)	SJ (Nov. 22)	1	0	1	0
Rodney Pelley (CAN)	NJ (Feb. 1)	0	0	0	0
Rich Peverley (CAN)	NAS (Mar. 4)	0	1	1	0
Joe Piskula (USA)	LA (Mar. 23)	0	0	0	2
Tomas Plihal (CZE)	SJ (Jan. 26)	0	0	0	0
Roman Polak (CZE)	STL (Oct. 9)	0	0	0	0
Tomas Popperle (CZE)	CBJ (Feb. 2)	25:42	1	ND	
Benoit Pouliot (CAN)	MIN (Nov. 22)	0	0	0	0
Brandon Prust (CAN)	CAL (Nov. 1)	0	0	0	0
Alexander Radulov (RUS)	NAS (Oct. 21)	0	0	0	2
Karri Ramo (FIN)	TB (Dec. 2)	51:43	2	ND	
Aaron Rome (CAN)	ANA (Jan. 2)	0	0	0	0
Michael Ryan (USA)	BUF (Nov.22)	0	0	0	0
Rob Schremp (USA)	EDM (Apr. 5)	0	0	0	0
Jeff Schultz (CAN)	WAS (Dec. 22)	0	0	0	0
Jesse Schultz (CAN)	VAN (Nov. 28)	0	0	0	0
Marek Schwarz (CZE)	STL (Dec. 12)	58:46	3	L	
Andrej Sekera (SVK)	BUF (Nov. 22)	0	0	0	2
Ryan Shannon (USA)	ANA (Oct. 6)	0	0	0	0
Jonathan Sigalet (CAN)	BOS (Jan. 9)	0	0	0	4

Player	Team (Date)				
Ladislav Smid (CZE)	EDM (Oct. 5)	0		0	0	2
Mike Smith (CAN)	DAL (Oct. 21)	60:00	0	W	
Janis Sprukts (LAT)	FLO (Oct. 20)	0	0	0	0
Jordan Staal (CAN)	PIT (Oct. 5)	0	0	0	0
Drew Stafford (USA)	BUF (Nov. 5)	0	1	1	0
Paul Stastny (CAN)	COL (Oct. 4)	0	0	0	2
Shay Stephenson (CAN)	LA (Mar. 1)	0	0	0	0
Zachery Stortini (CAN)	EDM (Jan. 20)	0	0	0	10
Nate Thompson (USA)	BOS (Oct. 21)	0	0	0	0
Patrick Thoresen (NOR)	EDM (Oct. 5)	0	0	0	2
Jussi Timonen (FIN)	PHI (Nov. 20)	0	0	0	2
Lauri Tukonen (FIN)	LA (Feb. 22)	0	0	0	0
Marc-Edouard Vlasic (CAN)	SJ (Oct. 5)	0	0	0	0
Michael Wall (CAN)	ANA (Nov. 26)	60:00	3	W	
Joel Ward (CAN)	MIN (Dec. 16)	0	0	0	0
Keith Yandle (USA)	PHO (Oct. 11)	0	0	0	0
Bryan Young (CAN)	EDM (Mar. 9)	0	0	0	0
Travis Zajac (CAN)	NJ (Oct. 6)	0	0	0	2
John Zeiler (USA)	LA (Feb. 17)	0	0	0	0

BY NATIONALITY

TOTAL	139
CANADA	66
USA	32
CZECH REPUBLIC	11
SWEDEN	8
FINLAND	7
RUSSIA	4
DENMARK	2
SLOVAKIA	2
GERMANY	1
JAPAN	1

LATVIA	1
NORWAY	1
SLOVENIA	1
SWITZERLAND	1
UKRAINE	1

PLAYER REGISTER, REGULAR SEASON, 2006–07

Player YEAR	GP	G	A	P	Pim		
Goalie YEAR	GP	W-L-OT	Mins	GA	SO	GAA	

Abid, Ramzi b. Montreal, Quebec, March 24, 1980

	GP	G	A	P	Pim
2006–07 NAS	13	1	4	5	13
NHL Totals	68	14	16	30	78

Adams, Craig b. Seria, Brunei (Malaysia), April 26, 1977

	GP	G	A	P	Pim
2006–07 CAR	82	7	7	14	54
NHL Totals	387	31	41	72	303

Adams, Kevyn b. Washington, D.C., October 8, 1974

	GP	G	A	P	Pim
2006–07 CAR/PHO	68	3	9	12	25
NHL Totals	513	59	75	134	304

* traded by Carolina on January 8, 2007, to Phoenix for Dennis Seidenberg

Aebischer, David b. Fribourg, Switzerland, February 7, 1978

	GP	W-L-OT	Mins	GA	SO	GAA
2006–07 MON	32	13–12–0–3	1,760	93	0	3.17
NHL Totals	213	106–73–12–5	12,169	510	13	2.51

Afanasenkov, Dmitry b. Arkhangelsk, Soviet Union (Russia), May 12, 1980

	GP	G	A	P	Pim
2006–07 TB/PHI	74	11	10	21	20
NHL Totals	227	27	27	54	52

* claimed off waivers by Philadelphia on December 30, 2006, from Tampa Bay

Afinogenov, Maxim b. Moscow, Soviet Union (Russia), September 4, 1979

2006–07 BUF	56	23	38	61	66
NHL Totals	465	118	168	286	378

Alberts, Andrew b. Minneapolis, Minnesota, June 30, 1981

2006–07 BOS	76	0	10	10	124
NHL Totals	149	1	16	17	192

Alexeev, Nikita b. Murmansk, Soviet Union (Russia), December 27, 1981

2006–07 TB/CHI	78	12	11	23	12
NHL Totals	159	20	17	37	28

* traded by Tampa Bay on February 27, 2007, to Chicago for Karl Stewart and a 6th-round draft choice in 2007

Alfredsson, Daniel b. Goteborg, Sweden, December 11, 1972

2006–07 OTT	77	29	58	87	42
NHL Totals	783	291	467	758	351

Allen, Bobby b. Weymouth, Massachusetts, November 14, 1978

2006–07 BOS	31	0	3	3	10
NHL Totals	32	0	3	3	10

Allen, Bryan b. Kingston, Ontario, August 21, 1980

2006–07 FLO	82	4	21	25	112
NHL Totals	298	18	39	57	400

Amonte, Tony b. Hingham, Massachusetts, August 2, 1970

2006–07 CAL	81	10	20	30	40
NHL Totals	1,174	416	484	900	752

Anderson, Craig b. Park Ridge, Illinois, May 21, 1981

2006–07 FLO	5	1–1–0–1	216	8	0	2.21
NHL Totals	61	13–30–2–5	3,245	169	2	3.12

Antropov, Nik b. Vost, Soviet Union (Kazakhstan), February 18, 1980

2006–07 TOR	54	18	15	33	44
NHL Totals	374	78	111	189	361

Arkhipov, Denis b. Kazan, Soviet Union (Russia), May 19, 1979

2006–07 CHI	79	10	17	27	54
NHL Totals	352	56	82	138	128

Armstrong, Colby b. Lloydminster, Saskatchewan, November 23, 1982

2006–07 PIT	80	12	22	34	67
NHL Totals	127	28	46	74	125

Armstrong, Derek b. Ottawa, Ontario, April 23, 1973

2006–07 LA	67	11	33	44	62
NHL Totals	338	59	118	177	227

Arnason, Tyler b. Oklahoma City, Oklahoma, March 16, 1979

2006–07 COL	82	16	33	49	26
NHL Totals	346	73	119	192	110

Arnott, Jason b. Collingwood, Ontario, October 11, 1974

2006–07 NAS	68	27	27	54	48
NHL Totals	892	303	395	698	1,047

Asham, Arron b. Portage La Prairie, Manitoba, April 13, 1978

2006–07 NYI	80	11	12	23	63
NHL Totals	421	58	67	125	453

Aubin, Jean-Sebastien b. Montreal, Quebec, July 19, 1977

2006–07 TOR	20	3–5–0–2	804	46	0	3.43
NHL Totals	199	75–77–11–4	10,370	503	7	2.91

Aucoin, Adrian b. Ottawa, Ontario, July 3, 1973

2006–07 CHI	59	4	12	16	50
NHL Totals	694	88	179	267	544

Aucoin, Keith b. Waltham, Massachusetts, November 6, 1978

2006–07 CAR	8	0	1	1	0
NHL Totals	15	0	2	12	4

Auld, Alexander b. Cold Lake, Alberta, January 7, 1981

2006–07 FLO	27	7–13–0–5	1,470	82	1	3.34
NHL Totals	108	46–44–2–11	6,120	295	2	2.89

Avery, Sean b. Pickering, Ontario, April 10, 1980

2006–07 LA/NYR	84	18	30	48	174
NHL Totals	322	50	84	134	913

* traded by Los Angeles on February 5, 2007, with John Seymour to New York Rangers for Jason Ward, Marc-Andre Cliché and Jan Marek

Axelsson, P-J b. Kungalv, Sweden, February 26, 1975

2006–07 BOS	55	11	16	27	52
NHL Totals	647	84	144	228	245

Babchuk, Anton b. Kiev, Soviet Union (Ukraine), May 6, 1984

2006–07 CAR	52	2	12	14	30
NHL Totals	96	7	19	26	54

Bacashihua, Jason b. Garden City, Michigan, September 20, 1982

2006–07 STL	19	3–7–0–3	893	47	0	3.15
NHL Totals	38	7–17–0–4	1,859	99	0	3.19

Backes, David b. Blaine, Minnesota, May 1, 1984

2006–07 STL	49	10	13	23	37
NHL Totals	49	10	13	23	37

Backman, Christian b. Alingsas, Sweden, April 28, 1980

| 2006–07 STL | 61 | 7 | 11 | 18 | 36 |
| NHL Totals | 183 | 18 | 36 | 54 | 100 |

Backstrom, Niklas b. Helsinki, Finland, February 13, 1978

| 2006–07 MIN | 41 | 23–8–0–6 | 2,226 | 73 | 5 | 1.97 |
| NHL Totals | 41 | 23–8–0–6 | 2,226 | 73 | 5 | 1.97 |

Balastik, Jaroslav b. Gottwaldov, Czechoslovakia (Czech Republic), November 28, 1979

| 2006–07 CBJ | 8 | 1 | 1 | 2 | 4 |
| NHL Totals | 74 | 13 | 11 | 24 | 30 |

Ballard, Keith b. Baudette, Minnesota, November 26, 1982

| 2006–07 PHO | 69 | 5 | 22 | 27 | 59 |
| NHL Totals | 151 | 13 | 53 | 66 | 158 |

Barch, Krys b. Guelph, Ontario, March 26, 1980

| 2006–07 DAL | 26 | 3 | 2 | 5 | 107 |
| NHL Totals | 26 | 3 | 2 | 5 | 107 |

Barker, Cam b. Winnipeg, Manitoba, April 4, 1986

| 2006–07 CHI | 35 | 1 | 7 | 8 | 44 |
| NHL Totals | 36 | 1 | 7 | 8 | 44 |

Barnaby, Matthew b. Ottawa, Ontario, May 4, 1973

| 2006–07 DAL | 39 | 1 | 6 | 7 | 127 |
| NHL Totals | 834 | 113 | 187 | 300 | 2,562 |

Barnes, Stu b. Spruce Grove, Alberta, December 25, 1970

| 2006–07 DAL | 82 | 13 | 12 | 25 | 40 |
| NHL Totals | 1,057 | 249 | 325 | 574 | 412 |

Bates, Shawn b. Melrose, Massachusetts, April 3, 1975

2006–07 NYI	48	4	6	10	34
NHL Totals	463	72	126	198	266

Battaglia, Bates b. Chicago, Illinois, December 13, 1975

2006–07 TOR	82	12	19	31	45
NHL Totals	567	80	118	198	378

Baumgartner, Nolan b. Calgary, Alberta, March 23, 1976

2006–07 PHI/DAL	13	0	3	3	21
NHL Totals	131	6	39	45	67

* claimed off waivers on February 24, 2007, by Dallas from Philadelphia

Bayda, Ryan b. Saskatoon, Saskatchewan, December 9, 1980

2006–07 CAR	9	1	1	2	2
NHL Totals	78	8	14	22	40

Beauchemin, Francois b. Sorel, Quebec, June 4, 1980

2006–07 ANA	71	7	21	28	49
NHL Totals	144	15	49	64	101

Beech, Kris b. Salmon Arm, British Columbia, February 5, 1981

2006–07 WAS	64	8	18	26	46
NHL Totals	173	19	37	56	109

Begin, Steve b. Trois-Rivieres, Quebec, June 14, 1978

2006–07 MON	52	5	5	10	46
NHL Totals	303	37	29	66	392

Belak, Wade b. Saskatoon, Saskatchewan, July 3, 1976

2006–07 TOR	65	0	3	3	110
NHL Totals	395	7	21	28	1,030

Belanger, Eric b. Sherbrooke, Quebec, December 16, 1977

2006–07 CAR/ATL	80	17	18	35	26	
NHL Totals	403	80	105	185	195	

* traded by Carolina on February 9, 2007, to Nashville for Josef Vasicek;
  traded by Nashville on February 10, 2007, to Atlanta for Vitaly Vishnevski

Belfour, Ed b. Carman, Manitoba, April 21, 1965

2006–07 FLO	58	27–17–0–0	3,289	152	1	2.77
NHL Totals	963	484–320–111–14	55,695	2,317	76	2.77

Bell, Brendan b. Ottawa, Ontario, March 31, 1983

2006–07 PHO	14	0	2	2	8
NHL Totals	46	1	6	7	27

Bell, Mark b. St. Paul's, Ontario, August 5, 1980

2006–07 SJ	71	11	10	21	83
NHL Totals	410	83	89	172	537

Belle, Shawn b. Edmonton, Alberta, January 3, 1985

2006–07 MIN	9	0	1	1	4
NHL Totals	9	0	1	1	4

Berard, Bryan b. Woonsocket, Rhode Island, March 5, 1977

2006–07 CBJ	11	0	3	3	8
NHL Totals	565	71	230	301	452

Bergeron, Marc-Andre b. St. Louis de France, Quebec,
October 13, 1980

2006–07 EDM/NYI	78	14	32	46	38
NHL Totals	212	39	70	109	111

* traded by Edmonton with a 3rd-round draft choice in 2008 by Edmonton
  to New York Islanders for Denis Grebeshkov

Bergeron, Patrice b. Ancienne-Lorette, Quebec, July 24, 1985

2006–07 BOS	77	22	48	70	26
NHL Totals	229	69	113	182	70

Bernier, Steve b. Quebec City, Quebec, March 31, 1985

2006–07 SJ	62	15	16	31	29
NHL Totals	101	29	29	58	64

Bertuzzi, Todd b. Sudbury, Ontario, February 2, 1975

2006–07 FLO/DET	15	3	8	11	19
NHL Totals	725	226	314	540	1,050

* traded by Florida on February 27, 2007, to Detroit for Shawn Matthias and conditional draft choices in 2007 and 2008

Betts, Blair b. Edmonton, Alberta, February 16, 1980

2006–07 NYR	82	9	4	13	24
NHL Totals	183	20	11	31	60

Bickell, Bryan b. Bowmanville, Ontario, March 9, 1986

2006–07 CHI	3	2	0	2	0
NHL Totals	3	2	0	2	0

Bieksa, Kevin b. Grimsby, Ontario, June 16, 1981

2006–07 VAN	81	12	30	42	134
NHL Totals	120	12	36	48	211

Biron, Martin b. Lac St. Charles, Quebec, August 15, 1977

2006–07 BUF/PHI	35	18–12–0–3	2,101	101	0	3.03
NHL Totals	316	140–123–25–6	17,708	754	18	2.55

* traded by Buffalo on February 27, 2007, to Philadelphia for a 2nd-round draft choice in 2007

Bisaillon, Sebastien b. Mont Laurier, Quebec, December 8, 1986

2006–07 EDM	2	0	0	0	0
NHL Totals	2	0	0	0	0

Blake, Jason b. Moorhead, Minnesota, September 2, 1973

2006–07 NYI	82	40	29	69	34
NHL Totals	508	134	152	286	304

Blake, Rob b. Simcoe, Ontario, December 10, 1969

2006–07 LA	72	14	20	34	82
NHL Totals	1,056	214	457	671	1,411

Blunden, Michael b. Toronto, Ontario, December 15, 1986

2006–07 CHI	9	0	0	0	10
NHL Totals	9	0	0	0	10

Bochenski, Brandon b. Blaine, Minnesota, April 4, 1982

2006–07 CHI/BOS	41	13	11	24	16
NHL Totals	81	21	20	41	38

* traded by Chicago on February 3, 2007, to Boston for Kris Versteeg and a conditional draft choice

Boguniecki, Eric b. New Haven, Connecticut, May 6, 1975

2006–07 NYI	11	0	0	0	8
NHL Totals	178	34	42	76	105

Bois, Danny b. Thunder Bay, Ontario, June 1, 1983

2006–07 OTT	1	0	0	0	7
NHL Totals	1	0	0	0	7

Bolland, Dave b. Toronto, Ontario, June 5, 1986

2006–07 CHI	1	0	0	0	0
NHL Totals	1	0	0	0	0

Bondra, Peter b. Luck, Soviet Union (Ukraine), February 7, 1968

2006–07 CHI	37	5	9	14	26
NHL Totals	1,081	503	389	892	761

Bonk, Radek b. Krnov, Czechoslovakia (Czech Republic), January 9, 1976

2006–07 MON	74	13	10	23	54
NHL Totals	824	171	272	443	507

Boogaard, Derek b. Saskatoon, Saskatchewan, June 23, 1982

2006–07 MIN	48	0	1	1	120
NHL Totals	113	2	5	7	278

Booth, David b. Detroit, Michigan, November 24, 1984

2006–07 FLO	48	3	7	10	12
NHL Totals	48	3	7	10	12

Bootland, Darryl b. Toronto, Ontario, November 2, 1981

2006–07 DET	6	0	0	0	9
NHL Totals	28	1	1	2	83

Bouchard, Pierre-Marc b. Sherbrooke, Quebec, April 27, 1984

2006–07 MIN	82	20	37	57	14
NHL Totals	273	48	110	158	82

Boucher, Brian b. Woonsocket, Rhode Island, January 2, 1977

2006–07 CHI/CBJ	18	2–11–0–3	968	54	1	3.35
NHL Totals	220	77–96–30–3	12,372	575	13	2.79

* claimed by Columbus off waivers on February 27, 2007, from Chicago

Boucher, Philippe b. Ste. Apollinaire, Quebec, March 24, 1973

2006–07 DAL	76	19	32	51	104
NHL Totals	669	89	188	277	637

Bouck, Tyler b. Camrose, Alberta, January 13, 1980

2006–07 VAN	6	0	0	0	16
NHL Totals	91	4	8	12	93

Bouillon, Francis b. New York, New York, October 17, 1975

2006–07 MON	62	3	11	14	52
NHL Totals	357	14	71	85	257

Boulton, Eric b. Halifax, Nova Scotia, August 17, 1976

2006–07 ATL	45	3	4	7	49
NHL Totals	268	12	21	33	647

Bourdon, Luc b. Shippagan, New Brunswick, February 16, 1987

2006–07 VAN	9	0	0	0	4
NHL Totals	9	0	0	0	4

Bourque, Rene b. Lac La Biche, Alberta, December 10, 1981

2006–07 CHI	44	7	10	17	38
NHL Totals	121	23	28	51	94

Bouwmeester, Jay b. Edmonton, Alberta, September 27, 1983

2006–07 FLO	82	12	30	42	66
NHL Totals	307	23	101	124	189

Boyd, Dustin b. Winnipeg, Manitoba, July 16, 1986

2006–07 CAL	13	2	2	4	4
NHL Totals	13	2	2	4	4

Boyes, Brad b. Mississauga, Ontario, April 17, 1982

2006–07 BOS/STL	81	17	29	46	29
NHL Totals	164	43	72	115	61

* traded by Boston on February 27, 2007, to St. Louis for Dennis Wideman

Boyle, Dan b. Ottawa, Ontario, July 12, 1976

2006–07 TB	82	20	43	63	62
NHL Totals	486	72	195	267	281

Boynton, Nick b. Nobleton, Ontario, January 14, 1979

2006–07 PHO	59	2	9	11	138
NHL Totals	358	24	71	95	535

Bradley, Matt b. Stittsville, Ontario, June 13, 1978

2006–07 WAS	57	4	9	13	47
NHL Totals	334	30	47	77	283

Brashear, Donald b. Bedford, Indiana, January 7, 1972

2006–07 WAS	77	4	9	13	156
NHL Totals	846	79	113	192	2,321

Brent, Tim b. Cambridge, Ontario, March 10, 1984

2006–07 ANA	15	1	0	1	6
NHL Totals	15	1	0	1	6

Brewer, Eric b. Vernon, British Columbia, April 17, 1979

2006–07 STL	82	6	23	29	69
NHL Totals	518	46	105	151	376

Briere, Daniel b. Gatineau, Quebec, October 6, 1977

2006–07 BUF	81	32	63	95	89
NHL Totals	483	162	214	376	365

Brind'Amour, Rod b. Ottawa, Ontario, August 9, 1970

2006–07 CAR	78	26	56	82	46
NHL Totals	1,265	408	655	1,063	990

Brisebois, Patrice b. Montreal, Quebec, January 27, 1971

2006–07 COL	33	1	10	11	22
NHL Totals	904	90	301	391	578

Brodeur, Martin b. Montreal, Quebec, May 6, 1972

2006–07 NJ	78	48–23–0–7	4,696	171	12	2.18
NHL Totals	891	494–263–105–14	52,572	1,931	92	2.20

Brodziak, Kyle b. St. Paul, Alberta, May 25, 1984

2006–07 EDM	6	1	0	1	2
NHL Totals	10	1	0	1	6

Brookbank, Sheldon b. Lanigan, Saskatchewan, October 3, 1980

2006–07 NAS	3	0	1	1	12
NHL Totals	3	0	1	1	12

Brookbank, Wade b. Lanigan, Saskatchewan, September 29, 1977

2006–07 BOS	7	1	0	1	15
NHL Totals	68	4	2	6	229

Brooks, Alexander b. Madison, Wisconsin, August 21, 1976

2006–07 NJ	19	0	1	1	4
NHL Totals	19	0	1	1	4

Brouwer, Troy b. Vancouver, British Columbia, August 17, 1985

2006–07 CHI	10	0	0	0	7
NHL Totals	10	0	0	0	7

Brown, Curtis b. Unity, Saskatchewan, February 12, 1976

2006–07 SJ	78	8	12	20	56
NHL Totals	703	124	167	291	388

Brown, Dustin b. Ithaca, New York, November 4, 1984

2006–07 LA	81	17	29	46	54
NHL Totals	191	32	47	79	150

Brule, Gilbert b. Edmonton, Alberta, January 1, 1987

2006–07 CBJ	78	9	10	19	28
NHL Totals	85	11	12	23	28

Brunette, Andrew b. Sudbury, Ontario, August 24, 1973

2006–07 COL	82	27	56	83	36
NHL Totals	706	172	318	490	250

Brust, Barry b. Swan River, Manitoba, August 8, 1983

2006–07 LA	11	2–4–0–1	486	30	0	3.70
NHL Totals	11	2–4–0–1	486	30	0	3.70

Brylin, Sergei b. Moscow, Soviet Union (Russia), January 13, 1974

2006–07 NJ	82	16	24	40	35
NHL Totals	683	123	169	292	253

Bryzgalov, Ilya b. Togliatti, Soviet Union (Russia), June 22, 1980

2006–07 ANA	27	10–8–0–6	1,508	62	1	2.47
NHL Totals	60	24–20–0–7	3,176	131	2	2.47

Budaj, Peter b. Banska Bystrica, Czechoslovakia (Slovakia), September 18, 1982

2006–07 COL	57	31–16–0–6	3,198	143	3	2.68
NHL Totals	91	45–26–0–12	5,001	229	5	2.75

Bulis, Jan b. Pardubice, Czechoslovakia (Czech Republic), March 18, 1978

2006–07 VAN	79	12	11	23	70
NHL Totals	552	96	149	245	268

Burish, Adam b. Madison, Wisconsin, January 6, 1983

2006–07 CHI	9	0	0	0	2
NHL Totals	9	0	0	0	2

Burke, Sean b. Windsor, Ontario, January 29, 1967

2006–07 LA	23	6–10–0–5	1,309	68	1	3.11
NHL Totals	820	324–341–101–9	46,440	2,290	38	2.96

Burns, Brent b. Ajax, Ontario, March 9, 1985

2006–07 MIN	77	7	18	25	26
NHL Totals	185	12	35	47	70

Burrows, Alexandre b. Pointe Claire, Quebec, April 11, 1981

2006–07 VAN	81	3	6	9	93
NHL Totals	124	10	11	21	154

Byfuglien, Dustin b. Minneapolis, Minnesota, March 27, 1985

2006–07 CHI	9	1	2	3	10
NHL Totals	34	4	4	8	34

Cairns, Eric b. Oakville, Ontario, June 27, 1974

2006–07 PIT	1	0	0	0	5
NHL Totals	457	10	32	42	1,182

Cajanek, Petr b. Gottwaldov, Czechoslovakia (Czech Republic), August 18, 1975

2006–07 STL	77	15	33	48	54
NHL Totals	269	46	107	153	144

Calder, Kyle b. Mannville, Alberta, January 5, 1979

2006–07 PHI/DET	78	14	21	35	58
NHL Totals	437	99	146	245	242

* traded by Philadelphia on February 26, 2007, to Chicago for Lasse Kukkonen and a 3rd-round draft choice in 2007; traded to Detroit on the same day for Jason Williams

Callahan, Ryan b. Rochester, New York, March 21, 1985

2006–07 NYR	14	4	2	6	9
NHL Totals	14	4	2	6	9

Cammalleri, Mike b. Richmond Hill, Ontario, June 8, 1982

2006–07 LA	81	34	46	80	48
NHL Totals	220	74	84	158	140

Campbell, Brian b. Strathroy, Ontario, May 23, 1979

2006–07 BUF	82	6	42	48	35
NHL Totals	328	27	106	133	101

Campbell, Darcy b. Airdrie, Alberta, May 12, 1984

2006–07 CBJ	1	0	0	0	0
NHL Totals	1	0	0	0	0

Campbell, Gregory b. London, Ontario, December 17, 1983

2006–07 FLO	79	6	3	9	66
NHL Totals	145	9	9	18	111

Campoli, Chris b. North York (Toronto), Ontario, July 9, 1984

2006–07 NYI	51	1	13	14	23
NHL Totals	131	10	38	48	69

Carcillo, Daniel b. King City, Ontario, January 28, 1985

2006–07 PHO	18	4	3	7	74
NHL Totals	18	4	3	7	74

Card, Mike b. Kitchener, Ontario, February 18, 1986

2006–07 BUF	4	0	0	0	0
NHL Totals	4	0	0	0	0

Carle, Matt b. Anchorage, Alaska, September 25, 1984

2006–07 SJ	77	11	31	42	30
NHL Totals	89	14	34	48	44

Carney, Keith b. Providence, Rhode Island, February 3, 1970

2006–07 MIN	80	4	13	17	58
NHL Totals	957	44	173	217	862

Caron, Sebastien b. Amqui, Quebec, June 25, 1980

	GP		MIN	GA	SO	GAA
2006–07 CHI/ANA	2	1–0–0–0	87	2	0	1.38
NHL Totals	92	25–47–7–5	5,021	289	4	3.45

* traded by Chicago with Matt Keith and Chris Durno on December 28, 2006, to Anaheim for Pierre Parenteau and Bruno St. Jacques

Carter, Anson b. Toronto, Ontario, June 6, 1974

	GP	G	A	PTS	PIM
2006–07 CBJ/CAR	64	11	17	28	18
NHL Totals	674	202	219	421	229

* traded by Columbus on February 23, 2007, to Carolina for a 5th-round draft choice in 2008

Carter, Jeff b. London, Ontario, January 1, 1985

	GP	G	A	PTS	PIM
2006–07 PHI	62	14	23	37	48
NHL Totals	143	37	42	79	88

Carter, Ryan b. White Bear Lake, Minnesota, August 3, 1983

	GP	G	A	PTS	PIM
2006–07 ANA	3	0	0	0	0
NHL Totals	3	0	0	0	0

Cassivi, Frederic b. Sorel, Quebec, June 12, 1975

	GP		MIN	GA	SO	GAA
2006–07 WAS	4	0–1–0–1	138	6	0	2.59
NHL Totals	13	3–6–0–1	627	38	0	3.64

Chara, Zdeno b. Trencin, Czechoslovakia (Slovakia), March 18, 1977

	GP	G	A	PTS	PIM
2006–07 BOS	80	11	32	43	100
NHL Totals	610	68	150	218	1,001

Cheechoo, Jonathan b. Moose Factory, Ontario, July 15, 1980

	GP	G	A	PTS	PIM
2006–07 SJ	76	37	32	69	69
NHL Totals	305	130	95	225	199

Chelios, Chris b. Chicago, Illinois, January 25, 1962

2006–07 DET	71	0	11	11	34
NHL Totals	1,547	182	754	936	2,837

Chimera, Jason b. Edmonton, Alberta, May 2, 1979

2006–07 CBJ	82	15	21	36	91
NHL Totals	292	51	51	102	279

Chistov, Stanislav b. Chelyabisnk, Soviet Union (Russia), April 17, 1983

2006–07 ANA/BOS	61	5	8	13	36
NHL Totals	196	19	42	61	116

* traded by Anaheim on November 13, 2006, to Boston for a 3rd-round draft choice in 2008

Chouinard, Marc b. Charlesbourg, Quebec, May 6, 1977

2006–07 VAN	42	2	2	4	10
NHL Totals	320	37	41	78	123

Christensen, Erik b. Edmonton, Alberta, December 17, 1983

2006–07 PIT	61	18	15	33	26
NHL Totals	94	24	22	46	60

Clark, Brett b. Wapella, Saskatchewan, December 23, 1976

2006–07 COL	82	10	29	39	50
NHL Totals	320	24	62	86	166

Clark, Chris b. South Windsor, Connecticut, March 8, 1976

2006–07 WAS	74	30	24	54	66
NHL Totals	430	85	79	165	539

Clarke, Noah b. LaVerne, California, June 11, 1979

2006–07 LA	13	2	0	2	4
NHL Totals	20	2	1	3	4

Clarkson, David b. Toronto, Ontario, March 31, 1984

| 2006–07 NJ | 7 | 3 | 1 | 4 | 6 |
| NHL Totals | 7 | 3 | 1 | 4 | 6 |

Cleary, Daniel b. Carbonear, Newfoundland, December 18, 1978

| 2006–07 DET | 71 | 20 | 20 | 40 | 24 |
| NHL Totals | 477 | 64 | 103 | 167 | 257 |

Clemmensen, Scott b. Des Moines, Iowa, July 23, 1977

| 2006–07 NJ | 6 | 1–1–0–2 | 305 | 16 | 0 | 3.15 |
| NHL Totals | 25 | 7–6–0–4 | 1,190 | 56 | 2 | 2.82 |

Cloutier, Dan b. Mont Laurier, Quebec, April 22, 1976

| 2006–07 LA | 24 | 6–14–0–2 | 1,281 | 85 | 0 | 3.98 |
| NHL Totals | 342 | 137–138–33–3 | 18,439 | 846 | 15 | 2.75 |

Clowe, Ryane b. St. John's, Newfoundland, September 30, 1982

| 2006–07 SJ | 58 | 16 | 18 | 34 | 78 |
| NHL Totals | 76 | 16 | 20 | 36 | 87 |

Clymer, Ben b. Bloomington, Minnesota, April 11, 1978

| 2006–07 WAS | 66 | 7 | 13 | 20 | 44 |
| NHL Totals | 438 | 52 | 77 | 129 | 367 |

Coburn, Braydon b. Calgary, Alberta, February 27, 1985

| 2006–07 ATL/PHI | 49 | 3 | 8 | 11 | 46 |
| NHL Totals | 58 | 3 | 9 | 12 | 50 |

* traded by Atlanta on February 24, 2007, to Philadelphia for Alexei Zhitnik

Colaiacovo, Carlo b. Toronto, Ontario, January 27, 1983

| 2006–07 TOR | 48 | 8 | 9 | 17 | 22 |
| NHL Totals | 73 | 10 | 16 | 26 | 41 |

Cole, Erik b. Oswego, New York, November 6, 1978

2006–07 CAR	71	29	32	61	76
NHL Totals	345	107	122	229	330

Colliton, Jeremy b. Blackie, Alberta, January 13, 1985

2006–07 NYI	1	0	0	0	0
NHL Totals	20	1	1	2	6

Comeau, Blake b. Meadow Lake, Saskatchewan, February 18, 1986

2006–07 NYI	3	0	0	0	0
NHL Totals	3	0	0	0	0

Commodore, Mike b. Fort Saskatchewan, Alberta, November 7, 1979

2006–07 CAR	82	7	22	29	113
NHL Totals	229	11	38	49	339

Comrie, Mike b. Edmonton, Alberta, September 11, 1980

2006–07 PHO/OTT	65	20	25	45	44
NHL Totals	386	123	139	262	276

* traded by Phoenix on January 3, 2007, to Ottawa for Alexei Kaigorodov

Conklin, Ty b. Anchorage, Alaska, March 30, 1976

2006–07 CBJ/BUF	16	3–5–0–2	718	40	0	3.34
NHL Totals	76	30–24–4–3	3,874	171	2	2.65

* traded by Columbus on February 27, 2007, to Buffalo for a 5th-round draft choice in 2007

Conner, Chris b. Westland, Michigan, December 23, 1983

2006–07 DAL	11	1	2	3	4
NHL Totals	11	1	2	3	4

Connolly, Tim b. Syracuse, New York, May 7, 1981

2006–07 BUF	2	1	0	1	2
NHL Totals	390	63	138	201	182

Conroy, Craig b. Potsdam, New York, September 4, 1971

2006–07 LA/CAL	80	13	24	37	56
NHL Totals	767	153	290	443	471

* traded by Los Angeles on January 29, 2007, to Calgary for Jamie Lundmark, a 4th-round draft choice in 2007 and a 2nd-round draft choice in 2008

Cooke, Matt b. Belleville, Ontario, September 7, 1978

2006–07 VAN	81	10	20	30	64
NHL Totals	505	76	111	187	561

Corazzini, Carl b. Framingham, Massachusetts, April 21, 1979

2006–07 CHI	7	0	1	1	2
NHL Totals	19	2	1	3	2

Corvo, Joe b. Oak Park, Illinois, June 20, 1977

2006–07 OTT	76	8	29	37	42
NHL Totals	279	35	79	114	130

Cote, Riley b. Winnipeg, Manitoba, March 16, 1982

2006–07 PHI	8	0	0	0	11
NHL Totals	8	0	0	0	11

Coulombe, Patrick b. St. Fabien, Quebec, April 23, 1985

2006–07 VAN	7	0	1	1	4
NHL Totals	7	0	1	1	4

Cowan, Jeff b. Scarborough (Toronto), Ontario, September 27, 1976

2006–07 LA/VAN	63	7	5	12	125
NHL Totals	367	47	33	80	585

* claimed off waivers by Vancouver on December 30, 2006, from Los Angeles

Craig, Ryan b. Abbotsford, British Columbia, January 6, 1982

2006–07 TB	72	14	13	27	55
NHL Totals	120	29	26	55	61

Crosby, Sidney b. Halifax, Nova Scotia, August 7, 1987

2006–07 PIT	79	36	84	120	60
NHL Totals	160	75	147	222	170

Cullen, Mark b. Moorhead, Minnesota, October 28, 1978

2006–07 PHI	3	0	0	0	0
NHL Totals	32	7	9	16	2

Cullen, Matt b. Virginia, Minnesota, November 2, 1976

2006–07 NYR	80	16	25	41	52
NHL Totals	671	118	203	321	306

Cullimore, Jassen b. Simcoe, Ontario, December 4, 1972

2006–07 CHI	65	1	6	7	64
NHL Totals	643	21	59	80	621

Cumiskey, Kyle b. Abbotsford, British Columbia, December 2, 1986

2006–07 COL	9	1	1	2	2
NHL Totals	9	1	1	2	2

Daley, Trevor b. Toronto, Ontario, October 9, 1983

2006–07 DAL	74	4	8	12	63
NHL Totals	182	8	24	32	164

Dallman, Kevin b. Niagara Falls, Ontario, February 26, 1981

2006–07 LA	53	1	9	10	12
NHL Totals	120	5	19	24	41

Dandenault, Mathieu b. Sherbrooke, Quebec, February 3, 1976

2006–07 MON	68	2	6	8	40
NHL Totals	766	55	122	177	465

Darche, Mathieu b. Montreal, Quebec, November 26, 1976

2006–07 SJ	2	0	0	0	0
NHL Totals	28	1	1	2	6

Datsyuk, Pavel b. Sverdlovsk, Soviet Union (Russia), July 20, 1978

2006–07 DET	79	27	60	87	20
NHL Totals	363	108	220	328	97

Davison, Rob b. St. Catharines, Ontario, May 1, 1980

2006–07 SJ	22	0	2	2	27
NHL Totals	161	2	12	14	217

Dawes, Nigel b. Winnipeg, Manitoba, February 9, 1985

2006–07 NYR	8	1	0	1	0
NHL Totals	8	1	0	1	0

Demitra, Pavol b. Dubnica, Czechoslovakia (Slovakia),
November 29, 1974

2006–07 MIN	71	25	39	64	28
NHL Totals	682	266	379	645	240

Dempsey, Nathan b. Spruce Grove, Alberta, July 14, 1974

2006–07 BOS	17	0	1	1	6
NHL Totals	260	21	67	88	120

Denis, Marc b. Montreal, Quebec, August 1, 1977

2006–07 TB	44	17–18–0–2	2,352	125	1	3.19
NHL Totals	338	111–174–28–3	19,091	953	16	3.00

Devereaux, Boyd b. Seaforth, Ontario, April 16, 1978

2006–07 TOR	33	8	11	19	12
NHL Totals	542	54	96	150	179

de Vries, Greg b. Sundridge, Ontario, January 4, 1973

2006–07 ATL	82	3	21	24	66
NHL Totals	730	43	131	174	644

Dimitrakos, Niko b. Boston, Massachusetts, May 21, 1979

2006–07 PHI	5	0	0	0	6
NHL Totals	158	24	38	62	95

DiPenta, Joe b. Barrie, Ontario, February 25, 1979

2006–07 ANA	76	2	6	8	48
NHL Totals	151	5	13	18	94

DiPietro, Rick b. Winthrop, Massachusetts, September 19, 1981

2006–07 NYI	62	32–19–0–9	3,626	156	5	2.58
NHL Totals	205	90–81–8–14	11,710	540	11	2.77

Doan, Shane b. Halkirk, Alberta, October 10, 1976

2006–07 PHO	73	27	28	55	73
NHL Totals	803	199	273	472	784

Donovan, Shean b. Timmins, Ontario, January 22, 1975

2006–07 BOS	76	6	11	17	56
NHL Totals	774	100	114	214	558

Dowd, Jim b. Brick, New Jersey, December 25, 1968

2006–07 NJ	66	4	4	8	20
NHL Totals	655	66	163	229	349

Downey, Aaron b. Shelburne, Ontario, August 27, 1974

2006–07 MON	21	1	0	1	48
NHL Totals	183	7	6	13	371

Drake, Dallas b. Trail, British Columbia, February 4, 1969

2006–07 STL	60	6	6	12	38
NHL Totals	944	174	297	471	844

Draper, Kris b. Toronto, Ontario, May 24, 1971

2006–07 DET	81	14	15	29	58
NHL Totals	885	132	165	297	642

Drury, Chris b. Trumbull, Connecticut, August 20, 1976

2006–07 BUF	77	37	32	69	30
NHL Totals	628	193	271	464	352

Dubielewicz, Wade b. Invermere, British Columbia, January 30, 1978

2006–07 NYI	8	4–1–0–0	378	13	0	2.06
NHL Totals	17	7–4–1–0	793	31	0	2.34

Dubinsky, Brandon b. Anchorage, Alaska, April 29, 1986

2006–07 NYR	6	0	0	0	2
NHL Totals	6	0	0	0	2

Dumont, J-P b. Montreal, Quebec, April 1, 1978

2006–07 NAS	82	21	45	66	28
NHL Totals	516	142	180	322	274

Dunham, Mike b. Johnson City, New York, June 1, 1972

2006–07 NYI	19	4–10–0–3	979	61	0	3.74
NHL Totals	394	141–178–39–5	21,653	989	19	2.74

Dupont, Micki b. Calgary, Alberta, April 15, 1980

2006–07 PIT	3	0	1	1	4
NHL Totals	21	1	3	4	10

Dupuis, Pascal b. Laval, Quebec, April 7, 1979

2006–07 ATL	17	3	2	5	4
NHL Totals	357	71	76	147	166

Dvorak, Radek b. Tabor, Czechoslovakia (Czech Republic), March 9, 1977

2006–07 STL	82	10	27	37	48
NHL Totals	828	171	278	449	292

Eager, Ben b. Ottawa, Ontario, January 22, 1984

2006–07 PHI	63	6	5	11	233
NHL Totals	88	9	10	19	251

Eaton, Mark b. Wilmington, Delaware, May 6, 1977

2006–07 PIT	35	0	3	3	16
NHL Totals	348	16	34	50	154

Eaves, Patrick b. Calgary, Alberta, May 1, 1984

2006–07 OTT	73	14	18	32	36
NHL Totals	131	34	27	61	58

Edler, Alexander b. Stockholm, Sweden, April 21, 1986

2006–07 VAN	22	1	2	3	6
NHL Totals	22	1	2	3	6

Ehrhoff, Christian b. Moers, West Germany (Germany), July 6, 1982

2006–07 SJ	82	10	23	33	63
NHL Totals	187	16	52	68	109

Ekman, Nils b. Stockholm, Sweden, March 11, 1976

2006–07 PIT	34	6	9	15	24
NHL Totals	264	60	91	151	188

Elias, Patrik b. Trebic, Czechoslovakia (Czech Republic), April 13, 1976

2006–07 NJ	75	21	48	69	38
NHL Totals	671	244	329	573	333

Ellis, Matt b. Welland, Ontario, August 31, 1981

2006–07 DET	16	0	1	1	6
NHL Totals	16	0	1	1	6

Ellison, Matt b. Duncan, British Columbia, December 8, 1983

2006–07 PHI	2	0	0	0	0
NHL Totals	43	3	11	14	19

Emery, Ray b. Cayuga, Ontario, September 28, 1982

2006–07 OTT	58	33–16–0–6	3,351	138	5	2.47
NHL Totals	103	59–27–0–10	5,729	247	8	2.59

Eminger, Steve b. Woodbridge, Ontario, October 31, 1983

2006–07 WAS	68	1	16	17	63
NHL Totals	192	6	35	41	213

Erat, Martin b. Trebic, Czechoslovakia (Czech Republic), August 28, 1981

2006–07 NAS	68	16	41	57	50
NHL Totals	331	62	134	196	210

Eriksson, Anders b. Bollnas, Sweden, January 9, 1975

2006–07 CBJ	79	0	23	23	46
NHL Totals	491	21	132	153	204

Eriksson, Loui b. Gothenburg, Sweden, July 17, 1985

2006–07 DAL	59	6	13	19	18
NHL Totals	59	6	13	19	18

Erskine, John b. Kingston, Ontario, June 26, 1980

2006–07 WAS	29	1	6	7	69
NHL Totals	170	4	8	12	405

Esche, Robert b. Whitesboro, New York, January 22, 1978

2006–07 PHI	18	5–9–0–1	860	62	1	4.33
NHL Totals	188	78–64–16–6	10,139	464	10	2.75

Exelby, Garnet b. Craik, Saskatchewan, August 16, 1981

2006–07 ATL	58	2	8	10	56
NHL Totals	219	4	28	32	306

Fahey, Jim b. Boston, Massachusetts, May 11, 1979

2006–07 NJ	13	0	1	1	2
NHL Totals	92	1	24	25	67

Fata, Drew b. Sault Ste. Marie, Ontario, July 28, 1983

2006–07 NYI	3	1	0	1	5
NHL Totals	3	1	0	1	5

Fata, Rico b. Sault Ste. Marie, Ontario, February 12, 1980

2006–07 WAS	10	1	1	2	2
NHL Totals	230	27	36	63	104

Fedorov, Sergei b. Pskov, Soviet Union (Russia), December 13, 1969

2006–07 CBJ	73	18	24	42	56
NHL Totals	1,128	461	644	1,105	751

Fedoruk, Todd b. Redwater, Alberta, February 13, 1979

2006–07 PHI	48	3	8	11	84
NHL Totals	354	17	48	65	785

Fedotenko, Ruslan b. Kiev, Soviet Union (Ukraine), January 18, 1979

2006–07 TB	80	12	20	32	52
NHL Totals	465	107	99	206	285

Fehr, Eric b. Winkler, Manitoba, September 7, 1985

2006–07 WAS	14	2	1	3	8
NHL Totals	25	2	1	3	10

Ference, Andrew b. Edmonton, Alberta, March 17, 1979

2006–07 BOS	26	1	2	3	31
NHL Totals	413	22	80	102	398

Ference, Brad b. Calgary, Alberta, April 2, 1979

2006–07 CAL	5	0	0	0	2
NHL Totals	250	4	30	34	565

Fernandez, Manny b. Etobicoke (Toronto), Ontario, August 26, 1974

2006–07 MIN	44	22–16–0–1	2,421	103	2	2.55
NHL Totals	293	125–113–24–8	16,692	688	13	2.47

Fiddler, Vernon b. Edmonton, Alberta, May 9, 1980

2006–07 NAS	72	11	15	26	40
NHL Totals	148	23	21	44	119

Filppula, Valtteri b. Vantaa, Finland, March 20, 1984

2006–07 DET	73	10	7	17	20
NHL Totals	77	10	8	18	22

Finger, Jeff b. Houghton, Michigan, December 18, 1979

2006–07 COL	22	1	4	5	11
NHL Totals	22	1	4	5	11

Finley, Brian b. Sault Ste. Marie, Ontario, July 3, 1981

2006–07 BOS	2	0–1–0–0	59	3	0	3.05
NHL Totals	4	0–2–0–0	165	13	0	4.70

Fischer, Patrick b. Zug, Switzerland, September 6, 1975

2006–07 PHO	27	4	6	10	24
NHL Totals	27	4	6	10	24

Fisher, Mike b. Peterborough, Ontario, June 5, 1980

2006–07 OTT	68	22	26	48	41
NHL Totals	384	92	100	192	314

Fitzpatrick, Rory b. Rochester, New York, January 11, 1975

2006–07 VAN	58	1	6	7	46
NHL Totals	268	10	24	34	190

Fleischmann, Tomas b. Koprivnice, Czechoslovakia (Czech Republic), May 16, 1984

2006–07 WAS	29	4	4	8	8
NHL Totals	43	4	6	10	8

Fleury, Marc-Andre b. Sorel, Quebec, November 28, 1984

2006–07 PIT	67	40–16–0–9	3,905	184	5	2.83
NHL Totals	138	57–57–2–15	7,868	406	7	3.10

Foote, Adam b. Toronto, Ontario, July 10, 1971

2006–07 CBJ	59	3	9	12	71
NHL Totals	923	64	204	268	1,300

Forsberg, Peter b. Ornskoldsvik, Sweden, July 20, 1973

2006–07 PHI/NAS	57	13	42	55	88
NHL Totals	697	248	623	871	678

* traded by Philadelphia on February 15, 2007, to Nashville for Ryan Parent, Scottie Upshall and a 1st-round and 3rd-round draft choice in 2007

Foster, Kurtis b. Carp, Ontario, November 24, 1981

2006–07 MIN	57	3	20	23	52
NHL Totals	120	13	39	52	112

Foy, Matt b. Oakville, Ontario, May 18, 1983

2006–07 MIN	9	0	0	0	4
NHL Totals	28	2	3	5	20

Franzen, Johan b. Landsbro, Sweden, December 23, 1979

2006–07 DET	69	10	20	30	37
NHL Totals	149	22	24	46	73

Fraser, Colin b. Sicamous, British Columbia, January 28, 1985

2006–07 CHI	1	0	0	0	2
NHL Totals	1	0	0	0	2

Fraser, Mark b. Ottawa, Ontario, September 29, 1986

2006–07 NJ	7	0	0	0	7
NHL Totals	7	0	0	0	7

Friesen, Jeff b. Meadow Lake, Saskatchewan, August 5, 1976

2006–07 CAL	72	6	6	12	34
NHL Totals	893	218	298	516	488

Fritsche, Dan b. Cleveland, Ohio, July 13, 1985

2006–07 CBJ	59	12	15	27	35
NHL Totals	137	19	22	41	69

Frolov, Alexander b. Moscow, Soviet Union (Russia), June 19, 1982

2006–07 LA	82	35	36	71	34
NHL Totals	307	94	110	204	132

Fukufuji, Yutaka b. Tokyo, Japan, September 17, 1982

2006–07 LA	4	0–3–0–0	96	7	0	4.38
NHL Totals	4	0–3–0–0	96	7	0	4.38

Funk, Michael b. Abbotsford, British Columbia, August 15, 1986

2006–07 BUF	5	0	2	2	0
NHL Totals	5	0	2	2	0

Gaborik, Marian b. Trencin, Czechoslovakia (Slovakia), February 14, 1982

2006–07 MIN	48	30	27	57	40
NHL Totals	408	164	167	331	236

Gagne, Simon b. Ste. Foy, Quebec, February 29, 1980

2006–07 PHI	76	41	27	68	30
NHL Totals	502	201	191	392	185

Garon, Mathieu b. Chandler, Quebec, January 9, 1978

2006–07 LA	32	13–10–0–6	1,778	79	2	2.66
NHL Totals	138	60–56–3–9	7,560	361	10	2.86

Gaustad, Paul b. Fargo, North Dakota, February 3, 1982

2006–07 BUF	54	9	13	22	74
NHL Totals	133	18	28	46	139

Gauthier, Denis b. Montreal, Quebec, October 1, 1976

2006–07 PHI	43	0	4	4	45
NHL Totals	489	15	58	73	658

Gauthier, Gabe b. Buena Park, California, January 20, 1984

2006–07 LA	5	0	0	0	2
NHL Totals	5	0	0	0	2

Gelinas, Martin b. Shawinigan, Quebec, June 5, 1970

2006–07 FLO	82	14	30	44	36
NHL Totals	1,216	300	340	640	800

Gerber, Martin b. Burgdorf, Switzerland, September 3, 1974

2006–07 OTT	29	15–9–0–3	1,598	74	1	2.78
NHL Totals	143	70–46–7–9	7,993	339	7	2.54

Germyn, Carsen b. Campbell River, British Columbia, February 22, 1985

2006–07 CAL	2	0	0	0	0
NHL Totals	4	0	0	0	0

Gervais, Bruno b. Longueuil, Quebec, October 3, 1984

2006–07 NYI	51	0	6	6	28
NHL Totals	78	3	10	13	36

Getzlaf, Ryan b. Regina, Saskatchewan, May 10, 1985

2006–07 ANA	82	25	33	58	66
NHL Totals	139	39	58	97	88

Giguere, Jean-Sebastien b. Montreal, Quebec, May 16, 1977

2006–07 ANA	56	36–10–0–8	3,244	122	4	2.26
NHL Totals	353	156–134–25–19	20,354	840	25	2.48

Gilbert, Tom b. Minneapolis, Minnesota, January 10, 1983

2006–07 EDM	12	1	5	6	0
NHL Totals	12	1	5	6	0

Gill, Hal b. Concord, Massachusetts, April 6, 1975

2006–07 TOR	82	6	14	20	91
NHL Totals	708	26	91	117	679

Gionta, Brian b. Rochester, New York, January 18, 1979

2006–07 NJ	62	25	20	45	36
NHL Totals	310	110	89	199	149

Giordano, Mark b. Toronto, Ontario, October 3, 1983

2006–07 CAL	48	7	8	15	36
NHL Totals	55	7	9	16	44

Girardi, Daniel b. Welland, Ontario, April 29, 1984

2006–07 NYR	34	0	6	6	8
NHL Totals	34	0	6	6	8

Giroux, Alexandre b. Quebec City, Quebec, June 16, 1981

2006–07 WAS	9	2	2	4	2
NHL Totals	10	2	2	4	2

Gleason, Tim b. Southfield, Michigan, January 29, 1983

2006–07 CAR	57	2	4	6	57
NHL Totals	182	4	30	34	155

Glencross, Curtis b. Kindersley, Saskatchewan, December 28, 1982

2006–07 ANA/CBJ	9	1	0	1	2
NHL Totals	9	1	0	1	2

* traded by Anaheim with Zenon Konopka and a 7th-round draft choice in either 2007 or 2008 on January 26, 2007, to Columbus for Joe Motzko, Mark Hartigan and a 4th-round draft choice in 2007

Globke, Rob b. Farmington, Michigan, October 24, 1982

2006–07 FLO	19	0	1	1	0
NHL Totals	37	1	1	2	6

Glumac, Mike b. Niagara Falls, Ontario, April 5, 1980

2006–07 STL	3	0	1	1	0
NHL Totals	36	7	6	13	33

Goc, Marcel b. Calw, West Germany (Germany), August 24, 1983

2006–07 SJ	78	5	8	13	24
NHL Totals	159	13	22	35	46

Godard, Eric b. Vernon, British Columbia, March 7, 1980

2006–07 CAL	19	0	1	1	50
NHL Totals	126	2	4	6	310

Goertzen, Steve b. Stony Plain, Alberta, May 26, 1984

2006–07 CBJ	7	0	0	0	10
NHL Totals	46	0	0	0	54

Gomez, Scott b. Anchorage, Alaska, December 23, 1979

2006–07 NJ	72	13	47	60	42
NHL Totals	548	116	334	450	362

Gonchar, Sergei b. Chelyabinsk, Soviet Union (Russia), April 13, 1974

2006–07 PIT	82	13	54	67	72
NHL Totals	826	173	377	550	701

Gordon, Boyd b. Unity, Saskatchewan, October 19, 1983

2006–07 WAS	71	7	22	29	14
NHL Totals	137	8	28	36	26

Goren, Lee b. Winnipeg, Manitoba, December 26, 1977

2006–07 VAN	2	0	0	0	0
NHL Totals	67	5	4	9	44

Gorges, Josh b. Kelowna, British Columbia, August 14, 1984

2006–07 SJ/MON	54	1	3	4	26
NHL Totals	103	1	9	10	57

* traded by San Jose with a 1st-round draft choice in 2007 on February 25, 2007, to Montreal for Craig Rivet and a 5th-round draft choice in 2008

Gove, David b. Centerville, Massachusetts, May 4, 1978

2006–07 CAR	1	0	0	0	0
NHL Totals	2	0	1	1	0

Grabovski, Mikhail b. Potsdam, East Germany (Germany), January 31, 1984

2006–07 MON	3	0	0	0	0
NHL Totals	3	0	0	0	0

Grahame, John b. Denver, Colorado, August 31, 1975

2006–07 CAR	28	10–13–0–2	1,514	72	0	2.85
NHL Totals	207	92–79–14–3	11,515	521	12	2.71

Grant, Triston b. Brandon, Manitoba, February 2, 1984

2006–07 PHI	8	0	1	1	10
NHL Totals	8	0	1	1	10

Gratton, Chris b. Brantford, Ontario, July 5, 1975

2006–07 FLO	81	13	22	35	94
NHL Totals	1,008	204	340	544	1,549

Gratton, Josh b. Scarborough (Toronto), Ontario, September 9, 1982

2006–07 PHO	52	1	1	2	188
NHL Totals	66	2	1	3	232

Green, Josh b. Camrose, Alberta, November 16, 1977

2006–07 VAN	57	2	5	7	25
NHL Totals	322	35	39	74	193

Green, Mike b. Calgary, Alberta, October 12, 1985

2006–07 WAS	70	2	10	12	36
NHL Totals	92	3	12	15	54

Green, Travis b. Castlegar, British Columbia, December 20, 1970

2006–07 ANA/TOR	31	1	1	2	27
NHL Totals	970	193	262	455	764

* claimed off waivers by Toronto on January 10, 2007, from Anaheim

Greene, Andy b. Trenton, Michigan, October 30, 1982

2006–07 NJ	23	1	5	6	6
NHL Totals	23	1	5	6	6

Greene, Matt b. Grand Ledge, Michigan, May 13, 1983

2006–07 EDM	78	1	9	10	109
NHL Totals	105	1	11	12	152

Grenier, Martin b. Laval, Quebec, November 2, 1980

2006–07 PHI	3	0	0	0	0
NHL Totals	18	1	0	1	14

Grier, Mike b. Detroit, Michigan, January 5, 1975

2006–07 SJ	81	16	17	33	43
NHL Totals	774	128	172	300	435

Grossman, Nicklas b. Stockholm, Sweden, January 22, 1985

2006–07 DAL	8	0	0	0	4
NHL Totals	8	0	0	0	4

Guenin, Nathan b. Sewickley, Pennsylvania, December 10, 1982

2006–07 PHI	9	0	2	2	4
NHL Totals	9	0	2	2	4

Guerin, Bill b. Worcester, Massachusetts, November 9, 1970

2006–07 STL/SJ	77	36	20	56	64
NHL Totals	1,026	364	355	719	1,439

* traded by St. Louis on February 27, 2007, to San Jose for Ville Nieminen, Jay Barriball and a 1st-round draft choice in 2007

Guite, Ben b. Montreal, Quebec, July 17, 1978

2006–07 COL	39	3	8	11	16
NHL Totals	40	3	8	11	16

Hagman, Niklas b. Espoo, Finland, December 5, 1979

2006–07 DAL	82	17	12	29	34
NHL Totals	399	53	71	124	102

Hainsey, Ron b. Bolton, Connecticut, March 24, 1981

2006–07 CBJ	80	9	25	34	69
NHL Totals	167	12	41	53	118

Halak, Jaroslav b. Bratislava, Czechoslovakia (Slovakia), May 13, 1985

2006–07 MON	16	10–6–0–0	912	44	2	2.89
NHL Totals	16	10–6–0–0	912	44	2	2.89

Hale, David b. Colorado Springs, Colorado, June 18, 1981

2006–07 NJ/CAL	54	0	1	1	36
NHL Totals	157	0	9	9	129

* traded by New Jersey with a 5th-round draft choice in 2007 on February 27, 2007, to Calgary for a 3rd-round draft choice in 2007

Hall, Adam b. Kalamazoo, Michigan, August 14, 1980

2006–07 NYR/MIN	72	6	11	17	26
NHL Totals	306	49	53	102	134

* traded by New York Rangers on February 9, 2007, to Minnesota for Pascal Dupuis

Halpern, Jeff b. Potomac, Maryland, May 3, 1976

2006–07 DAL	76	8	17	25	78
NHL Totals	514	95	144	239	429

Hamel, Denis b. Lachute, Quebec, May 10, 1977

2006–07 OTT/ATL/PHI	53	5	3	8	10
NHL Totals	192	19	12	31	77

* claimed off waivers by Atlanta on February 10, 2007, from Ottawa; claimed off waivers by Philadelphia on February 27, 2007, from Atlanta

Hamhuis, Dan b. Smithers, British Columbia, December 13, 1982

2006–07 NAS	81	6	14	20	66
NHL Totals	243	20	64	84	193

Hamilton, Jeff b. Englewood, Ohio, September 4, 1977

2006–07 CHI	70	18	21	39	22
NHL Totals	84	20	27	47	30

Hamrlik, Roman b. Zlin, Czechoslovakia (Czech Republic),
April 12, 1974

2006–07 CAL	75	7	31	38	88
NHL Totals	999	131	374	505	1,129

Handzus, Michal b. Banska Bystrica, Czechoslovakia (Slovakia),
March 11, 1977

2006–07 CHI	8	3	5	8	6
NHL Totals	517	115	185	300	313

Hannan, Scott b. Richmond, British Columbia, January 23, 1979

2006–07 SJ	79	4	20	24	38
NHL Totals	508	25	102	127	329

Hansen, Jannick b. Herlev, Denmark, March 15, 1986

2006–07 VAN	10	0	1	1	4
NHL Totals	10	0	1	1	4

Harding, Josh b. Regina, Saskatchewan, June 18, 1984

2006–07 MIN	7	3–2–0–1	360	7	1	1.16
NHL Totals	10	5–3–0–1	545	15	2	1.65

Harrison, Jay b. Oshawa, Ontario, November 3, 1982

2006–07 TOR	5	0	0	0	6
NHL Totals	13	0	1	1	8

Harrold, Peter b. Kirtland Hills, Ontario, June 8, 1983

2006–07 LA	12	0	2	2	8
NHL Totals	12	0	2	2	8

Hartigan, Mark b. Fort St. John, British Columbia, October 15, 1977

2006–07 CBJ/ANA	12	1	2	3	6
NHL Totals	79	16	10	26	42

* traded by Columbus with Joe Motzko and a 4th-round draft choice in 2007 on January 26, 2007, to Anaheim for Zenon Konopka, Curtis Glencross and a conditional draft choice in either 2007 or 2008

Hartnell, Scott b. Regina, Saskatchewan, April 18, 1982

2006–07 NAS	64	22	17	39	96
NHL Totals	436	93	118	211	544

Hasek, Dominik b. Pardubice, Czechoslovakia (Czech Republic), January 29, 1965

2006–07 DET	56	38–11–0–6	3,340	114	8	205
NHL Totals	694	362–213–82–10	40,486	1,488	76	2.21

Hatcher, Derian b. Sterling Heights, Michigan, June 4, 1972

2006–07 PHI	82	3	6	9	67
NHL Totals	1,001	78	246	324	1,548

Havelid, Niclas b. Stockholm, Sweden, April 12, 1973

2006–07 ATL	77	3	18	21	52
NHL Totals	469	31	107	138	252

Havlat, Martin b. Mlada Boleslav, Czechoslovakia (Czech Republic), April 19, 1981

2006–07 CHI	56	25	32	57	28
NHL Totals	354	130	162	292	194

Haydar, Darren b. Toronto, Ontario, October 22, 1979

2006–07 ATL	4	0	0	0	0
NHL Totals	6	0	0	0	0

Heatley, Dany b. Freiburg, West Germany (Germany), January 21, 1981

2006–07 OTT	82	50	55	105	74
NHL Totals	354	180	209	389	292

Hecht, Jochen b. Mannheim, West Germany (Germany), June 21, 1977

2006–07 BUF	76	19	37	56	39
NHL Totals	473	110	184	294	288

Hedberg, Johan b. Leksand, Sweden, May 3, 1973

2006–07 ATL	21	9–4–0–2	1,057	51	0	2.89
NHL Totals	177	75–71–14–3	10,065	473	10	2.82

Hedican, Bret b. St. Paul, Minnesota, August 10, 1970

2006–07 CAR	50	0	10	10	36
NHL Totals	922	52	219	271	787

Hejda, Jan b. Prague, Czechoslovakia (Czech Republic), June 18, 1978

2006–07 EDM	39	1	8	9	20
NHL Totals	39	1	8	9	20

Hejduk, Milan b. Usti-nad-Labem, Czechoslovakia (Czech Republic), February 14, 1976

2006–07 COL	80	35	35	70	44
NHL Totals	624	256	288	544	222

Helbling, Timo b. Basel, Switzerland, July 21, 1981

2006–07 WAS	2	0	0	0	2
NHL Totals	11	0	1	1	8

Hemsky, Ales b. Pardubice, Czechoslovakia (Czech Republic),
August 13, 1983

2006–07 EDM	64	13	40	53	40
NHL Totals	275	50	144	194	132

Hennessy, Joshua b. Brockton, Massachusetts, February 7, 1985

2006–07 OTT	10	1	0	1	4
NHL Totals	10	1	0	1	4

Heward, Jamie b. Regina, Saskatchewan, March 30, 1971

2006–07 WAS/LA	71	6	18	24	47
NHL Totals	381	38	84	122	217

* traded by Washington on February 27, 2007, to Los Angeles for a conditional draft choice

Higgins, Chris b. Smithtown, New York, June 2, 1983

2006–07 MON	61	22	16	38	26
NHL Totals	143	45	31	76	52

Hilbert, Andy b. Lansing, Michigan, February 6, 1981

2006–07 NYI	81	8	20	28	34
NHL Totals	166	23	38	61	90

Hill, Sean b. Duluth, Minnesota, February 14, 1970

2006–07 NYI	81	1	24	25	110
NHL Totals	841	60	229	289	976

Hinote, Dan b. Leesburg, Florida, January 30, 1977

2006–07 STL	41	5	5	10	23
NHL Totals	394	32	43	75	277

Hnidy, Shane b. Neepawa, Manitoba, November 8, 1975

2006–07 ATL	72	5	7	12	63
NHL Totals	336	9	28	37	449

Hoggan, Jeff b. Hope, British Columbia, February 1, 1978

2006–07 BOS	46	0	2	2	33
NHL Totals	98	2	8	10	67

Holik, Bobby b. Jihlava, Czechoslovakia (Czech Republic), January 1, 1971

2006–07 ATL	82	11	18	29	86
NHL Totals	1,170	307	397	704	1,267

Hollweg, Ryan b. Downey, California, April 23, 1983

2006–07 NYR	78	1	2	3	131
NHL Totals	130	3	5	8	215

Holmqvist, Johan b. Tolfta, Sweden, May 24, 1978

2006–07 TB	48	27–15–0–3	2,547	121	1	2.85
NHL Totals	52	27–18–0–3	2,714	133	1	2.94

Holmqvist, Mikael b. Stockholm, Sweden, June 8, 1979

2006–07 CHI	63	6	7	13	31
NHL Totals	156	18	17	35	72

Holmstrom, Tomas b. Pitea, Sweden, January 23, 1973

2006–07 DET	77	30	22	52	58
NHL Totals	699	155	192	347	511

Horcoff, Shawn b. Trail, British Columbia, September 17, 1978

2006–07 EDM	80	16	35	51	56
NHL Totals	427	82	153	235	297

Hordichuk, Darcy b. Kamsack, Saskatchewan, August 10, 1980

2006–07 NAS	53	1	3	4	90
NHL Totals	257	12	11	23	687

Horton, Nathan b. Welland, Ontario, May 29, 1985

2006–07 FLO	82	31	31	62	61
NHL Totals	208	73	58	131	207

Hossa, Marcel b. Ilava, Czechoslovakia (Slovakia), October 12, 1981

2006–07 NYR	64	10	8	18	26
NHL Totals	187	30	23	53	78

Hossa, Marian b. Stara Lubovna, Czechoslovakia (Slovakia), January 12, 1979

2006–07 ATL	82	43	57	100	49
NHL Totals	629	270	312	582	359

Houle, Martin b. Montreal, Quebec, February 12, 1985

2006–07 PHI	1	0–0–0–0	2:00	1	0	30.00
NHL Totals	1	0–0–0–0	2:00	1	0	30.00

Hudler, Jiri b. Olomouc, Czechoslovakia (Czech Republic), January 4, 1984

2006–07 DET	76	15	10	25	36
NHL Totals	92	16	12	28	48

Huet, Cristobal b. St. Martin d'Heres, France, September 3, 1975

2006–07 MON	42	19–16–0–3	2,286	107	2	2.81
NHL Totals	131	51–47–11–7	7,129	294	13	2.47

Hunt, Jameson b. Calgary, Alberta, April 20, 1984

2006–07 WAS	1	0	0	0	0
NHL Totals	1	0	0	0	0

Hunter, Trent b. Red Deer, Alberta, July 5, 1980

2006–07 NYI	77	20	15	35	22
NHL Totals	244	61	64	125	76

Huselius, Kristian b. Osterhaninge, Sweden, November 10, 1978

2006–07 ATL	81	34	43	77	26
NHL Totals	392	107	136	243	124

Huskins, Kent b. Almonte, Ontario, May 4, 1979

2006–07 ANA	33	0	3	3	14
NHL Totals	33	0	3	3	14

Hussey, Matt b. New Haven, Connecticut, May 28, 1979

2006–07 DET	5	0	0	0	2
NHL Totals	21	2	2	4	2

Hutchinson, Andrew b. Evanston, Illinois, March 24, 1980

2006–07 CAR	41	3	11	14	30
NHL Totals	95	10	23	33	52

Iginla, Jarome b. Edmonton, Alberta, July 1, 1977

2006–07 CAL	70	39	55	94	40
NHL Totals	778	324	340	664	548

Immonen, Jarkko b. Rantasalmi, Finland. April 19, 1982

2006–07 NYR	14	1	5	6	4
NHL Totals	20	3	5	8	4

Isbister, Brad b. Edmonton, Alberta, May 7, 1977

2006–07 NYR	19	1	4	5	14
NHL Totals	486	100	111	211	577

Ivanans, Raitis b. Riga, Soviet Union (Latvia), January 1, 1979

2006–07 LA	66	4	4	8	140
NHL Totals	70	4	4	8	149

Jacina, Greg b. Guelph, Ontario, May 22, 1982

2006–07 FLO	3	0	0	0	2
NHL Totals	14	0	1	1	6

Jackman, Barret b. Trail, British Columbia, March 5, 1981

2006–07 STL	70	3	24	27	82
NHL Totals	231	11	48	59	469

Jackman, Ric b. Toronto, Ontario, June 28, 1978

2006–07 FLO/ANA	31	2	10	12	20
NHL Totals	231	19	58	77	156

* traded by Florida on January 3, 2007, to Anaheim for a conditional draft
choice in 2007

Jackman, Tim b. Minot, North Dakota, November 14, 1981

2006–07 LA	5	0	0	0	10
NHL Totals	32	1	2	3	47

Jacques, Jean-Francois b. Terrebonne, Quebec, April 29, 1985

2006–07 EDM	37	0	0	0	33
NHL Totals	44	0	0	0	33

Jagr, Jaromir b. Kladno, Czechoslovakia (Czech Republic),
February 15, 1972

2006–07 NYR	82	30	66	96	78
NHL Totals	1,191	621	907	1,528	849

Janik, Doug b. Agawam, Massachusetts, March 26, 1980

2006–07 TB	75	2	9	11	53
NHL Totals	85	2	9	11	74

Janssen, Cam b. St. Louis, Missouri, April 15, 1984

2006–07 NJ	48	1	0	1	114
NHL Totals	95	1	0	1	205

Johnson, Aaron b. Port Hawkesbury, Nova Scotia, April 30, 1983

2006–07 CBJ	61	3	7	10	38
NHL Totals	116	7	19	26	93

Johnson, Brent b. Farmington, Michigan, March 12, 1977

2006–07 WAS	30	6–15–0–7	1,644	99	0	3.61
NHL Totals	207	92–80–13–8	11,599	505	13	2.61

Johnson, Jack b. Indianapolis, Indiana, January 13, 1987

2006–07 LA	5	0	0	0	18
NHL Totals	5	0	0	0	18

Johnson, Mike b. Scarborough (Toronto), Ontario, October 3, 1974

2006–07 MON	80	11	20	31	40
NHL Totals	640	127	243	370	307

Johnson, Ryan b. Thunder Bay, Ontario, June 14, 1976

2006–07 STL	59	7	4	11	47
NHL Totals	468	29	55	84	196

Johnsson, Kim b. Malmo, Sweden, March 16, 1976

2006–07 MIN	76	3	19	22	64
NHL Totals	518	54	162	216	290

Jokinen, Jussi b. Kalajoki, Finland, April 1, 1983

2006–07 DAL	82	14	34	48	18
NHL Totals	163	31	72	103	48

Jokinen, Olli b. Kuopio, Finland, December 5, 1978

2006–07 FLO	82	39	52	91	78
NHL Totals	641	174	216	390	660

Jones, Blair b. Central Butte, Saskatchewan, September 27, 1986

2006–07 TB	20	1	2	3	2
NHL Totals	20	1	2	3	2

Jones, Matt b. Downers Grove, Illinois, August 8, 1983

2006–07 PHO	45	1	6	7	39	
NHL Totals	61	1	8	9	53	

Jones, Randy b. Quispamsis, New Brunswick, July 23, 1981

2006–07 PHI	66	4	18	22	38	
NHL Totals	99	4	26	30	54	

Jonsson, Lars b. Borlange, Sweden, January 2, 1982

2006–07 PHI	8	0	2	2	6	
NHL Totals	8	0	2	2	6	

Joseph, Curtis b. Keswick, Ontario, April 29, 1967

2006–07 PHO	55	18–31–0–2	2,993	159	4	3.19
NHL Totals	913	446–341–90–5	52,813	2,449	51	2.78

Jovanovski, Ed b. Windsor, Ontario, June 26, 1976

2006–07 PHO	54	11	18	29	63	
NHL Totals	741	97	249	346	1,148	

Jurcina, Milan b. Liptovsky Mikulas, Czechoslovakia (Slovakia), June 7, 1983

2006–07 WAS	30	2	7	9	24	
NHL Totals	121	10	13	23	98	

Kaberle, Frantisek b. Kladno, Czechoslovakia (Czech Republic), November 8, 1973

2006–07 CAR	27	2	6	8	20	
NHL Totals	413	28	135	163	180	

Kaberle, Tomas b. Rakovnik, Czechoslovakia (Czech Republic), March 2, 1978

2006–07 TOR	74	11	47	58	20	
NHL Totals	599	61	288	349	176	

Kaigorodov, Alexei b. Chelyabinsk, Soviet Union (Russia), July 29, 1983

2006–07 OTT	6	0	1	1	0
NHL Totals	6	0	1	1	0

Kaleta, Patrick b. Buffalo, New York, June 8, 1986

2006–07 BUF	7	0	2	2	21
NHL Totals	7	0	2	2	21

Kalinin, Dmitri b. Chelyabinsk, Soviet Union (Russia), July 22, 1980

2006–07 BUF	82	7	22	29	36
NHL Totals	420	33	104	137	257

Kalus, Petr b. Ostrava, Czechoslovakia (Czech Republic), June 29, 1987

2006–07 BOS	9	4	1	5	6
NHL Totals	9	4	1	5	6

Kane, Boyd b. Swift Current, Saskatchewan, April 18, 1978

2006–07 PHI	15	0	2	2	28
NHL Totals	27	0	3	3	37

Kapanen, Niko b. Hattula, Finland, April 29, 1978

2006–07 PHO	19	2	7	9	8
NHL Totals	318	26	72	98	126

Kapanen, Sami b. Vantaa, Finland, June 14, 1973

2006–07 PHI	77	11	14	25	22
NHL Totals	757	184	266	450	159

Kariya, Paul b. Vancouver, British Columbia, October 16, 1974

2006–07 NAS	82	24	52	76	36
NHL Totals	821	366	500	866	311

Karlsson, Andreas b. Luvika, Sweden, August 19, 1975

2006–07 TB	53	3	6	9	12
NHL Totals	206	14	33	47	62

Kasparaitis, Darius b. Elektrenai, Soviet Union (Lithuania), October 16, 1972

2006–07 NYR	24	2	2	4	30
NHL Totals	863	27	136	163	1,379

Keith, Duncan b. Winnipeg, Manitoba, July 16, 1983

2006–07 CHI	82	2	29	31	76
NHL Totals	163	11	41	52	155

Keith, Matt b. Edmonton, Alberta, April 11, 1983

2006–07 CHI	2	0	0	0	4
NHL Totals	24	2	3	5	14

Kelly, Chris b. Toronto, Ontario, November 11, 1980

2006–07 OTT	82	15	23	38	40
NHL Totals	168	25	43	68	116

Kesler, Ryan b. Detroit, Michigan, August 31, 1984

2006–07 VAN	48	6	10	16	40
NHL Totals	158	18	26	44	135

Kessel, Phil b. Madison, Wisconsin, October 2, 1987

2006–07 BOS	70	11	18	29	12
NHL Totals	70	11	18	29	12

Khabibulin, Nikolai b. Sverdlovsk, Soviet Union (Russia), January 13, 1973

2006–07 CHI	60	25–26–0–5	3,424	163	1	2.86
NHL Totals	586	251–239–58–11	33,345	1,497	36	2.69

Kilger, Chad b. Cornwall, Ontario, November 27, 1976

2006–07 TOR	82	14	14	28	58
NHL Totals	661	97	104	201	345

King, D.J. b. Meadow Lake, Saskatchewan, January 27, 1984

2006–07 STL	27	1	1	2	52
NHL Totals	27	1	1	2	52

Kiprusoff, Miikka b. Turku, Finland, October 26, 1976

2006–07 CAL	74	40–24–0–9	4,419	181	7	2.46
NHL Totals	233	120–75–7–20	13,489	510	24	2.27

Klee, Ken b. Indianapolis, Indiana, April 24, 1971

2006–07 COL	81	3	16	19	68
NHL Totals	791	53	121	174	792

Klein, Kevin b. Kitchener, Ontario, December 13, 1984

2006–07 NAS	3	1	0	1	0
NHL Totals	5	1	0	1	0

Klemm, Jon b. Cranbrook, British Columbia, January 8, 1970

2006–07 DAL	38	1	2	3	24
NHL Totals	751	42	100	142	426

Klepis, Jakub b. Prague, Czechoslovakia (Czech Republic), June 5, 1984

2006–07 WAS	41	3	7	10	28
NHL Totals	66	4	10	14	36

Klesla, Rostislav b. Novy Jicin, Czechoslovakia (Czech Republic), March 21, 1982

2006–07 CBJ	75	9	13	22	105
NHL Totals	328	29	59	88	358

Knuble, Mike b. Toronto, Ontario, July 4, 1972

2006–07 PHI	64	24	30	54	56
NHL Totals	656	159	168	327	360

Kobasew, Chuck b. Osoyoos, British Columbia, April 17, 1982

2006–07 CAL/BOS	50	5	14	19	62
NHL Totals	220	35	38	73	185

* traded by Calgary with Andrew Ference on February 10, 2007, to Boston for Brad Stuart and Wayne Primeau

Koci, David b. Prague, Czechoslovakia (Czech Republic), May 12, 1981

2006–07 CHI	9	0	0	0	88
NHL Totals	9	0	0	0	88

Koivu, Mikko b. Turku, Finland, March 12, 1983

2006–07 MIN	82	20	34	54	58
NHL Totals	146	26	49	75	98

Koivu, Saku b. Turku, Finland, November 23, 1974

2006–07 MON	81	22	53	75	74
NHL Totals	650	159	376	535	486

Kolnik, Juraj b. Nitra, Czechoslovakia (Slovakia), November 13, 1980

2006–07 FLO	64	11	14	25	18
NHL Totals	240	46	49	95	84

Kolzig, Olaf b. Johannesburg, South Africa, April 9, 1970

2006–07 WAS	54	22–24–0–6	3,184	159	1	3.00
NHL Totals	657	276–272–63–17	38,105	1,707	34	2.69

Komisarek, Mike b. Islip Terrace, New York, January 19, 1982

2006–07 MON	82	4	15	19	96
NHL Totals	220	6	24	30	274

Konopka, Zenon b. Niagara-on-the-Lake, Ontario, January 2, 1981

2006–07 CBJ	6	0	0	0	20
NHL Totals	29	4	3	7	68

Kopecky, Tomas b. Ilava, Czechoslovakia (Slovakia), February 5, 1982

2006–07 DET	26	1	0	1	22
NHL Totals	27	1	0	1	24

Kopitar, Anze b. Jesenice, Yugoslavia (Slovenia), August 24, 1987

2006–07 LA	72	20	41	61	24
NHL Totals	72	20	41	61	24

Kostitsyn, Andrei b. Novopolosk, Soviet Union (Belarus), February 3, 1985

2006–07 MON	22	1	10	11	6
NHL Totals	34	3	11	14	8

Kostopoulos, Tom b. Mississauga, Ontario, January 24, 1979

2006–07 LA	76	7	15	22	73
NHL Totals	231	25	45	70	249

Kotalik, Ales b. Jindrichuv Hradec, Czechoslovakia (Czech Republic), December 23, 1978

2006–07 BUF	66	16	22	38	46
NHL Totals	291	78	87	165	181

Kovalchuk, Ilya b. Tver, Soviet Union (Russia), April 15, 1983

2006–07 ATL	82	42	34	76	66
NHL Totals	387	202	177	379	282

Kovalev, Alexei b. Togliatti, Soviet Union (Russia), February 24, 1973

2006–07 MON	73	18	29	47	78
NHL Totals	991	333	459	792	1,056

Kozlov, Viktor b. Togliatti, Soviet Union (Russia), February 14, 1975

2006–07 NYI	81	25	26	51	28
NHL Totals	749	169	273	442	214

Kozlov, Vyacheslav b. Voskresensk, Soviet Union (Russia), May 3, 1972

2006–07 ATL	81	28	52	80	36
NHL Totals	963	305	405	710	601

Krajicek, Lukas b. Prostejov, Czechoslovakia (Czech Republic), March 11, 1983

2006–07 VAN	78	3	13	16	64
NHL Totals	168	6	33	39	126

Krejci, David b. Sternberk, Czechoslovakia (Czech Republic), April 28, 1986

2006–07 BOS	6	0	0	0	2
NHL Totals	6	0	0	0	2

Kreps, Kamil b. Litomerice, Czechoslovakia (Czech Republic), November 18, 1984

2006–07 FLO	14	1	1	2	6
NHL Totals	14	1	1	2	6

Krog, Jason b. Fernie, British Columbia, October 9, 1975

2006–07 NYR	9	2	0	2	4
NHL Totals	198	21	37	58	44

Kronwall, Niklas b. Stockholm, Sweden, January 12, 1981

2006–07 DET	68	1	21	22	54
NHL Totals	115	3	33	36	98

Kuba, Filip b. Ostrava, Czechoslovakia (Czech Republic), December 29, 1976

2006–07 TB	81	15	22	37	36
NHL Totals	456	49	127	176	199

Kubina, Pavel b. Celadna, Czechoslovakia (Czech Republic), April 15, 1977

2006–07 TOR	61	7	14	21	48
NHL Totals	592	72	158	230	711

Kukkonen, Lasse b. Oulu, Finland, September 18, 1981

2006–07 CHI/PHI	74	5	9	14	38
NHL Totals	84	5	10	15	42

* traded by Chicago with a 3rd-round draft choice in 2007 on February 26, 2007, to Philadelphia for Kyle Calder

Kunitz, Chris b. Regina, Saskatchewan, September 26, 1979

2006–07 ANA	81	25	35	60	81
NHL Totals	171	44	63	107	164

Kwiatkowski, Joel b. Kindersley, Saskatchewan, March 22, 1977

2006–07 FLO/PIT	42	5	5	10	20
NHL Totals	264	16	24	40	225

* traded by Florida on February 27, 2007, to Pittsburgh for a 4th-round draft choice in 2007

Laaksonen, Antti b. Tammela, Finland, October 3, 1973

2006–07 COL	41	3	1	4	16
NHL Totals	483	81	87	168	152

LaCouture, Dan b. Hyannis, Massachusetts, April 18, 1977

2006–07 NJ	6	0	0	0	7
NHL Totals	326	18	25	43	338

Ladd, Andrew b. Maple Ridge, British Columbia, December 12, 1985

2006–07 CAR	65	11	10	21	46
NHL Totals	94	17	15	32	50

Laich, Brooks b. Medicine Hat, Alberta, June 23, 1983

2006–07 WAS	73	8	10	18	29
NHL Totals	151	15	25	40	57

Lalime, Patrick b. St. Bonaventure, Quebec, July 7, 1974

2006–07 CHI	12	4–6–0–1	644	33	1	3.07
NHL Totals	365	175–136–32–9	20,897	874	34	2.51

Lampman, Bryce b. Rochester, Minnesota, August 31, 1982

2006–07 NYR	1	0	0	0	0
NHL Totals	10	0	0	0	2

Lang, Robert b. Teplice, Czechoslovakia (Czech Republic), December 19, 1970

2006–07 DET	81	19	33	52	66
NHL Totals	799	213	368	581	308

Langenbrunner, Jamie b. Duluth, Minnesota, July 24, 1975

2006–07 NJ	82	23	37	60	64
NHL Totals	739	167	268	435	630

Langfeld, Josh b. Fridley, Minnesota, July 17, 1977

2006–07 DET	33	0	2	2	0
NHL Totals	141	9	23	32	60

Langkow, Daymond b. Edmonton, Alberta, September 27, 1976

2006–07 CAL	81	33	44	77	44
NHL Totals	788	194	296	490	464

Laperriere, Ian b. Montreal, Quebec, January 19, 1974

2006–07 COL	81	8	21	29	133
NHL Totals	857	107	171	278	1,491

Lapierre, Maxim b. St. Leonard, Quebec, March 29, 1985

2006–07 MON	46	6	6	12	24
NHL Totals	47	6	6	12	24

Lapointe, Martin b. Ville St. Pierre, Quebec, September 12, 1973

2006–07 CHI	82	13	11	24	98
NHL Totals	921	175	193	368	1,347

Laraque, Georges b. Montreal, Quebec, December 7, 1976

2006–07 PHO/PIT	73	5	19	24	70
NHL Totals	563	48	87	135	896

* traded by Phoenix on February 27, 2007, to Pittsburgh for Daniel Carcillo and a 3rd-round draft choice in 2008

Larman, Drew b. Canton, Michigan, May 15, 1985

2006–07 FLO	16	2	0	2	2
NHL Totals	16	2	0	2	2

LaRose, Chad b. Fraser, Michigan, March 27, 1982

2006–07 CAR	80	6	12	18	10
NHL Totals	129	7	24	31	45

Larsen, Brad b. Nakusp, British Columbia, June 28, 1977

2006–07 ATL	72	7	6	13	39
NHL Totals	232	18	26	44	122

Lashoff, Matt b. East Greenbush, New York, September 29, 1986

2006–07 BOS	12	0	2	2	12
NHL Totals	12	0	2	2	12

Latendresse, Guillaume b. Ste. Catherine, Quebec, May 24, 1987

2006–07 MON	80	16	13	29	47
NHL Totals	80	16	13	29	47

Leahy, Pat b. Brighton, Massachusetts, June 9, 1979

2006–07 NAS	1	0	0	0	0
NHL Totals	50	4	4	8	19

Lebda, Brett b. Buffalo Grove, Illinois, January 15, 1982

2006–07 DET	74	5	13	18	61
NHL Totals	120	8	22	30	81

Lecavalier, Vincent b. Ile Bizard, Quebec, April 21, 1980

2006–07 TB	82	52	56	108	44
NHL Totals	629	233	277	510	418

LeClair, John b. St. Albans, Vermont, July 5, 1969

2006–07 PIT	21	2	5	7	12
NHL Totals	967	406	413	819	501

Leclaire, Pascal b. Repentigny, Quebec, November 7, 1982

2006–07 CBJ	24	6–15–0–2	1,315	65	1	2.97
NHL Totals	59	17–32–0–5	3,238	169	1	3.13

Legace, Manny b. Toronto, Ontario, February 4, 1973

2006–07 STL	45	23–15–0–5	2,521	109	5	2.59
NHL Totals	242	137–58–18–8	13,549	516	18	2.28

Legwand, David b. Detroit, Michigan, August 17, 1980

| 2006–07 NAS | 78 | 27 | 36 | 63 | 44 |
| NHL Totals | 484 | 106 | 177 | 283 | 280 |

Lehoux, Yanick b. Montreal, Quebec, April 8, 1982

| 2006–07 PHO | 7 | 1 | 2 | 3 | 4 |
| NHL Totals | 10 | 2 | 2 | 4 | 6 |

Lehtinen, Jere b. Espoo, Finland, June 24, 1973

| 2006–07 DAL | 73 | 26 | 17 | 43 | 16 |
| NHL Totals | 721 | 216 | 220 | 436 | 180 |

Lehtonen, Kari b. Helsinki, Finland, November 16, 1983

| 2006–07 ATL | 68 | 34–24–0–9 | 3,934 | 183 | 4 | 2.79 |
| NHL Totals | 110 | 58–39–0–9 | 6,339 | 294 | 7 | 2.78 |

Lehtonen, Mikko b. Oulu, Finland, June 12, 1978

| 2006–07 NAS | 15 | 1 | 2 | 3 | 8 |
| NHL Totals | 15 | 1 | 2 | 3 | 8 |

Leighton, Michael b. Petrolia, Ontario, May 19, 1981

| 2006–07 NAS/PHI | 5 | 2–2–0–0 | 194 | 12 | 0 | 3.71 |
| NHL Totals | 47 | 10–23–10–0 | 2,648 | 134 | 3 | 3.04 |

* claimed off waivers by Nashville on November 27, 2006, from Anaheim;
  claimed off waivers by Philadelphia on January 11, 2007, from Nashville;
  claimed off waivers by Montreal on February 27, 2007, from Philadelphia

LeNeveu, David b. Fernie, British Columbia, May 23, 1983

| 2006–07 PHO | 6 | 2–1–0–0 | 233 | 15 | 0 | 3.86 |
| NHL Totals | 21 | 5–9–0–2 | 1,047 | 59 | 0 | 3.38 |

Leopold, Jordan b. Golden Valley, Minnesota, August 3, 1980

| 2006–07 COL | 15 | 2 | 3 | 5 | 14 |
| NHL Totals | 229 | 17 | 55 | 72 | 118 |

Lessard, Junior b. St. Joseph de Beauce, Quebec, May 26, 1980

2006–07 DAL	1	1	0	1	0
NHL Totals	6	2	0	2	12

Letang, Kris b. Montreal, Quebec, April 24, 1987

2006–07 PIT	7	2	0	2	4
NHL Totals	7	2	0	2	4

Letowski, Trevor b. Thunder Bay, Ontario, April 5, 1977

2006–07 CAR	61	2	6	8	18
NHL Totals	541	75	108	183	179

Lidstrom, Nicklas b. Vasteras, Sweden, April 28, 1970

2006–07 DET	80	13	49	62	46
NHL Totals	1,176	202	666	868	372

Liffiton, David b. Windsor, Ontario, October 18, 1984

2006–07 NYR	2	0	0	0	7
NHL Totals	3	0	0	0	9

Liles, John-Michael b. Zionsville, Indiana, November 25, 1980

2006–07 COL	71	14	30	44	24
NHL Totals	232	38	89	127	96

Lilja, Andreas b. Landskrona, Sweden, July 13, 1975

2006–07 DET	57	0	5	5	54
NHL Totals	319	10	37	47	338

Linden, Trevor b. Medicine Hat, Alberta, April 11, 1970

2006–07 VAN	80	12	13	25	34
NHL Totals	1,323	368	487	855	880

Lindros, Eric b. London, Ontario, February 28, 1973

2006–07 DAL	49	5	21	26	70
NHL Totals	760	372	493	865	1,398

Lindstrom, Joakim b. Skelleftea, Sweden, December 5, 1983

2006–07 CBJ	9	1	0	1	4
NHL Totals	12	1	0	1	4

Lisin, Enver b. Moscow, Soviet Union (Russia), April 22, 1986

2006–07 PHO	17	1	1	2	16
NHL Totals	17	1	1	2	16

Lojek, Martin b. Brno, Czechoslovakia (Czech Republic), August 19, 1985

2006–07 FLO	3	0	1	1	0
NHL Totals	3	0	1	1	0

Lombardi, Matt b. Montreal, Quebec, March 18, 1982

2006–07 CAL	81	20	26	46	48
NHL Totals	215	42	59	101	128

Low, Reed b. Moose Jaw, Saskatchewan, June 21, 1976

2006–07 CHI	6	0	0	0	31
NHL Totals	256	3	16	19	725

Lukowich, Brad b. Cranbrook, British Columbia, August 12, 1976

2006–07 NJ	75	4	8	12	36
NHL Totals	523	21	75	96	333

Lundmark, Jamie b. Edmonton, Alberta, January 16, 1981

2006–07 CAL/LA	68	7	6	13	56
NHL Totals	232	27	44	71	167

* traded by Calgary with a 4th-round draft choice in 2007 and a 4th-round draft choice in 2008 to Los Angeles on January 29, 2007, for Craig Conroy

Lundqvist, Henrik b. Are, Sweden, March 2, 1982

2006–07 NYR	70	37–22–0–8	4,108	160	5	2.34
NHL Totals	123	67–34–0–17	7,220	276	7	2.29

Lundqvist, Joel b. Are, Sweden, March 2, 1982

2006–07 DAL	36	3	3	6	14
NHL Totals	36	3	3	6	14

Luongo, Roberto b. Montreal, Quebec, April 4, 1979

2006–07 VAN	76	47–22–0–6	4,490	171	5	2.29
NHL Totals	417	162–190–33–15	23,624	1,037	32	2.63

Lupul, Joffrey b. Edmonton, Alberta, September 23, 1983

2006–07 EDM	81	16	12	28	45
NHL Totals	237	57	58	115	121

Lydman, Toni b. Lahti, Finland, September 25, 1977

2006–07 BUF	67	2	17	19	55
NHL Totals	431	22	107	129	277

MacArthur, Clarke b. Lloydminster, Alberta, April 6, 1985

2006–07 BUF	19	3	4	7	4
NHL Totals	19	3	4	7	4

MacDonald, Craig b. Antigonish, Nova Scotia, April 7, 1977

2006–07 CHI	25	3	2	5	14
NHL Totals	160	8	14	22	75

MacDonald, Joey b. Pictou, Nova Scotia, February 7, 1980

2006–07 DET/BOS	15	3–7–0–2	826	43	0	3.12
NHL Totals	15	3–7–0–2	826	43	0	3.12

* claimed off waivers by Boston on February 24, 2007, from Detroit

MacKenzie, Derek b. Sudbury, Ontario, June 11, 1981

2006–07 ATL	4	0	0	0	0
NHL Totals	28	0	2	2	20

MacLean, Don b. Sydney, Nova Scotia, January 14, 1977

2006–07 PHO	9	1	1	2	0
NHL Totals	41	8	5	13	6

Madden, John b. Barrie, Ontario, May 4, 1973

2006–07 NJ	74	12	20	32	14
NHL Totals	556	113	118	231	141

Mair, Adam b. Hamilton, Ontario, February 15, 1979

2006–07 BUF	82	2	9	11	128
NHL Totals	334	18	42	60	550

Maki, Tomi b. Helsinki, Finland, August 19, 1983

2006–07 CAL	1	0	0	0	0
NHL Totals	1	0	0	0	0

Malakhov, Vladimir b. Sverdlovsk, Soviet Union (Russia), August 30, 1968

2006–07 NJ	29	4	5	9	26
NHL Totals	712	86	260	346	697

Malec, Tomas b. Skalica, Czechoslovakia (Slovakia), May 13, 1982

2006–07 OTT	1	0	0	0	0
NHL Totals	46	0	2	2	47

Malhotra, Manny b. Mississauga, Ontario, May 18, 1980

2006–07 CBJ	82	9	16	25	76
NHL Totals	486	54	79	133	282

Malik, Marek b. Ostrava, Czechoslovakia (Czech Republic), June 24, 1975

2006–07 NYR	69	2	19	21	70
NHL Totals	607	31	122	153	536

Malkin, Evgeni b. Magnitogorsk, Soviet Union (Russia), July 31, 1986

2006–07 PIT	78	33	52	85	80
NHL Totals	78	33	52	85	80

Malone, Ryan b. Pittsburgh, Pennsylvania, December 1, 1979

2006–07 PIT	64	16	15	31	71
NHL Totals	222	60	58	118	198

Maltby, Kirk b. Guelph, Ontario, December 22, 1972

2006–07 DET	82	6	5	11	50
NHL Totals	881	113	120	233	775

Mancari, Mark b. London, Ontario, July 11, 1985

2006–07 BUF	3	0	1	1	2
NHL Totals	3	0	1	1	2

Mara, Paul b. Ridgewood, New Jersey, September 7, 1979

2006–07 BOS/NYR	78	5	18	23	113
NHL Totals	502	57	144	201	494

* traded by Boston on February 27, 2007, to New York Rangers for Aaron Ward

Marchant, Todd b. Buffalo, New York, August 12, 1973

2006–07 ANA	56	8	15	23	44
NHL Totals	891	162	272	434	634

Markkanen, Jussi b. Imatra, Finland, May 8, 1975

2006–07 EDM	22	5-9-00-1	992	52	0	3.15
NHL Totals	128	43-47-8-7	6,610	297	7	2.70

Markov, Andrei b. Voskresensk, Soviet Union (Russia), December 20, 1978

2006–07 MON	77	6	43	49	56
NHL Totals	411	46	161	207	226

Markov, Danny b. Moscow, Soviet Union (Russia), July 30, 1976

2006–07 DET	66	4	12	16	59
NHL Totals	538	29	118	147	456

Marleau, Patrick b. Aneroid, Saskatchewan, September 15, 1979

2006–07 SJ	77	32	46	78	33
NHL Totals	717	219	272	491	252

Martin, Paul b. Minneapolis, Minnesota, March 5, 1981

2006–07 NJ	82	3	23	26	18
NHL Totals	232	14	73	87	54

Martinek, Radek b. Havlickuv Brod, Czechoslovakia (Czech Republic), August 31, 1976

2006–07 NYI	43	2	15	17	40
NHL Totals	253	10	49	59	157

Mason, Chris b. Red Deer, Alberta, April 20, 1976

2006–07 NAS	40	24–11–0–4	2,341	93	5	2.38
NHL Totals	84	40–21–1–5	4,439	180	8	2.43

Matvichuk, Richard b. Edmonton, Alberta, February 5, 1973

2006–07 NJ	1	0	0	0	0
NHL Totals	796	39	139	178	624

May, Brad b. Toronto, Ontario, November 29, 1971

2006–07 COL/ANA	24	0	4	4	21
NHL Totals	882	123	153	276	2,040

* traded by Colorado on February 27, 2007, to Anaheim for Mike Wall

Mayers, Jamal b. Toronto, Ontario, October 24, 1974

2006–07 STL	80	8	14	22	89
NHL Totals	515	59	72	131	665

McAmmond, Dean b. Grand Cache, Alberta, June 15, 1973

2006–07 OTT	81	14	15	29	28
NHL Totals	804	164	229	393	414

McCabe, Bryan b. St. Catharines, Ontario, June 8, 1975

2006–07 TOR	82	15	42	57	115
NHL Totals	863	110	285	395	1,493

McCarthy, Steve b. Trail, British Columbia, February 3, 1981

2006–07 ATL	46	4	12	16	24
NHL Totals	247	16	32	48	120

McCarty, Darren b. Burnaby, British Columbia, April 1, 1972

2006–07 CAL	32	0	0	0	58
NHL Totals	742	126	160	286	1,450

McCauley, Alyn b. Brockville, Ontario, May 29, 1977

2006–07 LA	10	1	0	1	2
NHL Totals	488	69	97	166	116

McClement, Jay b. Kingston, Ontario, March 2, 1983

2006–07 STL	81	8	28	36	55
NHL Totals	148	14	49	63	85

McCormick, Cody b. London, Ontario, April 18, 1983

2006–07 COL	6	0	1	1	6
NHL Totals	95	6	8	14	108

McDonald, Andy b. Strathroy, Ontario, August 25, 1977

2006–07 ANA	82	27	51	78	46
NHL Totals	358	88	155	243	132

McGratton, Brian b. Hamilton, Ontario, September 2, 1981

2006–07 OTT	45	0	2	2	100
NHL Totals	105	2	5	7	241

McIver, Nathan b. Kinkora, Prince Edward Island, January 6, 1985

2006–07 VAN	1	0	0	0	7
NHL Totals	1	0	0	0	7

McKee, Jay b. Kingston, Ontario, September 8, 1977

2006–07 STL	23	0	0	0	12
NHL Totals	605	17	81	98	482

McLaren, Kyle b. Humboldt, Saskatchewan, June 18, 1977

2006–07 SJ	67	5	12	17	61
NHL Totals	658	43	153	196	587

McLean, Brett b. Comox, British Columbia, August 14, 1978

2006–07 COL	78	15	20	35	36
NHL Totals	238	35	71	106	141

McLennan, Jamie b. Edmonton, Alberta, June 30, 1971

2006–07 CAL	9	3–5–0–1	532	32	0	3.60
NHL Totals	254	80–109–33–3	13,834	617	13	2.68

Meech, Derek b. Winnipeg, Manitoba, April 21, 1984

2006–07 DET	4	0	0	0	2
NHL Totals	4	0	0	0	2

Melichar, Josef b. Ceske Budejovice, Czechoslovakia (Czech Republic), January 20, 1979

2006–07 PIT	70	1	11	12	44
NHL Totals	310	7	33	40	263

Melin, Bjorn b. Jonkoping, Sweden, July 4, 1981

2006–07 ANA	3	1	0	1	0
NHL Totals	3	1	0	1	0

Mellanby, Scott b. Montreal, Quebec, June 11, 1966

2006–07 ATL	69	12	24	36	63
NHL Totals	1,431	364	476	840	2,479

Meloche, Eric b. Montreal, Quebec, May 1, 1976

2006–07 PHI	13	1	2	3	4
NHL Totals	74	9	11	20	36

Meszaros, Andrei b. Povazska Bystrica, Czechoslovakia (Slovakia), October 13, 1985

2006–07 OTT	82	7	28	35	102
NHL Totals	164	17	57	74	163

Methot, Marc b. Ottawa, Ontario, June 21, 1985

2006–07 CBJ	20	0	4	4	12
NHL Totals	20	0	4	4	12

Metropolit, Glen b. Toronto, Ontario, June 25, 1974

2006–07 ATL/STL	77	14	19	33	34
NHL Totals	180	24	56	80	60

* traded by Atlanta with a 1st- and 3rd-round draft choice in 2007 and a 2nd-round draft choice in 2008 to St. Louis on February 25, 2007, for Keith Tkachuk

Meyer, Freddy b. Sanbornville, New Hampshire, January 4, 1981

2006–07 PHI/NYI	60	2	6	8	38
NHL Totals	118	8	27	35	71

* traded by Philadelphia with a conditional 3rd-round draft choice to New York Islanders on December 16, 2007, for Alexei Zhitnik

Mezei, Branislav b. Nitra, Czechoslovakia (Slovakia), October 8, 1980

2006–07 FLO	45	0	3	3	55
NHL Totals	183	3	17	20	247

Michalek, Milan b. Jindrichuv Hradec, Czechoslovakia (Czech Republic), December 7, 1984

2006–07 SJ	78	26	40	66	36
NHL Totals	161	44	58	102	85

Michalek, Zbynek b. Jindrichuv Hradec, Czechoslovakia (Czech Republic), December 23, 1982

2006–07 PHO	82	4	24	28	34
NHL Totals	186	14	40	54	100

Miettinen, Antti b. Hameenlinna, Finland, July 3, 1980

2006–07 DAL	74	11	14	25	38
NHL Totals	169	23	34	57	84

Mikhnov, Alexei b. Kiev, Soviet Union (Ukraine), August 31, 1982

2006–07 EDM	2	0	0	0	0
NHL Totals	2	0	0	0	0

Miller, Aaron b. Buffalo, New York, August 11, 1971

2006–07 LA	82	0	8	8	60
NHL Totals	620	24	86	110	390

Miller, Andrew b. Dover, New Jersey, February 17, 1984

* appeared only in the playoffs for Anaheim in 2006–07

Miller, Ryan b. East Lansing, Michigan, July 17, 1980

2006–07 BUF	63	40–16–0–6	3,692	168	2	2.73
NHL Totals	129	76–41–1–9	7,644	347	4	2.72

Milroy, Duncan b. Edmonton, Alberta, February 8, 1983

2006–07 MON	5	0	1	1	0
NHL Totals	5	0	1	1	0

Mitchell, Willie b. Port McNeill, British Columbia, April 23, 1977

2006–07 VAN	62	1	10	11	45
NHL Totals	384	10	62	72	433

Modano, Mike b. Livonia, Michigan, June 7, 1970

2006–07 DAL	59	22	21	43	34
NHL Totals	1,238	507	719	1,226	802

Modin, Fredrik b. Sundsvall, Sweden, October 8, 1974

2006–07 CBJ	79	22	20	42	50
NHL Totals	741	205	199	404	365

Modry, Jaroslav b. Ceske Budejovice, Czechoslovakia (Czech Republic), February 27, 1971

2006–07 DAL/LA	76	1	17	18	54
NHL Totals	645	48	193	241	460

* traded by Dallas with Johan Fransson, a 2nd- and 3rd-round draft choice in 2007 and a 1st-round draft choice in 2008 to Los Angeles on February 27, 2007, for Mattias Norstrom, Konstantin Pushkarev and a 3rd- and 4th-round draft choice in 2007

Moen, Travis b. Stewart Valley, Saskatchewan, April 6, 1982

| 2006–07 ANA | 82 | 11 | 10 | 21 | 101 |
| NHL Totals | 203 | 19 | 13 | 32 | 315 |

Mojzis, Tomas b. Kolin, Czechoslovakia (Czech Republic), May 2, 1982

| 2006–07 STL | 6 | 1 | 0 | 1 | 0 |
| NHL Totals | 13 | 1 | 1 | 2 | 12 |

Montador, Steve b. Vancouver, British Columbia, December 21, 1979

| 2006–07 FLO | 72 | 1 | 8 | 9 | 119 |
| NHL Totals | 217 | 6 | 18 | 24 | 388 |

Moore, Dominic b. Thornhill, Ontario, August 3, 1980

| 2006–07 PIT/MIN | 69 | 8 | 9 | 17 | 56 |
| NHL Totals | 156 | 17 | 21 | 38 | 84 |

* traded by Pittsburgh on February 27, 2007, to Minnesota for a 3rd-round draft choice in 2007

Moran, Brad b. Abbotsford, British Columbia, March 20, 1979

| 2006–07 VAN | 3 | 0 | 1 | 1 | 2 |
| NHL Totals | 8 | 1 | 2 | 3 | 4 |

Moran, Ian b. Cleveland, Ohio, August 24, 1972

| 2006–07 ANA | 1 | 0 | 0 | 0 | 0 |
| NHL Totals | 489 | 21 | 50 | 71 | 321 |

Moreau, Ethan b. Huntsville, Ontario, September 22, 1975

| 2006–07 EDM | 7 | 1 | 0 | 1 | 12 |
| NHL Totals | 685 | 117 | 107 | 224 | 832 |

Morgan, Jason b. St. John's, Newfoundland, October 9, 1976

| 2006–07 MIN | 4 | 0 | 0 | 0 | 4 |
| NHL Totals | 44 | 2 | 5 | 7 | 18 |

Morris, Derek b. Edmonton, Alberta, August 24, 1978

2006–07 PHO	82	6	19	25	115
NHL Totals	636	63	232	295	671

Morrison, Brendan b. Pitt Meadows, British Columbia, August 15, 1975

2006–07 VAN	82	20	31	51	60
NHL Totals	635	150	299	449	334

Morrison, Mike b. Medford, Maine, July 11, 1979

2006–07 PHO	4	0–3–0–0	127	13	0	6.14
NHL Totals	29	11–7–0–3	1,225	67	0	3.28

Morrisonn, Shaone b. Vancouver, British Columbia, December 23, 1982

2006–07 WAS	78	3	10	13	106
NHL Totals	202	5	30	35	215

Morrow, Brenden b. Carlyle, Saskatchewan, January 16, 1979

2006–07 DAL	40	16	15	31	33
NHL Totals	491	136	164	300	789

Moss, David b. Dearborn, Michigan, December 28, 1981

2006–07 CAL	41	10	8	18	12
NHL Totals	41	10	8	18	12

Motzko, Joe b. Bemidji, Minnesota, March 14, 1980

2006–07 CBJ	7	1	0	1	0
NHL Totals	11	1	0	1	0

Mowers, Mark b. Decature, Georgia, February 16, 1974

2006–07 BOS	78	5	12	17	26
NHL Totals	261	17	44	61	62

Muir, Bryan b. Winnipeg, Manitoba, June 8, 1973

2006–07 WAS	26	3	4	7	42
NHL Totals	279	16	37	53	281

Murray, Doug b. Bromma, Sweden, March 12, 1980

2006–07 SJ	35	0	3	3	31
NHL Totals	69	0	4	4	58

Murray, Garth b. Regina, Saskatchewan, September 17, 1982

2006–07 MON	43	2	1	3	32
NHL Totals	99	8	2	10	100

Murray, Glen b. Halifax, Nova Scotia, November 1, 1972

2006–07 BOS	59	28	17	45	44
NHL Totals	946	320	301	621	629

Murray, Marty b. Lyleton, Manitoba, February 16, 1975

2006–07 LA	19	0	2	2	4
NHL Totals	261	31	42	73	41

Nabokov, Evgeni b. Ust-Kamenogorsk, Soviet Union (Kazakhstan), July 25, 1975

2006–07 SJ	50	25–16–0–4	2,777	106	7	2.29
NHL Totals	353	162–129–29–11	20,049	811	34	2.43

Nagy, Ladislav b. Saca, Czechoslovakia (Slovakia), June 1, 1979

2006–07 PHO/DAL	80	12	43	55	54
NHL Totals	397	106	179	285	340

* traded by Phoenix on February 12, 2007, to Dallas for Mathias Tjarnqvist and a 1st-round draft choice in 2007

Nash, Rick b. Brampton, Ontario, June 16, 1984

2006–07 CBJ	75	27	30	57	73
NHL Totals	283	116	91	207	289

Naslund, Markus b. Ornskoldsvik, Sweden, July 30, 1973

2006–07 VAN	82	24	36	60	54
NHL Totals	953	346	422	768	633

Nasreddine, Alain b. Montreal, Quebec, July 10, 1975

2006–07 PIT	44	1	4	5	18
NHL Totals	68	1	4	5	80

Nedved, Petr b. Liberec, Czechoslovakia (Czech Republic), December 9, 1971

2006–07 PHI/EDM	40	2	10	12	28
NHL Totals	982	310	407	717	708

* claimed off waivers by Edmonton on January 2, 2007, from Philadelphia

Neil, Chris b. Markdale, Ontario, June 18, 1979

2006–07 OTT	82	12	16	28	177
NHL Totals	383	52	52	104	953

Newbury, Kris b. Brampton, Ontario, February 19, 1982

2006–07 TOR	15	2	2	4	26
NHL Totals	15	2	2	4	26

Nichol, Scott b. Edmonton, Alberta, December 31, 1974

2006–07 NAS	59	7	6	13	79
NHL Totals	301	30	34	64	573

Niedermayer, Rob b. Cassiar, British Columbia, December 28, 1974

2006–07 ANA	82	5	11	16	77
NHL Totals	854	149	242	391	741

Niedermayer, Scott b. Edmonton, Alberta, August 31, 1973

2006–07 ANA	79	15	54	69	86
NHL Totals	1,053	140	468	608	660

Nielsen, Frans b. Herning, Denmark, April 24, 1984

2006–07 NYI	15	1	1	2	0
NHL Totals	15	1	1	2	0

Nieminen, Ville b. Tampere, Finland, April 6, 1977

2006–07 SJ/STL	44	1	1	2	43
NHL Totals	385	48	69	117	333

* traded by San Jose with Jay Barriball and a 1st-round draft choice in 2007 to St. Louis on February 27, 2007, for Bill Guerin

Nieuwendyk, Joe b. Oshawa, Ontario, September 10, 1966

2006–07 FLO	15	5	3	8	4
NHL Totals	1,257	564	561	1,126	677

Niinimaa, Janne b. Raahe, Finland, May 22, 1975

2006–07 MON	41	0	3	3	36
NHL Totals	741	54	265	319	733

Niittymaki, Antero b. Turku, Finland, June 18, 1980

2006–07 PHI	52	9–29–0–9	2,942	166	0	3.38
NHL Totals	101	35–44–0–15	5,812	302	2	3.12

Nilson, Marcus b. Balsta, Sweden, March 1, 1978

2006–07 CAL	63	5	10	15	27
NHL Totals	474	64	99	163	266

Nilsson, Robert b. Calgary, Alberta, January 10, 1985

2006–07 EDM	4	1	0	1	4
NHL Totals	57	7	14	21	30

Nolan, Owen b. Belfast, Northern Ireland, February 12, 1972

2006–07 PHO	76	16	24	40	56
NHL Totals	991	365	410	775	1,656

Nordqvist, Jonas b. Leksand, Sweden, April 26, 1982

2006–07 CHI	3	0	2	2	2
NHL Totals	3	0	2	2	2

Norrena, Fredrik b. Pietarsaari, Finland, November 29, 1973

2006–07 CBJ	55	24–23–0–3	2,952	137	3	2.78
NHL Totals	55	24–23–0–3	2,952	137	3	2.78

Norstrom, Mattias b. Stockholm, Sweden, January 2, 1972

2006–07 LA/DAL	76	2	9	11	48
NHL Totals	837	16	136	152	621

* traded by Los Angeles with Konstantin Pushkarev and a 3rd- and 4th-round draft choice in 2007 to Dallas on February 27, 2007, for Jaroslav Modry, Johan Fransson, a 2nd- and 3rd-round draft choice in 2007 and a 1st-round draft choice in 2008

Norton, Brad b. Cambridge, Massachusetts, February 13, 1975

2006–07 DET	6	0	1	1	20
NHL Totals	124	3	8	11	287

Novak, Filip b. Ceske Budejovice, Czechoslovakia (Czech Republic), May 7, 1982

2006–07 CBJ	6	0	0	0	2
NHL Totals	17	0	0	0	6

Novotny, Jiri b. Pelhrimov, Czechoslovakia (Czech Republic), August 12, 1983

2006–07 BUF/WAS	68	6	13	19	28
NHL Totals	82	8	14	22	28

* traded by Buffalo with Jiri Novotny and a 1st-round draft choice in 2007 to Washington on February 27, 2007, for Dainius Zubrus and Timo Helbling

Nummelin, Petteri b. Turku, Finland, November 25, 1972

2006–07 MIN	51	3	17	20	22
NHL Totals	112	7	29	36	32

Numminen, Teppo b. Tampere, Finland, July 3, 1968

2006-07 BUF	79	2	27	29	32
NHL Totals	1,314	115	505	620	491

Nycholat, Lawrence b. Calgary, Alberta, May 7, 1979

2006-07 WAS/OTT	19	2	6	8	12
NHL Totals	28	2	6	8	18

* traded by Washington on February 26, 2007, to Ottawa for Andy Hedlund and a 6th-round draft choice in 2007

Nylander, Michael b. Stockholm, Sweden, October 3, 1972

2006-07 NYR	79	26	57	83	42
NHL Totals	808	189	420	609	412

O'Brien, Shane b. Port Hope, Ontario, August 9, 1983

2006-07 ANA/TB	80	2	14	16	176
NHL Totals	80	2	14	16	176

* traded by Anaheim with a 3rd-round draft choice in 2007 to Tampa Bay on February 24, 2007, for Gerald Coleman and a 1st-round draft choice in 2007

O'Donnell, Sean b. Ottawa, Ontario, October 13, 1971

2006-07 ANA	79	2	15	17	92
NHL Totals	850	25	143	168	1,474

Oduya, John b. Stockholm, Sweden, October 1, 1981

2006-07 NJ	76	2	9	11	61
NHL Totals	76	2	9	11	61

Ohlund, Mattias b. Pitea, Sweden, September 9, 1976

2006-07 VAN	77	11	20	31	80
NHL Totals	635	78	198	276	572

Olesz, Rostislav b. Bilovec, Czechoslovakia (Czech Republic), October 10, 1985

2006–07 FLO	75	11	19	30	28
NHL Totals	134	19	32	51	52

Ondrus, Ben b. Sherwood Park, Alberta, June 25, 1982

2006–07 TOR	16	0	2	2	20
NHL Totals	38	0	2	2	38

O'Neill, Jeff b. Richmond Hill, Ontario, February 23, 1976

2006–07 TOR	74	20	22	42	54
NHL Totals	821	237	259	496	670

Orpik, Brooks b. San Francisco, California, September 26, 1980

2006–07 PIT	70	0	6	6	82
NHL Totals	219	3	22	25	335

Orr, Colton b. Winnipeg, Manitoba, March 3, 1982

2006–07 NYR	53	2	1	3	126
NHL Totals	89	2	2	4	197

Ortmeyer, Jed b. Omaha, Nebraska, September 3, 1978

2006–07 NYR	41	2	9	11	22
NHL Totals	177	9	15	24	76

Osgood, Chris b. Peace River, Alberta, November 26, 1972

2006–07 DET	21	11–3–0–6	1,611	46	0	2.38
NHL Totals	621	336–186–66–11	35,609	1,455	43	2.45

O'Sullivan, Patrick b. Winston Salem, North Carolina, February 1, 1985

2006–07 LA	44	5	14	19	14
NHL Totals	44	5	14	19	14

Ott, Steve b. Summerside, Prince Edward Island, August 19, 1982

2006–07 DAL	19	0	4	4	35
NHL Totals	200	10	35	45	396

Ouellet, Michel b. Rimouski, Quebec, March 5, 1982

2006–07 PIT	73	19	29	48	30
NHL Totals	123	35	45	80	46

Ovechkin, Alexander b. Moscow, Soviet Union (Russia), September 17, 1985

2006–07 WAS	82	46	46	92	52
NHL Totals	163	98	100	198	104

Ozolinsh, Sandis b. Riga, Soviet Union (Latvia), August 3, 1972

2006–07 NYR	21	0	3	3	8
NHL Totals	836	164	384	548	614

Paetsch, Nathan b. Leroy, Saskatchewan, March 30, 1983

2006–07 BUF	63	2	22	24	50
NHL Totals	64	2	23	25	50

Pahlsson, Samuel b. Ornskoldsvik, Sweden, December 17, 1977

2006–07 ANA	82	8	18	26	42
NHL Totals	436	41	72	113	192

Paille, Daniel b. Welland, Ontario, April 15, 1984

2006–07 BUF	29	3	8	11	18
NHL Totals	43	4	10	14	20

Pandolfo, Jay b. Winchester, Massachusetts, December 27, 1974

2006–07 NJ	82	13	14	27	8
NHL Totals	652	78	102	180	116

Parent, Ryan b. Prince Albert, Saskatchewan, March 17, 1987

2006–07 PHI	1	0	0	0	0
NHL Totals	1	0	0	0	0

Parenteau, Pierre b. Hull, Quebec, March 24, 1983

2006–07 CHI	5	0	1	1	2
NHL Totals	5	0	1	1	2

Parise, Zach b. Minneapolis, Minnesota, July 28, 1984

2006–07 NJ	82	31	31	62	30
NHL Totals	163	45	49	94	58

Park, Richard b. Seoul, South Korea, May 27, 1976

2006–07 NYI	82	10	16	26	33
NHL Totals	450	60	73	133	172

Parker, Scott b. Hanford, California, January 29, 1978

2006–07 SJ/COL	21	1	1	2	28
NHL Totals	283	7	14	21	629

* traded by San Jose on February 27, 2007, to Colorado for a 6th-round draft choice in 2008

Parrish, Mark b. Edina, Minnesota, February 2, 1977

2006–07 MIN	76	19	20	39	18
NHL Totals	594	192	150	342	208

Parros, George b. Washington, Pennsylvania, December 29, 1979

2006–07 COL/ANA	34	1	0	1	102
NHL Totals	89	3	3	6	240

* traded by Colorado on November 13, 2006, to Anaheim for a 2nd-round draft choice in 2007

Pavelski, Joe b. Plover, Wisconsin, July 11, 1984

2006–07 SJ	46	14	14	28	18
NHL Totals	46	14	14	28	18

Payer, Serge b. Rockland, Ontario, May 7, 1979

2006–07 OTT	5	0	0	0
NHL Totals	124	7	6	13	49

Peca, Michael b. Toronto, Ontario, March 26, 1974

2006–07 TOR	35	4	11	15	60
NHL Totals	728	164	245	409	676

Pelley, Rodney b. Kitimat, British Columbia, September 1, 1984

2006–07 NJ	9	0	0	0	0
NHL Totals	9	0	0	0	0

Peltonen, Ville b. Vantaa, Finland, May 24, 1973

2006–07 FLO	72	17	20	37	28
NHL Totals	247	35	62	97	68

Penner, Dustin b. Winkler, Manitoba, September 28, 1982

2006–07 ANA	82	29	16	45	58
NHL Totals	101	33	19	52	72

Perezhogin, Alexander b. Ust-Kamenogorsk, Soviet Union (Kazakhstan), August 10, 1983

2006–07 MON	61	6	9	15	48
NHL Totals	128	15	19	34	86

Perrault, Joel b. Montreal, Quebec, April 6, 1983

2006–07 PHO/STL	26	1	2	3	14
NHL Totals	31	2	3	5	16

* claimed off waivers by St. Louis on October 31, 2006, from Phoenix; claimed off waivers by Phoenix on December 19, 2006, from St. Louis

Perreault, Yanic b. Sherbrooke, Quebec, April 4, 1971

2006–07 PHO/TOR	66		17	38	34
NHL Totals	806	238	264	502	378

* traded by Phoenix with a 5th-round draft choice in 2008 to Toronto on February 27, 2007, for Brandon Bell and a 2nd-round draft choice in 2008

Perrin, Eric b. Laval, Quebec, November 1, 1975

2006–07 TB	82	13	23	36	30
NHL Totals	86	13	23	36	30

Perry, Corey b. Peterborough, Ontario, May 16, 1985

2006–07 ANA	82	17	27	44	55
NHL Totals	138	30	39	69	105

Peters, Andrew b. St. Catharines, Ontario, May 5, 1980

2006–07 BUF	58	1	1	2	125
NHL Totals	128	3	1	4	376

Petersen, Toby b. Minneapolis, Minnesota, October 27, 1978

2006–07 EDM	64	6	9	15	4
NHL Totals	155	16	25	41	12

Petrovicky, Ronald b. Zilina, Czechoslovakia (Slovakia), February 15, 1977

2006–07 PIT	31	3	3	6	28
NHL Totals	342	41	51	92	429

Pettinger, Matt b. Edmonton, Alberta, October 22, 1980

2006–07 WAS	64	16	16	32	22
NHL Totals	278	50	42	92	144

Peverley, Rich b. Guelph, Ontario, July 8, 1982

2006–07 NAS	13	0	1	1	0
NHL Totals	13	0	1	1	0

Phaneuf, Dion b. Edmonton, Alberta, April 10, 1985

| 2006–07 CAL | 79 | 17 | 33 | 50 | 98 |
| NHL Totals | 161 | 37 | 62 | 99 | 191 |

Phillips, Chris b. Calgary, Alberta, March 9, 1978

| 2006–07 OTT | 82 | 8 | 18 | 26 | 80 |
| NHL Totals | 618 | 40 | 124 | 164 | 456 |

Picard, Alexandre b. Les Saules, Quebec, October 9, 1985

| 2006–07 CBJ | 23 | 0 | 1 | 1 | 6 |
| NHL Totals | 40 | 0 | 1 | 1 | 20 |

Picard, Alexandre b. Gatineau, Quebec, July 5, 1985

| 2006–07 PHI | 62 | 3 | 19 | 22 | 17 |
| NHL Totals | 68 | 3 | 19 | 22 | 21 |

Pihlman, Thomas b. Espoo, Finland, November 13, 1982

| 2006–07 NJ | 2 | 0 | 0 | 0 | 0 |
| NHL Totals | 15 | 1 | 1 | 2 | 12 |

Pisani, Fernando b. Edmonton, Alberta, December 27, 1976

| 2006–07 EDM | 77 | 14 | 14 | 28 | 40 |
| NHL Totals | 268 | 56 | 52 | 108 | 138 |

Piskula, Joe b. Antigo, Wisconsin, July 5, 1984

| 2006–07 LA | 5 | 0 | 0 | 0 | 6 |
| NHL Totals | 5 | 0 | 0 | 0 | 6 |

Pitkanen, Joni b. Oulu, Finland, September 19, 1983

| 2006–07 PHI | 77 | 4 | 39 | 43 | 88 |
| NHL Totals | 206 | 25 | 91 | 116 | 210 |

Platt, Geoff b. Toronto, Ontario, July 10, 1985

2006–07 CBJ	26	4	5	9	10
NHL Totals	41	4	10	14	26

Plekanec, Tomas b. Kladno, Czechoslovakia (Czech Republic), October 31, 1982

2006–07 MON	81	20	27	47	36
NHL Totals	150	29	47	76	68

Plihal, Tomas b. Frydlant, Czechoslovakia (Czech Republic), March 28, 1983

2006–07 SJ	3	0	0	0	0
NHL Totals	3	0	0	0	0

Pock, Thomas b. Klagenfurt, Austria, December 2, 1981

2006–07 NYR	44	4	4	8	16
NHL Totals	58	7	7	14	20

Pohl, John b. Rochester, Minnesota, June 29, 1979

2006–07 TOR	74	13	16	29	10
NHL Totals	82	16	17	33	14

Polak, Roman b. Ostrava, Czechoslovakia (Czech Republic), April 28, 1986

2006–07 STL	19	0	0	0	6
NHL Totals	19	0	0	0	6

Polak, Vojtech b. Ostrov nad Ohri, Czechoslovakia (Czech Republic), June 27, 1985

2006–07 DAL	2	0	0	0	0
NHL Totals	5	0	0	0	0

Pominville, Jason b. Repentigny, Quebec, November 30, 1982

2006–07 BUF	82	34	34	68	30
NHL Totals	140	52	46	98	52

Ponikarovsky, Alexei b. Kiev, Soviet Union (Ukraine), April 9, 1980

2006–07 TOR	71	21	24	45	63
NHL Totals	268	54	66	120	200

Popovic, Mark b. Stoney Creek, Ontario, October 11, 1982

2006–07 ATL	3	0	1	1	0
NHL Totals	11	0	1	1	0

Popperle, Tomas b. Broumov, Czechoslovakia (Czech Republic), October 10, 1984

2006–07 CBJ	2	0–0–0–0	44	1	0	1.33
NHL Totals	2	0–0–0–0	44	1	0	1.33

Pothier, Brian b. New Bedford, Massachusetts, April 15, 1977

2006–07 WAS	72	3	25	28	44
NHL Totals	254	15	71	86	157

Poti, Tom b. Worcester, Massachusetts, March 22, 1977

2006–07 NYI	78	6	38	44	74
NHL Totals	594	58	194	252	460

Potulny, Ryan b. Grand Forks, North Dakota, September 5, 1984

2006–07 PHI	35	7	5	12	22
NHL Totals	37	7	6	13	22

Pouliot, Benoit b. Alfred, Ontario, September 29, 1986

2006–07 MIN	3	0	0	0	0
NHL Totals	3	0	0	0	0

Pouliot, Marc-Antoine b. Quebec City, Quebec, May 22, 1985

2006–07 EDM	46	4	7	11	18
NHL Totals	54	5	7	12	18

Pratt, Nolan b. Fort McMurray, Alberta, August 14, 1975

2006–07 TB	81	1	7	8	44
NHL Totals	537	8	50	58	507

Preissing, Tom b. Rosemount, Minnesota, December 3, 1978

2006–07 OTT	80	7	31	38	18
NHL Totals	223	20	80	100	56

Primeau, Wayne b. Scarborough (Toronto), Ontario, June 4, 1976

2006–07 BOS/CAL	78	10	12	22	111
NHL Totals	648	63	109	172	714

* traded by Boston with Brad Stuart on February 10, 2007, to Calgary for Andrew Ference and Chuck Kobasew

Printz, David b. Stockholm, Sweden, July 24, 1980

2006–07 PHI	12	0	0	0	4
NHL Totals	13	0	0	0	4

Pronger, Chris b. Dryden, Ontario, October 10, 1974

2006–07 ANA	66	13	46	59	69
NHL Totals	868	119	396	515	1,241

Prospal, Vaclav b. Ceske Budejovice, Czechoslovakia (Czech Republic), February 17, 1975

2006–07 TB	82	14	41	55	36
NHL Totals	712	146	337	483	376

Prucha, Petr b. Chrudim, Czechoslovakia (Czech Republic),
September 14, 1982

2006–07 NYR	79	22	18	40	30
NHL Totals	147	52	35	87	62

Prust, Brandon b. London, Ontario, March 16, 1984

2006–07 CAL	10	0	0	0	25
NHL Totals	10	0	0	0	25

Pushkarev, Konstantin b. Ust-Kamenogorsk, Soviet Union
(Kazakhstan), February 12, 1985

2006–07 LA	16	2	2	4	8
NHL Totals	17	2	3	5	8

Pyatt, Taylor b. Thunder Bay, Ontario, August 19, 1981

2006–07 VAN	76	23	14	37	42
NHL Totals	384	65	70	135	212

Quincey, Kyle b. Kitchener, Ontario, August 12, 1985

2006–07 DET	6	1	0	1	0
NHL Totals	7	1	0	1	0

Quint, Deron b. Durham, New Hampshire, March 12, 1976

2006–07 NYI	5	0	0	0	0
NHL Totals	463	46	97	143	166

Rachunek, Karel b. Zlin, Czechoslovakia (Czech Republic),
August 27, 1979

2006–07 NYR	66	6	20	26	38
NHL Totals	324	18	109	127	187

Radivojevic, Branko b. Piestany, Czechoslovakia (Slovakia), November 24, 1980

2006–07 MIN	82	11	13	24	21
NHL Totals	320	45	58	103	204

Radulov, Alexander b. Nizhny Tagil, Soviet Union (Russia), July 5, 1986

2006–07 NAS	64	18	19	37	26
NHL Totals	64	18	19	37	26

Rafalski, Brian b. Dearborn, Michigan, September 28, 1973

2006–07 NJ	82	8	47	55	34
NHL Totals	541	44	267	311	180

Ramo, Karri b. Asikkala, Finland, July 1, 1986

2006–07 TB	2	0–0–0–0	69	4	0	3.43
NHL Totals	2	0–0–0–0	69	4	0	3.43

Ranger, Paul b. Whitby, Ontario, September 12, 1984

2006–07 TB	72	4	24	28	42
NHL Totals	148	5	41	46	100

Rasmussen, Erik b. Minneapolis, Minnesota, March 28, 1977

2006–07 NJ	71	3	7	10	25
NHL Totals	545	52	76	128	305

Rathje, Mike b. Mannville, Alberta, May 11, 1974

2006–07 PHI	18	0	1	1	6
NHL Totals	768	30	150	180	491

Raycroft, Andrew b. Belleville, Ontario, May 4, 1980

2006–07 TOR	72	37–25–0–9	4,108	205	2	2.99
NHL Totals	180	80–71–10–11	10,160	469	5	2.77

Reasoner, Marty b. Honeoye Falls, New York, February 26, 1977

2006–07 EDM	72	6	14	20	60
NHL Totals	383	53	98	151	209

Recchi, Mark b. Kamloops, British Columbia, February 1, 1968

2006–07 PIT	82	24	44	68	62
NHL Totals	1,338	508	825	1,333	910

Redden, Wade b. Lloydminster, Saskatchewan, June 12, 1977

2006–07 OTT	64	7	29	36	50
NHL Totals	758	95	277	372	516

Regehr, Richie b. Rosthern, Saskatchewan, January 17, 1983

2006–07 CAL	6	1	1	2	0
NHL Totals	20	1	3	4	6

Regehr, Robyn b. Recife, Brazil, April 19, 1980

2006–07 CAL	78	2	19	21	75
NHL Totals	509	20	81	101	512

Regier, Steve b. Edmonton, Alberta, August 31, 1984

2006–07 NYI	1	0	0	0	0
NHL Totals	10	0	0	0	0

Reich, Jeremy b. Craik, Saskatchewan, February 11, 1979

2006–07 BOS	32	0	1	1	63
NHL Totals	41	0	2	2	83

Reid, Brandon b. Kirkland, Quebec, March 9, 1981

2006–07 VAN	3	0	0	0	0
NHL Totals	13	2	4	6	0

Reid, Darren b. Lac La Biche, Alberta, May 8, 1983

2006–07 PHI	14	0	0	0	18
NHL Totals	21	0	1	1	18

Reinprecht, Steve b. Edmonton, Alberta, May 7, 1976

2006–07 PHO	49	9	24	33	28
NHL Totals	398	90	157	247	116

Reitz, Eric b. Detroit, Michigan, July 29, 1982

2006–07 MIN	1	0	0	0	0
NHL Totals	6	0	0	0	4

Ribeiro, Mike b. Montreal, Quebec, February 10, 1980

2006–07 DAL	81	18	41	59	22
NHL Totals	357	68	144	212	114

Ricci, Mike b. Scarborough (Toronto), Ontario, October 27, 1971

2006–07 PHO	7	0	1	1	4
NHL Totals	1,099	243	362	605	974

Richards, Brad b. Murray Harbour, Prince Edward Island, May 2, 1980

2006–07 TB	82	25	45	70	23
NHL Totals	490	132	306	438	118

Richards, Mike b. Kenora, Ontario, February 11, 1985

2006–07 PHI	59	10	22	32	52
NHL Totals	138	21	45	66	117

Richardson, Brad b. Belleville, Ontario, February 4, 1985

2006–07 COL	73	14	8	22	28
NHL Totals	114	17	18	35	40

Richardson, Luke b. Ottawa, Ontario, March 26, 1969

2006–07 TB	27	0	3	3	16
NHL Totals	1,339	33	159	192	2,012

Richmond, Danny b. Chicago, Illinois, August 1, 1984

2006–07 CHI	22	0	2	2	48
NHL Totals	42	0	3	3	73

Rissmiller, Pat b. Belmont, Massachusetts, October 26, 1978

2006–07 SJ	79	7	15	22	22
NHL Totals	101	10	18	28	30

Ritchie, Byron b. Burnaby, British Columbia, April 24, 1977

2006–07 CAL	64	8	6	14	68
NHL Totals	253	22	25	47	293

Rivers, Jamie b. Ottawa, Ontario, March 16, 1975

2006–07 STL	31	1	3	4	36
NHL Totals	454	17	49	66	385

Rivet, Craig b. North Bay, Ontario, September 13, 1974

2006–07 MON/SJ	71	7	17	24	69
NHL Totals	670	40	119	159	807

* traded by Montreal with a 5th-round draft choice in 2008 to San Jose for Josh Gorges and a 1st-round draft choice in 2007

Roberts, Gary b. North York (Toronto), Ontario, May 23, 1966

2006–07 FLO/PIT	69	20	22	42	97
NHL Totals	1,156	431	457	888	2,493

* traded by Florida on February 27, 2007, to Pittsburgh for Noah Welch

Robidas, Stephane b. Sherbrooke, Quebec, March 3, 1977

2006–07 DAL	75	0	17	17	86
NHL Totals	407	18	65	83	257

Robitaille, Randy b. Ottawa, Ontario, October 12, 1975

2006–07 PHI/NYI	78	11	29	40	44
NHL Totals	463	74	153	227	183

* traded by Philadelphia with a 5th-round draft choice in 2008 on December 20, 2006, to New York Islanders for Mike York

Roche, Travis b. Grand Cache, Alberta, June 17, 1978

2006–07 PHO	50	6	13	19	22
NHL Totals	60	6	14	20	24

Roenick, Jeremy b. Boston, Massachusetts, January 17, 1970

2006–07 PHO	70	11	17	28	32
NHL Totals	1,252	495	675	1,170	1,413

Roloson, Dwayne b. Simcoe, Ontario, October 12, 1969

2006–07 EDM	68	27–34–0–6	3,931	180	4	2.75
NHL Totals	356	124–157–42–11	20,164	856	22	2.55

Rolston, Brian b. Flint, Michigan, February 21, 1973

2006–07 MIN	78	31	33	64	46
NHL Totals	896	255	320	575	319

Rome, Aaron b. Nesbitt, Manitoba, September 27, 1983

2006–07 ANA	1	0	0	0	0
NHL Totals	1	0	0	0	0

Rourke, Allan b. Mississauga, Ontario, March 6, 1980

2006–07 NYI	11	0	1	1	4
NHL Totals	42	1	4	5	26

Roy, Andre b. Port Chester, New York, February 8, 1975

2006–07 PIT/TB	56	1	2	3	128
NHL Totals	408	28	30	58	978

* claimed off waivers by Tampa Bay on December 2, 2006, from Pittsburgh

Roy, Derek b. Ottawa, Ontario, May 4, 1983

2006–07 BUF	75	21	42	63	60
NHL Totals	194	48	80	128	129

Roy, Mathieu b. St. Georges, Quebec, August 10, 1983

2006–07 EDM	16	2	0	2	30
NHL Totals	17	2	0	2	30

Rozsival, Michal b. Vlasim, Czechoslovakia (Czech Republic), September 3, 1978

2006–07 NYR	80	10	30	40	52
NHL Totals	399	33	102	135	303

Rucchin, Steve b. Thunder Bay, Ontario, July 4, 1971

2006–07 ATL	47	5	16	21	14
NHL Totals	735	171	318	489	164

Rucinsky, Martin b. Most, Czechoslovakia (Czech Republic), March 11, 1971

2006–07 STL	52	12	21	33	48
NHL Totals	921	236	360	596	781

Rupp, Mike b. Cleveland, Ohio, January 13, 1980

2006–07 NJ	76	6	3	9	92
NHL Totals	199	21	14	35	218

Ruutu, Jarkko b. Vantaa, Finland, August 23, 1975

2006–07 PIT	81	7	9	16	125
NHL Totals	348	30	37	67	578

Ruutu, Tuomo b. Vantaa, Finland, February 16, 1983

2006–07 CHI	71	17	21	38	95
NHL Totals	168	42	45	87	184

Ruzicka, Stefan b. Nitra, Czechoslovakia (Slovakia), February 17, 1985

2006–07 PHI	40	3	10	13	18
NHL Totals	41	3	10	13	20

Ryan, Michael b. Boston, Massachusetts, May 16, 1980

2006–07 BUF	19	3	2	5	2
NHL Totals	19	3	2	5	2

Rycroft, Mark b. Penticton, British Columbia, July 12, 1978

2006–07 COL	66	6	6	12	31
NHL Totals	226	21	25	46	113

Ryder, Michael b. St. John's, Newfoundland, March 31, 1980

2006–07 MON	82	30	28	58	60
NHL Totals	244	85	91	176	126

Rypien, Rick b. Coleman, Alberta, May 16, 1984

2006–07 VAN	2	0	0	0	5
NHL Totals	7	1	0	1	9

Sabourin, Dany b. Val d'Or, Quebec, September 2, 1980

2006–07 VAN	9	2–4–0–1	479	21	0	2.63
NHL Totals	14	2–8–0–1	668	35	0	3.14

Sakic, Joe b. Burnaby, British Columbia, July 7, 1969

2006–07 COL	82	36	64	100	46
NHL Totals	1,319	610	979	1,589	588

Salei, Ruslan b. Minsk, Soviet Union (Belarus), November 2, 1974

2006–07 FLO	82	6	26	32	102
NHL Totals	676	32	105	137	837

Salmelainen, Tony b. Espoo, Finland, August 8, 1981

2006–07 CHI	57	6	11	17	26
NHL Totals	70	6	12	18	30

Salo, Sami b. Turku, Finland, September 2, 1974

2006–07 VAN	67	14	23	37	26
NHL Totals	474	59	136	195	146

Salvador, Bryce b. Brandon, Manitoba, February 11, 1976

2006–07 STL	64	2	5	7	55
NHL Totals	391	15	37	52	370

Samsonov, Sergei b. Moscow, Soviet Union (Russia), October 27, 1978

2006–07 MON	63	9	17	26	10
NHL Totals	596	178	240	418	119

Samuelsson, Mikael b. Mariefred, Sweden, December 23, 1976

2006–07 DET	53	14	20	34	28
NHL Totals	312	56	72	128	168

Sanderson, Geoff b. Hay River, Northwest Territories, February 1, 1972

2006–07 PHI	58	11	18	29	44
NHL Totals	1,063	352	335	687	495

Sanford, Curtis b. Owen Sound, Ontario, October 5, 1979

2006–07 STL	31	8–12–0–5	1,491	79	0	3.18
NHL Totals	73	26–26–0–10	3,719	173	4	2.79

Santala, Tommi b. Helsinki, Finland, June 27, 1979

2006–07 VAN	30	1	5	6	24
NHL Totals	63	2	7	9	46

Saprykin, Oleg b. Moscow, Soviet Union (Russia), February 12, 1981

2006–07 PHO/OTT	71	15	21	36	58
NHL Totals	325	55	82	137	240

* traded by Phoenix with a 7th-round draft choice in 2007 on February 27, 2007, to Ottawa for a 2nd-round draft choice in 2008

Sarich, Cory b. Saskatoon, Saskatchewan, August 16, 1978

2006–07 TB	82	0	15	15	70
NHL Totals	536	10	79	89	589

Satan, Miroslav b. Topolcany, Czechoslovakia (Slovakia), October 22, 1974

2006–07 NYI	81	27	32	59	46
NHL Totals	867	321	323	644	377

Sauer, Kurt b. St. Cloud, Minnesota, January 16, 1981

2006–07 COL	48	0	6	6	24
NHL Totals	234	3	17	20	173

Sauve, Philippe b. Buffalo, New York, February 27, 1980

2006–07 BOS	2	0–0–0–0	41	4	0	5.85
NHL Totals	32	10–14–3–0	1,616	93	0	3.45

Savard, Marc b. Ottawa, Ontario, July 17, 1977

2006–07 BOS	82	22	74	96	96
NHL Totals	585	155	342	497	558

Scatchard, Dave b. Hinton, Alberta, February 20, 1976

2006–07 PHO	46	3	5	8	72
NHL Totals	635	125	138	263	1,017

Schaefer, Peter b. Yellow Grass, Saskatchewan, July 12, 1977

2006–07 OTT	77	12	34	46	32
NHL Totals	493	89	144	233	180

Schneider, Mathieu b. New York, New York, June 12, 1969

2006–07 DET	68	11	41	52	66
NHL Totals	1,132	200	463	663	1,115

Schremp, Rob b. Syracuse, New York, July 1, 1986

2006–07 EDM	1	0	0	0	0
NHL Totals	1	0	0	0	0

Schubert, Christoph b. Munich, West Germany (Germany) February 5, 1982

2006–07 OTT	80	8	17	25	56
NHL Totals	136	12	23	35	104

Schultz, Jeff b. Calgary, Alberta, February 25, 1986

2006–07 WAS	38	0	3	3	16
NHL Totals	38	0	3	3	16

Schultz, Jesse b. Strasbourg, Saskatchewan, September 28, 1982

2006–07 VAN	2	0	0	0	0
NHL Totals	2	0	0	0	0

Schultz, Nick b. Strasbourg, Saskatchewan, August 25, 1982

2006–07 MIN	82	2	10	12	42
NHL Totals	367	17	45	62	138

Schwarz, Marek b. Mlada Boleslav, Czechoslovakia (Czech Republic), April 1, 1986

2006–07 STL	2	0–1–0–0	60	3	0	3.00
NHL Totals	2	0–1–0–0	60	3	0	3.00

Scuderi, Rob b. Syosset, New York, December 30, 1978

2006–07 PIT	78	1	10	11	28
NHL Totals	142	2	16	18	68

Seabrook, Brent b. Richmond, British Columbia, April 20, 1985

2006–07 CHI	81	4	20	24	104
NHL Totals	150	9	47	56	164

Sedin, Daniel b. Ornskoldsvik, Sweden, September 26, 1980

2006–07 VAN	81	36	48	84	36
NHL Totals	478	119	187	306	178

Sedin, Henrik b. Ornskoldsvik, Sweden, September 26, 1980

2006–07 VAN	82	10	71	81	66
NHL Totals	482	72	230	302	266

Seidenberg, Dennis b. Schwenningen, West Germany (Germany), July 18, 1981

2006–07 PHO/CAR	52	2	6	8	18
NHL Totals	178	9	30	39	58

* traded by Phoenix on January 8, 2007, to Carolina for Kevyn Adams

Sejna, Peter b. Liptovski Mikulas, Czechoslovakia (Slovakia), October 5, 1979

2006–07 STL	22	3	1	4	4
NHL Totals	49	7	4	11	12

Sekera, Andrej b. Bojnice, Czechoslovakia (Slovakia), June 8, 1986

2006–07 BUF	2	0	0	0	2
NHL Totals	2	0	0	0	2

Selanne, Teemu b. Helsinki, Finland, July 3, 1970

2006–07 ANA	82	48	46	94	82
NHL Totals	1,041	540	595	1,135	461

Semenov, Alexei b. Murmansk, Soviet Union (Russia), April 10, 1981

2006–07 FLO	23	0	5	5	28
NHL Totals	142	5	16	21	156

Semin, Alexander b. Krasjonarsk, Soviet Union (Russia), March 3, 1984

2006–07 WAS	77	38	35	73	90
NHL Totals	129	48	47	95	126

Shanahan, Brendan b. Mimico, Ontario, January 23, 1969

2006–07 NYR	67	29	33	62	47
NHL Totals	1,417	627	667	1,294	2,425

Shannon, Ryan b. Darien, Connecticut, March 2, 1983

2006–07 ANA	53	2	9	11	10
NHL Totals	53	2	9	11	10

Sharp, Patrick b. Thunder Bay, Ontario, December 27, 1981

2006–07 CHI	80	20	15	35	74
NHL Totals	196	39	34	73	177

Shelley, Jody b. Thompson, Manitoba, February 7, 1976

2006–07 CBJ	72	1	1	2	125
NHL Totals	349	11	18	29	981

Sigalet, Jonathan b. Vancouver, British Columbia, February 12, 1986

2006–07 BOS	1	0	0	0	4
NHL Totals	1	0	0	0	4

Sillinger, Mike b. Regina, Saskatchewan, June 29, 1971

2006–07 NYI	82	26	33	59	46
NHL Totals	990	224	296	520	616

Sim, Jon b. New Glasgow, Nova Scotia, September 29, 1977

2006–07 ATL	77	17	12	29	60
NHL Totals	307	52	45	97	204

Simon, Chris b. Wawa, Ontario, January 30, 1972

| 2006–07 NYI | 67 | 10 | 17 | 27 | 75 |
| NHL Totals | 744 | 143 | 159 | 302 | 1,765 |

Sjostrom, Fredrik b. Fargelanda, Sweden, May 6, 1983

| 2006–07 PHO | 78 | 9 | 9 | 18 | 48 |
| NHL Totals | 210 | 22 | 32 | 54 | 112 |

Skoula, Martin b. Litomerice, Czechoslovakia (Czech Republic), October 28, 1979

| 2006–07 MIN | 81 | 0 | 15 | 15 | 36 |
| NHL Totals | 563 | 34 | 124 | 158 | 282 |

Skrastins, Karlis b. Riga, Soviet Union (Latvia), July 9, 1974

| 2006–07 COL | 68 | 0 | 11 | 11 | 30 |
| NHL Totals | 539 | 21 | 71 | 92 | 251 |

Slater, Jim b. Petoskey, Michigan, December 9, 1982

| 2006–07 ATL | 74 | 5 | 14 | 19 | 62 |
| NHL Totals | 145 | 15 | 24 | 39 | 108 |

Smid, Ladislav b. Frydlant, Czechoslovakia (Czech Republic), February 1, 1986

| 2006–07 EDM | 77 | 3 | 7 | 10 | 37 |
| NHL Totals | 77 | 3 | 7 | 10 | 37 |

Smith, Jason b. Calgary, Alberta, November 2, 1973

| 2006–07 EDM | 82 | 2 | 9 | 11 | 103 |
| NHL Totals | 868 | 39 | 119 | 158 | 966 |

Smith, Mark b. Edmonton, Alberta, October 24, 1977

| 2006–07 SJ | 41 | 3 | 10 | 13 | 42 |
| NHL Totals | 323 | 22 | 44 | 66 | 398 |

Smith, Mike b. Kingston, Ontario, March 22, 1982

2006–07 DAL	23	12–5–0–2	1,213	45	3	2.23
NHL Totals	23	12–5–0–2	1,213	45	3	2.23

Smith, Nathan b. Edmonton, Alberta, February 9, 1982

2006–07 VAN	1	0	0	0	0
NHL Totals	4	0	0	0	0

Smith, Wyatt b. Thief River Falls, Minnesota, February 13, 1977

2006–07 MIN	61	3	3	6	16
NHL Totals	186	10	19	29	57

Smithson, Jerred b. Vernon, British Columbia, February 4, 1979

2006–07 NAS	64	5	7	12	42
NHL Totals	160	10	19	29	121

Smolinski, Bryan b. Toledo, Ohio, December 27, 1971

2006–07 CHI/VAN	82	18	26	44	37
NHL Totals	992	266	360	626	586

* traded by Chicago on February 26, 2007, to Vancouver for a conditional
  2nd-round draft choice

Smyth, Ryan b. Banff, Alberta, February 21, 1976

2006–07 EDM/NYI	71	36	32	68	52
NHL Totals	788	270	294	564	621

* traded by Edmonton on February 27, 2007, to New York Islanders for
  Robert Nilsson, Ryan O'Marra and a 1st-round draft choice in 2007

Sopel, Brent b. Calgary, Alberta, January 7, 1977

2006–07 LA/VAN	64	5	23	28	24
NHL Totals	434	39	142	181	223

* traded by Los Angeles on February 26, 2007, to Vancouver for a 2nd-round
  draft choice in either 2007 or 2008 and a 4th-round draft choice in 2008

Souray, Sheldon b. Elk Point, Alberta, July 13, 1976

2006–07 MON	81	26	38	64	135
NHL Totals	506	66	120	188	821

Spacek, Jaroslav b. Rokycany, Czechoslovakia (Czech Republic), February 11, 1974

2006–07 BUF	65	5	16	21	62
NHL Totals	561	56	170	226	435

Spezza, Jason b. Mississauga, Ontario, June 13, 1983

2006–07 OTT	67	34	53	87	45
NHL Totals	246	82	171	253	157

Sprukts, Janis b. Riga, Soviet Union (Latvia), January 31, 1982

2006–07 FLO	13	1	2	3	2
NHL Totals	13	1	2	3	2

Staal, Eric b. Thunder Bay, Ontario, October 29, 1984

2006–07 CAR	82	30	40	70	68
NHL Totals	245	86	115	201	189

Staal, Jordan b. Thunder Bay, Ontario, September 10, 1988

2006–07 PIT	81	29	13	42	24
NHL Totals	81	29	13	42	24

Stafford, Drew b. Milwaukee, Wisconsin, October 30, 1985

2006–07 BUF	41	13	14	27	33
NHL Totals	41	13	14	27	33

Staios, Steve b. Hamilton, Ontario, July 28, 1973

2006–07 EDM	58	2	15	17	97
NHL Totals	677	43	119	162	957

Stajan, Matt b. Mississauga, Ontario, December 19, 1983

2006–07 TOR	82	10	29	39	44
NHL Totals	232	40	54	94	116

Stastny, Paul b. Quebec City, Quebec, December 27, 1985

2006–07 COL	82	28	50	78	42
NHL Totals	82	28	50	78	42

Stastny, Yan b. Quebec City, Quebec, September 30, 1982

2006–07 BOS	21	0	2	2	19
NHL Totals	41	1	5	6	29

Steckel, David b. Milwaukee, Wisconsin, March 15, 1982

2006–07 WAS	5	0	0	0	2
NHL Totals	12	0	0	0	2

Steen, Alexander b. Winnipeg, Manitoba, March 1, 1984

2006–07 TOR	82	15	20	35	26
NHL Totals	157	33	47	80	68

Stefan, Patrik b. Pribram, Czechoslovakia (Czech Republic), September 16, 1980

2006–07 DAL	41	5	6	11	10
NHL Totals	455	64	124	188	158

Stempniak, Lee b. Buffalo, New York, February 4, 1983

2006–07 STL	82	27	25	52	33
NHL Totals	139	41	38	79	55

Stephenson, Shay b. Outlook, Saskatchewan, September 13, 1983

2006–07 LA	2	0	0	0	0
NHL Totals	2	0	0	0	0

Stewart, Anthony b. La Salle, Quebec, January 5, 1985

2006–07 FLO	10	0	1	1	2
NHL Totals	20	2	2	4	4

Stewart, Karl b. Scarborough (Toronto), Ontario, June 30, 1983

2006–07 CHI/TB	44	2	3	5	45
NHL Totals	60	2	4	6	66

* traded by Chicago with a 6th-round draft choice in 2007 on February 27, 2007, to Tampa Bay for Nikita Alexeev

Stillman, Cory b. Peterborough, Ontario, December 20, 1973

2006–07 CAR	43	5	22	27	24
NHL Totals	760	210	327	537	382

St. Louis, Martin b. Laval, Quebec, June 18, 1975

2006–07 TB	82	43	59	102	28
NHL Totals	526	183	239	422	186

Stoll, Jarret b. Melville, Saskatchewan, June 25, 1982

2006–07 EDM	51	13	26	39	48
NHL Totals	205	45	84	129	164

Stortini, Zachery b. Elliot Lake, Ontario, September 11, 1985

2006–07 EDM	29	1	0	1	105
NHL Totals	29	1	0	1	105

St. Pierre, Martin b. Ottawa, Ontario, August 11, 1983

2006–07 CHI	14	1	3	4	8
NHL Totals	16	1	3	4	8

Straka, Martin b. Plzen, Czechoslovakia (Czech Republic), September 3, 1972

2006–07 NYR	77	29	41	70	24
NHL Totals	889	243	433	676	338

Streit, Mark b. Englisberg, Switzerland, December 11, 1977

2006–07 MON	76	10	26	36	14
NHL Totals	124	12	35	47	42

Strudwick, Jason b. Edmonton, Alberta, July 17, 1975

2006–07 NYR	8	0	0	0	2
NHL Totals	436	10	26	36	638

Stuart, Brad b. Rocky Mountain House, Alberta, November 6, 1979

2006–07 BOS/CAL	75	7	15	22	44
NHL Totals	507	53	153	206	303

* traded by Boston with Wayne Primeau to Calgary on February 10, 2007, for Andrew Ference and Chuck Kobasew

Stuart, Mark b. Rochester, Minnesota, April 27, 1984

2006–07 BOS	15	0	1	1	14
NHL Totals	32	1	2	3	24

Stumpel, Jozef b. Nitra, Czechoslovakia (Slovakia), July 20, 1972

2006–07 FLO	73	23	34	57	22
NHL Totals	905	189	468	657	235

Sturm, Marco b. Dingolfing, West Germany (Germany), September 8, 1978

2006–07 BOS	76	27	17	44	46
NHL Totals	680	178	182	360	320

Suglobov, Aleksander b. Elektrostal, Soviet Union (Russia), January 15, 1982

2006–07 TOR	14	0	0	0	4
NHL Totals	18	1	0	1	4

Sullivan, Steve b. Timmins, Ontario, July 6, 1974

| 2006–07 NAS | 57 | 22 | 38 | 60 | 20 |
| NHL Totals | 723 | 228 | 349 | 577 | 450 |

Sundin, Mats b. Bromma, Sweden, February 13, 1971

| 2006–07 TOR | 75 | 27 | 49 | 76 | 62 |
| NHL Totals | 1,231 | 523 | 720 | 1,243 | 989 |

Suter, Ryan b. Madison, Wisconsin, January 21, 1985

| 2006–07 NAS | 82 | 8 | 16 | 24 | 54 |
| NHL Totals | 153 | 9 | 31 | 40 | 120 |

Sutherby, Brian b. Edmonton, Alberta, March 1, 1982

| 2006–07 WAS | 69 | 7 | 10 | 17 | 78 |
| NHL Totals | 254 | 25 | 35 | 60 | 274 |

Sutton, Andy b. Kingston, Ontario, March 10, 1975

| 2006–07 ATL | 55 | 2 | 14 | 16 | 76 |
| NHL Totals | 432 | 27 | 78 | 105 | 785 |

Svatos, Marek b. Kosice, Czechoslovakia (Slovakia), July 17, 1982

| 2006–07 COL | 66 | 15 | 15 | 30 | 46 |
| NHL Totals | 131 | 49 | 33 | 82 | 106 |

Svitov, Alexander b. Omsk, Soviet Union (Russia), November 3, 1982

| 2006–07 CBJ | 76 | 7 | 11 | 18 | 145 |
| NHL Totals | 179 | 13 | 24 | 37 | 223 |

Sydor, Darryl b. Edmonton, Alberta, May 13, 1972

| 2006–07 DAL | 74 | 5 | 16 | 21 | 36 |
| NHL Totals | 1,097 | 94 | 377 | 471 | 696 |

Sykora, Petr b. Plzen, Czechoslovakia (Czech Republic), November 19, 1976

2006–07 EDM	82	22	31	53	40
NHL Totals	764	247	318	565	330

Syvret, Danny b. Millgrove, Ontario, June 13, 1985

2006–07 EDM	16	0	1	1	6
NHL Totals	26	0	1	1	12

Taffe, Jeff b. Hastings, Minnesota, February 19, 1981

2006–07 PHO	17	4	2	6	2
NHL Totals	100	15	13	28	26

Talbot, Maxime b. Lemoyne, Quebec, February 11, 1984

2006–07 PIT	75	13	11	24	53
NHL Totals	123	18	14	32	112

Tallackson, Barry b. Grafton, North Dakota, April 14, 1983

2006–07 NJ	3	0	0	0	0
NHL Totals	13	1	1	2	2

Tallinder, Henrik b. Stockholm, Sweden, January 10, 1979

2006–07 BUF	47	4	10	14	34
NHL Totals	249	14	44	58	162

Tambellini, Jeff b. Calgary, Alberta, April 13, 1984

2006–07 NYI	23	2	7	9	6
NHL Totals	48	3	10	13	16

Tanabe, David b. White Bear Lake, Minnesota, July 19, 1980

2006–07 CAR	60	5	12	17	44
NHL Totals	431	29	82	111	237

Tanguay, Alex b. Ste. Justine, Quebec, November 21, 1979

2006–07 CAL	81	22	59	81	44
NHL Totals	531	159	322	481	263

Tarnasky, Nick b. Rocky Mountain House, Alberta, November 25, 1984

2006–07 TB	77	5	4	9	80
NHL Totals	89	5	5	10	84

Taylor, Tim b. Stratford, Ontario, February 6, 1969

2006–07 TB	71	1	5	6	16
NHL Totals	746	73	94	167	433

Tellqvist, Mikael b. Sundbyberg, Sweden, September 19, 1979

2006–07 TOR/PHO	31	11–12–0–3	1,650	92	2	3.35
NHL Totals	70	27–27–2–5	3,781	200	4	3.17

Tenkrat, Petr b. Kladno, Czechoslovakia (Czech Republic), May 31, 1977

2006–07 BOS	64	9	5	14	34
NHL Totals	177	22	30	52	84

Theodore, Jose b. Laval, Quebec, September 13, 1976

2006–07 COL	33	13–15–0–1	1,748	95	0	3.26
NHL Totals	391	155–176–30–7	22,096	986	23	2.68

Thibault, Jocelyn b. Montreal, Quebec, January 12, 1975

2006–07 PIT	22	7–8–0–2	1,101	52	1	2.83
NHL Totals	574	235–234–68–5	32,386	1,480	37	2.74

Thomas, Bill b. Pittsburgh, Pennsylvania, June 20, 1983

2006–07 PHO	24	8	6	14	2
NHL Totals	33	9	8	17	10

Thomas, Tim b. Flint, Michigan, April 15, 1974

2006–07 BOS	66	30–29–0–4	3,619	189	3	3.13
NHL Totals	108	45–43–0–14	6,025	301	4	3.00

Thompson, Nate b. Anchorage, Alaska, October 5, 1984

2006–07 BOS	4	0	0	0	0
NHL Totals	4	0	0	0	0

Thorburn, Chris b. Sault Ste. Marie, Ontario, June 3, 1983

2006–07 PIT	39	3	2	5	69
NHL Totals	41	3	3	6	76

Thoresen, Patrick b. Hamar, Norway, November 7, 1983

2006–07 EDM	68	4	12	16	52
NHL Totals	68	4	12	16	52

Thornton, Joe b. London, Ontario, July 2, 1979

2006–07 SJ	82	22	92	114	44
NHL Totals	672	211	449	660	716

Thornton, Scott b. London, Ontario, January 9, 1971

2006–07 LA	58	7	6	13	85
NHL Totals	894	139	138	277	1,420

Thornton, Shawn b. Oshawa, Ontario, July 23, 1977

2006–07 ANA	48	2	7	9	88
NHL Totals	79	4	8	12	158

Timonen, Jussi b. Kuopio, Finland, June 29, 1983

2006–07 PHI	14	0	4	4	6
NHL Totals	14	0	4	4	6

Timonen, Kimmo b. Kuopio, Finland, March 18, 1975

2006–07 NAS	80	13	42	55	42
NHL Totals	573	79	222	301	348

Tjarnqvist, Daniel b. Umea, Sweden, October 14, 1976

2006–07 EDM	37	3	12	15	30
NHL Totals	315	16	70	86	122

Tjarnqvist, Mathias b. Umea, Sweden, April 15, 1979

2006–07 DAL/PHO	44	6	7	13	6
NHL Totals	95	9	12	21	26

* traded by Dallas with a 1st-round draft choice in 2007 to Phoenix on
February 12, 2007, for Ladislav Nagy

Tkachuk, Keith b. Melrose, Massachusetts, March 28, 1972

2006–07 STL/ATL	79	27	31	58	126
NHL Totals	976	473	453	926	2,033

* traded by St. Louis on February 25, 2007, to Atlanta for Glen Metropolit,
a 1st-round draft choice in 2007 and a 2nd-round draft choice in 2008

Toivonen, Hannu b. Kalvola, Finland, May 18, 1984

2006–07 BOS	18	3–9–0–1	893	63	0	4.23
NHL Totals	38	12–14–0–5	2,056	114	1	3.33

Tollefsen, Ole-Kristian b. Oslo, Norway, March 29, 1984

2006–07 CBJ	70	2	3	5	123
NHL Totals	75	2	3	5	125

Tootoo, Jordin b. Churchill, Manitoba, February 2, 1983

2006–07 NAS	65	3	6	9	116
NHL Totals	169	11	16	27	308

Torres, Raffi b. Toronto, Ontario, October 8, 1981

2006–07 EDM	82	15	19	34	88
NHL Totals	275	62	53	115	219

Toskala, Vesa b. Tampere, Finland, May 20, 1977

2006–07 SJ	38	26–10–0–1	2,141	84	4	2.35
NHL Totals	115	65–28–5–5	6,268	245	8	2.35

Tremblay, Yannick b. Pointe aux Trembles, Quebec, November 15, 1975

2006–07 VAN	12	1	2	3	12
NHL Totals	390	38	87	125	178

Tucker, Darcy b. Castor, Alberta, March 15, 1975

2006–07 TOR	56	24	19	43	81
NHL Totals	739	179	223	402	1,196

Tukonen, Lauri b. Hyvinkaa, Finland, September 1, 1986

2006–07 LA	4	0	0	0	0
NHL Totals	4	0	0	0	0

Turco, Marty b. Sault Ste. Marie, Ontario, August 13, 1975

2006–07 DAL	67	38–20–0–5	3,763	140	6	2.23
NHL Totals	320	175–82–26–10	18,020	635	30	2.11

Turgeon, Pierre b. Rouyn, Quebec, August 28, 1969

2006–07 COL	17	4	3	7	10
NHL Totals	1,294	515	812	1,327	452

Tverdovsky, Oleg b. Donetsk, Soviet Union (Ukraine), May 18, 1976

2006–07 LA	26	0	4	4	10
NHL Totals	713	77	240	317	291

Tyutin, Fedor b. Izhevsk, Soviet Union (Russia), July 19, 1983

2006–07 NYR	66	2	12	14	44
NHL Totals	168	10	36	46	116

Umberger, R.J. b. Pittsburgh, Pennsylvania, May 3, 1982

2006–07 PHI	81	16	12	28	41
NHL Totals	154	36	30	66	59

Upshall, Scottie b. Fort McMurray, Alberta, October 7, 1983

2006–07 NAS/PHI	32	8	8	16	26
NHL Totals	95	17	25	42	60

* traded by Nashville with Ryan Parent and a 1st- and 3rd-round draft
  choice in 2007 to Philadelphia on February 15, 2007, for Peter Forsberg

Vaananen, Ossi b. Vantaa, Finland, August 18, 1980

2006–07 COL	74	2	6	8	69
NHL Totals	430	12	45	57	460

Valiquette, Stephen b. Etobicoke (Toronto), Ontario, August 20, 1977

2006–07 NYR	3	1–2–0–0	114	6	0	3.13
NHL Totals	12	4–3–0–0	441	20	0	2.72

Vandermeer, Jim b. Caroline, Alberta, February 21, 1980

2006–07 CHI	46	1	6	7	53
NHL Totals	192	14	37	51	279

Vanek, Thomas b. Vienna, Austria, January 19, 1984

2006–07 BUF	82	43	41	84	40
NHL Totals	163	68	64	132	112

Van Ryn, Mike b. London, Ontario, May 14, 1979

2006–07 FLO	78	4	25	29	64
NHL Totals	306	27	89	116	232

Vasicek, Josef b. Havlickuv Brod, Czechoslovakia (Czech Republic), September 12, 1980

2006–07 NAS/CAR	63	6	16	22	51
NHL Totals	379	61	87	148	258

* traded by Nashville on February 9, 2007, to Carolina for Eric Belanger

Veilleux, Stephane b. Beauceville, Quebec, November 16, 1981

2006–07 MIN	75	7	11	18	47
NHL Totals	203	19	30	49	153

Vermette, Antoine b. St. Agapit, Quebec, July 20, 1982

2006–07 OTT	77	19	20	39	52
NHL Totals	216	47	39	86	112

Vigier, J.P. b. Notre Dame de Lourdes, Manitoba, September 11, 1976

2006–07 ATL	72	5	8	13	27
NHL Totals	213	23	23	46	97

Vishnevski, Vitali b. Kharkov, Soviet Union (Ukraine), March 18, 1980

2006–07 ATL/NAS	67	3	10	13	41
NHL Totals	483	14	47	61	444

* traded by Atlanta on February 10, 2007, to Nashville for Eric Belanger

Visnovsky, Lubomir b. Topolcany, Czechoslovakia (Slovakia), August 11, 1976

2006–07 LA	69	18	40	58	26
NHL Totals	417	62	176	238	180

Vlasic, Marc-Edouard b. Montreal, Quebec, March 30, 1987

2006–07 SJ	81	3	23	26	18
NHL Totals	81	3	23	26	18

Vokoun, Tomas b. Karlovy Vary, Czechoslovakia (Czech Republic), July 2, 1976

2006–07 NAS	44	27–12–0–4	2,601	104	5	2.40
NHL Totals	384	161–159–35–11	21,808	926	21	2.55

Volchenkov, Anton b. Moscow, Soviet Union (Russia),
February 25, 1982

2006–07 OTT	78	1	18	19	67
NHL Totals	229	9	46	55	168

Vrbata, Radim b. Mlada Boleslav, Czechoslovakia (Czech
Republic), June 13, 1981

2006–07 CHI	77	14	27	41	26
NHL Totals	346	75	95	170	104

Vyborny, David b. Jihlava, Czechoslovakia (Czech Republic),
June 2, 1975

2006–07 CBJ	82	16	48	64	60
NHL Totals	477	106	185	291	194

Walker, Matt b. Beaverlodge, Alberta, April 7, 1980

2006–07 STL	48	0	5	5	72
NHL Totals	132	0	9	9	214

Walker, Scott b. Cambridge, Ontario, July 19, 1973

2006–07 CAR	81	21	30	51	45
NHL Totals	688	127	215	342	976

Wall, Michael b. Telkwa, British Columbia, July 25, 1985

2006–07 ANA	4	2–2–0–0	201	10	0	2.97
NHL Totals	4	2–2–0–0	201	10	0	2.97

Wallin, Niclas b. Boden, Sweden, February 20, 1975

2006–07 CAR	67	2	8	10	48
NHL Totals	340	14	32	46	269

Walser, Derrick b. New Glasgow, Nova Scotia, May 12, 1978

2006–07 CBJ	9	2	0	2	0
NHL Totals	91	8	21	29	56

Walter, Ben b. Beaconsfield, Ontario, May 11, 1984

2006–07 BOS	4	0	0	0	0
NHL Totals	10	0	0	0	2

Walz, Wes b. Calgary, Alberta, May 15, 1970

2006–07 MIN	62	9	15	24	30
NHL Totals	596	108	148	256	337

Wanvig, Kyle b. Calgary Alberta, January 29, 1981

2006–07 TB	4	0	0	0	0
NHL Totals	68	5	9	14	87

Ward, Aaron b. Windsor, Ontario, January 17, 1973

2006–07 NYR/BOS	80	4	12	16	75
NHL Totals	632	35	80	115	576

* traded by New York Rangers on February 27, 2007, to Boston for Paul Mara

Ward, Cam b. Sherwood Park, Alberta, February 29, 1984

2006–07 CAR	60	30–21–0–6	3,422	167	2	2.93
NHL Totals	88	44–29–0–8	4,906	258	2	3.16

Ward, Jason b. Chapleau, Ontario, January 16, 1979

2006–07 NYR/LA/TB	70	8	11	19	40
NHL Totals	256	28	39	67	127

* traded by New York Rangers with Marc-Andre Cliché and Jan Marek to
  Los Angeles on February 5, 2007, for Sean Avery and John Seymour;
  traded by Los Angeles on February 27, 2007, to Tampa Bay for a 5th-
  round draft choice in 2007

Ward, Joel b. Toronto, Ontario, December 2, 1980

2006–07 MIN	11	0	1	1	0
NHL Totals	11	0	1	1	0

Warrener, Rhett b. Shaunavon, Saskatchewan, January 27, 1976

| 2006–07 CAL | 62 | 4 | 6 | 10 | 67 |
| NHL Totals | 683 | 23 | 79 | 102 | 878 |

Weaver, Mike b. Bramalea, Ontario, May 2, 1978

| 2006–07 LA | 39 | 3 | 6 | 9 | 16 |
| NHL Totals | 149 | 3 | 21 | 24 | 60 |

Weber, Shea b. Sicamous, British Columbia, August 14, 1985

| 2006–07 NAS | 79 | 17 | 23 | 40 | 60 |
| NHL Totals | 107 | 19 | 31 | 50 | 102 |

Weekes, Kevin b. Toronto, Ontario, April 4, 1975

| 2006–07 NYR | 14 | 4–6–0–2 | 761 | 43 | 0 | 3.39 |
| NHL Totals | 323 | 96–156–33–5 | 17,698 | 854 | 19 | 2.90 |

Weight, Doug b. Warren, Michigan, January 21, 1971

| 2006–07 STL | 82 | 16 | 43 | 59 | 56 |
| NHL Totals | 1,064 | 255 | 689 | 944 | 865 |

Weinhandl, Mattias b. Ljungby, Sweden, June 1, 1980

| 2006–07 MIN | 12 | 1 | 1 | 2 | 10 |
| NHL Totals | 182 | 19 | 37 | 56 | 70 |

Weiss, Stephen b. Toronto, Ontario, April 3, 1983

| 2006–07 FLO | 74 | 20 | 28 | 48 | 28 |
| NHL Totals | 249 | 48 | 73 | 121 | 77 |

Welch, Noah b. Brighton, Massachusetts, August 26, 1982

| 2006–07 PIT/FLO | 24 | 2 | 1 | 3 | 24 |
| NHL Totals | 29 | 3 | 4 | 7 | 26 |

* traded by Pittsburgh on February 27, 2007, to Florida for Gary Roberts

Wellwood, Kyle b. Windsor, Ontario, May 16, 1983

2006–07 TOR	48	12	30	42	0
NHL Totals	130	23	64	87	14

Wesley, Glen b. Red Deer, Alberta, October 2, 1968

2006–07 CAR	68	1	12	13	56
NHL Totals	1,379	127	402	529	993

Westcott, Duvie b. Winnipeg, Manitoba, October 30, 1977

2006–07 CBJ	23	4	6	10	18
NHL Totals	178	10	42	52	269

Westrum, Erik b. Minneapolis, Minnesota, July 26, 1979

2006–07 TOR	2	0	0	0	0
NHL Totals	27	1	2	3	22

White, Colin b. New Glasgow, Nova Scotia, December 12, 1977

2006–07 NJ	69	0	8	8	69
NHL Totals	465	15	64	79	682

White, Ian b. Winnipeg, Manitoba, June 4, 1984

2006–07 TOR	76	3	23	26	40
NHL Totals	88	4	28	32	50

White, Todd b. Kanata, Ontario, May 21, 1975

2006–07 MIN	77	13	31	44	24
NHL Totals	414	97	146	243	142

Whitney, Ray b. Fort Saskatchewan, Alberta, May 8, 1972

2006–07 CAR	81	32	51	83	46
NHL Totals	844	254	419	673	307

Whitney, Ryan b. Boston, Massachusetts, February 19, 1983

2006–07 PIT	81	14	45	59	77
NHL Totals	149	20	77	97	162

Wideman, Dennis b. Kitchener, Ontario, March 20, 1983

2006–07 STL/BOS	75	6	19	25	71
NHL Totals	142	14	35	49	154

* traded by St. Louis on February 27, 2007, to Boston for Brad Boyes

Williams, Jason b. London, Ontario, August 11, 1980

2006–07 DET/CHI	78	15	17	32	44
NHL Totals	253	53	69	122	93

* traded by Detroit on February 26, 2007, to Chicago for Kyle Calder

Williams, Jeremy b. Regina, Saskatchewan, January 26, 1984

2006–07 TOR	1	1	0	1	0
NHL Totals	2	2	0	2	0

Williams, Justin b. Cobourg, Ontario, October 4, 1981

2006–07 CAR	82	33	34	67	73
NHL Totals	422	112	164	276	273

Willsie, Brian b. London, Ontario, March 16, 1978

2006–07 LA	81	11	10	21	49
NHL Totals	281	47	45	92	173

Winchester, Brad b. Madison, Wisconsin, March 1, 1981

2006–07 EDM	59	4	5	9	86
NHL Totals	78	4	6	10	107

Wisniewski, James b. Canton, Michigan, February 21, 1984

2006–07 CHI	50	2	8	10	39
NHL Totals	69	4	13	17	75

Witt, Brendan b. Humboldt, Saskatchewan, February 20, 1975

2006–07 NYI	81	1	13	14	131
NHL Totals	724	21	79	100	1,234

Wolski, Wojtek b. Zabrze, Poland, February 24, 1986

2006–07 COL	76	22	28	50	14
NHL Totals	85	24	32	56	18

Woywitka, Jeff b. Vermilion, Alberta, September 1, 1983

2006–07 STL	34	1	6	7	12
NHL Totals	60	1	8	9	37

Wozniewski, Andy b. Buffalo Grove, Illinois, May 25, 1980

2006–07 TOR	15	0	2	2	14
NHL Totals	28	0	3	3	27

Yandle, Keith b. Boston, Massachusetts, September 9, 1986

2006–07 PHO	7	0	2	2	8
NHL Totals	7	0	2	2	8

Yashin, Alexei b. Sverdlovsk, Soviet Union (Russia),
November 5, 1973

2006–07 NYI	58	18	32	50	44
NHL Totals	850	337	444	781	401

Yelle, Stephane b. Ottawa, Ontario, May 9, 1974

2006–07 CAL	56	10	14	24	32
NHL Totals	770	82	145	227	406

York, Jason b. Nepean, Ontario, May 20, 1970

2006–07 BOS	49	1	7	8	32
NHL Totals	757	42	187	229	619

York, Mike b. Pontiac, Michigan, January 3, 1978

2006–07 BOS	49	1	7	8	32
NHL Totals	757	42	187	229	621

Young, Bryan b. Kitchener, Ontario, August 6, 1986

2006–07 EDM	15	0	0	0	10
NHL Totals	15	0	0	0	10

Zajac, Travis b. Winnipeg, Manitoba, May 13, 1985

2006–07 NJ	80	17	25	42	16
NHL Totals	80	17	25	42	16

Zanon, Greg b. Burnaby, British Columbia, June 5, 1980

2006–07 NAS	66	3	5	8	32
NHL Totals	70	3	7	10	38

Zednik, Richard b. Bystrica, Czechoslovakia (Slovakia), January 6, 1976

2006–07 WAS/NYI	42	7	14	21	18
NHL Totals	621	168	152	320	474

* traded by Washington on February 26, 2007, to New York Islanders for a 2nd-round draft choice in 2007

Zeiler, John b. Pittsburgh, Pennsylvania, November 21, 1982

2006–07 LA	23	1	2	3	22
NHL Totals	23	1	2	3	22

Zetterberg, Henrik b. Njurunda, Sweden, October 9, 1980

2006–07 DET	63	33	35	68	36
NHL Totals	280	109	131	240	88

Zherdev, Nikolai b. Kiev, Soviet Union (Ukraine), November 5, 1984

2006–07 CBJ	71	10	22	32	26
NHL Totals	201	50	70	120	130

Zhitnik, Alexei b. Kiev, Soviet Union (Russia), October 10, 1972

2006–07 NYI/PHI/ATL	79	7	31	38	92
NHL Totals	1,020	93	370	463	1,210

* traded by New York Islanders on December 16, 2006, to Philadelphia for Freddy Meyer and a conditional 3rd-round draft choice; traded by Philadelphia on February 24, 2007, to Atlanta for Braydon Coburn

Zidlicky, Marek b. Most, Czechoslovakia (Czech Republic), February 3, 1977

2006–07 NAS	79	4	26	30	72
NHL Totals	228	30	102	132	236

Zigomanis, Mike b. North York (Toronto), Ontario, January 17, 1981

2006–07 PHO	75	14	9	23	46
NHL Totals	134	17	13	30	52

Zubov, Sergei b. Moscow, Soviet Union (Russia), July 22, 1970

2006–07 DAL	78	12	42	54	26
NHL Totals	1,012	148	584	732	325

Zubrus, Dainius b. Elektrenai, Soviet Union (Lithuania), June 16, 1978

2006–07 WAS/BUF	79	24	36	60	62
NHL Totals	689	138	222	360	449

* traded by Washington with Timo Helbling on February 27, 2007, to Buffalo fro Jiri Novotny and a 1st-round draft choice in 2007

Zyuzin, Andrei b. Ufa, Soviet Union (Russia), January 21, 1978

2006–07 CAL	49	1	5	6	30
NHL Totals	464	36	79	115	408

COACHES' REGISTER, 2006–07

(OTL are listed in lost column)

	Games	W	L	T
Agnew, Jim b. Deloraine, Manitoba, March 21, 1966				
2006–07 CBJ	5	0	4	1
NHL Totals	5	0	4	1

* interim coach of Columbus until Ken Hitchcock hired November 21, 2006

Babcock, Mike b. Manitouwadge, Ontario, April 29, 1963				
2006–07 DET	82	50	19	13
NHL Totals	328	177	111	40

* hired July 14, 2005

Carbonneau, Guy b. Sept-Iles, Quebec, March 18, 1960				
2006–07 MON	82	42	34	6
NHL Totals	82	42	34	6

* hired May 5, 2006

Carlyle, Randy b. Sudbury, Ontario, April 19, 1956				
2006–07 ANA	82	48	20	14
NHL Totals	164	91	47	26

* hired August 1, 2005

Crawford, Marc b. Belleville, Ontario, February 13, 1961				
2006–07 LA	82	27	41	14
NHL Totals	905	438	342	125

* hired May 22, 2006

Gallant, Gerard b. Summerside, Prince Edward Island, September 2, 1963				
2006–07 CBJ	15	5	9	1
NHL Totals	142	56	77	9

* hired January 1, 2004; fired November 13, 2006

Gretzky, Wayne b. Brantford, Ontario, January 26, 1961

2006-07 PHO	82	31	46	5
NHL Totals	164	69	85	10

* assumed coaching duties on August 8, 2005

Hanlon, Glen b. Brandon, Manitoba, February 20, 1957

2006-07 WAS	82	28	40	14
NHL Totals	218	81	109	28

* hired December 10, 2003, to replace Bruce Cassidy

Hartley, Bob b. Hawkesbury, Ontario, September 7, 1960

2006-07 ATL	82	43	28	11
NHL Totals	644	329	235	80

* hired January 14, 2003

Hitchcock, Ken b. Edmonton, Alberta, December 17, 1951

2006-07 PHI	8	1	6	1
2006-07 CBJ	62	28	29	5
NHL Totals	819	436	278	105

* fired by Philadelphia on October 22, 2006; hired by Columbus on November 21, 2006

Julien, Claude b. Orleans, Ontario, April 23, 1960

2006-07 NJ	79	47	24	8
NHL Totals	238	119	95	24

* hired June 13, 2006; fired April 2, 2007

Kitchen, Mike b. Newmarket, Ontario, February 1, 1956

2006-07 STL	28	7	17	4
NHL Totals	131	38	70	23

* hired February 24, 2004; replaced by Andy Murray on December 11, 2006

Lamoriello, Lou b. Providence, Rhode Island, October 21, 1942

2006–07 NJ	3	2	0	1
NHL Totals	53	34	14	5

* fired coach Claude Julien on April 2, 2007, and took over as coach for rest of season

Laviolette, Peter b. Norwood, Massachusetts, December 7, 1964

2006–07 CAR	82	40	34	8
NHL Totals	380	189	150	41

* hired December 15, 2003, to replace Paul Maurice

Lemaire, Jacques b. LaSalle, Quebec, September 7, 1945

2006–07 MIN	82	48	26	8
NHL Totals	967	460	370	137

* hired June 19, 2000

Lewis, Dave b. Kindersley, Saskatchewan, July 3, 1953

2006–07 BOS	82	35	41	6
NHL Totals	251	135	89	27

* hired June 29, 2006; fired June 15, 2007

MacTavish, Craig b. London, Ontario, August 15, 1958

2006–07 EDM	82	32	43	7
NHL Totals	492	222	203	67

* hired June 22, 2000

Martin, Jacques b. Bowmanville, Ontario, October 21, 1949

2006–07 FLO	82	35	31	16
NHL Totals	1,016	479	391	146

* hired May 26, 2004

Maurice, Paul b. Sault Ste. Marie, Ontario, January 30, 1967

2006–07 TOR	82	40	31	11
NHL Totals	756	308	338	110

* hired May 12, 2006

Murray, Andy b. Gladstone, Manitoba, March 3, 1951

2006–07 STL	54	27	18	9
NHL Totals	534	242	220	72

* replaced Mike Kitchen on December 11, 2006

Murray, Bryan b. Shawville, Quebec, December 5, 1942

2006–07 OTT	82	48	25	9
NHL Totals	1,221	613	459	149

* hired June 8, 2004; resigned as coach when hired as team's GM on June 18, 2007

Nolan, Ted b. Sault Ste. Marie, Ontario, April 7, 1958

2006–07 NYI	82	40	30	12
NHL Totals	246	113	102	31

* hired June 8, 2006

Playfair, Jim b. Fort St. James, British Columbia, May 22, 1964

2006–07 CAL	82	43	29	10
NHL Totals	82	43	29	10

* hired July 12, 2006; replaced by Mike Keenan on June 14, 2007

Quenneville, Joel b. Windsor, Ontario, September 15, 1958

2006–07 COL	82	44	31	7
NHL Totals	757	394	270	93

* hired July 7, 2004

Renney, Tom b. Cranbrook, British Columbia, January 3, 1955

2006–07 NYR	82	42	30	10
NHL Totals	285	130	124	31

* hired February 25, 2004, to replace Glen Sather

Ruff, Lindy b. Warburg, Alberta, February 17, 1960

2006–07 BUF	82	53	22	7
NHL Totals	738	358	289	91

* hired July 21, 1997

Savard, Denis b. Pointe Gatineau, Quebec, February 4, 1961

2006–07 CHI	61	24	30	7
NHL Totals	61	24	30	7

* replaced Trent Yawney on November 27, 2006

Stevens, John b. Campbellton, New Brunswick, May 4, 1966

2006–07 PHI	74	21	42	11
NHL Totals	74	21	42	11

* replaced Ken Hitchcock on October 22, 2006

Therrien, Michel b. Montreal, Quebec, November 4, 1963

2006–07 PIT	82	47	24	11
NHL Totals	323	138	143	42

* named head coach on December 15, 2005

Tippett, Dave b. Moosomin, Saskatchewan, August 25, 1961

2006–07 DAL	82	50	25	7
NHL Totals	328	190	97	41

* hired May 16, 2002

Tortorella, John b. Boston, Massachusetts, June 24, 1958

2006–07 TB	82	44	33	5
NHL Totals	457	208	201	48

* hired January 6, 2001

Trotz, Barry b. Winnipeg, Manitoba, July 15, 1962

2006–07 NAS	82	51	23	8
NHL Totals	656	283	297	76

* hired August 6, 1997, a year before the Predators played their first NHL game

Vigneault, Alain b. Quebec City, Quebec, May 14, 1961

2006–07 VAN	82	49	26	7
NHL Totals	348	158	148	42

* hired June 20, 2006

Wilson, Ron b. Windsor, Ontario, May 28, 1955

2006–07 SJ	82	51	26	5
NHL Totals	1,009	469	423	117

* hired December 4, 2003

Yawney, Trent b. Hudson Bay, Saskatchewan, September 29, 1965

2006–07 CHI	21	7	12	2
NHL Totals	103	33	55	15

* replaced by Denis Savard on November 27, 2006

2007 NHL ENTRY DRAFT

Columbus, Ohio, June 22–23, 2007

Draft-Day Trades

June 22

* Anaheim trades a 1st-round draft choice in 2007 to Minnesota for a 1st-round draft choice in 2007 and a 2nd-round draft choice in 2007

* Atlanta trades 3rd-round draft choice in 2007 to Pittsburgh for Chris Thorburn

* Calgary trades 1st-round draft choice in 2007 to St. Louis for a 1st-round draft choice in 2007 and a 3rd-round draft choice in 2007

* Carolina trades a 7th-round draft choice in 2007 to Montreal for Michael Leighton

* Chicago trades a 2nd-round draft choice in 2007 to Boston for a 2nd-round draft choice and 3rd-round draft choice in 2007

* Chicago trades Adrian Aucoin and a 7th-round draft choice in 2007 to Calgary for Andrei Zyuzin and Steve Marr

* Nashville trades Tomas Vokoun to Florida for a 2nd-round draft choice in 2007, a 1st-round draft choice in 2008 and a conditional 2nd-round draft choice in either 2007 or 2008

* Ottawa trades a 5th-round draft choice in 2007 and two 7th-round draft choices in 2007 to Tampa Bay for a 4th-round draft choice in 2008

* Phoenix trades a 1st-round draft choice in 2007 to Edmonton for a 1st-round draft choice in 2007 and a 2nd-round draft choice in 2007

* San Jose trades Vesa Toskala and Mark Bell to Toronto for a 1st-round draft choice in 2007, a 2nd-round draft choice in 2007 and a 4th-round draft choice in 2009

* San Jose trades a 4th-round draft choice and 5th-round draft

choice in 2007 and a 6th-round draft choice in 2008 to Anaheim for a 3rd-round draft choice in 2007

* St. Louis trades 1st-round draft choice in 2007 to San Jose for a 1st-round draft choice in 2007, a 2nd-round draft choice in 2007 and a 3rd-round draft choice in 2008
* Washington trades a 1st-round draft choice in 2007 to San Jose for a 2nd-round draft choice in 2007 and a 2nd-round draft choice in 2008

June 23

* Atlanta trades Jim Sharrow to Vancouver for Jesse Schultz
* Boston trades 2nd-round draft choice and 3rd-round draft choice in 2007 to Chicago for a 2nd-round draft choice
* Boston trades a 6th-round draft choice in 2008 to Colorado for a 6th-round draft choice in 2007
* Buffalo trades a 4th-round draft choice in 2007 to Calgary for two 5th-round draft choices in 2007
* Colorado trades a 3rd-round draft choice in 2007 to San Jose for a 4th-round draft choice and 5th-round draft choice in 2007 and a 6th-round draft choice in 2008
* Colorado trades a 6th-round draft choice in 2007 to Boston for a 6th-round draft choice in 2008
* Dallas trades a 4th-round draft choice in 2007 to Columbus for three 5th-round draft choices in 2007
* Los Angeles trades a 6th-round draft choice in 2007 and a 4th-round draft choice in 2008 to Washington for a 4th-round draft choice in 2007
* Pittsburgh trades Stephen Dixon to Anaheim for Tim Brent
* Vancouver trades Jason King and a conditional 3rd-round draft choice in 2009 to Anaheim for Ryan Shannon
* Washington trades a 2nd-round draft choice in 2007 to Philadelphia for a 3rd-round draft choice in 2007 and a 2nd-round draft choice in 2008

The Draft

First Round

1. Pat Kane (USA)—Chicago
2. James Van Riemsdyk (USA)—Philadelphia
3. Kyle Turris (CAN)—Phoenix
4. Thomas Hickey (CAN)—Los Angeles
5. Karl Alzner (CAN)—Washington
6. Sam Gagner (CAN)—Edmonton
7. Jakub Voracek (CZE)—Columbus
8. Zach Hamill (CAN)—Boston
9. Logan Couture (CAN)—San Jose
10. Keaton Ellerby (CAN)—Florida
11. Brandon Sutter (CAN)—Carolina
12. Ryan McDonagh (USA)—Montreal
13. Lars Eller (DEN)—St. Louis
14. Kevin Shattenkirk (USA)—Colorado
15. Alex Plante (CAN)—Edmonton
16. Colton Gillies (CAN)—Minnesota
17. Alexei Cherepanov (RUS)—NY Rangers
18. Ian Cole (USA)—St. Louis
19. Logan MacMillan (CAN)—Anaheim
20. Angelo Esposito (CAN)—Pittsburgh
21. Riley Nash (CAN)—Edmonton
22. Max Pacioretty (USA)—Montreal
23. Jonathon Blum (USA)—Nashville
24. Mikael Backlund (SWE)—Calgary
25. Patrick White (USA)—Vancouver
26. David Perron (CAN)—St. Louis
27. Brendan Smith (CAN)—Detroit
28. Nicholas Petrecki (USA)—San Jose
29. James O'Brien (USA)—Ottawa
30. Nick Ross (CAN)—Phoenix

Second Round

31. T.J. Brennan (USA)—Buffalo
32. Brett MacLean (CAN)—Phoenix
33. Taylor Ellington (CAN)—Vancouver
34. Josh Godfrey (CAN)—Washington
35. Tommy Cross (USA)—Boston
36. Joel Gistedt (SWE)—Phoenix
37. Stefan Legein (CAN)—Columbus
38. William Sweatt (USA)—Chicago
39. Simon Hjalmarsson (SWE)—St. Louis
40. Michal Repik (CZE)—Florida
41. Kevin Marshall (CAN)—Philadelphia
42. Eric Tangradi (USA)—Anaheim
43. P.K. Subban (CAN)—Montreal
44. Aaron Palushaj (USA)—St. Louis
45. Colby Cohen (USA)—Colorado
46. Ted Ruth (USA)—Washington
47. Dana Tyrell (CAN)—Tampa Bay
48. Antoine Lafleur (CAN)—NY Rangers
49. Trevor Cann (CAN)—Colorado
50. Nico Sacchetti (USA)—Dallas
51. Kevin Veilleux (CAN)—Pittsburgh
52. Oscar Moller (SWE)—Los Angeles
53. Will Weber (USA)—Columbus
54. Jeremy Smith (USA)—Nashville
55. T.J. Galiardi (CAN)—Colorado
56. Akim Aliu (NIG)—Chicago
57. Mike Hoeffel (USA)—New Jersey
58. Nick Spaling (CAN)—Nashville
59. Drew Schiestel (CAN)—Buffalo
60. Ruslan Bashkirov (RUS)—Ottawa
61. Wayne Simmonds (CAN)—Los Angeles

Third Round

62. Mark Katic (CAN)—NY Islanders
63. Maxime Macenauer (CAN)—Anaheim
64. Sergei Korostin (RUS)—Dallas
65. Olivier Fortier (CAN)—Montreal
66. Garrett Klotz (CAN)—Philadelphia
67. Spencer Machacek (CAN)—Atlanta
68. Jake Hansen (USA)—Columbus
69. Maxime Tanguay (CAN)—Chicago
70. John Negrin (CAN)—Calgary
71. Evgeni Dadonov (RUS)—Florida
72. Drayson Bowman (USA)—Carolina
73. Yannick Weber (SUI)—Montreal
74. Dale Mitchell (CAN)—Toronto
75. Luca Cunti (SUI)—Tampa Bay
76. Jason Gregoire (CAN)—NY Islanders
77. Alexander Killorn (CAN)—Tampa Bay
78. Robert Bortuzzo (CAN)—Pittsburgh
79. Nick Palmieri (USA)—New Jersey
80. Casey Pierro-Zabotel (CAN)—Pittsburgh
81. Ryan Thang (USA)—Nashville
82. Bryan Cameron (CAN)—Los Angeles
83. Timo Pielmeier (GER)—San Jose
84. Phil Desimone (USA)—Washington
85. Brett Sonne (CAN)—St. Louis
86. Josh Unice (USA)—Chicago
87. Corbin McPherson (USA)—New Jersey
88. Joakim Andersson (SWE)—Detroit
89. Corey Tropp (USA)—Buffalo
90. Louie Caporusso (CAN)—Ottawa
91. Tyson Sexsmith (CAN)—San Jose

Fourth Round

92. Justin Vaive (USA)—Anaheim
93. Steven Kampfer (USA)—Anaheim
94. Maxim Mayorov (RUS)—Columbus
95. Alec Martinez (USA)—Los Angeles
96. Cade Fairchild (USA)—St. Louis
97. Linus Omark (SWE)—Edmonton
98. Sebastian Sefaniszin (GER)—Anaheim
99. Matt Frattin (CAN)—Toronto
100. Travis Erstad (USA)—St. Louis
101. Matt Rust (USA)—Florida
102. Justin McCrae (CAN)—Carolina
103. Vladimir Ruzicka (CZE)—Phoenix
104. Ben Winnett (CAN)—Toronto
105. Brad Malone (CAN)—Colorado
106. Maxim Gratchev (RUS)—NY Islanders
107. Mitch Fadden (CAN)—Tampa Bay
108. Brett Bruneteau (USA)—Washington
109. Dwight King (CAN)—Los Angeles
110. Justin Falk (CAN)—Minnesota
111. Luca Caputi (CAN)—Pittsburgh
112. Colton Sceviour (CAN)—Dallas
113. Kent Patterson (USA)—Colorado
114. Ben Ryan (USA)—Nashville
115. Niklas Lucenius (FIN)—Atlanta
116. Keith Aulie (CAN)—Calgary
117. Matt Halischuk (CAN)—New Jersey
118. Alex Grant (CAN)—Pittsburgh
119. Mark Santorelli (CAN)—Nashville
120. Ben Blood (USA)—Ottawa
121. Mattias Modig (SWE)—Anaheim

Fifth Round

122. Mario Kempe (SWE)—Philadelphia
123. Maxim Goncharov (RUS)—Phoenix
124. Linden Rowat (CAN)—Los Angeles
125. Brett Leffler (CAN)—Washington
126. Joseph Lavin (USA)—Chicago
127. Milan Kytnar (SVK)—Edmonton
128. Austin Smith (USA)—Dallas
129. Jamie Benn (CAN)—Dallas
130. Denis Reul (GER)—Boston
131. John Lee (USA)—Florida
132. Chris Terry (CAN)—Carolina
133. Joe Stejskal (USA)—Montreal
134. Juraj Mikus (SVK)—Toronto
135. Paul Carey (USA)—Colorado
136. Ondrej Roman (CZE)—Dallas
137. Joshua Turnbull (USA)—Los Angeles
138. Max Campbell (CAN)—NY Rangers
139. Bradley Eidsness (CAN)—Buffalo
140. Cody Almond (CAN)—Minnesota
141. Jake Muzzin (CAN)—Pittsburgh
142. Andrew Conboy (USA)—Montreal
143. Mickey Renaud (CAN)—Calgary
144. Andreas Thuresson (SWE)—Nashville
145. Charles-Antoine Messier (CAN)—Vancouver
146. Ilja Kablukov (RUS)—Vancouver
147. Jean-Simon Allard (CAN)—Buffalo
148. Randy Cameron (CAN)—Detroit
149. Michael Neal (CAN)—Dallas
150. Matt Marshall (USA)—Tampa Bay
151. Brett Morrison (CAN)—Anaheim

Sixth Round

152. Jonathon Kalinski (CAN)—Philadelphia
153. Scott Darling (USA)—Phoenix
154. Dan Dunn (CAN)—Washington
155. Jens Hellgren (SWE)—Colorado
156. Richard Greenop (CAN)—Chicago
157. William Quist (SWE)—Edmonton
158. Allen York (CAN)—Columbus
159. Alain Goulet (CAN)—Boston
160. Anthony Peluso (CAN)—St. Louis
161. Patrick Maroon (USA)—Philadelphia
162. Brett Bellemore (CAN)—Carolina
163. Nichlas Torp (SWE)—Montreal
164. Christopher DiDomenico (CAN)—Toronto
165. Patrik Zackrisson (SWE)—San Jose
166. Blake Kessel (USA)—NY Islanders
167. Johan Harju (SWE)—Tampa Bay
168. Carl Hagelin (SWE)—NY Rangers
169. Radim Ostrcil (CZE)—Boston
170. Harri Ilvonen (FIN)—Minnesota
171. Dustin Jeffrey (CAN)—Pittsburgh
172. Luke Gazdic (CAN)—Dallas
173. Nick Bonino (CAN)—San Jose
174. Robert Dietrich (GER)—Nashville
175. John Albert (USA)—Atlanta
176. Taylor Matson (USA)—Vancouver
177. Vili Sopanen (FIN)—New Jersey
178. Zack Torquato (CAN)—Detroit
179. Paul Byron (CAN)—Buffalo
180. Justin Taylor (CAN)—Washington
181. Corey Syvret (CAN)—Florida

Seventh Round

182. Brad Phillips (USA)—Philadelphia
183. Torrie Jung (CAN)—Tampa Bay
184. Josh Kidd (CAN)—Los Angeles
185. Nick Larson (USA)—Washington
186. C.J. Severyn (USA)—Calgary
187. Nick Eno (USA)—Buffalo
188. Matt Fillier (CAN)—Los Angeles
189. Jordan Knackstedt (CAN)—Boston
190. Trevor Nill (USA)—St. Louis
191. Ryan Watson (CAN)—Florida
192. Scott Kishel (USA)—Montreal
193. David Skokan (SVK)—NY Rangers
194. Carl Gunnarsson (SWE)—Toronto
195. Johan Alcen (SWE)—Colorado
196. Simon Lacroix (CAN)—NY Islanders
197. Michael Ward (CAN)—Tampa Bay
198. Danny Hobbs (CAN)—NY Rangers
199. Andrew Glass (USA)—Washington
200. Carson McMillan (CAN)—Minnesota
201. Justin Braun (USA)—San Jose
202. Sergei Gayduchenko (RUS)—Florida
203. Frazer McLaren (CAN)—San Jose
204. Atte Engren (FIN)—Nashville
205. Paul Postma (CAN)—Atlanta
206. Dan Gendur (CAN)—Vancouver
207. Ryan Molle (CAN)—New Jersey
208. Bryan Rufenach (CAN)—Detroit
209. Drew MacKenzie (USA)—Buffalo
210. Justin Courtnall (CAN)—Tampa Bay
211. Trent Vogelhuber (USA)—Columbus

Notes:

6th overall—Sam Gagner, son of former NHLer Dave

10th overall—Keaton Ellerby, cousin of Shane Doan (Phoenix Coyotes) and Carey Price (5th overall, Montreal Canadiens, 2005)

11th overall—Brandon Sutter, son of former NHLer Brent

13th overall—Lars Eller, highest-drafted Danish player ever

16th overall—Colton Gillies, nephew of former NHLer Clark

19th overall—Logan MacMillan, son of former NHLer Bobby

69th overall—Maxime Tanguay, brother of Alex (Calgary Flames)

92nd overall—Justin Vaive, son of former NHLer Rick

166th overall—Blake Kessel, brother of Phil (Boston Bruins)

181st overall—Corey Syvret, brother of Danny (Edmonton Oilers)

190th overall—Trevor Nill, son of former NHLer Jim

ALL-TIME LEADERS

MOST GAMES

1,767	Gordie Howe
1,756	Mark Messier
1,731	Ron Francis
1,639	Dave Andreychuk
1,635	Scott Stevens

MOST POINTS, REGULAR SEASON

2,857	Wayne Gretzky
1,887	Mark Messier
1,850	Gordie Howe
1,798	Ron Francis
1,771	Marcel Dionne

MOST GOALS, REGULAR SEASON

894	Wayne Gretzky
801	Gordie Howe
741	Brett Hull
731	Marcel Dionne
717	Phil Esposito

MOST ASSISTS, REGULAR SEASON

1,963	Wayne Gretzky
1,249	Ron Francis
1,193	Mark Messier
1,169	Ray Bourque
1,135	Paul Coffey

MOST PENALTY MINUTES, REGULAR SEASON

3,966	Dave "Tiger" Williams
3,565	Dale Hunter

3,515	Tie Domi
3,381	Marty McSorley
3,300	Bob Probert

MOST GAMES, GOALIE, REGULAR SEASON

1,029	Patrick Roy
971	Terry Sawchuk
963	Ed Belfour
906	Glenn Hall
891	Martin Brodeur

MOST SHUTOUTS, GOALIE, REGULAR SEASON

103	Terry Sawchuk
94	George Hainsworth
92	Martin Brodeur
84	Glenn Hall
82	Jacques Plante

YEAR-BY-YEAR STANDINGS AND STANLEY CUP FINALS RESULTS

After playoff scores, goalies who have registered a shutout will appear in square brackets (i.e., [Broda] means Turk Broda registered a shutout). All overtime goals are also recorded.

1917–18

First Half

	GP	W	L	GF	GA	PTS
Canadiens	14	10	4	81	47	20
Arenas	14	8	6	71	75	16
Ottawa	14	5	9	67	79	10
Wanderers+	6	1	5	17	35	2

Second Half

	GP	W	L	GF	GA	PTS
Arenas	8	5	3	37	34	10
Ottawa	8	4	4	35	35	8
Canadiens	8	3	5	34	37	6

+ Wanderers' rink burned down on January 2, 1918, and team withdrew from league. Arenas and Canadiens each counted a win for defaulted games with the Wanderers.

* winner of first half played winner of second half in a two-game total-goals series for a place in the Stanley Cup finals against the winner of the Pacific Coast Hockey Association and the Western Canada Hockey League. If one team won both halves, it went to the best-of-five Stanley Cup finals automatically.

* from 1917–21 games were played until a winner decided

NHL Finals

March 11   Canadiens 3 at Arenas 7
March 13   Arenas 3 at Canadiens 4
Arenas won two-game total-goals series 10–7

Stanley Cup Finals

March 20	Vancouver 3 at Toronto 5
March 23	Vancouver 6 at Toronto 4
March 26	Vancouver 3 at Toronto 6
March 28	Vancouver 8 at Toronto 1
March 30	Vancouver 1 at Toronto 2

Toronto won best-of-five finals 3–2

1918–19

First Half

	GP	W	L	GF	GA	PTS
Canadiens	10	7	3	57	50	14
Ottawa	10	5	5	39	39	10
Arenas	10	3	7	42	49	6

Second Half

Ottawa	8	7	1	32	14	14
Canadiens	8	3	5	31	28	6
Arenas	8	2	6	22	43	4

* Spanish influenza epidemic caused the cancellation of the Stanley Cup finals
* the 1918–19 season was supposed to be, like the ones before and after it, a 24–game schedule. However, when Canadiens and Ottawa clinched first place in both halves early, Arenas manager Charlie Querrie refused to play the remaining games, fearing a lack of fan interest. The league almost sued the Arenas, but instead Canadiens and Ottawa played a best-of-seven, rather than a two-game total-goals series, to create extra home dates for the clubs.

NHL Finals

February 22	Ottawa 4 at Canadiens 8
February 27	Canadiens 5 at Ottawa 3
March 1	Ottawa 3 at Canadiens 6
March 3	Canadiens 3 at Ottawa 6
March 6	Ottawa 2 at Canadiens 4

Canadiens won best-of-seven series 4–1

Stanley Cup Finals

March 19	Canadiens 0 at Seattle 7 [Holmes]
March 22	Canadiens 4 at Seattle 2
March 24	Canadiens 2 at Seattle 7
March 26	Canadiens 0 at Seattle 0 (20:00 OT) [Vezina/Holmes]
March 30	Canadiens 4 at Seattle 3 (Odie Cleghorn 15:57 OT)

Finals cancelled after five games because of Spanish influenza and the death of Canadiens player Joe Hall

1919–20

First Half

	GP	W	L	GP	GA	PTS
Ottawa	12	9	3	59	23	18
Canadiens	12	8	4	62	51	16
St. Pats	12	5	7	52	62	10
Bulldogs	12	2	10	44	81	4

Second Half

	GP	W	L	GP	GA	PTS
Ottawa	12	10	2	62	41	20
St. Pats	12	7	5	67	44	14
Canadiens	12	5	7	67	62	10
Bulldogs	12	2	10	47	96	4

No NHL finals because Ottawa won both halves

Stanley Cup Finals

March 22	Seattle 2 at Ottawa 3
March 24	Seattle 0 at Ottawa 3 [Benedict]
March 27	Seattle 3 at Ottawa 1
March 30	Seattle 5 Ottawa 2*
April 1	Ottawa 6 Seattle 1*

Ottawa won best-of-five finals 3–2

* played in Toronto because of poor ice conditions in Ottawa

1920–21

First Half

	GP	W	L	GP	GA	PTS
Ottawa	10	8	2	49	23	16
St. Pats	10	5	5	39	47	10
Canadiens	10	4	6	37	51	8
Hamilton	10	3	7	34	38	6

Second Half

	GP	W	L	GP	GA	PTS
St. Pats	14	10	4	66	53	20
Canadiens	14	9	5	75	48	18
Ottawa	14	6	8	48	52	12
Hamilton	14	3	11	58	94	6

NHL Finals

March 10   St. Pats 0 at Ottawa 5 [Benedict]
March 15   Ottawa 2 at St. Pats 0 [Benedict]
Ottawa won two-game total-goals series 7–0

Stanley Cup Finals

March 21   Ottawa 1 at Vancouver 3
March 24   Ottawa 4 at Vancouver 3
March 28   Ottawa 3 at Vancouver 2
March 31   Ottawa 2 at Vancouver 3
April 4   Ottawa 2 at Vancouver 1
Ottawa won best-of-five finals 3–2

1921–22

	GP	W	L	T	GF	GA	PTS
Ottawa	24	14	8	2	106	84	30
St. Pats	24	13	10	1	98	97	27
Canadiens	24	12	11	1	88	94	25
Hamilton	24	7	17	0	88	105	14

* overtime limited to 20 minutes (not sudden-death); minor penalties reduced from three to two minutes
* top two teams advance to playoffs; winner met the Pacific Coast Hockey Association–Western Canadian Hockey League Champion for the Stanley Cup

NHL Finals
March 11   Ottawa 4 at St. Pats 5
March 13   St. Pats 0 at Ottawa 0 [Roach/Benedict]
St. Pats won two-game total-goals series 5–4

Stanley Cup Finals
March 17   Vancouver 4 at St. Pats 3
March 21   Vancouver 1 at St. Pats 2 (Dye 4:50 OT)
March 23   Vancouver 3 at St. Pats 0 [Lehman]
March 25   Vancouver 0 at St. Pats 6 [Roach]
March 28   Vancouver 1 at St. Pats 5
St. Pats won best-of-five finals 3–2

1922–23

	GP	W	L	T	GF	GA	PTS
Ottawa	24	14	9	1	77	54	29
Canadiens	24	13	9	2	73	61	28
St. Pats	24	13	10	1	82	88	27
Hamilton	24	6	18	0	81	110	12

NHL Finals
March 7   Ottawa 2 at Canadiens 0 [Benedict]
March 9   Canadiens 2 at Ottawa 1
Ottawa won two-game total-goals series 3–2

Stanley Cup Playoffs
March 16   Ottawa 1 at Vancouver 0 [Benedict]
March 19   Ottawa 1 at Vancouver 4
March 23   Ottawa 3 at Vancouver 2
March 26   Ottawa 5 at Vancouver 1
Ottawa won best-of-five semifinals 3–1

Stanley Cup Finals
March 29   Ottawa 2 Edmonton 1 (Cy Denneny 2:08 OT)*
March 31   Ottawa 1 Edmonton 0 [Benedict]*
Ottawa won best-of-three finals 2–0

* games played at Vancouver

1923–24

	GP	W	L	T	GF	GA	PTS
Ottawa	24	16	8	0	74	54	32
Canadiens	24	13	11	0	59	48	26
St. Pats	24	10	14	0	59	85	20
Hamilton	24	9	15	0	63	68	18

NHL Finals
March 8   Ottawa 0 at Canadiens 1 [Vezina]
March 11   Canadiens 4 at Ottawa 2
Canadiens won two-game total-goals series 5–2

Stanley Cup Playoffs
March 18   Vancouver 2 at Canadiens 3
March 20   Vancouver 1 at Canadiens 2
Canadiens won best-of-three semifinals 2–0

Stanley Cup Finals
March 22   Calgary 1 at Canadiens 6

March 25   Canadiens 3 Calgary 0 [Vezina]*
Canadiens won best-of-three finals 2–0

* played at Ottawa

1924–25

	GP	W	L	T	GF	GA	PTS
Hamilton	30	19	10	1	90	60	39
St. Pats	30	19	11	0	90	84	38
Canadiens	30	17	11	2	93	56	36
Ottawa	30	17	12	1	83	66	35
Maroons	30	9	19	2	45	65	20
Boston	30	6	24	0	49	119	12

* the top two teams (Hamilton and Toronto) were supposed to compete for
the NHL championship and the right to advance to the Stanley Cup Finals
against the WCHL winners. However, the Tigers' players demanded more
money for these extra games and the NHL simply disqualified the team.
Thus, the St. Pats played the Canadiens.

NHL Finals
March 19   St. Pats 2 at Canadiens 3
March 13   Canadiens 2 at St. Pats 0
Canadiens won two-game total-goals series 5–2

Stanley Cup Finals
March 21   Canadiens 2 at Victoria 5
March 23   Canadiens 1 at Victoria 3*
March 27   Canadiens 4 at Victoria 2
March 30   Canadiens 1 at Victoria 6
Victoria won best-of-five finals 3–1

* played at Vancouver

1925–26

	GP	W	L	T	GF	GA	PTS
Ottawa	36	24	8	4	77	42	52
Maroons	36	20	11	5	91	73	45
Pirates	36	19	16	1	82	70	39
Boston	36	17	15	4	92	85	38
Americans	36	12	20	4	68	89	28
St. Pats	36	12	21	3	92	114	27
Canadiens	36	11	24	1	79	108	23

NHL Finals
March 25   Ottawa 1 at Maroons 1
March 27   Maroons 1 at Ottawa 0 [Benedict]
Maroons win two-game total-goals finals 2–1

Stanley Cup Finals
March 30   Victoria 0 at Maroons 3 [Benedict]
April 1   Victoria 0 at Maroons 3 [Benedict]
April 3   Victoria 3 at Maroons 2
April 6   Victoria 0 at Maroons 2 [Benedict]
Maroons won best-of-five finals 3–1

1926–27

Canadian Division

	GP	W	L	T	GF	GA	PTS
Ottawa	44	30	10	4	86	69	64
Canadiens	44	28	14	2	99	67	58
Maroons	44	20	20	4	71	68	44
Americans	44	17	25	2	82	91	36
Toronto*	44	15	24	5	79	94	35

American Division

Rangers	44	25	13	6	95	72	56
Boston	44	21	20	3	97	89	45
Chicago	44	19	22	3	115	116	41
Pirates	44	15	26	3	79	108	33
Cougars	44	12	28	4	76	105	28

* on February 14, 1927, the St. Pats changed their name to Maple Leafs

Stanley Cup Finals

April 7   Ottawa 0 at Boston 0* [Connell/Winkler]
April 9   Ottawa 3 at Boston 1
April 11   Boston 1 at Ottawa 1**
April 13   Boston 1 at Ottawa 3
Ottawa won best-of-five finals 2–0–2

* two 10-minute overtime periods
** one 20-minute overtime period

1927–28

Canadian Division

	GP	W	L	T	GF	GA	PTS
Canadiens	44	26	11	7	116	48	59
Maroons	44	24	14	6	96	77	54
Ottawa	44	20	14	10	78	57	50
Toronto	44	18	18	8	89	88	44
Americans	44	11	27	6	63	128	28

American Division

Boston	44	20	13	11	77	70	51
Rangers	44	19	16	9	94	79	47
Pirates	44	19	17	8	67	76	46
Cougars	44	19	19	6	88	79	44
Chicago	44	7	34	3	68	134	17

* overtime limited to 10 minutes of sudden-death; forward passing now
  allowed in defending zone

Finals

April 5	Rangers 0 at Maroons 2 [Benedict]
April 7	Rangers 2 at Maroons 1 (Frank Boucher 7:05 OT)
April 10	Rangers 0 at Maroons 2 [Benedict]
April 12	Rangers 1 at Maroons 0 [Miller]
April 14	Rangers 2 at Maroons 1

Rangers won best-of-five finals 3–2

1928–29

Canadian Division

	GP	W	L	T	GF	GA	PTS
Canadiens	44	22	7	15	71	43	59
Americans	44	19	13	12	53	53	50
Toronto	44	21	18	5	85	69	47
Ottawa	44	14	17	13	54	67	41
Maroons	44	15	20	9	67	65	39

American Division

	GP	W	L	T	GF	GA	PTS
Boston	44	26	13	5	89	52	57
Rangers	44	21	13	10	72	65	52
Cougars	44	19	16	9	72	63	47
Pirates	44	9	27	8	46	80	26
Chicago	44	7	29	8	33	85	22

* overtime set at 10 minutes without sudden-death; passing allowed into, but not within, the offensive zone
* the two division winners played a best-of-five and the two second place teams and third-place teams played two-game total-goals series. Those two winners then played to see who would play the winner of the two division champions' series.

Stanley Cup Finals

| March 28 | Rangers 0 at Boston 2 [Thompson] |
| March 29 | Boston 2 at Rangers 1 |

Boston won best-of-three finals 2–0

1929–30

Canadian Division

	GP	W	L	T	GF	GA	PTS
Maroons	44	23	16	5	141	114	51
Canadiens	44	21	14	9	142	114	51
Ottawa	44	21	15	8	138	118	50
Toronto	44	17	21	6	116	124	40
Americans	44	14	25	5	113	161	33

American Division

	GP	W	L	T	GF	GA	PTS
Boston	44	38	5	1	179	98	77
Chicago	44	21	18	5	117	111	47
Rangers	44	17	17	10	136	143	44
Falcons	44	14	24	6	117	133	34
Pirates	44	5	36	3	102	185	13

* forward passing allowed in all three zones, producing twice the number of goals this season over last

Stanley Cup Finals

April 1   Canadiens 3 at Boston 0 [Hainsworth]
April 3   Boston 3 at Canadiens 4
Canadiens won best-of-three finals 2–0

1930–31

Canadian Division

	GP	W	L	T	GF	GA	PTS
Canadiens	44	26	10	8	129	89	60
Toronto	44	22	13	9	118	99	53
Maroons	44	20	18	6	105	106	46
Americans	44	18	16	10	76	74	46
Ottawa	44	10	30	4	91	142	24

American Division

Boston	44	28	10	6	143	90	62
Chicago	44	24	17	3	108	78	51
Rangers	44	19	16	9	106	87	47
Falcons	44	16	21	7	102	105	39
Quakers	44	4	36	4	76	184	12

Stanley Cup Finals

April 3	Canadiens 2 at Chicago 1
April 5	Canadiens 1 at Chicago 2 (24:50 OT)
April 9	Chicago 3 at Canadiens 2 (53:50 OT)
April 11	Chicago 2 at Canadiens 4
April 14	Chicago 0 at Canadiens 2 [Hainsworth]

Canadiens won best-of-five finals 3–2

1931–32

Canadian Division

	GP	W	L	T	GF	GA	PTS
Canadiens	48	25	16	7	128	111	57
Toronto	48	23	18	7	155	127	53
Maroons	48	19	22	7	142	139	45
Americans	48	16	24	8	95	142	40

American Division

Rangers	48	23	17	8	134	112	54
Chicago	48	18	19	11	86	101	47
Falcons	48	18	20	10	95	108	46
Boston	48	15	21	12	122	117	42

Stanley Cup Finals

April 5	Toronto 6 at Rangers 4
April 7	Toronto 6 at Rangers 2*
April 9	Rangers 4 at Toronto 6

Toronto won best-of-five finals 3–0

* played at Boston because Madison Square Garden unavailable April 7 because of circus. Because of the scores in the finals (6–4, 6–2, 6–4) this series has long been dubbed the "Tennis Series"
* all members of this Toronto team were given gold coins by Conn Smythe as lifetime passes to the Gardens

1932–33

Canadian Division

	GP	W	L	T	GF	GA	PTS
Toronto	48	24	18	6	119	111	54
Maroons	48	22	20	6	135	119	50
Canadiens	48	18	25	5	92	115	41
Americans	48	15	22	11	91	118	41
Ottawa	48	11	27	10	88	131	32

American Division

	GP	W	L	T	GF	GA	PTS
Boston	48	25	15	8	124	88	58
Detroit	48	25	15	8	111	93	58
Rangers	48	23	17	8	135	107	54
Chicago	48	16	20	12	88	101	44

Stanley Cup Finals

April 4	Toronto 1 at Rangers 5
April 8	Rangers 3 at Toronto 1
April 11	Rangers 2 at Toronto 3
April 13	Rangers 1 at Toronto 0 (Bill Cook 7:33 OT) [Aitkenhead]

Rangers won best-of-five finals 3–1

1933–34
Canadian Division

	GP	W	L	T	GF	GA	PTS
Toronto	48	26	13	9	174	119	61
Canadiens	48	22	20	6	99	101	50
Maroons	48	19	18	11	117	122	49
Americans	48	15	23	10	104	132	40
Ottawa	48	13	29	6	115	143	32

American Division

	GP	W	L	T	GF	GA	PTS
Detroit	48	24	14	10	113	98	58
Chicago	48	20	17	11	88	83	51
Rangers	48	21	19	8	120	113	50
Boston	48	18	25	5	111	130	41

Stanley Cup Finals
April 3   Chicago 2 at Detroit 1 (Paul Thompson 21:10 OT)
April 5   Chicago 4 at Detroit 1
April 8   Detroit 5 at Chicago 2
April 10   Detroit 0 at Chicago 1 (Mush March 30:05 OT) [Gardiner]
Chicago won best-of-five finals 3–1

1934–35
Canadian Division

	GP	W	L	T	GF	GA	PTS
Toronto	48	30	14	4	157	111	64
Maroons	48	24	19	5	123	92	53
Canadiens	48	19	23	6	110	145	44
Americans	48	12	27	9	100	142	33
Eagles	48	11	31	6	86	144	28

American Division

	GP	W	L	T	GF	GA	PTS
Boston	48	26	16	6	129	112	58
Chicago	48	26	17	5	118	88	57
Rangers	48	22	20	6	137	139	50
Detroit	48	19	22	7	127	114	45

Stanley Cup Finals

April 4   Maroons 3 at Toronto 2 (Dave Trottier 5:28 OT)
April 6   Maroons 3 at Toronto 1
April 9   Toronto 1 at Maroons 4
Maroons won best-of-five finals 3–0

1935–36
Canadian Division

	GP	W	L	T	GF	GA	PTS
Maroons	48	22	16	10	114	106	54
Toronto	48	23	19	6	126	106	52
Americans	48	16	25	7	109	122	39
Canadiens	48	11	26	11	82	123	33

American Division

Detroit	48	24	16	8	124	103	56
Boston	48	22	20	6	92	83	50
Chicago	48	21	19	8	93	92	50
Rangers	48	19	17	12	91	96	50

Stanley Cup Finals

April 5   Toronto 1 at Detroit 3
April 7   Toronto 4 at Detroit 9
April 9   Detroit 3 at Toronto 4 (Buzz Boll 0:31 OT)
April 11 Detroit 3 at Toronto 2
Detroit won best-of-five finals 3–1

1936–37

Canadian Division

	GP	W	L	T	GF	GA	PTS
Canadiens	48	24	18	6	115	111	54
Maroons	48	22	17	9	126	110	53
Toronto	48	22	21	5	119	115	49
Americans	48	15	29	4	122	161	34

American Division

	GP	W	L	T	GF	GA	PTS
Detroit	48	25	14	9	128	102	59
Boston	48	23	18	7	120	110	53
Rangers	48	19	20	9	117	106	47
Chicago	48	14	27	7	99	131	35

Stanley Cup Finals

April 6	Detroit 1 at Rangers 5
April 8	Rangers 2 at Detroit 4
April 11	Rangers 1 at Detroit 0 [Kerr]
April 13	Rangers 0 at Detroit 1 [Robertson]
April 15	Rangers 0 at Detroit 3 [Robertson]

Detroit won best-of-five finals 3–2

1937–38

Canadian Division

	GP	W	L	T	GF	GA	PTS
Toronto	48	24	15	9	151	127	57
Americans	48	19	18	11	110	111	49
Canadiens	48	18	17	13	123	128	49
Maroons	48	12	30	6	101	149	30

American Division

Boston	48	30	11	7	142	89	67
Rangers	48	27	15	6	149	96	60
Chicago	48	14	25	9	97	139	37
Detroit	48	12	25	11	99	133	35

Stanley Cup Finals

April 5	Chicago 3 at Toronto 1
April 7	Chicago 1 at Toronto 5
April 10	Toronto 1 at Chicago 2
April 12	Toronto 1 at Chicago 4

Chicago won best-of-five finals 3–1

1938–39

	GP	W	L	T	GF	GA	PTS
Boston	48	36	10	2	156	76	74
Rangers	48	26	16	6	149	105	58
Toronto	48	19	20	9	114	107	47
Americans	48	17	21	10	119	157	44
Detroit	48	18	24	6	107	128	42
Canadiens	48	15	24	9	115	146	39
Chicago	48	12	28	8	91	132	32

* only the last-place team did not qualify for the playoffs under the new one-division, 7-team format. The first- and second-place team played a best-of-seven series to advance to the finals. The second played third and fourth played fifth in best-of-three, the two winners playing another best-of-three to advance to the finals.

Stanley Cup Finals

April 6	Toronto 1 at Boston 2
April 9	Toronto 3 at Boston 2 (Doc Romnes 10:38 OT)
April 11	Boston 3 at Toronto 1
April 13	Boston 2 at Toronto 0 [Brimsek]
April 16	Toronto 1 at Boston 3

Boston won best-of-seven finals 4–1

1939–40

	GP	W	L	T	GF	GA	PTS
Boston	48	31	12	5	170	98	67
Rangers	48	27	11	10	136	77	64
Toronto	48	25	17	6	134	110	56
Chicago	48	23	19	6	112	120	52
Detroit	48	16	26	6	90	126	38
Americans	48	15	29	4	106	140	34
Canadiens	48	10	33	5	90	167	25

Stanley Cup Finals

April 2	Toronto 1 at Rangers 2 (Alf Pike 15:30 OT)
April 3	Toronto 2 at Rangers 6
April 6	Rangers 1 at Toronto 2
April 9	Rangers 0 at Toronto 3 [Broda]
April 11	Rangers 2 at Toronto 1 (Muzz Patrick 31:43 OT)*
April 13	Rangers 3 at Toronto 2 (Bryan Hextall 2:07 OT)

Rangers won best-of-seven finals 4–2

* game could not be played at Madison Square Garden as it was previously
booked for the circus

1940–41

	GP	W	L	T	GF	GA	PTS
Boston	48	27	8	13	168	102	67
Toronto	48	28	14	6	145	99	62
Detroit	48	21	16	11	112	102	53
Rangers	48	21	19	8	143	125	50
Chicago	48	16	25	7	112	139	39
Canadiens	48	16	26	6	121	147	38
Americans	48	8	29	11	99	186	27

Stanley Cup Finals

April 6   Detroit 2 at Boston 3
April 8   Detroit 1 at Boston 2
April 10   Boston 4 at Detroit 2
April 12   Boston 3 at Detroit 1
Boston won best-of-seven finals 4–0

1941–42

	GP	W	L	T	GF	GA	PTS
Rangers	48	29	17	2	177	143	60
Toronto	48	27	18	3	158	136	57
Boston	48	25	17	6	160	118	56
Chicago	48	22	23	3	145	155	47
Detroit	48	19	25	4	140	147	42
Canadiens	48	18	27	3	134	173	39
Brooklyn	48	16	29	3	133	175	35

Stanley Cup Finals

April 4   Detroit 3 at Toronto 2
April 7   Detroit 4 at Toronto 2
April 9   Toronto 2 at Detroit 5
April 12   Toronto 4 at Detroit 3
April 14   Detroit 3 at Toronto 9
April 16   Toronto 3 at Detroit 0 [Broda]
April 18   Detroit 1 at Toronto 3
Toronto won best-of-seven finals 4–3

* only time in NHL history that a team has trailed 3–0 in the finals and won
  the Stanley Cup

1942–43

	GP	W	L	T	GF	GA	PTS
Detroit	50	25	14	11	169	124	61
Boston	50	24	17	9	195	176	57
Toronto	50	22	19	9	198	159	53
Canadiens	50	19	19	12	181	191	50
Chicago	50	17	18	15	179	180	49
Rangers	50	11	31	8	161	253	30

* because of wartime restrictions on train schedules overtime was eliminated as of November 21, 1942
* the top four teams qualified for the playoffs in the six-team league, and both rounds were best-of-seven

Stanley Cup Finals

April 1	Boston 2 at Detroit 6
April 4	Boston 3 at Detroit 4
April 7	Detroit 4 at Boston 0 [Mowers]
April 8	Detroit 2 at Boston 0 [Mowers]

Detroit won best-of-seven finals 4–0

1943–44

	GP	W	L	T	GF	GA	PTS
Canadiens	50	38	5	7	234	109	83
Detroit	50	26	18	6	214	177	58
Toronto	50	23	23	4	214	174	50
Chicago	50	22	23	5	178	187	49
Boston	50	19	26	5	223	268	43
Rangers	50	6	39	5	162	310	17

Stanley Cup Finals

April 4	Chicago 1 at Canadiens 5
April 6	Chicago 1 at Canadiens 3
April 9	Chicago 2 at Canadiens 3
April 13	Chicago 4 at Canadiens 5 (Toe Blake 9:12 OT)

Canadiens won best-of-seven finals 4–0

1944–45

	GP	W	L	T	GF	GA	PTS
Canadiens	50	38	8	4	228	121	80
Detroit	50	31	14	5	218	161	67
Toronto	50	24	22	4	183	161	52
Boston	50	16	30	4	179	219	36
Chicago	50	13	30	7	141	194	33
Rangers	50	11	29	10	154	247	32

Stanley Cup Finals

April 6	Toronto 1 at Detroit 0 [McCool]
April 8	Toronto 2 at Detroit 0 [McCool]
April 12	Detroit 0 at Toronto 1 [McCool]
April 14	Detroit 5 at Toronto 3
April 19	Toronto 0 at Detroit 2 [Lumley]
April 21	Detroit 1 at Toronto 0 (Ed Bruneteau 14:16 OT) [Lumley]
April 22	Toronto 2 at Detroit 1

Toronto won best-of-seven finals 4–3

1945–46

	GP	W	L	T	GF	GA	PTS
Canadiens	50	28	17	5	172	134	61
Boston	50	24	18	8	167	156	56
Chicago	50	23	20	7	200	178	53
Detroit	50	20	20	10	146	159	50
Toronto	50	19	24	7	174	185	45
Rangers	50	13	28	9	144	191	35

Stanley Cup Finals

March 30	Boston 3 at Canadiens 4 (Maurice Richard 9:08 OT)
April 2	Boston 2 at Canadiens 3 (Jimmy Peters 16:55 OT)
April 4	Canadiens 4 at Boston 2
April 7	Canadiens 2 at Boston 3 (Terry Reardon 15:13 OT)
April 9	Boston 3 at Canadiens 6

Canadiens won best-of-seven finals 4–1

1946–47

	GP	W	L	T	GF	GA	PTS
Canadiens	60	34	16	10	189	138	78
Toronto	60	31	19	10	209	172	72
Boston	60	26	23	11	190	175	63
Detroit	60	22	27	11	190	193	55
Rangers	60	22	32	6	167	186	50
Chicago	60	19	37	4	193	274	42

Stanley Cup Finals

April 8	Toronto 0 at Canadiens 6 [Durnan]
April 10	Toronto 4 at Canadiens 0 [Broda]
April 12	Canadiens 2 at Toronto 4
April 15	Canadiens 1 at Toronto 2 (Syl Apps 16:36 OT)
April 17	Toronto 1 at Canadiens 3
April 19	Canadiens 1 at Toronto 2

Toronto won best-of-seven finals 4–2

1947–48

	GP	W	L	T	GF	GA	PTS
Toronto	60	32	15	13	182	143	77
Detroit	60	30	18	12	187	148	72
Boston	60	23	24	13	167	168	59
Rangers	60	21	26	13	176	201	55
Canadiens	60	20	29	11	147	169	51
Chicago	60	20	34	6	195	225	46

Stanley Cup Finals

April 7	Detroit 3 at Toronto 5
April 10	Detroit 2 at Toronto 4
April 11	Toronto 2 at Detroit 0 [Broda]
April 14	Toronto 7 at Detroit 2

Toronto won best-of-seven finals 4–0

1948–49

	GP	W	L	T	GF	GA	PTS
Detroit	60	34	19	7	195	145	75
Boston	60	29	23	8	178	163	66
Canadiens	60	28	23	9	152	126	65
Toronto	60	22	25	13	147	161	57
Chicago	60	21	31	8	173	211	50
Rangers	60	18	31	11	133	172	47

Stanley Cup Finals

April 8   Toronto 3 at Detroit 2 (Joe Klukay 17:31 OT)
April 10   Toronto 3 at Detroit 1
April 13   Detroit 1 at Toronto 3
April 16   Detroit 1 at Toronto 3
Toronto won best-of-seven finals 4–0

1949–50

	GP	W	L	T	GF	GA	PTS
Detroit	70	37	19	14	229	164	88
Canadiens	70	29	22	19	172	150	77
Toronto	70	31	27	12	176	173	74
Rangers	70	28	31	11	170	189	67
Boston	70	22	32	16	198	228	60
Chicago	70	22	38	10	203	244	54

Stanley Cup Finals

April 11   Rangers 1 at Detroit 4
April 13   Detroit 1 Rangers 3*
April 15   Detroit 4 Rangers 0*[Lumley]
April 18   Rangers 4 at Detroit 3 (Don Raleigh 8:34 OT)
April 20   Rangers 2 at Detroit 1 (Don Raleigh 1:38 OT)
April 22   Rangers 4 at Detroit 5
April 23   Rangers 3 at Detroit 4 (Pete Babando 28:31 OT)**
Detroit won best-of-seven finals 4–3

* played at Toronto because Madison Square Garden was previously booked for
  the circus. Games 6 and 7 played in Detroit because league by-laws stipulated

a Stanley Cup-winning game cannot be played on neutral ice.
** first time in history the Cup was won on an OT goal in game 7

1950–51

	GP	W	L	T	GF	GA	PTS
Detroit	70	44	13	13	236	139	101
Toronto	70	41	16	13	212	138	95
Canadiens	70	25	30	15	173	184	65
Boston	70	22	30	18	178	197	62
Rangers	70	20	29	21	169	201	61
Chicago	70	13	47	10	171	280	36

Stanley Cup Finals

April 11   Canadiens 2 at Toronto 3 (Sid Smith 5:51 OT)
April 14   Canadiens 3 at Toronto 2 (Maurice Richard 2:55 OT)
April 17   Toronto 2 at Canadiens 1 (Ted Kennedy 4:47 OT)
April 19   Toronto 3 at Canadiens 2 (Harry Watson 5:15 OT)
April 21   Canadiens 2 at Toronto 3 (Bill Barilko 2:53 OT)
Toronto won best-of-seven finals 4–1

1951–52

	GP	W	L	T	GF	GA	PTS
Detroit	70	44	14	12	215	133	100
Canadiens	70	34	26	10	195	164	78
Toronto	70	29	25	16	168	157	74
Boston	70	25	29	16	162	176	66
Rangers	70	23	34	13	192	219	59
Chicago	70	17	44	9	158	241	43

Stanley Cup Finals

April 10   Detroit 3 at Canadiens 1
April 12   Detroit 2 at Canadiens 1
April 13   Canadiens 0 at Detroit 3 [Sawchuk]
April 15   Canadiens 0 at Detroit 3 [Sawchuk]
Detroit won best-of-seven finals 4–0

1952–53

	GP	W	L	T	GF	GA	PTS
Detroit	70	36	16	18	222	133	90
Canadiens	70	28	23	19	155	148	75
Boston	70	28	29	13	152	172	69
Chicago	70	27	28	15	169	175	69
Toronto	70	27	30	13	156	167	67
Rangers	70	17	37	16	152	211	50

Stanley Cup Finals

April 9   Boston 2 at Canadiens 4
April 11 Boston 4 at Canadiens 1
April 12 Canadiens 3 at Boston 0 [McNeil]
April 14 Canadiens 7 at Boston 3
April 16 Boston 0 at Canadiens 1 (Elmer Lach 1:22 OT) [McNeil]
Canadiens won best-of-seven finals 4–1

1953–54

	GP	W	L	T	GF	GA	PTS
Detroit	70	37	19	14	191	132	88
Canadiens	70	35	24	11	195	141	81
Toronto	70	32	24	14	152	131	78
Boston	70	32	28	10	177	181	74
Rangers	70	29	31	10	161	182	68
Chicago	70	12	51	7	133	242	31

Stanley Cup Finals

April 4   Canadiens 1 at Detroit 3
April 6   Canadiens 3 at Detroit 1
April 8   Detroit 5 at Canadiens 2
April 10 Detroit 2 at Canadiens 0 [Sawchuk]
April 11 Canadiens 1 at Detroit 0 (Ken Mosdell 5:45 OT) [McNeil]
April 13 Detroit 1 at Canadiens 4
April 16 Canadiens 1 at Detroit 2 (Tony Leswick 4:29 OT)
Detroit won best-of-seven finals 4–3

1954–55

	GP	W	L	T	GF	GA	PTS
Detroit	70	42	17	11	204	134	95
Canadiens	70	41	18	11	228	157	93
Toronto	70	24	24	22	147	135	70
Boston	70	23	26	21	169	188	67
Rangers	70	17	35	18	150	210	52
Chicago	70	13	40	17	161	235	43

Stanley Cup Finals

April 3   Canadiens 2 at Detroit 4
April 5   Canadiens 1 at Detroit 7
April 7   Detroit 2 at Canadiens 4
April 9   Detroit 3 at Canadiens 5
April 10   Canadiens 1 at Detroit 5
April 12   Detroit 3 at Canadiens 6
April 14   Canadiens 1 at Detroit 3
Detroit won best-of-seven finals 4–3

1955–56

	GP	W	L	T	GF	GA	PTS
Canadiens	70	45	15	10	222	131	100
Detroit	70	30	24	16	183	148	76
Rangers	70	32	28	10	204	203	74
Toronto	70	24	33	13	153	181	61
Boston	70	23	34	13	147	185	59
Chicago	70	19	39	12	155	216	50

Stanley Cup Finals

March 31   Detroit 4 at Canadiens 6
April 3   Detroit 1 at Canadiens 5
April 5   Canadiens 1 at Detroit 3
April 8   Canadiens 3 at Detroit 0 [Plante]
April 10   Detroit 1 at Canadiens 3
Canadiens won best-of-seven finals 4–1

1956–57

	GP	W	L	T	GF	GA	PTS
Detroit	70	38	20	12	198	157	88
Canadiens	70	35	23	12	210	155	82
Boston	70	34	24	12	195	174	80
Rangers	70	26	30	14	184	227	66
Toronto	70	21	34	15	174	192	57
Chicago	70	16	39	15	169	225	47

* penalized player allowed to return to the ice after a power-play goal has been
  scored by the opposition

Stanley Cup Finals
April 6   Boston 1 at Canadiens 5
April 9   Boston 0 at Canadiens 1 [Plante]
April 11   Canadiens 4 at Boston 2
April 14   Canadiens 0 at Boston 2 [Simmons]
April 16   Boston 1 at Canadiens 5
Canadiens won best-of-seven finals 4–1

1957–58

	GP	W	L	T	GF	GA	PTS
Canadiens	70	43	17	10	250	158	96
Rangers	70	32	25	13	195	188	77
Detroit	70	29	29	12	176	207	70
Boston	70	27	28	15	199	194	69
Chicago	70	24	39	7	163	202	55
Toronto	70	21	38	11	192	226	53

Stanley Cup Finals
April 8   Boston 1 at Canadiens 2
April 10   Boston 5 at Canadiens 2
April 13   Canadiens 3 at Boston 0 [Plante]
April 15   Canadiens 1 at Boston 3
April 17   Boston 2 at Canadiens 3 (Maurice Richard 5:45 OT)

April 20   Canadiens 5 at Boston 3
Canadiens won best-of-seven finals 4–2

1958–59

	GP	W	L	T	GF	GA	PTS
Canadiens	70	39	18	13	258	158	91
Boston	70	32	29	9	205	215	73
Chicago	70	28	29	13	197	208	69
Toronto	70	27	32	11	189	201	65
Rangers	70	26	32	12	201	217	64
Detroit	70	25	37	8	167	218	58

Stanley Cup Finals
April 9   Toronto 3 at Canadiens 5
April 11   Toronto 1 at Canadiens 3
April 14   Canadiens 2 at Toronto 3 (Dick Duff 10:06 OT)
April 16   Canadiens 3 at Toronto 2
April 18   Toronto 3 at Canadiens 5
Canadiens won best-of-seven finals 4–1

1959–60

	GP	W	L	T	GF	GA	PTS
Canadiens	70	40	18	12	255	178	92
Toronto	70	35	26	9	199	195	79
Chicago	70	28	29	13	191	180	69
Detroit	70	26	29	15	186	197	67
Boston	70	28	34	8	220	241	64
Rangers	70	17	38	15	187	247	49

Stanley Cup Finals

April 7	Toronto 2 at Canadiens 4
April 9	Toronto 1 at Canadiens 2
April 12	Canadiens 5 at Toronto 2
April 14	Canadiens 4 at Toronto 0 [Plante]

Canadiens won best-of-seven finals 4–0

1960–61

	GP	W	L	T	GF	GA	PTS
Canadiens	70	41	19	10	254	188	92
Toronto	70	39	19	12	234	176	90
Chicago	70	29	24	17	198	180	75
Detroit	70	25	29	16	195	215	66
Rangers	70	22	38	10	204	248	54
Boston	70	15	42	13	176	254	43

Stanley Cup Finals

April 6	Detroit 2 at Chicago 3
April 8	Chicago 1 at Detroit 3
April 10	Detroit 1 at Chicago 3
April 12	Chicago 1 at Detroit 2
April 14	Detroit 3 at Chicago 6
April 16	Chicago 5 at Detroit 1

Chicago won best-of-seven finals 4–2

1961–62

	GP	W	L	T	GF	GA	PTS
Canadiens	70	42	14	14	259	166	98
Toronto	70	37	22	11	232	180	85
Chicago	70	31	26	13	217	186	75
Rangers	70	26	32	12	195	207	64
Detroit	70	23	33	14	184	219	60
Boston	70	15	47	8	177	306	38

Stanley Cup Finals

April 10	Chicago 1 at Toronto 4
April 12	Chicago 2 at Toronto 3
April 15	Toronto 0 at Chicago 3 [Hall]
April 17	Toronto 1 at Chicago 4
April 19	Chicago 4 at Toronto 8
April 22	Toronto 2 at Chicago 1

Toronto won best-of-seven finals 4–2

1962–63

	GP	W	L	T	GF	GA	PTS
Toronto	70	35	23	12	221	180	82
Chicago	70	32	21	17	194	178	81
Canadiens	70	28	19	23	225	183	79
Detroit	70	32	25	13	200	194	77
Rangers	70	22	36	12	211	233	56
Boston	70	14	39	17	198	281	45

Stanley Cup Finals

April 9	Detroit 2 at Toronto 4
April 11	Detroit 2 at Toronto 4
April 14	Toronto 2 at Detroit 3
April 16	Toronto 4 at Detroit 2
April 18	Detroit 1 at Toronto 3

Toronto won best-of-seven finals 4–1

1963–64

	GP	W	L	T	GF	GA	PTS
Canadiens	70	36	21	13	209	167	85
Chicago	70	36	22	12	218	169	84
Toronto	70	33	25	12	192	172	78
Detroit	70	30	29	11	191	204	71
Rangers	70	22	38	10	186	242	54
Boston	70	18	40	12	170	212	48

Stanley Cup Finals

April 11	Detroit 2 at Toronto 3
April 14	Detroit 4 at Toronto 3 (Larry Jeffrey 7:52 OT)
April 16	Toronto 3 at Detroit 4
April 18	Toronto 4 at Detroit 2
April 21	Detroit 2 at Toronto 1
April 23	Toronto 4 at Detroit 3 (Bobby Baun 1:43 OT)
April 25	Detroit 0 at Toronto 4 [Bower]

Toronto won best-of-seven finals 4–3

1964–65

	GP	W	L	T	GF	GA	PTS
Detroit	70	40	23	7	224	175	87
Canadiens	70	36	23	11	211	185	83
Chicago	70	34	28	8	224	176	76
Toronto	70	30	26	14	204	173	74
Rangers	70	20	38	12	179	246	52
Boston	70	21	43	6	166	253	48

Stanley Cup Finals

April 17	Chicago 2 at Canadiens 3
April 20	Chicago 0 at Canadiens 2 [Worsley]
April 22	Canadiens 1 at Chicago 3
April 25	Canadiens 1 at Chicago 5
April 27	Chicago 0 at Canadiens 6 [Hodge]
April 29	Canadiens 1 at Chicago 2
May 1	Chicago 0 at Canadiens 4 [Worsley]

Canadiens won best-of-seven finals 4–3

1965–66

	GP	W	L	T	GF	GA	PTS
Canadiens	70	41	21	8	239	173	90
Chicago	70	37	25	8	240	187	82
Toronto	70	34	25	11	208	187	79
Detroit	70	31	27	12	221	194	74
Boston	70	21	43	6	174	275	48
Rangers	70	18	41	11	195	261	47

Stanley Cup Finals

April 24	Detroit 3 at Canadiens 2
April 26	Detroit 5 at Canadiens 2
April 28	Canadiens 4 at Detroit 2
May 1	Canadiens 2 at Detroit 1
May 3	Detroit 1 at Canadiens 5
May 5	Canadiens 3 at Detroit 2 (Henri Richard 2:20 OT)

Canadiens won best-of-seven finals 4–2

1966–67

	GP	W	L	T	GF	GA	PTS
Chicago	70	41	17	12	264	170	94
Canadiens	70	32	25	13	202	188	77
Toronto	70	32	27	11	204	211	75
Rangers	70	30	28	12	188	189	72
Detroit	70	27	39	4	212	241	58
Boston	70	17	43	10	182	253	44

Stanley Cup Finals

April 20	Toronto 2 at Canadiens 6
April 22	Toronto 3 at Canadiens 0 [Bower]
April 25	Canadiens 2 at Toronto 3 (Bob Pulford 28:26 OT)
April 27	Canadiens 6 at Toronto 2
April 29	Toronto 4 at Canadiens 1
May 2	Canadiens 1 at Toronto 3

Toronto won best-of-seven finals 4–2

1967–68

East Division

	GP	W	L	T	GF	GA	PTS
Canadiens	74	42	22	10	236	167	94
Rangers	74	39	23	12	226	183	90
Boston	74	37	27	10	259	216	84
Chicago	74	32	26	16	212	222	80
Toronto	74	33	31	10	209	176	76
Detroit	74	27	35	12	245	257	66

West Division

	GP	W	L	T	GF	GA	PTS
Philadelphia	74	31	32	11	173	179	73
Los Angeles	74	31	33	10	200	224	72
St. Louis	74	27	31	16	177	191	70
North Stars	74	27	32	15	191	226	69
Pittsburgh	74	27	34	13	195	216	67
Oakland	74	15	42	17	153	219	47

* top four teams in each division qualified for the playoffs

Stanley Cup Finals

May 5	Canadiens 3 at St. Louis 2 (Jacques Lemaire 1:41 OT)
May 7	Canadiens 1 at St. Louis 0 [Worsley]
May 9	St. Louis 3 at Canadiens 4 (Bobby Rousseau 1:13 OT)
May 11	St. Louis 2 at Canadiens 3

Canadiens won best-of-seven finals 4–0

1968–69

East Division

	GP	W	L	T	GF	GA	PTS
Canadiens	76	46	19	11	271	202	103
Boston	76	42	18	16	303	221	100
Rangers	76	41	26	9	231	196	91
Toronto	76	35	26	15	234	217	85
Detroit	76	33	31	12	239	221	78
Chicago	76	34	33	9	280	246	77

West Division

	GP	W	L	T	GF	GA	PTS
St. Louis	76	37	25	14	204	157	88
Oakland	76	29	36	11	219	251	69
Philadelphia	76	20	35	21	174	225	61
Los Angeles	76	24	42	10	185	260	58
Pittsburgh	76	20	45	11	189	252	51
North Stars	76	18	43	15	189	270	51

Stanley Cup Finals

April 27   St. Louis 1 at Canadiens 3
April 29   St. Louis 1 at Canadiens 3
May 1   Canadiens 4 at St. Louis 0 [Vachon]
May 4   Canadiens 2 at St. Louis 1
Canadiens won best-of-seven finals 4–0

1969–70

East Division

	GP	W	L	T	GF	GA	PTS
Chicago	76	45	22	9	250	170	99
Boston	76	40	17	19	277	216	99
Detroit	76	40	21	15	246	199	95
Rangers	76	38	22	16	246	189	92
Canadiens	76	38	22	16	244	201	92
Toronto	76	29	34	13	222	242	71

West Division

	GP	W	L	T	GF	GA	PTS
St. Louis	76	37	27	12	224	179	86
Pittsburgh	76	26	38	12	182	238	64
North Stars	76	19	35	22	224	257	60
Oakland	76	22	40	14	169	243	58
Philadelphia	76	17	35	24	197	225	58
Los Angeles	76	14	52	10	168	290	38

Stanley Cup Finals

May 3	Boston 6 at St. Louis 1
May 5	Boston 6 at St. Louis 2
May 7	St. Louis 1 at Boston 4
May 10	St. Louis 3 at Boston 4 (Bobby Orr 0:40 OT)

Boston won best-of-seven finals 4–0

1970–71

East Division

	GP	W	L	T	GF	GA	PTS
Boston	78	57	14	7	399	207	121
Rangers	78	49	18	11	259	177	109
Canadiens	78	42	23	13	291	216	97
Toronto	78	37	33	8	248	211	82
Buffalo	78	24	39	15	217	291	63
Vancouver	78	24	46	8	229	296	56
Detroit	78	22	45	11	209	308	55

West Division

	GP	W	L	T	GF	GA	PTS
Chicago	78	49	20	9	277	184	107
St. Louis	78	34	25	19	223	208	87
Philadelphia	78	28	33	17	207	225	73
North Stars	78	28	34	16	191	223	72
Los Angeles	78	25	40	13	239	303	63
Pittsburgh	78	21	37	20	221	240	62
California	78	20	53	5	199	320	45

Stanley Cup Finals

May 4	Canadiens 1 at Chicago 2 (Jim Pappin 21:11 OT)
May 6	Canadiens 3 at Chicago 5
May 9	Chicago 2 at Canadiens 4
May 11	Chicago 2 at Canadiens 5
May 13	Canadiens 0 at Chicago 2 [Esposito]
May 16	Chicago 3 at Canadiens 4
May 18	Canadiens 3 at Chicago 2

Canadiens won best-of-seven finals 4–3

1971–72

East Division

	GP	W	L	T	GF	GA	PTS
Boston	78	54	13	11	330	204	119
Rangers	78	48	17	13	317	192	109
Canadiens	78	46	16	16	307	205	108
Toronto	78	33	31	14	209	208	80
Detroit	78	33	35	10	261	262	76
Buffalo	78	16	43	19	203	289	51
Vancouver	78	20	50	8	203	297	48

West Division

	GP	W	L	T	GF	GA	PTS
Chicago	78	46	17	15	256	166	107
North Stars	78	37	29	12	212	191	86
St. Louis	78	28	39	11	208	247	67
Pittsburgh	78	26	38	14	220	258	66
Philadelphia	78	26	38	14	200	236	66
California	78	21	39	18	216	288	60
Los Angeles	78	20	49	9	206	305	49

Stanley Cup Finals

April 30	Rangers 5 at Boston 6
May 2	Rangers 1 at Boston 2
May 4	Boston 2 at Rangers 5
May 7	Boston 3 at Rangers 2
May 9	Rangers 3 at Boston 2
May 11	Boston 3 at Rangers 0 [Johnston]

Boston won best-of-seven finals 4–2

1972–73

East Division

	GP	W	L	T	GF	GA	PIM	PTS
Canadiens	78	52	10	16	329	184	783	120
Boston	78	51	22	5	330	235	1097	107
Rangers	78	47	23	8	297	208	765	102
Buffalo	78	37	27	14	257	219	940	88
Detroit	78	37	29	12	265	243	893	86
Toronto	78	27	41	10	247	279	716	64
Vancouver	78	22	47	9	233	339	943	53
Islanders	78	12	60	6	170	347	881	30

West Division

	GP	W	L	T	GF	GA	PIM	PTS
Chicago	78	42	27	9	284	225	864	93
Philadelphia	78	37	30	11	296	256	1756	85
North Stars	78	37	30	11	254	230	881	85
St. Louis	78	32	34	12	233	251	1195	76
Pittsburgh	78	32	37	9	257	265	866	73
Los Angeles	78	31	36	11	232	245	888	73
Flames	78	25	38	15	191	239	852	65
California	78	16	46	16	213	323	840	48

Stanley Cup Finals

April 29	Chicago 3 at Canadiens 8
May 1	Chicago 1 at Canadiens 4
May 3	Canadiens 4 at Chicago 7
May 6	Canadiens 4 at Chicago 0 [Dryden]
May 8	Chicago 8 at Canadiens 7
May 10	Canadiens 6 at Chicago 4

Canadiens won best-of-seven finals 4–2

1973–74

East Division

	GP	W	L	T	GF	GA	PTS
Boston	78	52	17	9	349	221	113
Canadiens	78	45	24	9	293	240	99
Rangers	78	40	24	14	300	251	94
Toronto	78	35	27	16	274	230	86
Buffalo	78	32	34	12	242	250	76
Detroit	78	29	39	10	255	319	68
Vancouver	78	24	43	11	224	296	59
Islanders	78	19	41	18	182	247	56

West Division

	GP	W	L	T	GF	GA	PTS
Philadelphia	78	50	16	12	273	164	112
Chicago	78	41	14	23	272	164	105
Los Angeles	78	33	33	12	233	231	78
Flames	78	30	34	14	214	238	74
Pittsburgh	78	28	41	9	242	273	65
St. Louis	78	26	40	12	206	248	64
North Stars	78	23	38	17	235	275	63
California	78	13	55	10	195	342	36

Stanley Cup Finals

May 7	Philadelphia 2 at Boston 3
May 9	Philadelphia 3 at Boston 2 (Bobby Clarke 12:01 OT)
May 12	Boston 1 at Philadelphia 4
May 14	Boston 2 at Philadelphia 4
May 16	Philadelphia 1 at Boston 5
May 19	Boston 0 at Philadelphia 1 [Parent]

Philadelphia won best-of-seven finals 4–2

1974–75

PRINCE OF WALES CONFERENCE
Adams Division

	GP	W	L	T	GF	GA	PTS
Buffalo	80	49	16	15	354	240	113
Boston	80	40	26	14	345	245	94
Toronto	80	31	33	16	280	309	78
California	80	19	48	13	212	316	51

Norris Division

Canadiens	80	47	14	19	374	225	113
Los Angeles	80	42	17	21	269	185	105
Pittsburgh	80	37	28	15	326	289	89
Detroit	80	23	45	12	259	335	58
Washington	80	8	67	5	181	446	21

CLARENCE CAMPBELL CONFERENCE
Patrick Division

Philadelphia	80	51	18	11	293	181	113
Rangers	80	37	29	14	319	276	88
Islanders	80	33	25	22	264	221	88
Flames	80	34	31	15	243	233	83

Smythe Division

Vancouver	80	38	32	10	271	254	86
St. Louis	80	35	31	14	269	267	84
Chicago	80	37	35	8	268	241	82
North Stars	80	23	50	7	221	341	53
Kansas City	80	15	54	11	184	328	41

* the top three teams in each division qualified for the playoffs. The four division champions received byes to the second round and all second- and third-place clubs were seeded 1–8 by points, #1 playing # 8, #2 and #7, etc. The first round was best-of-three, the subsequent rounds best-of-seven.

Stanley Cup Finals

May 15	Buffalo 1 at Philadelphia 4
May 18	Buffalo 1 at Philadelphia 2
May 20	Philadelphia 4 at Buffalo 5 (Rene Robert 18:29 OT)
May 22	Philadelphia 2 at Buffalo 4
May 25	Buffalo 1 at Philadelphia 5
May 27	Philadelphia 2 at Buffalo 0 [Parent]

Philadelphia won best-of-seven finals 4–2

1975–76

PRINCE OF WALES CONFERENCE
Adams Division

	GP	W	L	T	GF	GA	PTS
Boston	80	48	15	17	313	237	113
Buffalo	80	46	21	13	339	240	105
Toronto	80	34	31	15	294	276	83
California	80	27	42	11	250	278	65

Norris Division

	GP	W	L	T	GF	GA	PTS
Canadiens	80	58	11	11	337	174	127
Los Angeles	80	38	33	9	263	265	85
Pittsburgh	80	35	33	12	339	303	82
Detroit	80	26	44	10	226	300	62
Washington	80	11	59	10	224	394	32

CLARENCE CAMPBELL CONFERENCE
Patrick Division

	GP	W	L	T	GF	GA	PTS
Philadelphia	80	51	13	16	348	209	118
Islanders	80	42	21	17	297	190	101
Flames	80	35	33	12	262	237	82
Rangers	80	29	42	9	262	333	67

Smythe Division

Chicago	80	32	30	18	254	261	82
Vancouver	80	33	32	15	271	272	81
St. Louis	80	29	37	14	249	290	72
North Stars	80	20	53	7	195	303	47
Kansas City	80	12	56	12	190	351	36

Stanley Cup Finals

May 9	Philadelphia 3 at Canadiens 4
May 11	Philadelphia 1 at Canadiens 2
May 13	Canadiens 3 at Philadelphia 2
May 16	Canadiens 5 at Philadelphia 3

Canadiens won best-of-seven finals 4–0

1976–77

PRINCE OF WALES CONFERENCE

Adams Division

	GP	W	L	T	GF	GA	PTS
Boston	80	49	23	8	312	240	106
Buffalo	80	48	24	8	301	220	104
Toronto	80	33	32	15	301	285	81
Cleveland	80	25	42	13	240	292	63

Norris Division

Canadiens	80	60	8	12	387	171	132
Los Angeles	80	34	31	15	271	241	83
Pittsburgh	80	34	33	13	240	252	81
Washington	80	24	42	14	221	307	62
Detroit	80	16	55	9	183	309	41

CLARENCE CAMPBELL CONFERENCE

Patrick Division

Philadelphia	80	48	16	16	323	213	112
Islanders	80	47	21	12	288	193	106
Flames	80	34	34	12	264	265	80
Rangers	80	29	37	14	272	310	64

Smythe Division

St. Louis	80	32	39	9	239	276	73
North Stars	80	23	39	18	240	310	64
Chicago	80	26	43	11	240	298	63
Vancouver	80	25	42	13	235	294	63
Rockies	80	20	46	14	226	307	54

Stanley Cup Finals

May 7	Boston 3 at Canadiens 7
May 10	Boston 0 at Canadiens 3 [Dryden]
May 12	Canadiens 4 at Boston 2
May 14	Canadiens 2 at Boston 1

Canadiens won best-of-seven finals 4–0

1977–78

PRINCE OF WALES CONFERENCE

Adams Division

	GP	W	L	T	GF	GA	PTS
Boston	80	51	18	11	333	218	113
Buffalo	80	44	19	17	288	215	105
Toronto	80	41	29	10	271	237	92
Cleveland	80	22	45	13	230	325	57

Norris Division

Canadiens	80	59	10	11	359	183	129
Detroit	80	32	34	14	252	266	78
Los Angeles	80	31	34	15	243	245	77
Pittsburgh	80	25	37	18	254	321	68
Washington	80	17	49	14	195	321	48

CLARENCE CAMPBELL CONFERENCE

Patrick Division

Islanders	80	48	17	15	334	210	111
Philadelphia	80	45	20	15	296	200	105
Flames	80	34	27	19	274	252	87
Rangers	80	30	37	13	279	280	73

Smythe Division

Chicago	80	32	29	19	230	220	83
Rockies	80	19	40	21	257	305	59
Vancouver	80	20	43	17	239	320	57
St. Louis	80	20	47	13	195	304	53
North Stars	80	18	53	9	218	325	45

* all 1st- and 2nd-place teams qualified for playoffs and the next best four regardless of division also qualified

Stanley Cup Finals

May 13	Boston 1 at Canadiens 4
May 16	Boston 2 at Canadiens 3 (Guy Lafleur 13:09 OT)
May 18	Canadiens 0 at Boston 4 [Cheevers]
May 21	Canadiens 3 at Boston 4 (Bobby Schmautz 6:22 OT)
May 23	Boston 1 at Canadiens 4
May 25	Canadiens 4 at Boston 1

Canadiens won best-of-seven finals 4–2

1978–79

PRINCE OF WALES CONFERENCE

Adams Division

	GP	W	L	T	GF	GA	PTS
Boston	80	43	23	14	316	270	100
Buffalo	80	36	28	16	280	263	88
Toronto	80	34	33	13	267	252	81
North Stars	80	28	40	12	257	289	68

Norris Division

Canadiens	80	52	17	11	337	204	115
Pittsburgh	80	36	31	13	281	279	85
Los Angeles	80	34	34	12	292	286	80
Washington	80	24	41	15	273	338	63
Detroit	80	23	41	16	252	295	62

CLARENCE CAMPBELL CONFERENCE
PATRICK DIVISION

Islanders	80	51	15	14	358	214	116
Philadelphia	80	40	25	15	281	248	95
Rangers	80	40	29	11	316	292	91
Flames	80	41	31	8	327	280	90

Smythe Division

Chicago	80	29	36	15	244	277	73
Vancouver	80	25	42	13	217	291	63
St. Louis	80	18	50	12	249	348	48
Rockies	80	15	53	12	210	331	42

Stanley Cup Finals

May 13	Rangers 4 at Canadiens 1
May 15	Rangers 2 at Canadiens 6
May 17	Canadiens 4 at Rangers 1
May 19	Canadiens 4 at Rangers 3 (Serge Savard 7:25 OT)
May 21	Rangers 1 at Canadiens 4

Canadiens won best-of-seven finals 4–1

1979–80

PRINCE OF WALES CONFERENCE
Adams Division

	GP	W	L	T	GF	GA	PTS
Buffalo	80	47	17	16	318	201	110
Boston	80	46	21	13	310	234	105
North Stars	80	36	28	16	311	253	88
Toronto	80	35	40	5	304	327	75
Quebec	80	25	44	11	248	313	61

Norris Division

	GP	W	L	T	GF	GA	PTS
Canadiens	80	47	20	13	328	240	107
Los Angeles	80	30	36	14	290	313	74
Pittsburgh	80	30	37	13	251	303	73
Hartford	80	27	34	19	303	312	73
Detroit	80	26	43	11	268	306	63

CLARENCE CAMPBELL CONFERENCE
PATRICK DIVISION

	GP	W	L	T	GF	GA	PTS
Philadelphia	80	48	12	20	327	254	116
Islanders	80	39	28	13	281	247	91
Rangers	80	38	32	10	308	284	86
Flames	80	35	32	13	282	269	83
Washington	80	27	40	13	261	293	67

Smythe Division

	GP	W	L	T	GF	GA	PTS
Chicago	80	34	27	19	241	250	87
St. Louis	80	34	34	12	266	278	80
Vancouver	80	27	37	16	256	281	70
Edmonton	80	28	39	13	301	322	69
Winnipeg	80	20	49	11	214	314	51
Rockies	80	19	48	13	234	308	51

* top four teams in each division qualified for the playoffs

Stanley Cup Finals

May 13	Islanders 4 at Philadelphia 3 (Denis Potvin 4:07 OT)
May 15	Islanders 3 at Philadelphia 8
May 17	Philadelphia 2 at Islanders 6
May 19	Philadelphia 2 at Islanders 5
May 22	Islanders 3 at Philadelphia 6
May 24	Philadelphia 4 at Islanders 5 (Bob Nystrom 7:11 OT)

Islanders won best-of-seven finals 4–2

1980–81

PRINCE OF WALES CONFERENCE

Adams Division

	GP	W	L	T	GF	GA	PTS
Buffalo	80	39	20	21	327	250	99
Boston	80	37	30	13	316	272	87
North Stars	80	35	28	17	291	263	87
Quebec	80	30	32	18	314	318	78
Toronto	80	28	37	15	322	367	71

Norris Division

Canadiens	80	45	22	13	332	232	103
Los Angeles	80	43	24	13	337	290	99
Pittsburgh	80	30	37	13	302	345	73
Hartford	80	21	41	18	292	372	60
Detroit	80	19	43	18	252	339	56

CLARENCE CAMPBELL CONFERENCE

Patrick Division

Islanders	80	48	18	14	355	260	110
Philadelphia	80	41	24	15	313	249	97
Calgary	80	39	27	14	329	298	92
Rangers	80	30	36	14	312	317	74
Washington	80	26	36	18	286	317	70

Smythe Division

St. Louis	80	45	18	17	352	281	107
Chicago	80	31	33	16	304	315	78
Vancouver	80	28	32	20	289	301	76
Edmonton	80	29	35	16	328	327	74
Rockies	80	22	45	13	258	344	57
Winnipeg	80	9	57	14	246	400	32

Stanley Cup Finals

May 12	North Stars 3 at Islanders 6
May 14	North Stars 3 at Islanders 6
May 17	Islanders 7 at North Stars 5
May 19	Islanders 2 at North Stars 4
May 21	North Stars 1 at Islanders 5

Islanders won best-of-seven finals 4–1

1981–82

CLARENCE CAMPBELL CONFERENCE

Norris Division

	GP	W	L	T	GF	GA	PTS
North Stars	80	37	23	20	346	288	94
Winnipeg	80	33	33	14	319	332	80
St. Louis	80	32	40	8	315	349	72
Chicago	80	30	38	12	332	363	72
Toronto	80	20	44	16	298	380	56
Detroit	80	21	47	12	270	351	54

Smythe Division

Edmonton	80	48	17	15	417	295	111
Vancouver	80	30	33	17	290	286	77
Calgary	80	29	34	17	334	345	75
Los Angeles	80	24	41	15	314	369	63
Rockies	80	18	49	13	241	362	49

PRINCE OF WALES CONFERENCE

Adams Division

Canadiens	80	46	17	17	360	223	109
Boston	80	43	27	10	323	285	96
Buffalo	80	39	26	15	307	273	93
Quebec	80	33	31	16	356	345	82
Hartford	80	21	41	18	264	351	60

Patrick Division

Islanders	80	54	16	10	385	250	118
Rangers	80	39	27	14	316	306	92
Philadelphia	80	38	31	11	325	313	87
Pittsburgh	80	31	36	13	310	337	75
Washington	80	26	41	13	319	338	65

Stanley Cup Finals

May 8	Vancouver 5 at Islanders 6 (Mike Bossy 19:58 OT)
May 11	Vancouver 4 at Islanders 6
May 13	Islanders 3 at Vancouver 0 [Smith]
May 16	Islanders 3 at Vancouver 1

Islanders won best-of-seven finals 4–0

1982–83

CLARENCE CAMPBELL CONFERENCE

Norris Division

	GP	W	L	T	GF	GA	PTS
Chicago	80	47	23	10	338	268	104
North Stars	80	40	24	16	321	290	96
Toronto	80	28	40	12	293	330	68
St. Louis	80	25	40	15	285	316	65
Detroit	80	21	44	15	263	344	57

Smythe Division

Edmonton	80	47	21	12	424	315	106
Calgary	80	32	34	14	321	317	78
Vancouver	80	30	35	15	303	309	75
Winnipeg	80	33	39	8	311	333	74
Los Angeles	80	27	41	12	308	365	66

PRINCE OF WALES CONFERENCE

Adams Division

Boston	80	50	20	10	327	228	110
Canadiens	80	42	24	14	350	286	98
Buffalo	80	38	29	13	318	285	89
Quebec	80	34	34	12	343	336	80
Hartford	80	19	54	7	261	403	45

Patrick Division

Philadelphia	80	49	23	8	326	240	106
Islanders	80	42	26	12	302	226	96
Washington	80	39	25	16	306	283	94
Rangers	80	35	35	10	306	287	80
New Jersey	80	17	49	14	230	338	48
Pittsburgh	80	18	53	9	257	394	45

Stanley Cup Finals

May 10	Islanders 2 at Edmonton 0 [Smith]
May 12	Islanders 6 at Edmonton 3
May 14	Edmonton 1 at Islanders 5
May 17	Edmonton 2 at Islanders 4

Islanders won best-of-seven finals 4–0

1983–84

CLARENCE CAMPBELL CONFERENCE

Norris Division

	GP	W	L	T	GF	GA	PTS
North Stars	80	39	31	10	345	344	88
St. Louis	80	32	41	7	293	316	71
Detroit	80	31	42	7	298	323	69
Chicago	80	30	42	8	277	311	68
Toronto	80	26	45	9	303	387	61

Smythe Division

	GP	W	L	T	GF	GA	PTS
Edmonton	80	57	18	5	446	314	119
Calgary	80	34	32	14	311	314	82
Vancouver	80	32	39	9	306	328	73
Winnipeg	80	31	38	11	340	374	73
Los Angeles	80	23	44	13	309	376	59

PRINCE OF WALES CONFERENCE

Adams Division

	GP	W	L	T	GF	GA	PTS
Boston	80	49	25	6	336	261	104
Buffalo	80	48	25	7	315	257	103
Quebec	80	42	28	10	360	278	94
Canadiens	80	35	40	5	286	295	75
Hartford	80	28	42	10	288	320	66

Patrick Division

	GP	W	L	T	GF	GA	PTS
Islanders	80	50	26	4	357	269	104
Washington	80	48	27	5	308	226	101
Philadelphia	80	44	26	10	350	290	98
Rangers	80	42	29	9	314	304	93
New Jersey	80	17	56	7	231	350	41
Pittsburgh	80	16	58	6	254	390	38

* five-minute sudden-death overtime introduced for regular-season games

Stanley Cup Finals

May 10	Edmonton 1 at Islanders 0 [Fuhr]
May 12	Edmonton 1 at Islanders 6
May 15	Islanders 2 at Edmonton 7
May 17	Islanders 2 at Edmonton 7
May 19	Islanders 2 at Edmonton 5

Edmonton won best-of-seven finals 4–1

1984–85

CLARENCE CAMPBELL CONFERENCE

Norris Division

	GP	W	L	T	GF	GA	PTS
St. Louis	80	37	31	12	299	288	86
Chicago	80	38	35	7	309	299	83
Detroit	80	27	41	12	313	357	66
North Stars	80	25	43	12	268	321	62
Toronto	80	20	52	8	253	358	48

Smythe Division

	GP	W	L	T	GF	GA	PTS
Edmonton	80	49	20	11	401	298	109
Winnipeg	80	43	27	10	358	332	96
Calgary	80	41	27	12	363	302	94
Los Angeles	80	34	32	14	339	326	82
Vancouver	80	25	46	9	284	401	59

PRINCE OF WALES CONFERENCE

Adams Division

	GP	W	L	T	GF	GA	PTS
Canadiens	80	41	27	12	309	262	94
Quebec	80	41	30	9	323	275	91
Buffalo	80	38	28	14	290	237	90
Boston	80	36	34	10	303	287	82
Hartford	80	30	41	9	268	318	69

Patrick Division

Philadelphia	80	53	20	7	348	241	113
Washington	80	46	25	9	322	240	101
Islanders	80	40	34	6	345	312	86
Rangers	80	26	44	10	295	345	62
New Jersey	80	22	48	10	264	346	54
Pittsburgh	80	24	51	5	276	385	53

Stanley Cup Finals

May 21	Edmonton 1 at Philadelphia 4
May 23	Edmonton 3 at Philadelphia 1
May 25	Philadelphia 3 at Edmonton 4
May 28	Philadelphia 3 at Edmonton 5
May 30	Philadelphia 3 at Edmonton 8

Edmonton won best-of-seven finals 4–1

1985–86

CLARENCE CAMPBELL CONFERENCE

Norris Division

	GP	W	L	T	GF	GA	PTS
Chicago	80	39	33	8	351	349	86
North Stars	80	38	33	9	327	305	85
St. Louis	80	37	34	9	302	291	83
Toronto	80	25	48	7	311	386	57
Detroit	80	17	57	6	266	415	40

Smythe Division

Edmonton	80	56	17	7	426	310	119
Calgary	80	40	31	9	354	315	89
Winnipeg	80	26	47	7	295	372	59
Vancouver	80	23	44	13	282	333	59
Los Angeles	80	23	49	8	284	389	54

PRINCE OF WALES CONFERENCE
Adams Division

Quebec	80	43	31	6	330	289	92
Canadiens	80	40	33	7	330	280	87
Boston	80	37	31	12	311	288	86
Hartford	80	40	36	4	332	302	84
Buffalo	80	37	37	6	296	291	80

Patrick Division

Philadelphia	80	53	23	4	335	241	110
Washington	80	50	23	7	315	272	107
Islanders	80	39	29	12	327	284	90
Rangers	80	36	38	6	280	276	78
Pittsburgh	80	34	38	8	313	305	76
New Jersey	80	28	49	3	300	374	59

Stanley Cup Finals

May 16	Canadiens 2 at Calgary 5
May 18	Canadiens 3 at Calgary 2 (Brian Skrudland 0:09 OT)
May 20	Calgary 3 at Canadiens 5
May 22	Calgary 0 at Canadiens 1 [Roy]
May 24	Canadiens 4 at Calgary 3

Canadiens won best-of-seven finals 4–1

1986–87

CLARENCE CAMPBELL CONFERENCE
Norris Division

	GP	W	L	T	GF	G	PTS
St. Louis	80	32	33	15	281	293	79
Detroit	80	34	36	10	260	274	78
Chicago*	80	29	37	14	290	310	72
Toronto	80	32	42	6	286	319	70
North Stars	80	30	40	10	296	314	70

Smythe Division

Edmonton	80	50	24	6	372	284	106
Calgary	80	46	31	3	318	289	95
Winnipeg	80	40	32	8	279	271	88
Los Angeles	80	31	41	8	318	341	70
Vancouver	80	29	43	8	282	314	66

PRINCE OF WALES CONFERENCE

Adams Division

Hartford	80	43	30	7	287	270	93
Canadiens	80	41	29	10	277	241	92
Boston	80	39	34	7	301	276	85
Quebec	80	31	39	10	267	276	72
Buffalo	80	28	44	8	280	308	64

Patrick Division

Philadelphia	80	46	26	8	310	245	100
Washington	80	38	32	10	285	278	86
Islanders	80	35	33	12	279	281	82
Rangers	80	34	38	8	307	323	76
Pittsburgh	80	30	38	12	297	290	72
New Jersey	80	29	45	6	293	368	64

* Chicago changed spelling of nickname from Black Hawks to Blackhawks at start of season

Stanley Cup Finals

May 17	Philadelphia 2 at Edmonton 4
May 20	Philadelphia 2 at Edmonton 3 (Jari Kurri 6:50 OT)
May 22	Edmonton 3 at Philadelphia 5
May 24	Edmonton 4 at Philadelphia 1
May 26	Philadelphia 4 at Edmonton 3
May 28	Edmonton 2 at Philadelphia 3
May 31	Philadelphia 1 at Edmonton 3

Edmonton won best-of-seven finals 4–3

1987–88

CLARENCE CAMPBELL CONFERENCE
Norris Division

	GP	W	L	T	GF	GA	PTS
Detroit	80	41	28	11	322	269	93
St. Louis	80	34	38	8	278	294	76
Chicago	80	30	41	9	284	326	69
Toronto	80	21	49	10	273	345	52
North Stars	80	19	48	13	242	349	51

Smythe Division

	GP	W	L	T	GF	GA	PTS
Calgary	80	48	23	9	397	305	105
Edmonton	80	44	25	11	363	288	99
Winnipeg	80	33	36	11	292	310	77
Los Angeles	80	30	42	8	318	359	68
Vancouver	80	25	46	9	272	320	59

PRINCE OF WALES CONFERENCE
Adams Division

	GP	W	L	T	GF	GA	PTS
Canadiens	80	45	22	13	298	238	103
Boston	80	44	30	6	300	251	94
Buffalo	80	37	32	11	283	305	85
Hartford	80	35	38	7	249	267	77
Quebec	80	32	43	5	271	306	69

Patrick Division

	GP	W	L	T	GF	GA	PTS
Islanders	80	39	31	10	308	267	88
Washington	80	38	33	9	281	249	85
Philadelphia	80	38	33	9	292	282	85
New Jersey	80	38	36	6	295	296	82
Rangers	80	36	34	10	300	283	82
Pittsburgh	80	36	35	9	319	316	81

Stanley Cup Finals

May 18	Boston 1 at Edmonton 2
May 20	Boston 2 at Edmonton 4
May 22	Edmonton 6 at Boston 3
May 24	Edmonton 3 at Boston 3*
May 26	Boston 3 at Edmonton 6

Edmonton won best-of-seven finals 4–0

* game suspended because of power failure but statistics counted (if necessary, this game would have been made up at the end of the series)

1988–1989

CLARENCE CAMPBELL CONFERENCE

Norris Division

	GP	W	L	T	GF	GA	PTS
Detroit	80	34	34	12	313	316	80
St. Louis	80	33	35	12	275	285	78
North Stars	80	27	37	16	258	278	70
Chicago	80	27	41	12	297	335	66
Toronto	80	28	46	6	259	342	62

Smythe Division

Calgary	80	54	17	9	354	226	117
Los Angeles	80	42	31	7	376	335	91
Edmonton	80	38	34	8	325	306	84
Vancouver	80	33	39	8	251	253	74
Winnipeg	80	26	42	12	300	355	64

PRINCE OF WALES CONFERENCE

Adams Division

Canadiens	80	53	18	9	315	218	115
Boston	80	37	29	14	289	256	88
Buffalo	80	38	35	7	291	299	83
Hartford	80	37	38	5	299	290	79
Quebec	80	27	46	7	269	342	61

Patrick Division

Washington	80	41	29	10	305	259	92
Pittsburgh	80	40	33	7	347	349	87
Rangers	80	37	35	8	310	307	82
Philadelphia	80	36	36	8	307	285	80
New Jersey	80	27	41	12	281	325	66
Islanders	80	28	47	5	265	325	61

Stanley Cup Finals

May 14	Canadiens 2 at Calgary 3
May 17	Canadiens 4 at Calgary 2
May 19	Calgary 3 at Canadiens 4 (Ryan Walter 38:08 OT)
May 21	Calgary 4 at Canadiens 2
May 23	Calgary 2 at Canadiens 3
May 25	Calgary 4 at Canadiens 2

Calgary won best-of-seven finals 4–2

1989–90
CLARENCE CAMPBELL CONFERENCE
Norris Division

	GP	W	L	T	GF	GA	PTS
Chicago	80	41	33	6	316	294	88
St. Louis	80	37	34	9	295	279	83
Toronto	80	38	38	4	337	358	80
North Stars	80	36	40	4	284	291	76
Detroit	80	28	38	14	288	323	70

Smythe Division

Calgary	80	42	23	15	348	265	99
Edmonton	80	38	28	14	315	283	90
Winnipeg	80	37	32	11	298	290	85
Los Angeles	80	34	39	7	338	337	75
Vancouver	80	25	41	14	245	306	64

PRINCE OF WALES CONFERENCE
Adams Division

Boston	80	46	25	9	289	232	101
Buffalo	80	45	27	8	286	248	98
Canadiens	80	41	28	11	288	234	93
Hartford	80	38	33	9	275	268	85
Quebec	80	12	61	7	240	407	31

Patrick Division

Rangers	80	36	31	13	279	267	85
New Jersey	80	37	34	9	295	288	83
Washington	80	36	38	6	284	275	78
Islanders	80	31	38	11	281	288	73
Pittsburgh	80	32	40	8	318	359	72
Philadelphia	80	30	39	11	290	297	71

Stanley Cup Finals

May 15	Edmonton 3 at Boston 2 (Petr Klima 55:13 OT)
May 18	Edmonton 7 at Boston 2
May 20	Boston 2 at Edmonton 1
May 22	Boston 1 at Edmonton 5
May 24	Edmonton 4 at Boston 1

Edmonton won best-of-seven finals 4–1

1990–91

CLARENCE CAMPBELL CONFERENCE
Norris Division

	GP	W	L	T	GF	GA	PTS
Chicago	80	49	23	8	284	211	106
St. Louis	80	47	22	11	310	250	105
Detroit	80	34	38	8	273	298	76
North Stars	80	27	39	14	256	266	68
Toronto	80	23	46	11	241	318	57

Smythe Division

Los Angeles	80	46	24	10	340	254	102
Calgary	80	46	26	8	344	263	100
Edmonton	80	37	37	6	272	272	80
Vancouver	80	28	43	9	243	315	65
Winnipeg	80	26	43	11	260	288	63

Prince of Wales Conference

Adams Division

Boston	80	44	24	12	299	264	100
Canadiens	80	39	30	11	273	249	89
Buffalo	80	31	30	19	292	278	81
Hartford	80	31	38	11	238	276	73
Quebec	80	16	50	14	236	354	46

Patrick Division

Pittsburgh	80	41	33	6	342	305	88
Rangers	80	36	31	13	297	265	85
Washington	80	37	36	7	258	258	81
New Jersey	80	32	33	15	272	264	79
Philadelphia	80	33	37	10	252	267	76
Islanders	80	25	45	10	223	290	60

Stanley Cup Finals

May 15	Minnesota 5 at Pittsburgh 4
May 17	Minnesota 1 at Pittsburgh 4
May 19	Pittsburgh 1 at Minnesota 3
May 21	Pittsburgh 5 at Minnesota 3
May 23	Minnesota 4 at Pittsburgh 6
May 25	Pittsburgh 8 at Minnesota 0 [Barrasso]

Pittsburgh won best-of-seven finals 4–2

1991–92
CLARENCE CAMPBELL CONFERENCE
Norris Division

	GP	W	L	T	GF	GA	PTS
Detroit	80	43	25	12	320	256	98
Chicago	80	36	29	15	257	236	87
St. Louis	80	36	33	11	279	266	83
North Stars	80	32	42	6	246	278	70
Toronto	80	30	43	7	234	294	67

Smythe Division

	GP	W	L	T	GF	GA	PTS
Vancouver	80	42	26	12	285	250	96
Los Angeles	80	35	31	14	287	296	84
Edmonton	80	36	34	10	295	297	82
Winnipeg	80	33	32	15	251	244	81
Calgary	80	31	37	12	296	305	74
San Jose	80	17	58	5	219	359	39

PRINCE OF WALES CONFERENCE
Adams Division

	GP	W	L	T	GF	GA	PTS
Canadiens	80	41	28	11	267	207	93
Boston	80	36	32	12	270	275	84
Buffalo	80	31	37	12	289	299	74
Hartford	80	26	41	13	247	283	65
Quebec	80	20	48	12	255	318	52

Patrick Division

	GP	W	L	T	GF	GA	PTS
Rangers	80	50	25	5	321	246	105
Washington	80	45	27	8	330	275	98
Pittsburgh	80	39	32	9	343	308	87
New Jersey	80	38	31	11	289	259	87
Islanders	80	34	35	11	291	299	79
Philadelphia	80	32	37	11	252	273	75

Stanley Cup Finals

May 26	Chicago 4 at Pittsburgh 5
May 28	Chicago 1 at Pittsburgh 3
May 30	Pittsburgh 1 at Chicago 0 [Barrasso]
June 1	Pittsburgh 6 at Chicago 5

Pittsburgh won best-of-seven finals 4–0

1992–93

CLARENCE CAMPBELL CONFERENCE
Norris Division

	GP	W	L	T	GF	GA	PTS
Chicago	84	47	25	12	279	230	106
Detroit	84	47	28	9	369	280	103
Toronto	84	44	29	11	288	241	99
St. Louis	84	37	36	11	282	278	85
North Stars	84	36	38	10	272	293	82
Tampa Bay	84	23	54	7	245	332	53

Smythe Division

	GP	W	L	T	GF	GA	PTS
Vancouver	84	46	29	9	346	278	101
Calgary	84	43	30	11	322	282	97
Los Angeles	84	39	35	10	338	340	88
Winnipeg	84	40	37	7	322	320	87
Edmonton	84	26	50	8	242	337	60
San Jose	84	11	71	2	218	414	24

PRINCE OF WALES CONFERENCE
Adams Division

	GP	W	L	T	GF	GA	PTS
Boston	84	51	26	7	332	268	109
Quebec	84	47	27	10	351	300	104
Canadiens	84	48	30	6	326	280	102
Buffalo	84	38	36	10	335	297	86
Hartford	84	26	52	6	284	369	58
Ottawa	84	10	70	4	202	395	24

Patrick Division

Pittsburgh	84	56	21	7	367	268	119
Washington	84	43	34	7	325	286	93
Islanders	84	40	37	7	335	297	87
New Jersey	84	40	37	7	308	299	87
Philadelphia	84	36	37	11	319	319	83
Rangers	84	34	39	11	304	308	79

Stanley Cup Finals

June 1	Los Angeles 4 at Canadiens 1
June 3	Los Angeles 2 at Canadiens 3 (Eric Desjardins 0:51 OT)
June 5	Canadiens 4 at Los Angeles 3 (John LeClair 0:34 OT)
June 7	Canadiens 3 at Los Angeles 2 (John LeClair 14:37 OT)
June 9	Los Angeles 1 at Canadiens 4

Canadiens won best-of-seven finals 4–1

1993–94

WESTERN CONFERENCE
Central Division

	GP	W	L	T	GF	GA	PTS
Detroit	84	46	30	8	356	275	100
Toronto	84	43	29	12	280	243	98
Dallas	84	42	29	13	286	265	97
St. Louis	84	40	33	11	270	283	91
Chicago	84	39	36	9	254	240	87
Winnipeg	84	24	51	9	245	344	57

Pacific Division

Calgary	84	42	29	13	302	256	97
Vancouver	84	41	40	3	279	276	85
San Jose	84	33	35	16	252	265	82
Anaheim	84	33	46	5	229	251	71
Los Angeles	84	27	45	12	294	322	66
Edmonton	84	25	45	14	261	305	64

EASTERN CONFERENCE
Northeast Division

Pittsburgh	84	44	27	13	299	285	101
Boston	84	42	29	13	289	252	97
Canadiens	84	41	29	14	283	248	96
Buffalo	84	43	32	9	282	218	95
Quebec	84	34	42	8	277	292	76
Hartford	84	27	48	9	227	288	63
Ottawa	84	14	61	9	201	397	37

Atlantic Division

Rangers	84	52	24	8	299	231	112
New Jersey	84	47	25	12	306	220	106
Washington	84	39	35	10	277	263	88
Islanders	84	36	36	12	282	264	84
Florida	84	33	34	17	233	233	83
Philadelphia	84	35	39	10	294	314	80
Tampa Bay	84	30	43	11	224	251	71

* the top eight teams in each conference qualified for the playoffs

Stanley Cup Finals

May 31	Vancouver 3 at Rangers 2 (Greg Adams 19:26 OT)
June 2	Vancouver 1 at Rangers 3
June 4	Rangers 5 at Vancouver 1
June 7	Rangers 4 at Vancouver 2
June 9	Vancouver 6 at Rangers 3
June 11	Rangers 1 at Vancouver 4
June 14	Vancouver 2 at Rangers 3

Rangers won best-of-seven finals 4–3

1994–95

WESTERN CONFERENCE
Central Division

	GP	W	L	T	GF	GA	PTS
Detroit	48	33	11	4	180	117	70
St. Louis	48	28	15	5	178	135	61
Chicago	48	24	19	5	156	115	53
Toronto	48	21	19	8	135	146	50
Dallas	48	17	23	8	136	135	42
Winnipeg	48	16	25	7	157	177	39

Pacific Division

	GP	W	L	T	GF	GA	PTS
Calgary	48	24	17	7	163	135	55
Vancouver	48	18	18	12	153	148	48
San Jose	48	19	25	4	129	161	42
Los Angeles	48	16	23	9	142	174	41
Edmonton	48	17	27	4	136	183	38
Anaheim	48	16	27	5	125	164	37

EASTERN CONFERENCE
Northeast Division

	GP	W	L	T	GF	GA	PTS
Quebec	48	30	13	5	185	134	65
Pittsburgh	48	29	16	3	181	158	61
Boston	48	27	18	3	150	127	57
Buffalo	48	22	19	7	130	119	51
Hartford	48	19	24	5	127	141	43
Canadiens	48	18	23	7	125	148	43
Ottawa	48	9	34	5	116	174	23

Atlantic Division

Philadelphia	48	28	16	4	150	132	60
New Jersey	48	22	18	8	136	121	52
Washington	48	22	18	8	136	120	52
Rangers	48	22	23	3	139	134	47
Florida	48	20	22	6	115	127	46
Tampa Bay	48	17	28	3	120	144	37
Islanders	48	15	28	5	126	158	35

Stanley Cup Finals

June 17	New Jersey 2 at Detroit 1
June 20	New Jersey 4 at Detroit 2
June 22	Detroit 2 at New Jersey 5
June 24	Detroit 2 at New Jersey 5

New Jersey won best-of-seven finals 4–0

1995–96

WESTERN CONFERENCE

Central Division

	GP	W	L	T	GF	GA	PTS
Detroit	82	62	13	7	325	181	131
Chicago	82	40	28	14	273	220	94
Toronto	82	34	36	12	247	252	80
St. Louis	82	32	34	16	219	248	80
Winnipeg	82	36	40	6	275	291	78
Dallas	82	26	42	14	227	280	66

Pacific Division

Colorado	82	47	25	10	326	240	104
Calgary	82	34	37	11	241	240	79
Vancouver	82	32	35	15	278	278	79
Anaheim	82	35	39	8	234	247	78
Edmonton	82	30	44	8	240	304	68
Los Angeles	82	24	40	18	256	302	66
San Jose	82	20	55	7	252	357	47

EASTERN CONFERENCE

Northeast Division

Pittsburgh	82	49	29	4	362	284	102
Boston	82	40	31	11	282	269	91
Canadiens	82	40	32	10	265	248	90
Hartford	82	34	39	9	237	259	77
Buffalo	82	33	42	7	247	262	73
Ottawa	82	18	59	5	191	291	41

Atlantic Division

Philadelphia	82	45	24	13	282	208	103
Rangers	82	41	27	14	272	237	96
Florida	82	41	31	10	254	234	92
Washington	82	39	32	11	234	204	89
Tampa Bay	82	38	32	12	238	248	88
New Jersey	82	37	33	12	215	202	86
Islanders	82	22	50	10	229	315	54

Stanley Cup Finals

June 4	Florida 1 at Colorado 3
June 6	Florida 1 at Colorado 8
June 8	Colorado 3 at Florida 2
June 10	Colorado 1 at Florida 0 (Uwe Krupp 44:31 OT) [Roy]

Colorado won best-of seven finals 4–0

1996–97

WESTERN CONFERENCE
Central Division

	GP	W	L	T	GF	GA	PTS
Dallas	82	48	26	8	252	198	104
Detroit	82	38	26	18	253	197	94
Phoenix	82	38	37	7	240	243	83
St. Louis	82	36	35	11	236	239	83
Chicago	82	34	35	13	223	210	81
Toronto	82	30	44	8	230	273	68

Pacific Division

	GP	W	L	T	GF	GA	PTS
Colorado	82	49	24	9	277	205	107
Anaheim	82	36	33	13	245	233	85
Edmonton	82	36	37	9	252	247	81
Vancouver	82	35	40	7	257	273	77
Calgary	82	32	41	9	214	239	73
Los Angeles	82	28	43	11	214	268	67
San Jose	82	27	47	8	211	278	62

EASTERN CONFERENCE
Northeast Division

	GP	W	L	T	GF	GA	PTS
Buffalo	82	40	30	12	237	208	92
Pittsburgh	82	38	36	8	285	280	84
Ottawa	82	31	36	15	226	234	77
Canadiens	82	31	36	15	249	276	77
Hartford	82	32	39	11	226	256	75
Boston	82	26	47	9	234	300	61

Atlantic Division

	GP	W	L	T	GF	GA	PTS
New Jersey	82	45	23	14	231	182	104
Philadelphia	82	45	24	13	274	217	103
Florida	82	35	28	19	221	201	89
Rangers	82	38	34	10	258	231	86

	GP	W	L	T	GF	GA	
Washington	82	33	40	9	214	231	75
Tampa Bay	82	32	40	10	217	247	74
Islanders	82	29	41	12	240	250	70

Stanley Cup Finals

May 31	Detroit 4 at Philadelphia 2
June 3	Detroit 4 at Philadelphia 2
June 5	Philadelphia 1 at Detroit 6
June 7	Philadelphia 1 at Detroit 2

Detroit won best-of-seven finals 4–0

1997–98

WESTERN CONFERENCE

Central Division

	GP	W	L	T	GF	GA	PTS
Dallas	82	49	22	11	242	167	109
Detroit	82	44	23	15	250	196	103
St. Louis	82	45	29	8	256	204	98
Phoenix	82	35	35	12	224	227	82
Chicago	82	30	39	13	192	199	73
Toronto	82	30	43	9	194	237	69

Pacific Division

	GP	W	L	T	GF	GA	PTS
Colorado	82	39	26	17	231	205	95
Los Angeles	82	38	33	11	227	225	87
Edmonton	82	35	37	10	215	224	80
San Jose	82	34	38	10	210	216	78
Calgary	82	26	41	15	217	252	67
Anaheim	82	26	43	13	205	261	65
Vancouver	82	25	43	14	224	273	64

EASTERN CONFERENCE
Northeast Division

Pittsburgh	82	40	24	18	228	188	98
Boston	82	39	30	13	221	194	91
Buffalo	82	36	29	17	211	187	89
Canadiens	82	37	32	13	235	208	87
Ottawa	82	34	33	15	193	20	83
Carolina	82	33	41	8	200	219	74

Atlantic Division

New Jersey	82	48	23	11	225	166	107
Philadelphia	82	42	29	11	242	193	95
Washington	82	40	30	12	219	202	92
Islanders	82	30	41	11	212	225	71
Rangers	82	25	39	18	197	231	68
Florida	82	24	43	15	203	256	63
Tampa Bay	82	17	55	10	151	269	44

Stanley Cup Finals

June 9	Washington 1 at Detroit 2
June 11	Washington 4 at Detroit 5 (Kris Draper 15:24 OT)
June 13	Detroit 2 at Washington 1
June 16	Detroit 4 at Washington 1

Detroit won best-of-seven finals 4–0

1998–99

EASTERN CONFERENCE

Northeast Division

	GP	W	L	T	GF	GA	PTS
Ottawa	82	44	23	15	239	179	103
Toronto	82	45	30	7	268	231	97
Boston	82	39	30	13	214	181	91
Buffalo	82	37	28	17	207	175	91
Canadiens	82	32	39	11	184	209	75

Atlantic Division

	GP	W	L	T	GF	GA	PTS
New Jersey	82	47	24	11	248	196	105
Philadelphia	82	37	26	19	231	196	93
Pittsburgh	82	38	30	14	242	225	90
Rangers	82	33	38	11	217	227	77
Islanders	82	24	48	10	194	244	58

Southeast Division

	GP	W	L	T	GF	GA	PTS
Carolina	82	34	30	18	210	202	86
Florida	82	30	34	18	210	228	78
Washington	82	31	45	6	200	218	68
Tampa Bay	82	19	54	9	179	292	47

WESTERN CONFERENCE

Central Division

	GP	W	L	T	GF	GA	PTS
Detroit	82	43	32	7	245	202	93
St. Louis	82	37	32	13	237	209	87
Chicago	82	29	41	12	202	248	70
Nashville	82	28	47	7	190	261	63

Pacific Division

Dallas	82	51	19	12	236	168	114
Phoenix	82	39	31	12	205	197	90
Anaheim	82	35	34	13	215	206	83
San Jose	82	31	33	18	196	191	80
Los Angeles	82	32	45	5	189	222	69

Northwest Division

Colorado	82	44	28	10	239	205	98
Edmonton	82	33	37	12	230	226	78
Calgary	82	30	40	12	211	234	72
Vancouver	82	23	47	12	192	258	58

Stanley Cup Finals

June 8	Buffalo 3 at Dallas 2 (Jason Woolley 15:30 OT)
June 10	Buffalo 2 at Dallas 4
June 12	Dallas 2 at Buffalo 1
June 15	Dallas 1 at Buffalo 2
June 17	Buffalo 0 at Dallas 2 [Belfour]
June 19	Dallas 2 at Buffalo 1 (Brett Hull 54:51 OT)

Dallas won best-of-seven finals 4–2

1999–2000

EASTERN CONFERENCE

Northeast Division

	GP	W	L	T	OTL	GF	GA	PTS
Toronto	82	45	30	7	3	246	222	100
Ottawa	82	41	30	11	2	244	210	95
Buffalo	82	35	36	11	4	213	204	85
Canadiens	82	35	38	9	4	196	194	83
Boston	82	24	39	19	6	210	248	73

Atlantic Division

Philadelphia	82	45	25	12	3	237	179	105
New Jersey	82	45	29	8	5	251	203	103
Pittsburgh	82	37	37	8	6	241	236	88
Rangers	82	29	42	12	3	218	246	73
Islanders	82	24	49	9	1	194	275	58

Southeast Division

Washington	82	44	26	12	2	227	194	102
Florida	82	43	33	6	6	244	209	98
Carolina	82	37	35	10	0	217	216	84
Tampa Bay	82	19	54	9	7	204	309	54
Atlanta	82	14	61	7	4	170	313	39

WESTERN CONFERENCE

Central Division

St. Louis	82	51	20	11	1	248	165	114
Detroit	82	48	24	10	2	278	210	108
Chicago	82	33	39	10	2	242	245	78
Nashville	82	28	47	7	7	199	240	70

Northwest Division

Colorado	82	42	29	11	1	233	201	96
Edmonton	82	32	34	16	8	226	212	88
Vancouver	82	30	37	15	8	227	237	83
Calgary	82	31	41	10	5	211	256	77

Pacific Division

Dallas	82	43	29	10	6	211	184	102
Los Angeles	82	39	31	12	4	245	228	94
Phoenix	82	39	35	8	4	232	228	90
San Jose	82	35	37	10	7	225	214	87
Anaheim	82	34	36	12	3	217	227	83

Stanley Cup Finals

May 30	Dallas 3 at New Jersey 7
June 1	Dallas 2 at New Jersey 1
June 3	New Jersey 2 at Dallas 1
June 5	New Jersey 3 at Dallas 1
June 8	Dallas 1 at New Jersey 0 (Mike Modano 46:21 OT) [Belfour]
June 10	New Jersey 2 at Dallas 1 (Jason Arnott 28:20 OT)

New Jersey won best-of-seven finals 4–2

2000–01

EASTERN CONFERENCE
Northeast Division

	GP	W	L	T	OTL	GF	GA	PTS
Ottawa	82	48	21	9	4	274	205	109
Buffalo	82	46	30	5	1	218	184	98
Toronto	82	37	29	11	5	232	207	90
Boston	82	36	30	8	8	227	249	88
Montreal	82	28	40	8	6	206	232	70

Atlantic Division

	GP	W	L	T	OTL	GF	GA	PTS
New Jersey	82	48	19	12	3	295	195	111
Philadelphia	82	43	25	11	3	240	207	100
Pittsburgh	82	42	28	9	3	281	256	96
Rangers	82	33	43	5	1	250	290	72
Islanders	82	21	51	7	3	185	268	52

Southeast Division

	GP	W	L	T	OTL	GF	GA	PTS
Washington	82	41	27	10	4	233	211	96
Carolina	82	38	32	9	3	212	225	88
Florida	82	22	38	13	9	200	246	66
Atlanta	82	23	45	12	2	211	289	60
Tampa Bay	82	24	47	6	5	201	280	59

WESTERN CONFERENCE
Central Division

Detroit	82	49	20	9	4	253	202	111
St. Louis	82	43	22	12	5	249	195	103
Nashville	82	34	36	9	3	186	200	80
Chicago	82	29	40	8	5	210	246	71
Columbus	82	28	39	9	6	190	233	71

Northwest Division

Colorado	82	52	16	10	4	270	192	118
Edmonton	82	39	28	12	3	243	222	93
Vancouver	82	36	28	11	7	239	238	90
Calgary	82	27	36	15	4	197	236	73
Minnesota	82	25	39	13	5	168	210	68

Pacific Division

Dallas	82	48	24	8	2	241	187	106
San Jose	82	40	27	12	3	217	192	95
Los Angeles	82	38	28	13	3	252	228	92
Phoenix	82	35	27	17	3	214	212	90
Anaheim	82	25	41	11	5	188	245	66

Stanley Cup Finals

May 26	New Jersey 0 at Colorado 5 [Roy]
May 29	New Jersey 2 at Colorado 1
May 31	Colorado 3 at New Jersey 1
June 2	Colorado 2 at New Jersey 3
June 4	New Jersey 4 at Colorado 1
June 7	Colorado 4 at New Jersey 0 [Roy]
June 9	New Jersey 1 at Colorado 3

Colorado won best-of-seven finals 4–3

2001–02

EASTERN CONFERENCE
Northeast Division

	GP	W	L	T	OTL	GF	GA	PTS
Boston	82	43	24	6	9	236	201	101
Toronto	82	43	25	10	4	249	207	100
Ottawa	82	39	27	9	7	243	208	94
Montreal	82	36	31	12	3	207	209	87
Buffalo	82	35	35	11	1	213	200	82

Atlantic Division

	GP	W	L	T	OTL	GF	GA	PTS
Philadelphia	82	42	27	10	3	234	192	97
Islanders	82	42	28	8	4	239	220	96
New Jersey	82	41	28	9	4	205	187	95
Rangers	82	36	38	4	4	227	258	80
Pittsburgh	82	28	41	8	5	198	249	69

Southeast Division

	GP	W	L	T	OTL	GF	GA	PTS
Carolina	82	35	26	16	5	217	217	91
Washington	82	36	33	11	2	228	240	85
Tampa Bay	82	27	40	11	4	178	219	69
Florida	82	22	44	10	6	180	250	60
Atlanta	82	19	47	11	5	187	288	54

WESTERN CONFERENCE
Central Division

	GP	W	L	T	OTL	GF	GA	PTS
Detroit	82	51	17	10	4	251	187	116
St. Louis	82	43	27	8	4	227	188	98
Chicago	82	41	27	13	1	216	207	96
Nashville	82	28	41	13	0	196	230	69
Columbus	82	22	47	8	5	164	255	57

Pacific Division

San Jose	82	44	27	8	3	248	199	99
Phoenix	82	40	27	9	6	228	210	95
Los Angeles	82	40	27	11	4	214	190	95
Dallas	82	36	28	13	5	215	213	90
Anaheim	82	29	42	8	3	175	198	69

Northwest Division

Colorado	82	42	28	8	1	212	169	99
Vancouver	82	42	30	7	3	254	211	94
Edmonton	82	38	28	12	4	205	182	92
Calgary	82	32	35	12	3	201	220	79
Minnesota	82	26	35	12	9	195	238	73

Stanley Cup Finals

June 4	Carolina 3 at Detroit 2
June 6	Carolina 1 at Detroit 3
June 8	Detroit 3 at Carolina 2
June 10	Detroit 3 at Carolina 0
June 13	Carolina 1 at Detroit 3

Detroit won best-of-seven finals 4–1

2002–03

EASTERN CONFERENCE

Northeast Division

	GP	W	L	T	OTL	GF	GA	PTS
Ottawa	82	52	21	8	1	263	182	113
Toronto	82	44	28	7	3	236	208	98
Boston	82	36	31	11	4	245	237	87
Montreal	82	30	35	8	9	206	234	77
Buffalo	82	27	37	10	8	190	219	72

Atlantic Division

New Jersey	82	46	20	10	6	216	166	108
Philadelphia	82	45	20	13	4	211	166	107
Islanders	82	35	34	11	2	224	231	83
Rangers	82	32	36	10	4	210	231	78
Pittsburgh	82	27	44	6	5	189	255	65

Southeast Division

Tampa Bay	82	36	25	16	5	219	210	93
Washington	82	39	29	8	6	224	220	92
Atlanta	82	31	39	7	5	226	284	74
Florida	82	24	36	13	9	176	237	70
Carolina	82	22	43	11	6	171	240	61

WESTERN CONFERENCE

Central Division

Detroit	82	48	20	10	4	269	203	110
St. Louis	82	41	24	11	6	253	222	99
Chicago	82	30	33	13	6	207	226	79
Nashville	82	27	35	13	7	183	206	74
Columbus	82	29	42	8	3	213	263	69

Pacific Division

Dallas	82	46	17	15	4	245	169	111
Anaheim	82	40	27	9	6	203	193	95
Los Angeles	82	33	37	6	6	203	221	78
Phoenix	82	31	35	11	5	204	230	78
San Jose	82	28	37	9	8	214	239	73

Northwest Division

Colorado	82	42	19	13	8	251	194	105
Vancouver	82	45	23	13	1	264	208	104
Minnesota	82	42	29	10	1	198	178	95

| Edmonton | 82 | 36 | 26 | 11 | 9 | 231 | 230 | 92 |
| Calgary | 82 | 29 | 36 | 13 | 4 | 186 | 228 | 75 |

Stanley Cup Finals

May 27	Anaheim 0 at New Jersey 3 [Brodeur]
May 29	Anaheim 0 at New Jersey 3 [Brodeur]
May 31	New Jersey 2 at Anaheim 3 (Ruslan Salei 6:59 OT)
June 2	New Jersey 0 at Anaheim 1 (Steve Thomas 0:39 OT) [Giguere]
June 5	Anaheim 3 at New Jersey 6
June 7	New Jersey 2 at Anaheim 5
June 9	Anaheim 0 at New Jersey 3 [Brodeur]

New Jersey won best-of-seven finals 4–3

2003–04

EASTERN CONFERENCE

Atlantic Division

	GP	W	L	T	OTL	PTS	GF	GA
Philadelphia	82	40	21	15	6	101	229	186
New Jersey	82	43	25	12	2	100	213	164
Islanders	82	38	29	11	4	91	237	210
Rangers	82	27	40	7	8	69	206	250
Pittsburgh	82	23	47	8	4	58	190	303

Northeast Division

	GP	W	L	T	OTL	PTS	GF	GA
Boston	82	41	19	15	7	104	209	188
Toronto	82	45	24	10	3	103	242	204
Ottawa	82	43	23	10	6	102	262	189
Montreal	82	41	30	7	4	93	208	192
Buffalo	82	37	34	7	4	85	220	221

Southeast Division

Tampa Bay	82	46	22	8	6	106	245	192
Atlanta	82	33	37	8	4	78	214	243
Carolina	82	28	34	14	6	76	172	209
Florida	82	28	35	15	4	75	188	221
Washington	82	23	46	10	3	59	186	253

WESTERN CONFERENCE

Central Division

Detroit	82	48	21	11	2	109	255	189
St. Louis	82	39	30	11	2	91	191	198
Nashville	82	38	29	11	4	91	216	217
Columbus	82	25	45	8	4	62	177	238
Chicago	82	20	43	11	8	59	188	259

Northwest Division

Vancouver	82	43	24	10	5	101	235	194
Colorado	82	40	22	13	7	100	236	198
Calgary	82	42	30	7	3	94	200	176
Edmonton	82	36	29	12	5	89	221	208
Minnesota	82	30	29	20	3	83	188	183

Pacific Division

San Jose	82	43	21	12	6	104	219	183
Dallas	82	41	26	13	2	97	194	175
Los Angeles	82	28	29	16	9	81	205	217
Anaheim	82	29	35	10	8	76	184	213
Phoenix	82	22	36	18	6	68	188	245

Note: overtime losses (OTL) are worth one point in the standings and are not included in the loss column (L)

Stanley Cup Finals

May 25	Calgary 4 at Tampa Bay 1
May 27	Calgary 1 at Tampa Bay 4

May 29	Tampa Bay 0 at Calgary 3 [Kiprusoff]
May 31	Tampa Bay 1 at Calgary 0 (Richards 2:48 1st) [Khabibulin]
June 3	Calgary 3 at Tampa Bay 2 (Saprykin 14:40 OT)
June 5	Tampa Bay 3 at Calgary 2 (St. Louis 20:33 OT)
June 7	Calgary 1 at Tampa Bay 2

Tampa Bay won best-of-seven finals 4–3

2005–06

EASTERN CONFERENCE

Northeast Division	GP	W	L	OTL	SOL	GF	GA	P
Ottawa Senators	82	52	21	3	6	314	211	113
Buffalo Sabres	82	52	24	1	5	281	239	110
Montreal Canadiens	82	42	31	6	3	243	247	93
Toronto Maple Leafs	82	41	33	1	7	257	270	90
Boston Bruins	82	29	37	8	8	230	266	74

Atlantic Division								
New Jersey Devils	82	46	27	5	4	242	229	101
Philadelphia Flyers	82	45	26	5	6	267	259	101
New York Rangers	82	44	26	8	4	257	215	100
New York Islanders	82	36	40	3	3	230	278	78
Pittsburgh Penguins	82	22	46	8	6	244	316	58

Southeast Division								
Carolina Hurricanes	82	52	22	6	2	294	260	112
Tampa Bay Lightning	82	43	33	2	4	252	260	92
Atlanta Thrashers	82	41	33	3	5	281	275	90
Florida Panthers	82	37	34	6	5	240	257	85
Washington Capitals	82	29	41	6	6	237	306	70

WESTERN CONFERENCE

Central Division	GP	W	L	OTL	SOL	GF	GA	P
Detroit Red Wings	82	58	16	5	3	305	209	124
Nashville Predators	82	49	25	5	3	259	227	106
Columbus Blue Jackets	82	35	43	1	3	223	279	74
Chicago Blackhawks	82	26	43	7	6	211	285	65
St. Louis Blues	82	21	46	6	9	197	292	57

Northwest Division								
Calgary Flames	82	46	25	4	7	218	200	103
Colorado Avalanche	82	43	30	3	6	283	257	95
Edmonton Oilers	82	41	28	4	9	256	251	95
Vancouver Canucks	82	42	32	4	4	256	255	92
Minnesota Wild	82	38	36	5	3	231	215	84

Pacific Division								
Dallas Stars	82	53	23	5	1	265	218	112
San Jose Sharks	82	44	27	4	7	266	242	99
Mighty Ducks of Anaheim	82	43	27	5	7	254	229	98
Los Angeles Kings	82	42	35	4	1	249	270	89
Phoenix Coyotes	82	38	39	2	3	246	271	81

Stanley Cup Finals

June 5	Edmonton 4 at Carolina 5
June 7	Edmonton 0 at Carolina 5 [Ward]
June 10	Carolina 1 at Edmonton 2
June 12	Carolina 2 at Edmonton 1
June 14	Edmonton 4 at Carolina 3 (Pisani 3:31 OT)]
June 17	Carolina 0 at Edmonton 4 [Ward]
June 19	Edmonton 1 at Carolina 3

Carolina wins best-of-seven finals 4–3

NHL AWARDS

Art Ross Trophy

1917–18	Joe Malone	Montreal Canadiens (48 points)
1918–19	Newsy Lalonde	Montreal Canadiens (32 points)
1919–20	Joe Malone	Quebec Bulldogs (49 points)
1920–21	Newsy Lalonde	Montreal Canadiens (43 points)
1921–22	Punch Broadbent	Ottawa Senators (46 points)
1922–23	Babe Dye	Toronto St. Pats (37 points)
1923–24	Cy Denneny	Ottawa Senators (24 points)
1924–25	Babe Dye	Toronto St. Pats (46 points)
1925–26	Nels Stewart	Montreal Maroons (42 points)
1926–27	Bill Cook	New York Rangers (37 points)
1927–28	Howie Morenz	Montreal Canadiens (51 points)
1928–29	Ace Bailey	Toronto Maple Leafs (32 points)
1929–30	Cooney Weiland	Boston Bruins (73 points)
1930–31	Howie Morenz	Montreal Canadiens (51 points)
1931–32	Busher Jackson	Toronto Maple Leafs (53 points)
1932–33	Bill Cook	New York Rangers (50 points)
1933–34	Charlie Conacher	Toronto Maple Leafs (52 points)
1934–35	Charlie Conacher	Toronto Maple Leafs (57 points)
1935–36	Sweeney Schriner	New York Americans (45 points)
1936–37	Sweeney Schriner	New York Americans (46 points)
1937–38	Gordie Drillon	Toronto Maple Leafs (52 points)
1938–39	Toe Blake	Montreal Canadiens (47 points)
1939–40	Milt Schmidt	Boston Bruins (52 points)
1940–41	Bill Cowley	Boston Bruins (62 points)
1941–42	Bryan Hextall	New York Rangers (56 points)
1942–43	Doug Bentley	Chicago Black Hawks (73 points)
1943–44	Herb Cain	Boston Bruins (82 points)
1944–45	Elmer Lach	Montreal Canadiens (80 points)
1945–46	Max Bentley	Chicago Black Hawks (61 points)
1946–47	Max Bentley	Chicago Black Hawks (72 points)

1947–48	Elmer Lach	Montreal Canadiens (61 points)
1948–49	Roy Conacher	Chicago Black Hawks (68 points)
1949–50	Ted Lindsay	Detroit Red Wings (78 points)
1950–51	Gordie Howe	Detroit Red Wings (86 points)
1951–52	Gordie Howe	Detroit Red Wings (86 points)
1952–53	Gordie Howe	Detroit Red Wings (95 points)
1953–54	Gordie Howe	Detroit Red Wings (81 points)
1954–55	Bernie Geoffrion	Montreal Canadiens (75 points)
1955–56	Jean Beliveau	Montreal Canadiens (88 points)
1956–57	Gordie Howe	Detroit Red Wings (89 points)
1957–58	Dickie Moore	Montreal Canadiens (84 points)
1958–59	Dickie Moore	Montreal Canadiens (96 points)
1959–60	Bobby Hull	Chicago Black Hawks (81 points)
1960–61	Bernie Geoffrion	Montreal Canadiens (95 points)
1961–62	Bobby Hull	Chicago Black Hawks (84 points)
1962–63	Gordie Howe	Detroit Red Wings (86 points)
1963–64	Stan Mikita	Chicago Black Hawks (89 points)
1964–65	Stan Mikita	Chicago Black Hawks (87 points)
1965–66	Bobby Hull	Chicago Black Hawks (97 points)
1966–67	Stan Mikita	Chicago Black Hawks (97 points)
1967–68	Stan Mikita	Chicago Black Hawks (87 points)
1968–69	Phil Esposito	Boston Bruins (126 points)
1969–70	Bobby Orr	Boston Bruins (120 points)
1970–71	Phil Esposito	Boston Bruins (152 points)
1971–72	Phil Esposito	Boston Bruins (133 points)
1972–73	Phil Esposito	Boston Bruins (130 points)
1973–74	Phil Esposito	Boston Bruins (145 points)
1974–75	Bobby Orr	Boston Bruins (135 points)
1975–76	Guy Lafleur	Montreal Canadiens (125 points)
1976–77	Guy Lafleur	Montreal Canadiens (136 points)
1977–78	Guy Lafleur	Montreal Canadiens (132 points)
1978–79	Bryan Trottier	New York Islanders (134 points)
1979–80	Marcel Dionne	Los Angeles Kings (137 points)
1980–81	Wayne Gretzky	Edmonton Oilers (164 points)

1981–82	Wayne Gretzky	Edmonton Oilers (212 points)
1982–83	Wayne Gretzky	Edmonton Oilers (196 points)
1983–84	Wayne Gretzky	Edmonton Oilers (205 points)
1984–85	Wayne Gretzky	Edmonton Oilers (208 points)
1985–86	Wayne Gretzky	Edmonton Oilers (215 points)
1986–87	Wayne Gretzky	Edmonton Oilers (183 points)
1987–88	Mario Lemieux	Pittsburgh Penguins (168 points)
1988–89	Mario Lemieux	Pittsburgh Penguins (199 points)
1989–90	Wayne Gretzky	Los Angeles Kings (142 points)
1990–91	Wayne Gretzky	Los Angeles Kings (163 points)
1991–92	Mario Lemieux	Pittsburgh Penguins (131 points)
1992–93	Mario Lemieux	Pittsburgh Penguins (160 points)
1993–94	Wayne Gretzky	Los Angeles Kings (130 points)
1994–95	Jaromir Jagr	Pittsburgh Penguins (70 points)
1995–96	Mario Lemieux	Pittsburgh Penguins (161 points)
1996–97	Mario Lemieux	Pittsburgh Penguins (122 points)
1997–98	Jaromir Jagr	Pittsburgh Penguins (102 points)
1998–99	Jaromir Jagr	Pittsburgh Penguins (127 points)
1999–00	Jaromir Jagr	Pittsburgh Penguins (96 points)
2000–01	Jaromir Jagr	Pittsburgh Penguins (121 points)
2001–02	Jarome Iginla	Calgary Flames (96 points)
2002–03	Peter Forsberg	Colorado Avalanche (106 points)
2003–04	Martin St. Louis	Tampa Bay Lightning (94 points)
2004–05	*no winner*	
2005–06	Joe Thornton	Boston Bruins/San Jose Sharks (125 points)
2006–07	Sidney Crosby	Pittsburgh Penguins (120 points)

Hart Trophy

1923–24	Frank Nighbor	Ottawa Senators
1924–25	Billy Burch	Hamilton Tigers
1925–26	Nels Stewart	Montreal Maroons
1926–27	Herb Gardiner	Montreal Canadiens
1927–28	Howie Morenz	Montreal Canadiens

1928–29	Roy Worters	New York Americans
1929–30	Nels Stewart	Montreal Maroons
1930–31	Howie Morenz	Montreal Canadiens
1931–32	Howie Morenz	Montreal Canadiens
1932–33	Eddie Shore	Boston Bruins
1933–34	Aurel Joliat	Montreal Canadiens
1934–35	Eddie Shore	Boston Bruins
1935–36	Eddie Shore	Boston Bruins
1936–37	Babe Siebert	Montreal Canadiens
1937–38	Eddie Shore	Boston Bruins
1938–39	Toe Blake	Montreal Canadiens
1939–40	Ebbie Goodfellow	Detroit Red Wings
1940–41	Bill Cowley	Boston Bruins
1941–42	Tom Anderson	Brooklyn Americans
1942–43	Bill Cowley	Boston Bruins
1943–44	Babe Pratt	Toronto Maple Leafs
1944–45	Elmer Lach	Montreal Canadiens
1945–46	Max Bentley	Chicago Black Hawks
1946–47	Maurice Richard	Montreal Canadiens
1947–48	Buddy O'Connor	New York Rangers
1948–49	Sid Abel	Detroit Red Wings
1949–50	Chuck Rayner	New York Rangers
1950–51	Milt Schmidt	Boston Bruins
1951–52	Gordie Howe	Detroit Red Wings
1952–53	Gordie Howe	Detroit Red Wings
1953–54	Al Rollins	Chicago Black Hawks
1954–55	Ted Kennedy	Toronto Maple Leafs
1955–56	Jean Beliveau	Montreal Canadiens
1956–57	Gordie Howe	Detroit Red Wings
1957–58	Gordie Howe	Detroit Red Wings
1958–59	Andy Bathgate	New York Rangers
1959–60	Gordie Howe	Detroit Red Wings
1960–61	Bernie Geoffrion	Montreal Canadiens
1961–62	Jacques Plante	Montreal Canadiens

1962–63	Gordie Howe	Detroit Red Wings
1963–64	Jean Beliveau	Montreal Canadiens
1964–65	Bobby Hull	Chicago Black Hawks
1965–66	Bobby Hull	Chicago Black Hawks
1966–67	Stan Mikita	Chicago Black Hawks
1967–68	Stan Mikita	Chicago Black Hawks
1968–69	Phil Esposito	Boston Bruins
1969–70	Bobby Orr	Boston Bruins
1970–71	Bobby Orr	Boston Bruins
1971–72	Bobby Orr	Boston Bruins
1972–73	Bobby Clarke	Philadelphia Flyers
1973–74	Phil Esposito	Boston Bruins
1974–75	Bobby Clarke	Philadelphia Flyers
1975–76	Bobby Clarke	Philadelphia Flyers
1976–77	Guy Lafleur	Montreal Canadiens
1977–78	Guy Lafleur	Montreal Canadiens
1978–79	Bryan Trottier	New York Islanders
1979–80	Wayne Gretzky	Edmonton Oilers
1980–81	Wayne Gretzky	Edmonton Oilers
1981–82	Wayne Gretzky	Edmonton Oilers
1982–83	Wayne Gretzky	Edmonton Oilers
1983–84	Wayne Gretzky	Edmonton Oilers
1984–85	Wayne Gretzky	Edmonton Oilers
1985–86	Wayne Gretzky	Edmonton Oilers
1986–87	Wayne Gretzky	Edmonton Oilers
1987–88	Mario Lemieux	Pittsburgh Penguins
1988–89	Wayne Gretzky	Edmonton Oilers
1989–90	Mark Messier	Edmonton Oilers
1990–91	Brett Hull	St. Louis Blues
1991–92	Mark Messier	New York Rangers
1992–93	Mario Lemieux	Pittsburgh Penguins
1993–94	Sergei Fedorov	Detroit Red Wings
1994–95	Eric Lindros	Philadelphia Flyers
1995–96	Mario Lemieux	Pittsburgh Penguins

1996–97	Dominik Hasek	Buffalo Sabres
1997–98	Dominik Hasek	Buffalo Sabres
1998–99	Jaromir Jagr	Pittsburgh Penguins
1999–00	Chris Pronger	St. Louis Blues
2000–01	Joe Sakic	Colorado Avalanche
2001–02	Jose Theodore	Montreal Canadiens
2002–03	Peter Forsberg	Colorado Avalanche
2003–04	Martin St. Louis	Tampa Bay Lightning
2004–05	*no winner*	
2005–06	Joe Thornton	Boston Bruins/San Jose Sharks
2006–07	Sidney Crosby	Pittsburgh Penguins

Lady Byng Trophy

1924–25	Frank Nighbor	Ottawa Senators
1925–26	Frank Nighbor	Ottawa Senators
1926–27	Billy Burch	New York Americans
1927–28	Frank Boucher	New York Rangers
1928–29	Frank Boucher	New York Rangers
1929–30	Frank Boucher	New York Rangers
1930–31	Frank Boucher	New York Rangers
1931–32	Joe Primeau	Toronto Maple Leafs
1932–33	Frank Boucher	New York Rangers
1933–34	Frank Boucher	New York Rangers
1934–35	Frank Boucher	New York Rangers
1935–36	Doc Romnes	Chicago Black Hawks
1936–37	Marty Barry	Detroit Red Wings
1937–38	Gordie Drillon	Toronto Maple Leafs
1938–39	Clint Smith	New York Rangers
1939–40	Bobby Bauer	Boston Bruins
1940–41	Bobby Bauer	Boston Bruins
1941–42	Syl Apps	Toronto Maple Leafs
1942–43	Max Bentley	Chicago Black Hawks
1943–44	Clint Smith	Chicago Black Hawks
1944–45	Bill Mosienko	Chicago Black Hawks

1945–46	Toe Blake	Montreal Canadiens
1946–47	Bobby Bauer	Boston Bruins
1947–48	Buddy O'Connor	New York Rangers
1948–49	Bill Quackenbush	Detroit Red Wings
1949–50	Edgar Laprade	New York Rangers
1950–51	Red Kelly	Detroit Red Wings
1951–52	Sid Smith	Toronto Maple Leafs
1952–53	Red Kelly	Detroit Red Wings
1953–54	Red Kelly	Detroit Red Wings
1954–55	Sid Smith	Toronto Maple Leafs
1955–56	Dutch Reibel	Detroit Red Wings
1956–57	Andy Hebenton	New York Rangers
1957–58	Camille Henry	New York Rangers
1958–59	Alex Delvecchio	Detroit Red Wings
1959–60	Don McKenney	Boston Bruins
1960–61	Red Kelly	Toronto Maple Leafs
1961–62	Dave Keon	Toronto Maple Leafs
1962–63	Dave Keon	Toronto Maple Leafs
1963–64	Kenny Wharram	Chicago Black Hawks
1964–65	Bobby Hull	Chicago Black Hawks
1965–66	Alex Delvecchio	Detroit Red Wings
1966–67	Stan Mikita	Chicago Black Hawks
1967–68	Stan Mikita	Chicago Black Hawks
1968–69	Alex Delvecchio	Detroit Red Wings
1969–70	Phil Goyette	St. Louis Blues
1970–71	John Bucyk	Boston Bruins
1971–72	Jean Ratelle	New York Rangers
1972–73	Gilbert Perreault	Buffalo Sabres
1973–74	John Bucyk	Boston Bruins
1974–75	Marcel Dionne	Detroit Red Wings
1975–76	Jean Ratelle	New York Rangers/Boston Bruins
1976–77	Marcel Dionne	Los Angeles Kings
1977–78	Butch Goring	Los Angeles Kings
1978–79	Bob MacMillan	Atlanta Flames

1979–80	Wayne Gretzky	Edmonton Oilers
1980–81	Rick Kehoe	Pittsburgh Penguins
1981–82	Rick Middleton	Boston Bruins
1982–83	Mike Bossy	New York Islanders
1983–84	Mike Bossy	New York Islanders
1984–85	Jari Kurri	Edmonton Oilers
1985–86	Mike Bossy	New York Islanders
1986–87	Joe Mullen	Calgary Flames
1987–88	Mats Naslund	Montreal Canadiens
1988–89	Joe Mullen	Calgary Flames
1989–90	Brett Hull	St. Louis Blues
1990–91	Wayne Gretzky	Los Angeles Kings
1991–92	Wayne Gretzky	Los Angeles Kings
1992–93	Pierre Turgeon	New York Islanders
1993–94	Wayne Gretzky	Los Angeles Kings
1994–95	Ron Francis	Pittsburgh Penguins
1995–96	Paul Kariya	Mighty Ducks of Anaheim
1996–97	Paul Kariya	Mighty Ducks of Anaheim
1997–98	Ron Francis	Pittsburgh Penguins
1998–99	Wayne Gretzky	New York Rangers
1999–00	Pavol Demitra	St. Louis Blues
2000–01	Joe Sakic	Colorado Avalanche
2001–02	Ron Francis	Carolina Hurricanes
2002–03	Alexander Mogilny	Toronto Maple Leafs
2003–04	Brad Richards	Tampa Bay Lightning
2004–05	*no winner*	
2005–06	Pavel Datsyuk	Detroit Red Wings
2006–07	Pavel Datsyuk	Detroit Red Wings

Vezina Trophy

1926–27	George Hainsworth	Montreal Canadiens (1.47 GAA)
1927–28	George Hainsworth	Montreal Canadiens (1.05 GAA)
1928–29	George Hainsworth	Montreal Canadiens (0.92 GAA)
1929–30	Tiny Thompson	Boston Bruins (2.19 GAA)

1930–31	Roy Worters	New York Americans (1.61 GAA)
1931–32	Charlie Gardiner	Chicago Black Hawks (1.85 GAA)
1932–33	Tiny Thompson	Boston Bruins (1.76 GAA)
1933–34	Charlie Gardiner	Chicago Black Hawks (1.63 GAA)
1934–35	Lorne Chabot	Chicago Black Hawks (1.80 GAA)
1935–36	Tiny Thompson	Boston Bruins (1.68 GAA)
1936–37	Normie Smith	Detroit Red Wings (2.05 GAA)
1937–38	Tiny Thompson	Boston Bruins (1.80 GAA)
1938–39	Frank Brimsek	Boston Bruins (1.56 GAA)
1939–40	Dave Kerr	New York Rangers (1.54 GAA)
1940–41	Turk Broda	Toronto Maple Leafs (2.00 GAA)
1941–42	Frank Brimsek	Boston Bruins (2.35 GAA)
1942–43	Johnny Mowers	Detroit Red Wings (2.47 GAA)
1943–44	Bill Durnan	Montreal Canadiens (2.18 GAA)
1944–45	Bill Durnan	Montreal Canadiens (2.42 GAA)
1945–46	Bill Durnan	Montreal Canadiens (2.60 GAA)
1946–47	Bill Durnan	Montreal Canadiens (2.30 GAA)
1947–48	Turk Broda	Toronto Maple Leafs (2.38 GAA)
1948–49	Bill Durnan	Montreal Canadiens (2.10 GAA)
1949–50	Bill Durnan	Montreal Canadiens (2.20 GAA)
1950–51	Al Rollins	Toronto Maple Leafs (1.77 GAA)
1951–52	Terry Sawchuk	Detroit Red Wings (1.90 GAA)
1952–53	Terry Sawchuk	Detroit Red Wings (1.90 GAA)
1953–54	Harry Lumley	Toronto Maple Leafs (1.86 GAA)
1954–55	Terry Sawchuk	Detroit Red Wings (1.96 GAA)
1955–56	Jacques Plante	Montreal Canadiens (1.86 GAA)
1956–57	Jacques Plante	Montreal Canadiens (2.00 GAA)
1957–58	Jacques Plante	Montreal Canadiens (2.11 GAA)
1958–59	Jacques Plante	Montreal Canadiens (2.16 GAA)
1959–60	Jacques Plante	Montreal Canadiens (2.54 GAA)
1960–61	Johnny Bower	Toronto Maple Leafs (2.50 GAA)
1961–62	Jacques Plante	Montreal Canadiens (2.37 GAA)
1962–63	Glenn Hall	Chicago Black Hawks (2.47 GAA)
1963–64	Charlie Hodge	Montreal Canadiens (2.26 GAA)

1964–65	Terry Sawchuk	Toronto Maple Leafs (2.56 GAA)
	Johnny Bower	Toronto Maple Leafs (2.38 GAA)
1965–66	Gump Worsley	Montreal Canadiens (2.36 GAA)
	Charlie Hodge	Montreal Canadiens (2.58 GAA)
1966–67	Glenn Hall	Chicago Black Hawks (2.38 GAA)
	Denis DeJordy	Chicago Black Hawks (2.46 GAA)
1967–68	Gump Worsley	Montreal Canadiens (1.98 GAA)
	Rogie Vachon	Montreal Canadiens (2.48 GAA)
1968–69	Jacques Plante	St. Louis Blues (1.96 GAA)
	Glenn Hall	St. Louis Blues (2.17 GAA)
1969–70	Tony Esposito	Chicago Black Hawks (2.17 GAA)
1970–71	Ed Giacomin	New York Rangers (2.16 GAA)
	Gilles Villemure	New York Rangers (2.30 GAA)
1971–72	Tony Esposito	Chicago Black Hawks (1.77 GAA)
	Gary Smith	Chicago Black Hawks (2.42 GAA)
1972–73	Ken Dryden	Montreal Canadiens (2.26 GAA)
1973–74	Bernie Parent	Philadelphia Flyers (1.89 GAA)
	Tony Esposito	Chicago Black Hawks (2.04 GAA)
1974–75	Bernie Parent	Philadelphia Flyers (2.03 GAA)
1975–76	Ken Dryden	Montreal Canadiens (2.03 GAA)
1976–77	Ken Dryden	Montreal Canadiens (2.14 GAA)
	Michel Larocque	Montreal Canadiens (2.09 GAA)
1977–78	Ken Dryden	Montreal Canadiens (2.05 GAA)
	Michel Larocque	Montreal Canadiens (2.67 GAA)
1978–79	Ken Dryden	Montreal Canadiens (2.30 GAA)
	Michel Larocque	Montreal Canadiens (2.84 GAA)
1979–80	Bob Sauve	Buffalo Sabres (2.36 GAA)
	Don Edwards	Buffalo Sabres (2.57 GAA)
1980–81	Richard Sevigny	Montreal Canadiens (2.40 GAA)
	Denis Herron	Montreal Canadiens (3.50 GAA)
	Michel Larocque	Montreal Canadiens (3.03 GAA)
1981–82	Billy Smith	New York Islanders (2.97 GAA)
1982–83	Pete Peeters	Boston Bruins (2.36 GAA)
1983–84	Tom Barrasso	Buffalo Sabres (2.84 GAA)

1984–85	Pelle Lindbergh	Philadelphia Flyers (3.02 GAA)
1985–86	John Vanbiesbrouck	New York Rangers (3.32 GAA)
1986–87	Ron Hextall	Philadelphia Flyers (3.00 GAA)
1987–88	Grant Fuhr	Edmonton Oilers (3.43 GAA)
1988–89	Patrick Roy	Montreal Canadiens (2.47 GAA)
1989–90	Patrick Roy	Montreal Canadiens (2.53 GAA)
1990–91	Ed Belfour	Chicago Blackhawks (2.47 GAA)
1991–92	Patrick Roy	Montreal Canadiens (2.36 GAA)
1992–93	Ed Belfour	Chicago Blackhawks (2.59 GAA)
1993–94	Dominik Hasek	Buffalo Sabres (1.95 GAA)
1994–95	Dominik Hasek	Buffalo Sabres (2.11 GAA)
1995–96	Jim Carey	Washington Capitals (2.26 GAA)
1996–97	Dominik Hasek	Buffalo Sabres (2.27 GAA)
1997–98	Dominik Hasek	Buffalo Sabres (2.09 GAA)
1998–99	Dominik Hasek	Buffalo Sabres (1.87 GAA)
1999–00	Olaf Kolzig	Washington Capitals (2.24 GAA)
2000–01	Dominik Hasek	Buffalo Sabres (2.11 GAA)
2001–02	Jose Theodore	Montreal Canadiens (2.11 GAA)
2002–03	Martin Brodeur	New Jersey Devils (2.02 GAA)
2003–04	Martin Brodeur	New Jersey Devils (2.62 GAA)
2004–05	*no winner*	
2005–06	Miikka Kiprusoff	Calgary Flames (2.07 GAA)
2006–07	Martin Brodeur	New Jersey Devils (2.18 GAA)

Calder Memorial Trophy

1932–33	Carl Voss	Detroit Red Wings
1933–34	Russ Blinco	Montreal Maroons
1934–35	Sweeney Schriner	New York Americans
1935–36	Mike Karakas	Chicago Black Hawks
1936–37	Syl Apps	Toronto Maple Leafs
1937–38	Cully Dahlstrom	Chicago Black Hawks
1938–39	Frank Brimsek	Boston Bruins
1939–40	Kilby MacDonald	New York Rangers
1940–41	John Quilty	Montreal Canadiens

1941–42	Grant Warwick	New York Rangers
1942–43	Gaye Stewart	Toronto Maple Leafs
1943–44	Gus Bodnar	Toronto Maple Leafs
1944–45	Frank McCool	Toronto Maple Leafs
1945–46	Edgar Laprade	New York Rangers
1946–47	Howie Meeker	Toronto Maple Leafs
1947–48	Jim McFadden	Detroit Red Wings
1948–49	Pentti Lund	New York Rangers
1949–50	Jack Gelineau	Boston Bruins
1950–51	Terry Sawchuk	Detroit Red Wings
1951–52	Bernie Geoffrion	Montreal Canadiens
1952–53	Gump Worsley	New York Rangers
1953–54	Camille Henry	New York Rangers
1954–55	Ed Litzenberger	Chicago Black Hawks
1955–56	Glenn Hall	Detroit Red Wings
1956–57	Larry Regan	Boston Bruins
1957–58	Frank Mahovlich	Toronto Maple Leafs
1958–59	Ralph Backstrom	Montreal Canadiens
1959–60	Bill Hay	Chicago Black Hawks
1960–61	Dave Keon	Toronto Maple Leafs
1961–62	Bobby Rousseau	Montreal Canadiens
1962–63	Kent Douglas	Toronto Maple Leafs
1963–64	Jacques Laperriere	Montreal Canadiens
1964–65	Roger Crozier	Detroit Red Wings
1965–66	Brit Selby	Toronto Maple Leafs
1966–67	Bobby Orr	Boston Bruins
1967–68	Derek Sanderson	Boston Bruins
1968–69	Danny Grant	Minnesota North Stars
1969–70	Tony Esposito	Chicago Black Hawks
1970–71	Gilbert Perreault	Buffalo Sabres
1971–72	Ken Dryden	Montreal Canadiens
1972–73	Steve Vickers	New York Rangers
1973–74	Denis Potvin	New York Islanders
1974–75	Eric Vail	Atlanta Flames

1975–76	Bryan Trottier	New York Islanders
1976–77	Willi Plett	Atlanta Flames
1977–78	Mike Bossy	New York Islanders
1978–79	Bobby Smith	Minnesota North Stars
1979–80	Raymond Bourque	Boston Bruins
1980–81	Peter Stastny	Quebec Nordiques
1981–82	Dale Hawerchuk	Winnipeg Jets
1982–83	Steve Larmer	Chicago Black Hawks
1983–84	Tom Barrasso	Buffalo Sabres
1984–85	Mario Lemieux	Pittsburgh Penguins
1985–86	Gary Suter	Calgary Flames
1986–87	Luc Robitaille	Los Angeles Kings
1987–88	Joe Nieuwendyk	Calgary Flames
1988–89	Brian Leetch	New York Rangers
1989–90	Sergei Makarov	Calgary Flames
1990–91	Ed Belfour	Chicago Blackhawks
1991–92	Pavel Bure	Vancouver Canucks
1992–93	Teemu Selanne	Winnipeg Jets
1993–94	Martin Brodeur	New Jersey Devils
1994–95	Peter Forsberg	Quebec Nordiques
1995–96	Daniel Alfredsson	Ottawa Senators
1996–97	Bryan Berard	New York Islanders
1997–98	Sergei Samsonov	Boston Bruins
1998–99	Chris Drury	Colorado Avalanche
1999–00	Scott Gomez	New Jersey Devils
2000–01	Evgeni Nabokov	San Jose Sharks
2001–02	Danny Heatley	Atlanta Thrashers
2002–03	Barret Jackman	St. Louis Blues
2003–04	Andrew Raycroft	Boston Bruins
2004–05	*no winner*	
2005–06	Alexander Ovechkin	Washington Capitals
2006–07	Evgeni Malkin	Pittsburgh Penguins

James Norris Trophy

1953–54	Red Kelly	Detroit Red Wings
1954–55	Doug Harvey	Montreal Canadiens
1955–56	Doug Harvey	Montreal Canadiens
1956–57	Doug Harvey	Montreal Canadiens
1957–58	Doug Harvey	Montreal Canadiens
1958–59	Tom Johnson	Montreal Canadiens
1959–60	Doug Harvey	Montreal Canadiens
1960–61	Doug Harvey	Montreal Canadiens
1961–62	Doug Harvey	Montreal Canadiens
1962–63	Pierre Pilote	Chicago Black Hawks
1963–64	Pierre Pilote	Chicago Black Hawks
1964–65	Pierre Pilote	Chicago Black Hawks
1965–66	Jacques Laperriere	Montreal Canadiens
1966–67	Harry Howell	New York Rangers
1967–68	Bobby Orr	Boston Bruins
1968–69	Bobby Orr	Boston Bruins
1969–70	Bobby Orr	Boston Bruins
1970–71	Bobby Orr	Boston Bruins
1971–72	Bobby Orr	Boston Bruins
1972–73	Bobby Orr	Boston Bruins
1973–74	Bobby Orr	Boston Bruins
1974–75	Bobby Orr	Boston Bruins
1975–76	Denis Potvin	New York Islanders
1976–77	Larry Robinson	Montreal Canadiens
1977–78	Denis Potvin	New York Islanders
1978–79	Denis Potvin	New York Islanders
1979–80	Larry Robinson	Montreal Canadiens
1980–81	Randy Carlyle	Pittsburgh Penguins
1981–82	Doug Wilson	Chicago Black Hawks
1982–83	Rod Langway	Washington Capitals
1983–84	Rod Langway	Washington Capitals
1984–85	Paul Coffey	Edmonton Oilers
1985–86	Paul Coffey	Edmonton Oilers

1986–87	Raymond Bourque	Boston Bruins
1987–88	Raymond Bourque	Boston Bruins
1988–89	Chris Chelios	Montreal Canadiens
1989–90	Raymond Bourque	Boston Bruins
1990–91	Raymond Bourque	Boston Bruins
1991–92	Brian Leetch	New York Rangers
1992–93	Chris Chelios	Chicago Blackhawks
1993–94	Raymond Bourque	Boston Bruins
1994–95	Paul Coffey	Detroit Red Wings
1995–96	Chris Chelios	Chicago Blackhawks
1996–97	Brian Leetch	New York Rangers
1997–98	Rob Blake	Los Angeles Kings
1998–99	Al MacInnis	St. Louis Blues
1999–00	Chris Pronger	St. Louis Blues
2000–01	Nicklas Lidstrom	Detroit Red Wings
2001–02	Nicklas Lidstrom	Detroit Red Wings
2002–03	Nicklas Lidstrom	Detroit Red Wings
2003–04	Scott Niedermayer	New Jersey Devils
2004–05	*no winner*	
2005–06	Nicklas Lidstrom	Detroit Red Wings
2006–07	Nicklas Lidstrom	Detroit Red Wings

Lester Patrick Trophy

1965–66	Jack Adams
1966–67	Gordie Howe
	Charles F. Adams
	James Norris, Sr.
1967–68	Tommy Lockhart
	Walter A. Brown
	Gen. John R. Kilpatrick
1968–69	Bobby Hull
	Ed Jeremiah
1969–70	Eddie Shore
	Jim Hendy

1970–71	Bill Jennings
	John B. Sollenberger
	Terry Sawchuk
1971–72	Clarence Campbell
	John A. Kelly
	Cooney Weiland
	James D. Norris
1972–73	Walter Bush, Jr.
1973–74	Alex Delvecchio
	Murray Murdoch
	Weston W. Adams Sr.
	Charles L. Crovat
1974–75	Donald M. Clark
	Bill Chadwick
	Tommy Ivan
1975–76	Stan Mikita
	George Leader
	Bruce A. Norris
1976–77	Johnny Bucyk
	Murray Armstrong
	John Mariucci
1977–78	Phil Esposito
	Tom Fitzgerald
	William T. Tutt
	Bill Wirtz
1978–79	Bobby Orr
1979–80	Bobby Clarke
	Ed Snider
	Fred Shero
	1980 U.S. Olympic Hockey Team
1980–81	Charles M. Schulz
1981–82	Emile Francis
1982–83	Bill Torrey

1983–84	John A. Ziegler Jr.
	Art Ross
1984–85	Jack Butterfield
	Arthur M. Wirtz
1985–86	John MacInnes
	Jack Riley
1986–87	Hobey Baker
	Frank Mathers
1987–88	Keith Allen
	Fred Cusick
	Bob Johnson
1988–89	Dan Kelly
	Lou Nanne
	Lynn Patrick
	Bud Poile
1989–90	Len Ceglarski
1990–91	Rod Gilbert
	Mike Ilitch
1991–92	Al Arbour
	Art Berglund
	Lou Lamoriello
1992–93	Frank Boucher
	Red Dutton
	Bruce McNall
	Gil Stein
1993–94	Wayne Gretzky
	Robert Ridder
1994–95	Joe Mullen
	Brian Mullen
	Bob Fleming
1995–96	George Gund
	Ken Morrow
	Milt Schmidt

1996–97	Seymour H. Knox III	
	Bill Cleary	
	Pat LaFontaine	
1997–98	Peter Karmanos	
	Neal Broten	
	John Mayasich	
	Max McNab	
1998–99	Harry Sinden	
	1998 U.S. Olympic Women's Hockey Team	
1999–00	Mario Lemieux	
	Craig Patrick	
	Lou Vairo	
2000–01	Scotty Bowman	
	David Poile	
	Gary Bettman	
2001–02	1960 U.S. Olympic Team	
	Herb Brooks	
	Larry Pleau	
2002–03	Ray Bourque	
	Ron DeGregorio	
	Willie O'Ree	
2003–04	Mike Emrick	
	John Davidson	
	Ray Miron	
2004–05	*none*	
2005–06	Red Berenson	
	Marcel Dionne	
	Reed Larson	
	Glen Sonmor	
	Steve Yzerman	

Conn Smythe Trophy

1964–65	Jean Beliveau	Montreal Canadiens
1965–66	Roger Crozier	Detroit Red Wings

1966–67	Dave Keon	Toronto Maple Leafs
1967–68	Glenn Hall	St. Louis Blues
1968–69	Serge Savard	Montreal Canadiens
1969–70	Bobby Orr	Boston Bruins
1970–71	Ken Dryden	Montreal Canadiens
1971–72	Bobby Orr	Boston Bruins
1972–73	Yvan Cournoyer	Montreal Canadiens
1973–74	Bernie Parent	Philadelphia Flyers
1974–75	Bernie Parent	Philadelphia Flyers
1975–76	Reggie Leach	Philadelphia Flyers
1976–77	Guy Lafleur	Montreal Canadiens
1977–78	Larry Robinson	Montreal Canadiens
1978–79	Bob Gainey	Montreal Canadiens
1979–80	Bryan Trottier	New York Islanders
1980–81	Butch Goring	New York Islanders
1981–82	Mike Bossy	New York Islanders
1982–83	Billy Smith	New York Islanders
1983–84	Mark Messier	Edmonton Oilers
1984–85	Wayne Gretzky	Edmonton Oilers
1985–86	Patrick Roy	Montreal Canadiens
1986–87	Ron Hextall	Philadelphia Flyers
1987–88	Wayne Gretzky	Edmonton Oilers
1988–89	Al MacInnis	Calgary Flames
1989–90	Bill Ranford	Edmonton Oilers
1990–91	Mario Lemieux	Pittsburgh Penguins
1991–92	Mario Lemieux	Pittsburgh Penguins
1992–93	Patrick Roy	Montreal Canadiens
1993–94	Brian Leetch	New York Rangers
1994–95	Claude Lemieux	New Jersey Devils
1995–96	Joe Sakic	Colorado Avalanche
1996–97	Mike Vernon	Detroit Red Wings
1997–98	Steve Yzerman	Detroit Red Wings
1998–99	Joe Nieuwendyk	Dallas Stars
1999–00	Scott Stevens	New Jersey Devils

2000–01	Patrick Roy	Colorado Avalanche
2001–02	Nicklas Lidstrom	Detroit Red Wings
2002–03	J-S Giguere	Mighty Ducks of Anaheim
2003–04	Brad Richards	Tampa Bay Lightning
2004–05	*no winner*	
2005–06	Cam Ward	Carolina Hurricanes
2006–07	Scott Niedermayer	Anaheim Ducks

Bill Masterton Trophy

1967–68	Claude Provost	Montreal Canadiens
1968–69	Ted Hampson	Oakland Seals
1969–70	Pit Martin	Chicago Black Hawks
1970–71	Jean Ratelle	New York Rangers
1971–72	Bobby Clarke	Philadelphia Flyers
1972–73	Lowell MacDonald	Pittsburgh Penguins
1973–74	Henri Richard	Montreal Canadiens
1974–75	Don Luce	Buffalo Sabres
1975–76	Rod Gilbert	New York Rangers
1976–77	Ed Westfall	New York Islanders
1977–78	Butch Goring	Los Angeles Kings
1978–79	Serge Savard	Montreal Canadiens
1979–80	Al MacAdam	Minnesota North Stars
1980–81	Blake Dunlop	St. Louis Blues
1981–82	Glenn Resch	Colorado Rockies
1982–83	Lanny McDonald	Calgary Flames
1983–84	Brad Park	Detroit Red Wings
1984–85	Anders Hedberg	New York Rangers
1985–86	Charlie Simmer	Boston Bruins
1986–87	Doug Jarvis	Hartford Whalers
1987–88	Bob Bourne	Los Angeles Kings
1988–89	Tim Kerr	Philadelphia Flyers
1989–90	Gord Kluzak	Boston Bruins
1990–91	Dave Taylor	Los Angeles Kings
1991–92	Mark Fitzpatrick	New York Islanders

1992–93	Mario Lemieux	Pittsburgh Penguins
1993–94	Cam Neely	Boston Bruins
1994–95	Pat LaFontaine	Buffalo Sabres
1995–96	Gary Roberts	Calgary Flames
1996–97	Tony Granato	San Jose Sharks
1997–98	Jamie McLennan	St. Louis Blues
1998–99	John Cullen	Tampa Bay Lightning
1999–00	Ken Daneyko	New Jersey Devils
2000–01	Adam Graves	New York Rangers
2001–02	Saku Koivu	Montreal Canadiens
2002–03	Steve Yzerman	Detroit Red Wings
2003–04	Bryan Berard	Chicago Blackhawks
2004–05	*no winner*	
2005–06	Teemu Selanne	Mighty Ducks of Anaheim
2006–07	Phil Kessel	Boston Bruins

Jack Adams Award

1973–74	Fred Shero	Philadelphia Flyers
1974–75	Bob Pulford	Los Angeles Kings
1975–76	Don Cherry	Boston Bruins
1976–77	Scotty Bowman	Montreal Canadiens
1977–78	Bobby Kromm	Detroit Red Wings
1978–79	Al Arbour	New York Islanders
1979–80	Pat Quinn	Philadelphia Flyers
1980–81	Red Berenson	St. Louis Blues
1981–82	Tom Watt	Winnipeg Jets
1982–83	Orval Tessier	Chicago Black Hawks
1983–84	Bryan Murray	Washington Capitals
1984–85	Mike Keenan	Philadelphia Flyers
1985–86	Glen Sather	Edmonton Oilers
1986–87	Jacques Demers	Detroit Red Wings
1987–88	Jacques Demers	Detroit Red Wings
1988–89	Pat Burns	Montreal Canadiens
1989–90	Bob Murdoch	Winnipeg Jets

1990–91	Brian Sutter	St. Louis Blues
1991–92	Pat Quinn	Vancouver Canucks
1992–93	Pat Burns	Toronto Maple Leafs
1993–94	Jacques Lemaire	New Jersey Devils
1994–95	Marc Crawford	Quebec Nordiques
1995–96	Scotty Bowman	Detroit Red Wings
1996–97	Ted Nolan	Buffalo Sabres
1997–98	Pat Burns	Boston Bruins
1998–99	Jacques Martin	Ottawa Senators
1999–00	Joel Quenneville	St. Louis Blues
2000–01	Bill Barber	Philadelphia Flyers
2001–02	Bob Francis	Phoenix Coyotes
2002–03	Jacques Lemaire	Minnesota Wild
2003–04	John Tortorella	Tampa Bay Lightning
2004–05	*no winner*	
2005–06	Lindy Ruff	Buffalo Sabres
2006–07	Alain Vigneault	Vancouver Canucks

Lester B. Pearson Award

1970–71	Phil Esposito	Boston Bruins
1971–72	Jean Ratelle	New York Rangers
1972–73	Bobby Clarke	Philadelphia Flyers
1973–74	Phil Esposito	Boston Bruins
1974–75	Bobby Orr	Boston Bruins
1975–76	Guy Lafleur	Montreal Canadiens
1976–77	Guy Lafleur	Montreal Canadiens
1977–78	Guy Lafleur	Montreal Canadiens
1978–79	Marcel Dionne	Los Angeles Kings
1979–80	Marcel Dionne	Los Angeles Kings
1980–81	Mike Liut	St. Louis Blues
1981–82	Wayne Gretzky	Edmonton Oilers
1982–83	Wayne Gretzky	Edmonton Oilers
1983–84	Wayne Gretzky	Edmonton Oilers
1984–85	Wayne Gretzky	Edmonton Oilers

1985–86	Mario Lemieux	Pittsburgh Penguins
1986–87	Wayne Gretzky	Edmonton Oilers
1987–88	Mario Lemieux	Pittsburgh Penguins
1988–89	Steve Yzerman	Detroit Red Wings
1989–90	Mark Messier	Edmonton Oilers
1990–91	Brett Hull	St. Louis Blues
1991–92	Mark Messier	New York Rangers
1992–93	Mario Lemieux	Pittsburgh Penguins
1993–94	Sergei Fedorov	Detroit Red Wings
1994–95	Eric Lindros	Philadelphia Flyers
1995–96	Mario Lemieux	Pittsburgh Penguins
1996–97	Dominik Hasek	Buffalo Sabres
1997–98	Dominik Hasek	Buffalo Sabres
1998–99	Jaromir Jagr	Pittsburgh Penguins
1999–00	Jaromir Jagr	Pittsburgh Penguins
2000–01	Joe Sakic	Colorado Avalanche
2001–02	Jarome Iginla	Calgary Flames
2002–03	Markus Naslund	Vancouver Canucks
2003–04	Martin St. Louis	Tampa Bay Lightning
2004–05	*no winner*	
2005–06	Jaromir Jagr	New York Rangers
2006–07	Sidney Crosby	Pittsburgh Penguins

Frank J. Selke Trophy

1977–78	Bob Gainey	Montreal Canadiens
1978–79	Bob Gainey	Montreal Canadiens
1979–80	Bob Gainey	Montreal Canadiens
1980–81	Bob Gainey	Montreal Canadiens
1981–82	Steve Kasper	Boston Bruins
1982–83	Bobby Clarke	Pittsburgh Penguins
1983–84	Doug Jarvis	Washington Capitals
1984–85	Craig Ramsay	Buffalo Sabres
1985–86	Troy Murray	Chicago Black Hawks
1986–87	Dave Poulin	Philadelphia Flyers

1987–88	Guy Carbonneau	Montreal Canadiens
1988–89	Guy Carbonneau	Montreal Canadiens
1989–90	Rick Meagher	St. Louis Blues
1990–91	Dirk Graham	Chicago Blackhawks
1991–92	Guy Carbonneau	Montreal Canadiens
1992–93	Doug Gilmour	Toronto Maple Leafs
1993–94	Sergei Fedorov	Detroit Red Wings
1994–95	Ron Francis	Pittsburgh Penguins
1995–96	Sergei Fedorov	Detroit Red Wings
1996–97	Michael Peca	Buffalo Sabres
1997–98	Jere Lehtinen	Dallas Stars
1998–99	Jere Lehtinen	Dallas Stars
1999–00	Steve Yzerman	Detroit Red Wings
2000–01	John Madden	New Jersey Devils
2001–02	Michael Peca	New York Islanders
2002–03	Jere Lehtinen	Dallas Stars
2003–04	Kris Draper	Detroit Red Wings
2004–05	*no winner*	
2005–06	Rod Brind 'Amour	Carolina Hurricanes
2006–07	Rod Brind 'Amour	Carolina Hurricanes

William M. Jennings Trophy

1981–82	Rick Wamsley & Denis Herron	Montreal Canadiens
1982–83	Rollie Melanson & Billy Smith	New York Islanders
1983–84	Al Jensen & Pat Riggin	Washington Capitals
1984–85	Tom Barrasso & Bob Sauve	Buffalo Sabres
1985–86	Bob Froese & Darren Jensen	Philadelphia Flyers
1986–87	Patrick Roy & Brian Hayward	Montreal Canadiens
1987–88	Patrick Roy & Brian Hayward	Montreal Canadiens
1988–89	Patrick Roy & Brian Hayward	Montreal Canadiens
1989–90	Andy Moog & Reggie Lemelin	Boston Bruins
1990–91	Ed Belfour	Chicago Blackhawks
1991–92	Patrick Roy	Montreal Canadiens
1992–93	Ed Belfour	Chicago Blackhawks

1993–94	Dominik Hasek & Grant Fuhr	Buffalo Sabres
1994–95	Ed Belfour	Chicago Blackhawks
1995–96	Chris Osgood & Mike Vernon	Detroit Red Wings
1996–97	Martin Brodeur & Mike Dunham	New Jersey Devils
1997–98	Martin Brodeur	New Jersey Devils
1998–99	Ed Belfour & Roman Turek	Dallas Stars
1999–00	Roman Turek	St. Louis Blues
2000–01	Dominik Hasek	Buffalo Sabres
2001–02	Patrick Roy	Colorado Avalanche
2002–03	Martin Brodeur	New Jersey Devils
	Roman Cechmanek	Philadelphia Flyers
	Robert Esche	Philadelphia Flyers
2003–04	Martin Brodeur	New Jersey Devils
2004–05	*no winner*	
2005–06	Miikka Kiprusoff	Calgary Flames
2006–07	Manny Fernandez & Niklas Backstrom	Minnesota Wild

King Clancy Memorial Trophy

1987–88	Lanny McDonald	Calgary Flames
1988–89	Bryan Trottier	New York Islanders
1989–90	Kevin Lowe	Edmonton Oilers
1990–91	Dave Taylor	Los Angeles Kings
1991–92	Raymond Bourque	Boston Bruins
1992–93	Dave Poulin	Boston Bruins
1993–94	Adam Graves	New York Rangers
1994–95	Joe Nieuwendyk	Calgary Flames
1995–96	Kris King	Winnipeg Jets
1996–97	Trevor Linden	Vancouver Canucks
1997–98	Kelly Chase	St. Louis Blues
1998–99	Rob Ray	Buffalo Sabres
1999–00	Curtis Joseph	Toronto Maple Leafs
2000–01	Shjon Podein	Colorado Avalanche

2001–02	Ron Francis	Carolina Hurricanes
2002–03	Brendan Shanahan	Detroit Red Wings
2003–04	Jarome Iginla	Calgary Flames
2004–05	*no winner*	
2005–06	Olaf Kolzig	Washington Capitals
2006–07	Saku Koivu	Montreal Canadiens

Rocket Richard Trophy

1998–99	Teemu Selanne	Mighty Ducks of Anaheim (47 goals)
1999–00	Pavel Bure	Florida Panthers (58 goals)
2000–01	Pavel Bure	Florida Panthers (59 goals)
2001–02	Jarome Iginla	Calgary Flames (52 goals)
2002–03	Milan Hejduk	Colorado Avalanche (50 goals)
2003–04	Rick Nash	Columbus Blue Jackets (41 goals)
	Jarome Iginla	Calgary Flames (41 goals)
	Ilya Kovalchuk	Atlanta Thrashers (41 goals)
2004–05	*no winner*	
2005–06	Jonathan Cheechoo	San Jose Sharks (56 goals)
2006–07	Vincent Lacavalier	Tampa Bay Lightning (52 goals)

HOCKEY HALLS OF FAME

Hockey Hall of Fame 2007 Elections, June 28, 2007
First-time eligible players: Ron Francis, Mark Messier, Al MacInnis, Adam Oates, Scott Stevens, Igor Larionov, Claude Lemieux

Other notable players still eligible: Doug Gilmour, Glenn Anderson, Dino Ciccarelli, Phil Housley, Kevin Lowe, Pavel Bure, Mike Vernon

Inductees:

Players

Mark Messier

Messier was the only player to captain two different teams to the Stanley Cup. In all, he won six Cups, five with Edmonton and one with the New York Rangers in 1993–94. His 1,887 career points in the regular season rank second all-time behind longtime teammate Wayne Gretzky, and his 1,193 assists rank third all-time. Messier was named Hart Trophy and Lester B. Pearson winner in 1989–90. He is second all-time in all major playoff scoring categories as well—goals, assists, points—and his number 11 was retired by both the Rangers and Oilers during the 2006–07 season. Messier also ranks second all-time in games played behind only Gordie Howe.

Ron Francis

A remarkably consistent player for his entire 23-year career, Francis averaged better than a point a game over 1,700 games. He recorded 1,249 career assists, second only to Wayne Gretzky. He won two Stanley Cups with Pittsburgh and was known and respected for his gentlemanly conduct on ice, winning the Lady Byng Trophy three times. Francis retired with 539 career goals and 1,798 total points. He was also remarkably durable, playing the full season eight times in his career.

Scott Stevens

The hardest hitter of his generation, Stevens was a dominant force on the blueline for 22 years. He was a blue-chip prospect from the Kitchener Rangers of the Ontario Hockey League and quickly developed into an on-ice leader, known for moving the puck effectively out of his own end and levelling oncoming forwards who skated with their heads down. He won three Stanley Cups with the New Jersey Devils, a team he played for the last 13 years of his career. Stevens won the Conn Smythe Trophy in 2000 but amazingly never won the Norris Trophy. Twice he was named to the First All-Star Team and three times to the Second Team. His 1,635 games played are the most ever by a defenceman.

Al MacInnis

MacInnis was known as the man with the hardest shot in the game for virtually his entire career—and he achieved that velocity using an old-fashioned wooden stick! More than that, MacInnis was an offensive force and an overpowering presence on the power play. In 1,416 games, he recorded an amazing 1,274 points, making him one of the game's all-time point producers from the blueline. He played all of his 23 years with just two teams, Calgary and St. Louis, winning his only Stanley Cup with the Flames in 1989. MacInnis was renowned for his conditioning and played nearly 30 minutes a game right up until the end of his career.

Builders
Jim Gregory

Gregory arrived in Toronto from Dunnville, Ontario, in 1953 to attend St. Michael's College School. He quickly became interested in managing rather than playing hockey, and worked his way up through the ranks in the 1960s, ultimately becoming general manager of the Toronto Maple Leafs. He later worked in the NHL's Central Scouting department and became the league's senior vice-president for hockey operations. Gregory also served as chairman of the Hockey Hall of Fame Selection Committee.

Hockey Hall of Fame Honoured Members

(member, category, year inducted)

Sid Abel—Player, 1969

Charles Adams—Builder, 1960

Jack Adams—Player, 1959

Weston Adams—Builder, 1972

Frank Ahearn—Builder, 1962

Bunny Ahearne—Builder, 1977

Sir Montagu Allan—Builder, 1945

Keith Allen—Builder, 1992

Syl Apps—Player, 1961

Al Arbour—Builder, 1996

George Armstrong—Player, 1975

Neil Armstrong—Official, 1991

John Ashley—Official, 1981

Ace Bailey—Player, 1975

Dan Bain—Player, 1945

Hobey Baker—Player, 1945

Harold Ballard—Builder, 1977

Bill Barber—Player, 1990

Marty Barry—Player, 1965

Andy Bathgate—Player, 1978

Bobby Bauer—Player, 1996

Father David Bauer—Builder, 1989

Jean Beliveau—Player, 1972

Clint Benedict—Player, 1965

Doug Bentley—Player, 1964

Max Bentley—Player, 1966

Jack Bickell—Builder, 1978

Toe Blake—Player, 1966

Leo Boivin—Player, 1986

Dickie Boon—Player, 1952

Mike Bossy—Player, 1991

Butch Bouchard—Player, 1966

Frank Boucher—Player, 1958

George Boucher—Player, 1960

Ray Bourque—Player, 2004

Johnny Bower—Player, 1976

Russell Bowie—Player, 1945

Scotty Bowman—Builder, 1991

Frank Brimsek—Player, 1966

Punch Broadbent—Player, 1962

Turk Broda—Player, 1967

Herb Brooks—Builder, 2006

George Brown—Builder, 1961

Walter Brown—Builder, 1962

Frank Buckland—Builder, 1975

Johnny Bucyk—Player, 1981

Billy Burch—Player, 1974

Walter Bush—Builder, 2000

Jack Butterfield—Builder, 1980

Frank Calder—Builder, 1947

Harry Cameron—Player, 1962

Angus Campbell—Builder, 1964

Clarence Campbell—Builder, 1966

Joe Cattarinich—Builder, 1977

Bill Chadwick—Official, 1964

Gerry Cheevers—Player, 1985

King Clancy—Player, 1958

Dit Clapper—Player, 1947

Bobby Clarke—Player, 1987

Sprague Cleghorn—Player, 1958

Paul Coffey—Player, 2004

Neil Colville—Player, 1967

Charlie Conacher—Player, 1961

Lionel Conacher—Player, 1994

Roy Conacher—Player, 1998

Alex Connell—Player, 1958

Bill Cook—Player, 1952

Bun Cook—Player, 1995

Murray Costello—Builder, 2005

Art Coulter—Player, 1974

Yvan Cournoyer—Player, 1982

Bill Cowley—Player, 1968

Rusty Crawford—Player, 1962

John D'Amico—Official, 1993

Leo Dandurand—Builder, 1963

Jack Darragh—Player, 1962

Scotty Davidson—Player, 1950

Hap Day—Player, 1961

Alex Delvecchio—Player, 1977

Cy Denneny—Player, 1959

Frank Dilio—Builder, 1964

Marcel Dionne—Player, 1992

Gord Drillon—Player, 1975

Graham Drinkwater—Player, 1950

Ken Dryden—Player, 1983

George Dudley—Builder, 1958

Dick Duff—Player, 2006

Woody Dumart—Player, 1992

Tommy Dunderdale—Player, 1974

James Dunn—Builder, 1968

Bill Durnan—Player, 1964

Red Dutton—Player, 1958

Babe Dye—Player, 1970

Chaucer Elliott—Official, 1961

Tony Esposito—Player, 1988

Phil Esposito—Player, 1984

Art Farrell—Player, 1965

Bernie Federko—Player, 2002

Slava Fetisov—Player, 2001

Fern Flaman—Player, 1990

Cliff Fletcher—Builder, 2004

Frank Foyston—Player, 1958

Emile Francis—Builder, 1982

Ron Francis—Player, 2007

Frank Fredrickson—Player, 1958

Grant Fuhr—Player, 2003

Bill Gadsby—Player, 1970

Bob Gainey—Player, 1992

Chuck Gardiner—Player, 1945

Herb Gardiner—Player, 1958

Jimmy Gardner—Player, 1962

Mike Gartner—Player, 2001

Bernie Geoffrion—Player, 1972

Eddie Gerard—Player, 1945

Ed Giacomin—Player, 1987

Dr. Jack Gibson—Builder, 1976

Rod Gilbert—Player, 1982

Clark Gillies—Player, 2002

Billy Gilmour—Player, 1962

Moose Goheen—Player, 1952

Ebbie Goodfellow—Player, 1963

Tommy Gorman—Builder, 1963

Michel Goulet—Player, 1998

Mike Grant—Player, 1950

Shorty Green—Player, 1962

Jim Gregory—Builder, 2007

Wayne Gretzky—Player, 1999

Si Griffis—Player, 1950

Frank Griffiths—Builder, 1993

George Hainsworth—Player, 1961

Glenn Hall—Player, 1975

Joe Hall—Player, 1961

William Hanley—Builder, 1986

Doug Harvey—Player, 1973

Dale Hawerchuk—Player, 2001

Charles Hay—Builder, 1974

George Hay—Player, 1958

George Hayes—Official, 1988

Jim Hendy—Builder, 1968

Riley Hern—Player, 1962

Bobby Hewitson—Official, 1963

Foster Hewitt—Builder, 1965

William Hewitt—Builder, 1947

Bryan Hextall—Player, 1969

Harry Holmes—Player, 1972

Tom Hooper—Player, 1962

Red Horner—Player, 1965

Tim Horton—Player, 1977

Harley Hotchkiss—Builder, 2006

Gordie Howe—Player, 1972

Syd Howe—Player, 1965

Harry Howell—Player, 197

Bobby Hull—Player, 1983

Fred Hume—Builder, 1962

Bouse Hutton—Player, 1962

Harry Hyland—Player, 1962

Mike Ilitch—Builder, 2003

Punch Imlach—Builder, 1984

Mickey Ion—Official, 1961

Dick Irvin—Player, 1958

Tommy Ivan—Builder, 1974

Harvey Jackson—Player, 1971

William Jennings—Builder, 1975

Bob Johnson—Builder, 1992

Moose Johnson—Player, 1952

Ching Johnson—Player, 1958

Tom Johnson—Player, 1970

Aurel Joliat—Player, 1947

Gordon Juckes—Builder, 1979

Duke Keats—Player, 1958

Red Kelly—Player, 1969

Ted Kennedy—Player, 1966

Dave Keon—Player, 1986

Valeri Kharlamov—Player, 2005

Gen. John Reed Kilpatrick—
Builder, 1960

Brian Kilrea—Builder, 2003

Seymour Knox—Builder, 1993

Jari Kurri—Player, 2001

Elmer Lach—Player, 1966

Guy Lafleur—Player, 1988

Pat LaFontaine—Player, 2003

Newsy Lalonde—Player, 1950

Rod Langway—Player, 2002

Jacques Laperriere—Player, 1987

Guy Lapointe—Player, 1993

Edgar Laprade—Player, 1993

Jack Laviolette—Player, 1962

George Leader—Builder, 1969

Robert LeBel—Builder, 1970

Hugh Lehman—Player, 1958

Jacques Lemaire—Player, 1984

Mario Lemieux—Player, 1997

Percy LeSueur—Player, 1961

Herbie Lewis—Player, 1989

Ted Lindsay—Player, 1966

Tommy Lockhart—Builder, 1965

Paul Loicq—Builder, 1961

Harry Lumley—Player, 1980

Al MacInnis—Player, 2007

Mickey MacKay—Player, 1952

Frank Mahovlich—Player, 1981

Joe Malone—Player, 1950

Sylvio Mantha—Player, 1960

John Mariucci—Builder, 1985

Jack Marshall—Player, 1965

Frank Mathers—Builder, 1992

Steamer Maxwell—Player, 1962

Lanny McDonald—Player, 1992

Frank McGee—Player, 1945

Billy McGimsie—Player, 1962

Major Frederic McLaughlin—
    Builder, 1963

George McNamara—Player, 1958

Mark Messier—Player, 2007

Stan Mikita—Player, 1983

Jake Milford—Builder, 1984

Hon. Hartland Molson—
    Builder, 1973

Dickie Moore—Player, 1974

Paddy Moran—Player, 1958

Howie Morenz—Player, 1945

Scotty Morrison—Builder, 1999

Bill Mosienko—Player, 1965

Joe Mullen—Player, 2000

Larry Murphy—Player, 2004

Monsignor Athol Murray—
    Builder, 1998

Cam Neely—Player, 2005

Roger Neilson—Builder, 2002

Francis Nelson—Builder, 1947

Frank Nighbor—Player, 1947

Reg Noble—Player, 1962

Bruce A. Norris—Builder, 1969

James Norris Jr.—Builder, 1962

James Norris Sr.—Builder, 1958

William Northey—Builder, 1947

Ambrose O'Brien—Builder, 1962

Buddy O'Connor—Player, 1988

Harry Oliver—Player, 1967

Bert Olmstead—Player, 1985

Brian O'Neill—Builder, 1994

Bobby Orr—Player, 1979

Fred Page—Builder, 1993

Bernie Parent—Player, 1984

Brad Park—Player, 1988

Craig Patrick—Builder, 2001

Frank Patrick—Builder, 1958

Lester Patrick—Player, 1947

Lynn Patrick—Player, 1980

Matt Pavelich—Official, 1987

Gilbert Perreault—Player, 1990

Tommy Phillips—Player, 1945

Allan Pickard—Builder, 1958

Pierre Pilote—Player, 1975

Rudy Pilous—Builder, 1985

Didier Pitre—Player, 1962

Jacques Plante—Player, 1978

Bud Poile—Builder, 1990

Sam Pollock—Builder, 1978

Denis Potvin—Player, 1991

Babe Pratt—Player, 1966

Joe Primeau—Player, 1963

Marcel Pronovost—Player, 1978

Bob Pulford—Player, 1991

Harvey Pulford—Player, 1945

Bill Quackenbush—Player, 1976

Frank Rankin—Player, 1961

Jean Ratelle—Player, 1985

Sen. Donat Raymond— Builder, 1958

Chuck Rayner—Player, 1973

Ken Reardon—Player, 1966

Henri Richard—Player, 1979

Maurice Richard—Player, 1961

George Richardson—Player, 1950

Gordon Roberts—Player, 1971

John Ross Robertson—Builder, 1947

Claude Robinson—Builder, 1947

Larry Robinson—Player, 1995

Mike Rodden—Official, 1962

Art Ross—Player, 1945

Philip D. Ross—Builder, 1976

Patrick Roy—Player, 2006

Blair Russel—Player, 1965

Ernie Russell—Player, 1965

Jack Ruttan—Player, 1962

Dr. Gunther Sabetzki— Builder, 1995

Borje Salming—Player, 1996

Glen Sather—Builder, 1997

Denis Savard—Player, 2000

Serge Savard—Player, 1986

Terry Sawchuk—Player, 1971

Fred Scanlan—Player, 1965

Milt Schmidt—Player, 1961

Sweeney Schriner—Player, 1962

Earl Seibert—Player, 1963

Oliver Seibert—Player, 1961

Frank Selke—Builder, 1960

Eddie Shore—Player, 1947

Steve Shutt—Player, 1993

Babe Siebert—Player, 1964

Joe Simpson—Player, 1962

Harry Sinden—Builder, 1983

Darryl Sittler—Player, 1989

Cooper Smeaton—Official, 1961

Alf Smith—Player, 1962

Billy Smith—Player, 1993

Clint Smith—Player, 1991

Frank Smith—Builder, 1962

Hooley Smith—Player, 1972

Tommy Smith—Player, 1973

Conn Smythe—Builder, 1958

Ed Snider—Builder, 1988

Allan Stanley—Player, 1981

Barney Stanley—Player, 1962

Peter Stastny—Player, 1998

Scott Stevens—Player, 2007

Jack Stewart—Player, 1964

Lord Stanley of Preston— Builder, 1945

Nels Stewart—Player, 1962

Red Storey—Official, 1967

Bruce Stuart—Player, 1961

Hod Stuart—Player, 1945

Capt. James T. Sutherland— Builder, 1947

Anatoli Tarasov—Builder, 1974
Cyclone Taylor—Player, 1947
Tiny Thompson—Player, 1959
Bill Torrey—Builder, 1995
Vladislav Tretiak—Player, 1989
Harry Trihey—Player, 1950
Bryan Trottier—Player, 1997
Lloyd Turner—Builder, 1958
William Tutt—Builder, 1978
Frank Udvari—Official, 1973
Norm Ullman—Player, 1982
Andy Van Hellemond—
    Official, 1999
Georges Vezina—Player, 1945
Carl Voss—Builder, 1974

Fred Waghorne—Builder, 1961
Jack Walker—Player, 1960
Marty Walsh—Player, 1962
Harry E. Watson—Player, 1962
Harry Watson—Player, 1994
Cooney Weiland—Player, 1971
Harry Westwick—Player, 1962
Fred Whitcroft—Player, 1962
Phat Wilson—Player, 1962
Arthur Wirtz—Builder, 1971
Bill Wirtz—Builder, 1976
Gump Worsley—Player, 1980
Roy Worters—Player, 1969
John Ziegler—Builder, 1987

IIHF Hall of Fame

(name, nationality, year inducted)

° denotes Referee; * denotes Builder; all others are Players

°Quido Adamec (Czech Republic),
    2005
*John "Bunny" Ahearne (Great
    Britain), 1997
Veniamin Alexandrov (Russia),
    2007
*Ernest Aljancic, Sr. (Slovenia),
    2002
Helmut Balderis (Latvia), 1998
Rudi Ball (Germany), 2004
*Father David Bauer (Canada),
    1997
*Curt Berglund (Sweden), 2003

Sven Bergqvist (Sweden), 1999
Lars Bjorn (Sweden), 1998
Vsevolod Bobrov (Russia), 1997
Vladimir Bouzek (Czech Republic),
    2007
Roger Bourbonnais (Canada), 1999
*Herb Brooks (USA), 1999
*Walter Brown (USA), 1997
Vlastimil Bubnik (Czech
    Republic), 1997
*Mike Buckna (Canada), 2004
*Ludek Bukac (Czech Republic),
    2007

*Enrico Calcaterra (Italy), 1999

Ferdinand Cattini (Switzerland), 1998

Hans Cattini (Switzerland), 1998

Josef Cerny (Czech Republic), 2007

*Arkady Chernyshev (Russia), 1999

Bill Christian (USA), 1998

Bill Cleary (USA), 1997

Gerry Cosby (USA), 1997

Jim Craig (USA), 1999

Mike Curran (USA), 1999

°Ove Dahlberg (Sweden), 2004

Vitali Davydov (Russia), 2004

Igor Dimitriev (Russia), 2007

Hans Dobida (Austria), 2007

Jaroslav Drobny (Czechoslovakia), 1997

Vladimir Dzurilla (Slovakia), 1998

*Rudolf Eklow (Sweden), 1999

Carl Erhardt (Great Britain), 1998

Slava Fetisov (Russia), 2005

Anatoli Firsov (Russia), 1998

Josef Golonka (Slovakia), 1998

Wayne Gretzky (Canada), 2000

*Arne Grunander (Sweden), 1997

Henryk Gruth (Poland), 2006

*Bengt-Ake Gustafsson (Sweden), 2003

Karel Gut (Czech Republic), 1998

Anders Hedberg (Sweden), 1997

*Heinz Henschel (Germany), 2003

William Hewitt (Canada), 1998

Ivan Hlinka (Czech Republic), 2002

Jiri Holecek (Czech Republic), 1998

Jiri Holik (Czech Republic), 1999

*Derek Holmes (Canada), 1999

Leif Holmqvist (Sweden), 1999

*Ladislav Horsky (Slovakia), 2004

Fran Huck (Canada), 1999

*Jorgen Hviid (Denmark), 2005

Gustav Jaenecke (Germany), 1998

*Tore Johannessen (Norway), 1999

Mark Johnson (USA), 1999

Marshall Johnston (Canada), 1998

Tomas Jonsson (Sweden), 2000

Gord Juckes (Canada), 1997

Timo Jutila (Finland), 2003

°Yuri Karandin (Russia), 2004

*Tsutomu Kawabuchi (Japan), 2004

Matti Keinonen (Finland), 2002

Valeri Kharlamov (Russia), 1998

*Anatoli Khorozov (Ukraine), 2006

Udo Kiessling (Germany), 2000

*Dave King (Canada), 2001

Jakob Kolliker (Switzerland), 2007

°Josef Kompalla (Germany), 2003

Viktor Konovalenko (Russia), 2007

*Vladimir Kostka (Czech Republic), 1997

Erich Kuhnhackl (Germany), 1997

Jari Kurri (Finland), 2000

Viktor Kuzkin (Russia), 2005

Jacques Lacarriere (France), 1998

*Bob Lebel (Canada), 1997

*Harry Lindblad (Finland), 1999

Vic Lindquist (Canada), 1997

*Paul Loicq (Belgium), 1997

Konstantin Loktev (Russia), 2007

Hakan Loob (Sweden), 1998

*Cesar Luthi (Switzerland), 1998

Oldrich Machac (Czech Republic), 1999

Barry MacKenzie (Canada), 1999

Sergei Makarov (Russia), 2001

Josef Malecek (Czech Republic), 2003

Alexander Maltsev (Russia), 1999

*Louis Magnus (France), 1997

Pekka Marjamaki (Finland), 1998

Seth Martin (Canada), 1997

Vladimir Martinec (Czech Republic), 2001

John Mayasich (USA), 1997

Boris Mayorov (Russia), 1999

Jack McCartan (USA), 1998

Jack McLeod (Canada), 1999

Boris Mikhailov (Russia), 2000

Lou Nanne (USA), 2004

Mats Naslund (Sweden), 2005

Vaclav Nedomansky (Czech Republic), 1997

Kent Nilsson (Sweden), 2006

Nisse Nilsson (Sweden), 2002

Lasse Oksanen (Finland), 1999

Terry O'Malley (Canada), 1998

Eduard Pana (Romania), 1998

*Gyorgy Pasztor (Hungary), 2001

*Peter Patton (Great Britain), 2002

Esa Peltonen (Finland), 2007

Vladimir Petrov (Russia), 2006

Ronald Pettersson (Sweden), 2004

Frantisek Pospisil (Czech Republic), 1999

Sepp Puschnig (Austria), 1999

Alexander Ragulin (Russia), 1997

Hans Rampf (Germany), 2001

*Gord Renwick (Canada), 2002

*Bob Ridder (USA), 1998

*Jack Riley (USA), 1998

Thomas Rundquist (Sweden), 2007

*Gunther Sabetzki (Germany), 1997

Borje Salming (Sweden), 1998

Alois Schloder (Germany), 2005

Harry Sinden (Canada), 1997

Nikolai Sologubov (Russia), 2004

*Andrei Starovoitov (Russia), 1997

Vyacheslav Starshinov (Russia), 2007

*Jan Starsi (Slovakia), 1999

Peter Stastny (Slovakia), 2000

Ulf Sterner (Sweden), 2001

Roland Stoltz (Sweden), 1999

*Arne Stromberg (Sweden), 1998

*Goran Stubb (Finland), 2000

*Miroslav Subrt (Czech Republic), 2004

*Anatoli Tarasov (Russia), 1997

Frantisek Tikal (Czech Republic), 2004

*Viktor Tikhonov (Russia), 1998

*Shoichi Tomita (Japan), 2006

Richard "Bibi" Torriani (Switzerland), 1997

Vladislav Tretiak (Russia), 1997
*Hal Trumble (USA), 1999
*Yoshiaki Tsutsumi (Japan), 1999
Sven Tumba (Sweden), 1997
*Thayer Tutt (USA), 2002
*Xaver Unsinn (Germany), 1998
Jorma Valtonen (Finland), 1999
Valeri Vasiliev (Russia), 1998
Juhani Wahlsten (Finland), 2006

*Walter Wasservogel (Austria), 1997
Harry Watson (Canada), 1998
°Unto Wiitala (Finland), 2003
Alexander Yakushev (Russia), 2003
Urpo Ylonen (Finland), 1997
*Vldimir Yurzinov (Russia), 2002
Vladimir Zabrodsky (Czech
    Republic), 1997
Joachim Ziesche (Germany), 1999

United States Hockey Hall of Fame Members

(year inducted in brackets)

Taffy Abel—Player (1973)
Oscar Almquist—Coach (1983)
Hobey Baker—Player (1973)
Earl Bartholome—Player (1977)
Amo Bessone—Player (1992)
Pete Bessone—Coach (1978)
Bob Blake—Player (1985)
Henry Boucha—Player (1995)
Frank Brimsek—Player (1973)
Herb Brooks—Coach (1990)
Neal Broten—Player (2000)
George Brown—Administrator
    (1973)
Walter Brown—Administrator
    (1973)

Walter Bush—Administrator
    (1980)
Joseph Cavanagh, Jr.—Player
    (1994)
Len Ceglarski—Coach (1992)
Bill Chadwick—Referee (1974)
Ray Chaisson—Player (1974)
John Chase—Player (1973)
Bill Christian—Player (1984)
Dave Christian—Player (2001)
Roger Christian—Player (1989)
Keith Christiansen—Player (2005)
Don Clark—Administrator (1978)
James Claypool—Administrator
    (1995)
Bill Cleary—Player (1976)
Bob Cleary—Player (1981)
Tony Conroy—Player (1975)
Paul Coppo—Player (2004)

John Cunniff—Coach (2003)
Mike Curranv (1998)
Cully Dahlstrom—Player (1973)
Vic Desjardins—Player (1974)
Richard Desmond—Player (1988)
Bob Dill—Player (1979)
Dick Dougherty—Player (2003)
Doug Everett—Player (1974)
Robbie Ftorek—Player (1991)
James Fullerton—Coach (1992)
Mark Fusco—Player (2002)
Scott Fusco—Player (2002)
Serge Gambucci—Coach (1996)
John Garrison—Player (1973)
Jack Garrity—Player (1986)
Doc Gibson—Administrator (1973)
Moose Goheen—Player (1973)
Malcolm Gordon—Coach (1973)
Wally Grant—Player (1994)
Austie Harding—Player (1975)
Ned Harkness—Coach (1994)
Vic Heyliger—Coach (1974)
Charlie Holt—Coach (1997)
Phil Housley—Player (2004)
Mark Howe—Player (2003)
Willard Ikola—Coach (1990)
Mike Ilitch—Administrator (2004)
Stewart Inglehart—Player (1975)
William Jennings—Administrator (1981)
Ed Jeremiah—Coach (1973)
Bob Johnson—Coach (1991)
Mark Johnson—Player (2004)
Paul Johnson—Player (2001)

Virgil Johnson—Player (1974)
Nick Kahler—Administrator (1980)
Mike Karakas—Player (1973)
Jack Kelley—Coach (1974)
Snooks Kelley—Coach (1993)
Jack Kirrane, Jr.—Player (1987)
Pat LaFontaine—Player (2003)
Myles Lane—Player (1973)
Dave Langevin—Player (1993)
Rod Langway—Player (1999)
Myles Lane—Player (1973)
Reed Larson—Player (1996)
Joe Linder—Player (1975)
Tom Lockhart—Administrator (1973)
Sam LoPresti—Player (1973)
Lane MacDonald—Player (2005)
John Mariucci—Player (1973)
Calvin Marvin—Administrator (1982)
John Matchefts—Player (1991)
Bruce Mather—Player (1998)
John Mayasich—Player (1976)
Jack McCartan—Player (1983)
Billy Moe—Player (1974)
Ken Morrow—Player (1995)
Fred Moseley—Player (1975)
Joe Mullen—Player (1998)
Muzz Murray—Player (1987)
Lou Nanne—Player/Administrator (1998)
Hub Nelson—Player (1978)
Bill Nyrop—Player (1997)

Eddie Olson —Player (1977)
George Owen—Player (1973)
Doug Palazzari—Administrator
    (2000)
Ding Palmer—Player (1973)
Bob Paradise—Player (1989)
Craig Patrick—Coach (1996)
Larry Pleau—Administrator (2000)
Connie Pleban—Coach (1990)
Fido Purpur—Player (1974)
Mike Ramsey—Player (2001)
Bob Ridder—Administrator (1976)
Bill Riley—Player (1977)
Jack Riley—Coach (1979)
Joe Riley—Player (2002)
Gordie Roberts—Player (1999)
Moe Roberts—Player (2005)
Doc Romnes—Player (1973)
Dick Rondeau—Player (1985)
Larry Ross—Coach (1988)
Charles Schulz—Administrator

    (1993)
Tim Sheehy—Player (1997)
Bill Stewart—Coach (1982)
Cliff Thompson—Coach (1973)
Hal Trumble—Administrator (1985)
Thayer Tutt—Administrator (1973)
Sid Watson—Administrator (1999)
Murray Williamson—Coach (2005)
Tommy Williams—Player (1981)
Ralph Winsor—Coach (1973)
Bill Wirtz—Administrator (1984)
Coddy Winters—Player (1973)
Doug Woog—Coach (2002)
Lyle Wright—Administrator (1973)
Ken Yackel—Player (1986)

1960 U.S. Olympic Team (2000)
1980 U.S. Olympic Team (2003)

2007 WORLD CHAMPIONSHIPS

World Championships, Women's

Winnipeg/Selkirk, Canada, April 3–10, 2007

FINAL PLACINGS

GOLD MEDAL	Canada
SILVER MEDAL	USA
BRONZE MEDAL	Sweden
Fourth Place	Finland
Fifth Place	Switzerland
Sixth Place	China
Seventh Place	Russia
Eighth Place	Germany
Ninth Place	Kazakhstan

All-Star Team

Goalie	Kim St. Pierre (Canada)
Defence	Delaney Collins (Canada)
	Angela Ruggiero (United States)
Forward	Natalie Darwitz (United States)
	Krissy Wendell (United States)
	Hayley Wickenheiser (Canada)

Directorate Awards

BEST GOALIE	Noora Raty (Finland)
BEST DEFENCEMAN	Molly Engstrom (United States)
BEST FORWARD	Hayley Wickenheiser (Canada)
MVP	Hayley Wickenheiser (Canada)

Tournament Format

Nine nations took part. They were divided into three groups of three and played a round-robin series within each. The top team from each group advanced to one group (D), the second-place teams advanced to a second (E) and the three third-place teams to yet another (F). Once again, they played a round-robin series within each new group. The top two teams from Group D advanced to the gold-medal game. The third team from this group played the top team from Group E for the bronze medal. The last-place team in Group F was relegated to Division I for the following year.

For the first time, teams received three points for a regulation-time victory. All games tied after 60 minutes went to overtime and, if needed, a shootout. The winner in OT/SO received two points and the loser one point.

Results & Final Standings

Group A (Selkirk)

	GP	W	OTW	OTL	L	GF	GA	P
USA	2	2	0	0	0	18	1	6
China	2	1	0	0	1	8	9	3
Kazakhstan	2	0	0	0	2	0	16	0

April 3	USA 9/Kazakhstan 0
April 4	China 7/Kazakhstan 0
April 5	USA 9/China 1

Group B (Winnipeg)

	GP	W	OTW	OTL	L	GF	GA	P
Canada	2	2	0	0	0	17	0	6
Switzerland	2	1	0	0	1	1	9	3
Germany	2	0	0	0	2	0	9	0

April 3	Canada 9/Switzerland 0
April 4	Switzerland 1/Germany 0
April 5	Canada 8/Germany 0

Group C (Winnipeg)

	GP	W	OTW	OTL	L	GF	GA	P
Finland	2	1	1	0	0	5	0	5
Sweden	2	1	0	1	0	3	3	4
Russia	2	0	0	0	2	2	7	0

April 3	Sweden 3/Russia 2
April 4	Finland 4/Russia 0
April 5	Finland 1/Sweden 0 (SO)

Group D (Winnipeg)

	GP	W	OTW	OTL	L	GF	GA	P
Canada	2	1	1	0	0	10	4	5
USA	2	1	0	1	0	8	5	4
Finland	2	0	0	0	2	0	9	0

April 7	Canada 5/USA 4
April 8	USA 4/Finland 0
April 9	Canada 5/Finland 0

Group E (Winnipeg)

	GP	W	OTW	OTL	L	GF	GA	P
Sweden	2	2	0	0	0	16	2	6
Switzerland	2	1	0	0	1	5	5	3
China	2	0	0	0	2	3	17	0

April 7	Switzerland 5/China 1
April 8	Sweden 12/China 2
April 9	Sweden 4/Switzerland 0

Group F (Winnipeg)

	GP	W	OTW	OTL	L	GF	GA	P
Russia	2	2	0	0	0	11	1	6
Germany	2	1	0	0	1	4	4	3
Kazakhstan	2	0	0	0	2	0	10	0

April 7	Germany 3/Kazakhstan 0
April 8	Russia 7/Kazakhstan 0
April 9	Russia 4/Germany 1

Bronze Medal Game

April 10   Sweden 1/Finland 0

Gold Medal Game

April 10   Canada 5/USA 1

World Championships, Men

Moscow/Mytischi, Russia, April 24–May 10, 2007

FINAL PLACINGS

GOLD MEDAL	Canada
SILVER MEDAL	Finland
BRONZE MEDAL	Russia
Fourth Place	Sweden
Fifth Place	United States
Sixth Place	Slovakia
Seventh Place	Czech Republic
Eighth Place	Switzerland
Ninth Place	Germany
Tenth Place	Denmark
Eleventh Place	Belarus
Twelfth Place	Italy
Thirteenth Place	Latvia

Fourteenth Place   Norway
Fifteenth Place   Austria
Sixteenth Place   Ukraine

All-Star Team

Goal	Kari Lehtonen (Finland)
Defence	Petteri Nummelin (Finland)
	Andrei Markov (Russia)
Forward	Rick Nash (Canada)
	Evgeni Malkin (Russia)
	Alexei Morozov (Russia)

Directorate Awards

BEST GOALIE	Kari Lehtonen (Finland)
BEST DEFENCEMAN	Andrei Markov (Russia)
BEST FORWARD	Alexei Morozov (Russia)
MVP	Rick Nash (Canada)

RESULTS & FINAL STANDINGS
Group A (Moscow)

	GP	W	OTW	OTL	L	GF	GA	P
Sweden	3	3	0	0	0	21	3	9
Switzerland	3	2	0	0	1	4	8	6
Italy	3	0	1	0	2	6	12	2
Latvia	3	0	0	1	2	6	14	1

April 28	Switzerland 2/Latvia 1
April 28	Sweden 7/Italy 1
April 30	Switzerland 2/Italy 1
April 30	Sweden 8/Latvia 2
May 2	Italy 4/Latvia 3 (OT)
May 2	Sweden 6/Switzerland 0

Group B (Mytischi)

	GP	W	OTW	OTL	L	GF	GA	P
Czech Republic	3	3	0	0	0	18	6	9
USA	3	2	0	0	1	14	7	6
Belarus	3	1	0	0	2	8	15	3
Austria	3	0	0	0	3	5	17	0

April 27	USA 6/Austria 2
April 27	Czech Republic 8/Belarus 2
April 29	Czech Republic 6/Austria 1
April 29	USA 5/Belarus 1
May 1	Belarus 5/Austria 2
May 1	Czech Republic 4/USA 3

Group C (Mytischi)

	GP	W	OTW	OTL	L	GF	GA	P
Canada	3	3	0	0	0	12	8	9
Slovakia	3	2	0	0	1	12	6	6
Germany	3	1	0	0	2	8	11	3
Norway	3	0	0	0	3	5	12	0

April 28	Canada 3/Germany 2
April 28	Slovakia 3/Norway 0
April 30	Slovakia 5/Germany 1
April 30	Canada 4/Norway 2
May 2	Germany 5/Norway 3
May 2	Canada 5/Slovakia 4

Group D (Moscow)

	GP	W	OTW	OTL	L	GF	GA	P
Russia	3	3	0	0	0	22	6	9
Finland	3	2	0	0	0	15	7	6
Denmark	3	1	0	0	0	7	18	3
Ukraine	3	0	0	0	0	4	17	0

April 27	Finland 5/Ukraine 0
April 27	Russia 9/Denmark 1
April 29	Finland 6/Denmark 2
April 29	Russia 8/Ukraine 1
May 1	Denmark 4/Ukraine 3
May 1	Russia 5/Finland 4

Group E (Moscow)

	GP	W	OTW	OTL	L	GF	GA	P
Russia	5	5	0	0	0	27	10	15
Sweden	5	4	0	0	1	21	7	12
Finland	5	3	0	0	2	15	8	9
Switzerland	5	2	0	0	3	9	16	6
Denmark	5	1	0	0	4	11	26	3
Italy	5	0	0	0	5	4	20	0

May 3	Finland 2/Switzerland 0
May 3	Sweden 5/Denmark 2
May 4	Russia 3/Italy 0
May 5	Switzerland 4/Denmark 1
May 5	Finland 3/Italy 0
May 6	Russia 6/Switzerland 3
May 6	Sweden 1/Finland 0
May 7	Denmark 5/Italy 2
May 7	Russia 4/Sweden 2

Group F

	GP	W	OTW	OTL	L	GF	GA	P
Canada	5	4	1	0	0	24	15	14
USA	5	3	0	0	2	18	13	9
Slovakia	5	3	0	0	2	18	15	9
Czech Rep.	5	2	0	1	2	17	14	7
Germany	5	2	0	0	3	11	16	6
Belarus	5	0	0	0	5	14	29	0

May 3	Mytischi	USA 4/Slovakia 2
May 3	Mytischi	Germany 2/Czech Republic 0
May 4	Moscow	Canada 6/Belarus 3
May 5	Mytischi	USA 3/Germany 0
May 5	Mytischi	Slovakia 3/Czech Republic 2
May 6	Mytischi	Slovakia 4/Belarus 3
May 6	Mytischi	Canada 4/Czech Republic 3 (OT)
May 7	Mytischi	Germany 6/Belarus 5
May 7	Mytischi	Canada 6/USA 3

Group G

	GP	W	OTW	OTL	L	GF	GA	P
Latvia	3	2	0	0	1	14	8	6
Norway	3	1	1	0	1	12	9	5
Austria	3	1	0	1	1	11	12	4
Ukraine	3	1	0	0	2	7	15	3

May 4	Mytischi	Norway 3/Austria 2
May 4	Mytischi	Latvia 5/Ukraine 0
May 6	Moscow	Latvia 5/Austria 1
May 6	Mytischi	Ukraine 3/Norway 2
May 7	Moscow	Austria 8/Ukraine 4
May 7	Mytischi	Norway 7/Latvia 4

Quarterfinals

May 9	Moscow	Russia 4/Czech Republic 0
May 9	Moscow	Sweden 7/Slovakia 4
May 10	Moscow	Canada 5/Switzerland 1
May 10	Moscow	Finland 5/USA 4 (SO)

Semifinals

| May 12 | Moscow | Finland 2/Russia 1 (OT) |
| May 12 | Moscow | Canada 4/Sweden 1 |

Bronze Medal Game

May 13   Moscow   Russia 3/Sweden 1

Gold Medal Game

May 13   Moscow   Canada 4/Finland 2

HISTORY OF THE IIHF

On May 15, 1908, at the invitation of French journalist Louis Magnus, ice hockey officials from four countries met in Paris: Robert Planque and Robert van der Hoeven of France; Eddie de Clercq and Eduard Malaret of Belgium; Eduard Mellor and Louis Dufour of Switzerland; and E.E. Mavrogrodato of Great Britain. These men established the Ligue Internationale de Hockey sur Glace (LIHG), electing Magnus as president and Planque as general secretary. France, Bohemia, Great Britain, Switzerland and Belgium became charter members of the LIHG.

The first European championship was played January 10–12, 1910, in the town of Les Avants, near Montreux, Switzerland, with four official participants—Great Britain, Germany, Belgium and Switzerland—plus the Oxford Canadians, a team of Canadians studying at Oxford that competed unofficially.

The European championship took place on a regular basis—interrupted only during the war years—at first as a standalone event and then, from 1930 onward, in conjunction with the World Championship. Between 1912 and 1914, besides the European championship, a so-called "LIHG championat" involving national teams was organized every year; however, this competition did not gain much importance.

An ice hockey tournament was included as part of the 1920 Summer Olympic Games in Antwerp and was played from April 23–29. For the first time, Canada and the United States competed—although at the time they were not yet LIHG members—and demonstrated a marked superiority over their European rivals.

On April 26, 1920, at the congress during that first Olympic ice hockey tournament, Canada and the U.S. were admitted to the LIHG, becoming its first non-European members. At the same congress in Antwerp it was also decided that the 1924 Olympic tournament would serve as the World Championship. In addition, a separate European championship was scheduled for 1924. In 1929, in Budapest, the congress decided to organize an annual World Championship to begin the following year, and the highest-placing team from Europe would be crowned the European champion.

This first World Championship—outside the Olympics, which were considered World Championships during the years of competition—was only partially successful. Once the natural ice melted in the championship venue of Chamonix, the decisive matches had to be moved to the Sports Palace in Berlin and to Vienna.

The 1932 Olympics in Lake Placid featured just four teams because most of the European associations could not raise the funds necessary to travel overseas. The European championship was played in the same year for the last time as a separate event. The World Championship of 1933 in Prague, played on the first artificial ice rink in Czechoslovakia, caused a sensation when the Canadians, perennial champions since their first international appearance in 1920, finished second to the U.S.

The 1936 Olympics in Garmisch-Partenkirchen brought a record 15 nations to the tournament. The winning team, Great Britain, counted a great number of Canadian-born and -trained players on its roster. While the main hockey venue was a modern artificial ice rink constructed especially for the Olympics, some matches were played on the natural ice of the frozen Riesser Lake. After snowfall affected quality of play, the IIHF (also no doubt remembering the lesson of Chamonix in 1930) decided that the Worlds would thenceforth be awarded only to countries that could provide artificial ice exclusively.

The IIHF also ruled that a World Championship should be played every year, but be recognized as such only if at least one association from outside Europe (i.e., Canada or the United States) took part.

Between the late 1950s and early 1960s, post–World War II politics intruded on the World Championship. As a result of the Hungarian revolt and Suez Crisis, both of which occurred in 1956, the tournament in Moscow in 1957 was boycotted by most of the western countries. At the 1961 World Championship in Switzerland, the West German team was urged by the federal government in Bonn to refrain from competing against the German Democratic Republic (East Germany), so that, in case the GDR won, the players would not be obliged to pay their respects to the East German flag. Instead, West Germany forfeited the game.

Two years later in Stockholm, the squad from the GDR turned their backs on the flagpole as the black, red and gold flag of the Federal Republic of Germany was hoisted during the awards ceremony.

The construction of the Berlin Wall in the summer of 1961 had an impact on the 1962 Worlds, held in Denver and Colorado Springs, Colorado. The United States denied entry to the East German team, and in solidarity, the other Eastern bloc countries boycotted the tournament.

Beginning with the 1961 World Championship, teams were divided into pools—A, B and C, in order of competitiveness—and a system of promotion and relegation meant that teams could move up or down in the pools. In 1987, a D pool was added. These groupings were renamed in 2001, when the A pool became simply the top pool, with no special name, while the B, C and D pools became Divisions I, II and III, respectively.

In 1970, Canada was due to host the World Championship for the first time. But when Canada was denied permission to use professionals in the tournament, the Canadians withdrew completely from international competition. Negotiations between IIHF president Gunther Sabetzki and the top officials in Canada paved the way for Canada's return to the Worlds in 1977. An agreement was reached allowing teams to use professionals, including NHLers, on their World Championship rosters. The World Championship was also scheduled to begin later so as to ensure the availability of players whose teams were eliminated from the Stanley Cup playoffs.

In turn, the Canadians pledged to participate regularly in the World Championship, and a new international competition, the Canada Cup, was inaugurated. This was an open tournament (meaning that all teams would be allowed to use their best players, whether amateur or professional) contested by Canada, the United States, and the four strongest European national teams according to the most recent World Championship standings. Between 1976 and 1991, the Canada Cup was played five times; in 1996, it was succeeded, with some modifications, by the World Cup of Hockey, which was staged again in 2004.

The number of IIHF member associations increased steadily during the 1980s and '90s, due in some part to the disintegration of the Soviet Union. The U.S.S.R.'s membership was assumed by Russia, while former Soviet republics Ukraine, Belarus, Azerbaijan and Kazakhstan were added after their countries declared independence. The memberships of Estonia, Latvia and Lithuania, which had lapsed after these countries were annexed by the Soviets, were renewed when they again became sovereign nations.

Today, international hockey has never been stronger or more popular. The game is played in countries around the world, and some 65 member nations of the IIHF compete annually in either ice hockey or InLine hockey.

CANADA HOSTS WORLD CHAMPIONSHIPS FOR FIRST TIME

For the first time since 1930, when the IIHF World Championships were inaugurated, Canada will play host to the tournament. It will be played in two cities—Quebec City and Halifax—and 16 teams will play a total of 56 games over 18 days (May 1–18, 2008).

The first series of games will consist of a round-robin Preliminary Round within each of four groups of four teams (Groups A, B, C, D—see below). The top three teams from each group will move on to a Qualifying Round, where they will be organized into two groups of six teams (Groups E, F). The last-place team in each Preliminary Round group will go to a Relegation Round to play another round robin. The bottom two teams in the Relegation Round will be demoted to Division I for 2009; the top two will remain at the top level.

The groups in the Qualifying Round will play another round robin, but only against those teams they didn't already face in the Preliminary Round (scores from the Preliminary Round are carried forward to the Qualifying Round).

The top four teams from these groups will then play a crossover quarterfinal series of games (i.e., E1 vs. F4, E2 vs. F3, etc.). These winners meet in the semifinals, and those winners advance to the final, the gold-medal game. The losers of the semifinal games play for the bronze medal.

As in the NHL, there are no longer any ties in international hockey. A tied game after 60 minutes results in an overtime and then a shootout, if necessary. Starting in 2008, the IIHF will also use a four-official system (i.e., two referees instead of one).

Canada has won gold three times in the last five years and been to the final four times (losing to the Czechs in the NHL-lockout year of 2004–05).

2008 World Championships

Group A (Quebec City)
Sweden
Switzerland
Belarus
France

Group C (Halifax)
Finland
Slovakia
Germany
Norway

Group B (Halifax)
Canada
USA
Latvia
Slovenia

Group D (Quebec City)
Russia
Czech Republic
Denmark
Italy

World Rankings
1. Sweden
2. Canada
3. Finland
4. Czech Republic
5. Russia
6. Slovakia
7. USA
8. Switzerland
9. Belarus
10. Latvia
11. Germany
12. Denmark
13. Italy
14. Norway
15. Slovenia
16. France

PRO CLASSICS RESULTS

1972 Summit Series
Canada/Moscow, September 2–28, 1972

	GP	W	L	T	GF	GA	P
Canada	8	4	3	1	31	32	9
Soviet Union	8	3	4	1	32	31	7

Results

Game 1	September 2	Montreal	Soviet Union 7/Canada 3
Game 2	September 4	Toronto	Canada 4/Soviet Union 1
Game 3	September 6	Winnipeg	Canada 4/Soviet Union 4
Game 4	September 8	Vancouver	Soviet Union 5/Canada 3

Exhibition September 16 Stockholm Canada 4/Swedish Nationals 1

Exhibition September 17 Stockholm Canada 4/Swedish Nationals 4

Game 5	September 22	Moscow	Soviet Union 5/Canada 4
Game 6	September 24	Moscow	Canada 3/Soviet Union 2
Game 7	September 26	Moscow	Canada 4/Soviet Union 3
Game 8	September 28	Moscow	Canada 6/Soviet Union 5

(Paul Henderson scores series winner at 19:26 of 3rd)

Exhibition September 30 Prague Canada 3/Czech Nationals 3

1976 Canada Cup
Canada, September 2–15, 1976
Series MVP: Bobby Orr (Canada)

Team MVPs
Canada	Rogie Vachon
Czechoslovakia	Milan Novy
Soviet Union	Alexander Maltsev
Sweden	Borje Salming
United States	Robbie Ftorek
Finland	Matti Hagman

Final Standings Round Robin
	GP	W	L	T	GF	GA	P
Canada	5	4	1	0	22	6	8
Czechoslovakia	5	3	1	1	19	9	7
Soviet Union	5	2	2	1	23	14	5
Sweden	5	2	2	1	16	18	5
United States	5	1	3	1	14	21	3
Finland	5	1	4	0	16	42	2

Results
September 2	Ottawa	Canada 11/Finland 2
September 3	Toronto	Sweden 5/United States 2
	Montreal	Czechoslovakia 5/Soviet Union 3
September 5	Montreal	Canada 4/United States 2
	Montreal	Soviet Union 3/Sweden 3
	Toronto	Czechoslovakia 8/Finland 0
September 7	Toronto	Canada 4/Sweden 0
	Montreal	Soviet Union 11/Finland 3
	Philadelphia	Czechoslovakia 4/United States 4

September 9	Montreal	Czechoslovakia 1/Canada 0
	Winnipeg	Finland 8/Sweden 6
	Philadelphia	Soviet Union 5/United States 0

September 11	Toronto	Canada 3/Soviet Union 1
	Quebec City	Sweden 2/Czechoslovakia 1
	Montreal	United States 6/Finland 3

FINALS (best two-of-three)

September 13	Toronto	Canada 6/Czechoslovakia 0
September 15	Montreal	Canada 5/Czechoslovakia 4
		(Sittler 11:33 OT)

1981 Canada Cup
Canada, September 1–13, 1981
Tournament MVP: Vladislav Tretiak
Team Canada MVP: Mike Bossy

All-Star Team

| Goal | Vladislav Tretiak (Soviet Union) |

| Defence | Alexei Kasatonov (Soviet Union) |
| | Arnold Kadlec (Czechoslovakia) |

Forward	Gil Perreault (Canada)
	Mike Bossy (Canada)
	Sergei Shepelev (Soviet Union)

Final Standings Round Robin

	GP	W	L	T	GF	GA	P
Canada	5	4	0	1	32	13	9
Soviet Union	5	3	1	1	20	13	7
Czechoslovakia	5	2	1	2	21	13	6
United States	5	2	2	1	17	19	5
Sweden	5	1	4	0	13	20	2
Finland	5	0	4	1	6	31	1

Results

September 1	Edmonton	Canada 9/Finland 0
	Edmonton	United States 3/Sweden 1
	Winnipeg	Czechoslovakia 1/Soviet Union 1
September 3	Edmonton	Canada 8/United States 3
	Edmonton	Czechoslovakia 7/Finland 1
	Winnipeg	Soviet Union 6/Sweden 3
September 5	Winnipeg	Canada 4/Czechoslovakia 4
	Winnipeg	Sweden 5/Finland 0
	Edmonton	Soviet Union 4/United States 1
September 7	Montreal	Canada 4/Sweden 3
	Winnipeg	Soviet Union 6/Finland 1
	Montreal	United States 6/Czechoslovakia 2
September 9	Montreal	Canada 7/Soviet Union 3
	Ottawa	Czechoslovakia 7/Sweden 1
	Montreal	Finland 4/United States 4

Semifinals

September 11	Montreal	Canada 4/United States 1
	Ottawa	Soviet Union 4/Czechoslovakia 1

Finals

September 13   Montreal   Soviet Union 8/Canada 1

1984 Canada Cup
Canada, September 1–18, 1984
Tournament MVP: John Tonelli

All-Star Team

Goal	Vladimir Myshkin (Soviet Union)
Defence	Paul Coffey (Canada)
	Rod Langway (United States)
Forward	Wayne Gretzky (Canada)
	John Tonelli (Canada)
	Sergei Makarov (Soviet Union)

Final Standings Round Robin

	GP	W	L	T	GF	GA	P
Soviet Union	5	5	0	0	22	7	10
United States	5	3	1	1	21	13	7
Sweden	5	3	2	0	15	16	6
Canada	5	2	2	1	23	18	5
West Germany	5	0	4	1	13	29	1
Czechoslovakia	5	0	4	1	10	21	1

Results

September 1	Montreal	Canada 7/West Germany 2
	Halifax	United States 7/Sweden 1
September 2	Montreal	Soviet Union 3/Czechoslovakia 0
September 3	Montreal	Canada 4/United States 4
September 4	London	Czechoslovakia 4/West Germany 4
	Calgary	Soviet Union 3/Sweden 2

September 6	Vancouver	Sweden 4/Canada 2
	Edmonton	Soviet Union 8/West Germany 1
	Buffalo	United States 3 /Czechoslovakia 2
September 8	Calgary	Canada 7/Czechoslovakia 2
	Calgary	Sweden 4/West Germany 2
	Edmonton	Soviet Union 2/United States 1
September 10	Edmonton	Soviet Union 6/Canada 3
	Vancouver	Sweden 4/Czechoslovakia 2
	Calgary	United States 6/West Germany 4

Semifinals

| September 12 | Edmonton | Sweden 9/United States 2 |
| September 13 | Calgary | Canada 3/Soviet Union 2 (Bossy 12:29 OT) |

Finals (best two-of-three)

| September 16 | Calgary | Canada 5/Sweden 2 |
| September 18 | Edmonton | Canada 6/Sweden 5 |

1987 Canada Cup
Canada, August 28–September 15, 1987

Tournament All-Star Team

Goal	Grant Fuhr (Canada)
Defence	Ray Bourque (Canada)
	Viacheslav Fetisov (Soviet Union)
Forward	Mario Lemieux (Canada)
	Wayne Gretzky (Canada)
	Vladimir Krutov (Soviet Union)

Final Standings Round Robin

	GP	W	L	T	GF	GA	P
Canada	5	3	0	2	19	13	8
Soviet Union	5	3	1	1	22	13	7
Sweden	5	3	2	0	17	14	6
Czechoslovakia	5	2	2	1	12	15	5
United States	5	2	3	0	13	14	4
Finland	5	0	5	0	9	23	0

Results

August 28	Calgary	Canada 4/Czechoslovakia 4
	Hartford	United States 4/Finland 1
August 29	Calgary	Sweden 5/Soviet Union 3
August 30	Hamilton	Canada 4/Finland 1
August 31	Regina	Soviet Union 4/Czechoslovakia 0
	Hamilton	United States 5/Sweden 2
September 2	Halifax	Soviet Union 7/Finland 4
	Hamilton	Canada 3/United States 2
	Regina	Sweden 4/Czechoslovakia 0
September 4	Hartford	Soviet Union 5/United States 1
	Sydney	Czechoslovakia 5/Finland 2
	Montreal	Canada 5/Sweden 3
September 6	Sydney	Sweden 3/Finland 1
	Sydney	Czechoslovakia 3/United States 1
	Hamilton	Canada 3/Soviet Union 3
September 8	Hamilton	Soviet Union 4/Sweden 2
	Montreal	Canada 5/Czechoslovakia 3

Finals (best two-of-three)

September 11	Montreal	Soviet Union 6/Canada 5 (Semak 5:33 OT)
September 13	Hamilton	Canada 6/Soviet Union 5 (Mario Lemieux 30:07 OT)
September 15	Hamilton	Canada 6/Soviet Union 5 (Lemieux scores winner at 18:34 of 3rd)

1991 Canada Cup
Canada, August 31–September 16, 1991
Tournament All-Star Team

Goal	Bill Ranford (Canada)
Defence	Al MacInnis (Canada)
	Chris Chelios (United States)
Forward	Wayne Gretzky (Canada)
	Jeremy Roenick (United States)
	Mats Sundin (Sweden)

Final Standings Round Robin

	GP	W	L	T	GF	GA	P
Canada	5	3	0	2	21	11	8
United States	5	4	1	0	19	15	8
Finland	5	2	2	1	10	13	5
Sweden	5	2	3	0	13	17	4
Soviet Union	5	1	3	1	14	14	3
Czechoslovakia	5	1	4	0	11	18	2

Results

August 31	Toronto	Canada 2/Finland 2
	Saskatoon	Czechoslovakia 5/Soviet Union 2
	Pittsburgh	United States 6/Sweden 3

September 2	Hamilton	Canada 6/United States 3
	Montreal	Sweden 3/Soviet Union 2
	Saskatoon	Finland 1/Czechoslovakia 0
September 5	Toronto	Canada 4/Sweden 1
	Hamilton	Soviet Union 6/Finland 1
	Detroit	United States 4/Czechoslovakia 2
September 7	Montreal	Canada 6/Czechoslovakia 2
	Toronto	Finland 3/Sweden 1
	Chicago	United States 2/Soviet Union 1
September 9	Quebec City	Canada 3/Soviet Union 3
	Toronto	Sweden 5/Czechoslovakia 2
	Chicago	United States 4/Finland 3

Semifinals

| September 11 | Hamilton | United States 7/Finland 3 |
| September 12 | Toronto | Canada 4/Sweden 0 |

Finals (best two-of-three)

| September 14 | Montreal | Canada 4/United States 1 |
| September 16 | Hamilton | Canada 4/United States 2 |

World Cup of Hockey 2004
Canada/Europe/United States, August 30–September 14, 2004

FINAL STANDINGS ROUND ROBIN
North American Pool

	GP	W	L	T	GF	GA	P
United States	3	3	0	0	19	8	6
Canada	3	2	1	0	11	10	4
Russia	3	1	2	0	12	14	2
Slovakia	3	0	3	0	9	19	0

European Pool

	GP	W	L	T	GF	GA	P
Sweden	3	3	0	0	14	3	6
Finland	3	2	1	0	17	11	4
Germany	3	1	2	0	11	15	2
Czech Republic	3	0	3	0	4	17	0

Results

August 26	Stockholm	Sweden 6/Germany 1
August 27	Helsinki	Finland 7/Czech Republic 3
August 28	Helsinki	Finland 8/Germany 3
	Prague	Sweden 3/Czech Republic 0
	Vancouver	Canada 5/Russia 3
August 31	Philadelphia	United States 5/Canada 3
	Garmisch	Germany 7/Czech Republic 1
	Montreal	Russia 7/Slovakia 4
September 1	Ottawa	Canada 3/Slovakia 2
	Stockholm	Sweden 5/Finland 2

September 2   New York   United States 5/Russia 2

September 3   New York   United States 9/Slovakia 3

Quarterfinals
September 5   Montreal   Canada 4/Germany 1

September 6   Ottawa   Russia 5/Finland 0

Semifinals
September 7   Philadelphia   Canada 3/Sweden 2
                             (Fleury 39:47 OT)
September 8   Ottawa   United States 5/Russia 2

Finals (best two-of-three)
September 10 Philadelphia   Canada 4/United States 3
                             (Yzerman 19:53 OT)
September 12 Montreal   United States 5/Canada 2
September 14 Montreal   United States 5/Canada 2

World Cup of Hockey 2004
August 30–September 14, 2004
Tournament MVP: Vincent Lecavalier (CAN)

All-Tournament Team
Goal   Martin Brodeur (CAN)

Defence   Adam Foote (CAN)
           Kimmo Timonen (FIN)

Forward   Vincent Lecavalier (CAN)
           Fredrik Modin (SWE)
           Saku Koivu (FIN)

PRELIMINARY ROUND STANDINGS
European Pool

	GP	W	L	T	GF	GA	P
Finland	3	2	0	1	11	4	5
Sweden	3	2	0	1	13	9	5
Czech Republic	3	1	2	0	10	10	2
Germany	3	0	3	0	4	15	0

August 30	Helsinki	Finland 4/Czech Republic 0
August 31	Stockholm	Sweden 5/Germany 2
September 1	Stockholm	Sweden 4/Czech Republic 3
September 2	Cologne	Finland 3/Germany 0
September 3	Prague	Czech Republic 7/Germany 2
September 4	Helsinki	Finland 4/Sweden 4 (5:00 OT)

North American Pool

	GP	W	L	T	GF	GA	P
Canada	3	3	0	0	10	3	6
Russia	3	2	1	0	9	6	4
USA	3	1	2	0	5	6	2
Slovakia	3	0	3	0	4	13	0

August 31	Montreal	Canada 2/USA 1
September 1	Montreal	Canada 5/Slovakia 1
September 2	St. Paul	Russia 3/USA 1
September 3	St. Paul	USA 3/Slovakia 1
September 4	Toronto	Canada 3/Russia 1
September 5	Toronto	Russia 5/Slovakia 2

Quarterfinals

September 6	Helsinki	Finland 2/Germany 1
September 7	Stockholm	Czech Republic 6/Sweden 1
September 7	St. Paul	USA 5/Russia 2
September 8	Toronto	Canada 5/Slovakia 1

Semifinals

September 11	St. Paul	Finland 2/USA 1
September 12	Toronto	Canada 4/Czech Republic 3
		(Vincent Lecavalier 3:45 OT)

Finals

| September 14 | Toronto | Canada 3/Finland 2 |

THE GAMES OF THE VII OLYMPIAD

ANTWERP, BELGIUM, April 23–September 12, 1920
(Winter Olympics held April 23–29, 1920)

FINAL PLACINGS

GOLD MEDAL	Canada
SILVER MEDAL	United States
BRONZE MEDAL	Czechoslovakia
Fourth Place	Sweden

THE FIRST OLYMPIC WINTER GAMES

CHAMONIX, FRANCE, January 25–February 5, 1924

FINAL PLACINGS

GOLD MEDAL	Canada
SILVER MEDAL	United States
BRONZE MEDAL	Great Britain
Fourth Place	Sweden
Fifth Place	Czechoslovakia
(tie)	France
Seventh Place	Belgium
(tie)	Switzerland

THE SECOND OLYMPIC WINTER GAMES

ST. MORITZ, SWITZERLAND, February 11–20, 1928

FINAL PLACINGS

GOLD MEDAL	Canada
SILVER MEDAL	Sweden
BRONZE MEDAL	Switzerland
Fourth Place	Great Britain
Fifth Place	France

Sixth Place	Czechoslovakia
Seventh Place	Belgium
(tie)	Austria
Ninth Place	Poland
Tenth Place	Germany
Eleventh Place	Hungary

THE THIRD OLYMPIC WINTER GAMES

LAKE PLACID, NEW YORK February 4–13, 1932

FINAL PLACINGS

GOLD MEDAL	Canada
SILVER MEDAL	United States
BRONZE MEDAL	Germany
Fourth Place	Poland

THE FOURTH OLYMPIC WINTER GAMES

GARMISCH–PARTENKIRCHEN, GERMANY February 6–16, 1936

FINAL PLACINGS

GOLD MEDAL	Great Britain
SILVER MEDAL	Canada
BRONZE MEDAL	United States
Fourth Place	Czechoslovakia
Fifth Place	Germany
(tie)	Sweden
Seventh Place	Austria
(tie)	Hungary
Ninth Place	Italy
(tie)	France
(tie)	Japan
(tie)	Poland
Thirteenth Place	Belgium
(tie)	Latvia
(tie)	Switzerland

THE FIFTH OLYMPIC WINTER GAMES

ST. MORITZ, SWITZERLAND January 30–February 8, 1948

FINAL PLACINGS

GOLD MEDAL	Canada
SILVER MEDAL	Czechoslovakia
BRONZE MEDAL	Switzerland
Fourth Place	United States
Fifth Place	Sweden
Sixth Place	Great Britain
Seventh Place	Poland
Eighth Place	Austria
Ninth Place	Italy

THE SIXTH OLYMPIC WINTER GAMES

OSLO, NORWAY February 15–25, 1952

FINAL PLACINGS

GOLD MEDAL	Canada
SILVER MEDAL	United States
BRONZE MEDAL	Sweden
Fourth Place	Czechoslovakia
Fifth Place	Switzerland
Sixth Place	Poland
Seventh Place	Finland
Eighth Place	West Germany
Ninth Place	Norway

THE SEVENTH OLYMPIC WINTER GAMES

CORTINA d'AMPEZZO, ITALY January 26–February 4, 1956

FINAL PLACINGS

GOLD MEDAL	Soviet Union
SILVER MEDAL	United States
BRONZE MEDAL	Canada
Fourth Place	Sweden

Fifth Place	Czechoslovakia
Sixth Place	Germany
Seventh Place	Italy
Eighth Place	Poland
Ninth Place	Switzerland
Tenth Place	Austria

THE EIGHTH OLYMPIC WINTER GAMES

SQUAW VALLEY, CALIFORNIA February 19–28, 1960

FINAL PLACINGS

GOLD MEDAL	United States
SILVER MEDAL	Canada
BRONZE MEDAL	Soviet Union
Fourth Place	Czechoslovakia
Fifth Place	Sweden
Sixth Place	Germany
Seventh Place	Finland
Eighth Place	Japan
Ninth Place	Australia

THE NINTH OLYMPIC WINTER GAMES

INNSBRUCK, AUSTRIA January 29–February 9, 1964

FINAL PLACINGS

GOLD MEDAL	Soviet Union
SILVER MEDAL	Sweden
BRONZE MEDAL	Czechoslovakia
Fourth Place	Canada
Fifth Place	United States
Sixth Place	Finland
Seventh Place	Germany
Eighth Place	Switzerland
Ninth Place	Poland
Tenth Place	Norway
Eleventh Place	Japan

Twelfth Place	Romania
Thirteenth Place	Austria
Fourteenth Place	Yugoslavia
Fifteenth Place	Italy
Sixteenth Place	Hungary

THE TENTH OLYMPIC WINTER GAMES

GRENOBLE, FRANCE February 6–17, 1968

FINAL PLACINGS

GOLD MEDAL	Soviet Union
SILVER MEDAL	Czechoslovakia
BRONZE MEDAL	Canada
Fourth Place	Sweden
Fifth Place	Finland
Sixth Place	United States
Seventh Place	West Germany
Eighth Place	East Germany
Ninth Place	Yugoslavia
Tenth Place	Japan
Eleventh Place	Norway
Twelfth Place	Romania
Thirteenth Place	Austria
Fourteenth Place	France

THE ELEVENTH OLYMPIC WINTER GAMES

SAPPORO, JAPAN February 5–12, 1972

FINAL PLACINGS

GOLD MEDAL	Soviet Union
SILVER MEDAL	United States
BRONZE MEDAL	Czechoslovakia
Fourth Place	Sweden
Fifth Place	Finland
Sixth Place	Poland
Seventh Place	West Germany

Eighth Place	Norway
Ninth Place	Japan
Tenth Place	Switzerland
Eleventh Place	Yugoslavia

THE TWELFTH OLYMPIC WINTER GAMES

INNSBRUCK, AUSTRIA February 4–13, 1976

FINAL PLACINGS

GOLD MEDAL	Soviet Union
SILVER MEDAL	Czechoslovakia
BRONZE MEDAL	West Germany
Fourth Place	Finland
Fifth Place	United States
Sixth Place	Poland
Seventh Place	Romania
Eighth Place	Austria
Ninth Place	Japan
Tenth Place	Yugoslavia
Eleventh Place	Switzerland
(tie)	Norway
Thirteenth Place	Bulgaria

THE THIRTEENTH OLYMPIC WINTER GAMES

LAKE PLACID, NEW YORK February 13–24, 1980

FINAL PLACINGS

GOLD MEDAL	United States
SILVER MEDAL	Soviet Union
BRONZE MEDAL	Sweden
Fourth Place	Finland
Fifth Place	Czechoslovakia
Sixth Place	Canada
Seventh Place	Poland
Eighth Place	Romania

Ninth Place	Netherlands
(tie)	Norway
Eleventh Place	West Germany
(tie)	Yugoslavia
Thirteenth Place	Japan

THE FOURTEENTH OLYMPIC WINTER GAMES

SARAJEVO, YUGOSLAVIA February 7–19, 1984

FINAL PLACINGS

GOLD MEDAL	Soviet Union
SILVER MEDAL	Czechoslovakia
BRONZE MEDAL	Sweden
Fourth Place	Canada
Fifth Place	West Germany
Sixth Place	Finland
Seventh Place	United States
Eighth Place	Poland
Ninth Place	Italy
Tenth Place	Norway
Eleventh Place	Austria
(tie)	Yugoslavia

THE FIFTEENTH OLYMPIC WINTER GAMES

CALGARY, ALBERTA February 13–28, 1988

FINAL PLACINGS

GOLD MEDAL	Soviet Union
SILVER MEDAL	Finland
BRONZE MEDAL	Sweden
Fourth Place	Canada
Fifth Place	West Germany
Sixth Place	Czechoslovakia
Seventh Place	United States
Eighth Place	Switzerland

Ninth Place	Austria
Tenth Place	Poland
Eleventh Place	France
Twelfth Place	Norway

THE SIXTEENTH OLYMPIC WINTER GAMES

ALBERTVILLE, FRANCE February 8–23, 1992

FINAL PLACINGS

GOLD MEDAL	Unified Team
SILVER MEDAL	Canada
BRONZE MEDAL	Czechoslovakia
Fourth Place	United States
Fifth Place	Sweden
Sixth Place	Germany
Seventh Place	Finland
Eighth Place	France
Ninth Place	Norway
Tenth Place	Switzerland
Eleventh Place	Poland
Twelfth Place	Italy

THE SEVENTEENTH OLYMPIC WINTER GAMES

LILLEHAMMER, NORWAY February 13–27, 1994

FINAL PLACINGS

GOLD MEDAL	Sweden
SILVER MEDAL	Canada
BRONZE MEDAL	Finland
Fourth Place	Russia
Fifth Place	Czech Republic
Sixth Place	Slovakia
Seventh Place	Germany
Eighth Place	United States
Ninth Place	Italy

Tenth Place	France
Eleventh Place	Norway
Twelfth Place	Austria

THE EIGHTEENTH OLYMPIC WINTER GAMES

NAGANO, JAPAN, February 7–22, 1998 (Men);
February 8–17, 1998 (Women)

FINAL PLACINGS: MEN

GOLD MEDAL	Czech Republic
SILVER MEDAL	Russia
BRONZE MEDAL	Finland
Fourth Place	Canada
Fifth Place (tie)	Sweden
	United States
	Belarus
	Kazakhstan
Ninth Place	Germany
Tenth Place	Slovakia
Eleventh Place	France
Twelfth Place	Italy
Thirteenth Place	Japan
Fourteenth Place	Austria

FINAL PLACINGS: WOMEN

GOLD MEDAL	United States
SILVER MEDAL	Canada
BRONZE MEDAL	Finland
Fourth Place	China
Fifth Place	Sweden
Sixth Place	Japan

THE NINETEENTH OLYMPIC WINTER GAMES

SALT LAKE CITY, UTAH, February 9–24, 2002 (Men);
February 11–21, 2002 (Women)

FINAL PLACINGS: MEN

GOLD MEDAL	Canada
SILVER MEDAL	United States
BRONZE MEDAL	Russia
Fourth Place	Belarus
Fifth Place	Sweden
Sixth Place	Finland
Seventh Place	Czech Republic
Eighth Place	Germany
Ninth Place	Latvia
Tenth Place	Ukraine
Eleventh Place	Switzerland
Twelfth Place	Austria
Thirteenth Place	Slovakia
Fourteenth Place	France

FINAL PLACINGS: WOMEN

GOLD MEDAL	Canada
SILVER MEDAL	United States
BRONZE MEDAL	Sweden
Fourth Place	Finland
Fifth Place	Russia
Sixth Place	Germany
Seventh Place	China
Eighth Place	Kazakhstan

THE TWENTIETH OLYMPIC WINTER GAMES

TORINO, ITALY, February 10–26, 2006 (Men);
February 11–20, 2006 (Women)

FINAL PLACINGS: MEN

GOLD MEDAL	Sweden
SILVER MEDAL	Finland
BRONZE MEDAL	Czech Republic
Fourth Place	Russia
Fifth Place	Slovakia
Sixth Place	Switzerland
Seventh Place	Canada
Eighth Place	United States
Ninth Place	Kazakhstan
Tenth Place	Germany
Eleventh Place	Italy
Twelfth Place	Latvia

FINAL PLACINGS: WOMEN

GOLD MEDAL	Canada
SILVER MEDAL	Sweden
BRONZE MEDAL	United States
Fourth Place	Finland
Fifth Place	Germany
Sixth Place	Russia
Seventh Place	Switzerland
Eighth Place	Italy

WORLD CHAMPIONSHIPS, 1930–2006

January 31–February 10, 1930

Chamonix, France/Berlin, Germany/Vienna, Austria

GOLD MEDAL	Canada
SILVER MEDAL	Germany
BRONZE MEDAL	Switzerland
Fourth Place	Austria
Fifth Place	Poland
Sixth Place (tie)	Czechoslovakia
	France
	Hungary
	Japan
Tenth Place (tie)	Belgium
	Great Britain
	Italy

March 1–8, 1931

Krynica, Poland

GOLD MEDAL	Canada
SILVER MEDAL	United States
BRONZE MEDAL	Austria
Fourth Place	Poland
Fifth Place	Czechoslovakia
Sixth Place	Sweden
Seventh Place	Hungary
Eighth Place	Great Britain
Ninth Place	France
Tenth Place	Romania

February 18–26, 1933

Prague, Czechoslovakia

GOLD MEDAL	United States
SILVER MEDAL	Canada
BRONZE MEDAL	Czechoslovakia
Fourth Place	Austria
Fifth Place (tie)	Germany
	Switzerland
Seventh Place (tie)	Hungary
	Poland
Ninth Place	Romania
Tenth Place	Latvia
Eleventh Place	Italy
Twelfth Place	Belgium

February 3–11, 1934

Milan, Italy

GOLD MEDAL	Canada
SILVER MEDAL	United States
BRONZE MEDAL	Germany
Fourth Place	Switzerland
Fifth Place	Czechoslovakia
Sixth Place	Hungary
Seventh Place	Austria
Eighth Place	Great Britain
Ninth Place	Italy
Tenth Place	Romania
Eleventh Place	France
Twelfth Place	Belgium

January 19–27, 1935

Davos, Switzerland

GOLD MEDAL	Canada
SILVER MEDAL	Switzerland
BRONZE MEDAL	Great Britain
Fourth Place	Czechoslovakia
Fifth Place	Sweden
Sixth Place	Austria
Seventh Place	France
Eighth Place	Italy
Ninth Place	Germany
Tenth Place	Poland
Eleventh Place (tie)	Hungary
	Romania
Thirteenth Place	Latvia
Fourteenth Place	Belgium
	Netherlands

February 17–27, 1937

London, Great Britain

GOLD MEDAL	Canada
SILVER MEDAL	Great Britain
BRONZE MEDAL	Switzerland
Fourth Place	Germany
Fifth Place	Hungary
Sixth Place	Czechoslovakia
Seventh Place	France
Eighth Place	Poland
Ninth Place (tie)	Norway
	Romania
	Sweden

February 11–20, 1938

Prague, Czechoslovakia

GOLD MEDAL	Canada
SILVER MEDAL	Great Britain
BRONZE MEDAL	Czechoslovakia
Fourth Place	Germany
Fifth Place	Sweden
Sixth Place	Switzerland
Seventh Place (tie)	Hungary
	Poland
	United States
Tenth Place (tie)	Austria
	Latvia
	Lithuania
Thirteenth Place (tie)	Norway
	Romania

February 3–12, 1939

Basel/Zurich, Switzerland

GOLD MEDAL	Canada
SILVER MEDAL	United States
BRONZE MEDAL	Switzerland
Fourth Place	Czechoslovakia
Fifth Place	Germany
Sixth Place	Poland
Seventh Place	Hungary
Eighth Place	Great Britain
Ninth Place	Italy
Tenth Place	Latvia
Eleventh Place (tie)	Belgium
	Netherlands
Thirteenth Place	Finland
	Yugoslavia

February 15–23, 1947

Prague, Czechoslovakia

GOLD MEDAL	Czechoslovakia
SILVER MEDAL	Sweden
BRONZE MEDAL	Austria
Fourth Place	Switzerland
Fifth Place	United States
Sixth Place	Poland
Seventh Place	Romania
Eighth Place	Belgium

February 12–20, 1949

Stockholm, Sweden

GOLD MEDAL	Czechoslovakia
SILVER MEDAL	Canada
BRONZE MEDAL	United States
Fourth Place	Sweden
Fifth Place	Switzerland
Sixth Place	Austria
Seventh Place	Finland
Eighth Place	Norway
Ninth Place	Belgium
Tenth Place	Denmark

March 13–22, 1950

London, Great Britain

GOLD MEDAL	Canada
SILVER MEDAL	United States
BRONZE MEDAL	Switzerland
Fourth Place	Great Britain
Fifth Place	Sweden
Sixth Place	Norway

Seventh Place	Belgium
Eighth Place	Netherlands
Ninth Place	France

March 9–17, 1951

Paris, France

GOLD MEDAL	Canada
SILVER MEDAL	Sweden
BRONZE MEDAL	Switzerland
Fourth Place	Norway
Fifth Place	Great Britain
Sixth Place	United States
Seventh Place	Finland

March 6–15, 1953

Zurich/Basel, Switzerland

GOLD MEDAL	Sweden
SILVER MEDAL	West Germany
BRONZE MEDAL	Switzerland
Fourth Place	Czechoslovakia

February 26–March 7, 1954

Stockholm, Sweden

GOLD MEDAL	Soviet Union
SILVER MEDAL	Canada
BRONZE MEDAL	Sweden
Fourth Place	Czechoslovakia
Fifth Place	West Germany
Sixth Place	Finland
Seventh Place	Switzerland
Eighth Place	Norway

February 25–March 6, 1955

Dusseldorf, West Germany

GOLD MEDAL	Canada
SILVER MEDAL	Soviet Union
BRONZE MEDAL	Czechoslovakia
Fourth Place	United States
Fifth Place	Sweden
Sixth Place	West Germany
Seventh Place	Poland
Eighth Place	Switzerland
Ninth Place	Finland

February 24–March 5, 1957

Moscow, Soviet Union

GOLD MEDAL	Sweden
SILVER MEDAL	Soviet Union
BRONZE MEDAL	Czechoslovakia
Fourth Place	Finland
Fifth Place	West Germany
Sixth Place	Poland
Seventh Place	Austria
Eighth Place	Japan

To protest the suppression of the Hungarian revolution by Soviet forces, Canadian Prime Minister Louis St. Laurent refused to allow a Canadian team to travel to Moscow to play at the World Championships.

February 25–March 9, 1958

Oslo, Norway

GOLD MEDAL	Canada
SILVER MEDAL	Soviet Union
BRONZE MEDAL	Sweden

Fourth Place	Czechoslovakia
Fifth Place	United States
Sixth Place	Finland
Seventh Place	Norway
Eighth Place	Poland

March 9–15, 1959

Prague, Czechoslovakia

GOLD MEDAL	Canada
SILVER MEDAL	Soviet Union
BRONZE MEDAL	Czechoslovakia
Fourth Place	United States
Fifth Place	Sweden
Sixth Place	Finland
Seventh Place	West Germany
Eighth Place	Norway
Ninth Place	East Germany
Tenth Place	Italy
Eleventh Place	Poland
Twelfth Place	Switzerland
Thirteenth Place	Romania
Fourteenth Place	Hungary
Fifteenth Place	Austria

March 1–12, 1961

Geneva/Lausanne, Switzerland

GOLD MEDAL	Canada
SIVER MEDAL	Czechoslovakia
BRONZE MEDAL	Soviet Union
Fourth Place	Sweden
Fifth Place	East Germany
Sixth Place	United States

Seventh Place   Finland
Eighth Place   West Germany

May 8–18, 1962

Colorado Springs, United States

GOLD MEDAL   Sweden
SILVER MEDAL   Canada
BRONZE MEDAL   United States
Fourth Place   Finland
Fifth Place   Norway
Sixth Place   West Germany
Seventh Place   Switzerland
Eighth Place   Great Britain

March 7–17, 1963

Stockholm, Sweden

GOLD MEDAL   Soviet Union
SILVER MEDAL   Sweden
BRONZE MEDAL   Czechoslovakia
Fourth Place   Canada
Fifth Place   Finland
Sixth Place   East Germany
Seventh Place   West Germany
Eighth Place   United States

March 3–14, 1965

Tampere, Finland

GOLD MEDAL   Soviet Union
SILVER MEDAL   Czechoslovakia
BRONZE MEDAL   Sweden
Fourth Place   Canada
Fifth Place   East Germany

Sixth Place	United States
Seventh Place	Finland
Eighth Place	Norway

March 3–14, 1966

Ljubljana, Yugoslavia

GOLD MEDAL	Soviet Union
SILVER MEDAL	Czechoslovakia
BRONZE MEDAL	Canada
Fourth Place	Sweden
Fifth Place	East Germany
Sixth Place	United States
Seventh Place	Finland
Eighth Place	Poland

March 18–29, 1967

Vienna, Austria

GOLD MEDAL	Soviet Union
SILVER MEDAL	Sweden
BRONZE MEDAL	Canada
Fourth Place	Czechoslovakia
Fifth Place	United States
Sixth Place	Finland
Seventh Place	West Germany
Eighth Place	East Germany

March 15–30, 1969

Stockholm, Sweden

GOLD MEDAL	Soviet Union
SILVER MEDAL	Sweden
BRONZE MEDAL	Czechoslovakia
Fourth Place	Canada

| Fifth Place | Finland |
| Sixth Place | United States |

To protest the ineligibility of professionals from the World Championships according to IIHF rules, Canada did not compete in IIHF sanctioned tournaments from 1970 through 1976.

March 14–30, 1970

Stockholm, Sweden

GOLD MEDAL	Soviet Union
SILVER MEDAL	Sweden
BRONZE MEDAL	Czechoslovakia
Fourth Place	Finland
Fifth Place	East Germany
Sixth Place	Poland

March 19–April 3, 1971

Bern/Geneva/Switzerland

GOLD MEDAL	Soviet Union
SILVER MEDAL	Czechoslovakia
BRONZE MEDAL	Sweden
Fourth Place	Finland
Fifth Place	East Germany
Sixth Place	United States

April 7–22, 1972

Prague, Czechoslovakia

GOLD MEDAL	Czechoslovakia
SILVER MEDAL	Soviet Union
BRONZE MEDAL	Sweden
Fourth Place	Finland
Fifth Place	East Germany
Sixth Place	Switzerland

March 31–April 15, 1973

Moscow, Soviet Union

GOLD MEDAL	Soviet Union
SILVER MEDAL	Sweden
BRONZE MEDAL	Czechoslovakia
Fourth Place	Finland
Fifth Place	Poland
Sixth Place	East Germany

April 5–20, 1974

Helsinki, Finland

GOLD MEDAL	Soviet Union
SILVER MEDAL	Czechoslovakia
BRONZE MEDAL	Sweden
Fourth Place	Finland
Fifth Place	Poland
Sixth Place	East Germany

April 3–19, 1975

Munich/Dusseldorf, West Germany

GOLD MEDAL	Soviet Union
SILVER MEDAL	Czechoslovakia
BRONZE MEDAL	Sweden
Fourth Place	Finland
Fifth Place	Poland
Sixth Place	United States

April 8–25, 1976

Katowice, Poland

GOLD MEDAL	Czechoslovakia
SILVER MEDAL	Soviet Union

BRONZE MEDAL	Sweden
Fourth Place	United States
Fifth Place	Finland
Sixth Place	West Germany
Seventh Place	Poland
Eighth Place	East Germany

April 21–May 8, 1977

Vienna, Austria

GOLD MEDAL	Czechoslovakia
SILVER MEDAL	Sweden
BRONZE MEDAL	Soviet Union
Fourth Place	Canada
Fifth Place	Finland
Sixth Place	United States
Seventh Place	West Germany
Eighth Place	Romania

April 25–May 8, 1978

Prague, Czechoslovakia

GOLD MEDAL	Soviet Union
SILVER MEDAL	Czechoslovakia
BRONZE MEDAL	Canada
Fourth Place	Sweden
Fifth Place	West Germany
Sixth Place	USA
Seventh Place	Finland
Eighth Place	East Germany

April 14–27, 1979

Moscow, Soviet Union

GOLD MEDAL	Soviet Union
SILVER MEDAL	Czechoslovakia
BRONZE MEDAL	Sweden
Fourth Place	Canada
Fifth Place	Finland
Sixth Place	West Germany
Seventh Place	United States
Eighth Place	Poland

April 12–26, 1981

Gothenburg/Stockholm, Sweden

GOLD MEDAL	Soviet Union
SILVER MEDAL	Sweden
BRONZE MEDAL	Czechoslovakia
Fourth Place	Canada
Fifth Place	United States
Sixth Place	Finland
Seventh Place	West Germany
Eighth Place	Netherlands

April 15–29, 1982

Helsinki/Tampere, Finland

GOLD MEDAL	Soviet Union
SILVER MEDAL	Czechoslovakia
BRONZE MEDAL	Canada
Fourth Place	Sweden
Fifth Place	Finland
Sixth Place	West Germany
Seventh Place	Italy
Eighth Place	United States

April 16–May 2, 1983

Dortmund/Dusseldorf/Munich, West Germany

GOLD MEDAL	Soviet Union
SILVER MEDAL	Czechoslovakia
BRONZE MEDAL	Canada
Fourth Place	Sweden
Fifth Place	East Germany
Sixth Place	West Germany
Seventh Place	Finland
Eighth Place	Italy

April 17–May 3, 1985

Prague, Czechoslovakia

GOLD MEDAL	Czechoslovakia
SILVER MEDAL	Canada
BRONZE MEDAL	Soviet Union
Fourth Place	United States
Fifth Place	Finland
Sixth Place	Sweden
Seventh Place	East Germany
Eighth Place	West Germany

April 12–28, 1986

Moscow, Soviet Union

GOLD MEDAL	Soviet Union
SILVER MEDAL	Sweden
BRONZE MEDAL	Canada
Fourth Place	Finland
Fifth Place	Czechoslovakia
Sixth Place	United States
Seventh Place	East Germany
Eighth Place	Poland

April 17–May 3, 1987

Vienna, Austria

GOLD MEDAL	Sweden
SILVER MEDAL	Soviet Union
BRONZE MEDAL	Czechoslovakia
Fourth Place	Canada
Fifth Place	Finland
Sixth Place	West Germany
Seventh Place	United States
Eighth Place	Switzerland

April 15–May 1, 1989

Stockholm, Sweden

GOLD MEDAL	Soviet Union
SILVER MEDAL	Canada
BRONZE MEDAL	Czechoslovakia
Fourth Place	Sweden
Fifth Place	Finland
Sixth Place	United States
Seventh Place	West Germany
Eighth Place	Poland

April 16–May 2, 1990

Bern, Switzerland

GOLD MEDAL	Soviet Union
SILVER MEDAL	Sweden
BRONZE MEDAL	Czechoslovakia
Fourth Place	Canada
Fifth Place	United States
Sixth Place	Finland
Seventh Place	West Germany
Eighth Place	Norway

April 14–May 5, 1991

Helsinki, Finland

GOLD MEDAL	Sweden
SILVER MEDAL	Canada
BRONZE MEDAL	Soviet Union
Fourth Place	United States
Fifth Place	Finland
Sixth Place	Czechoslovakia
Seventh Place	Switzerland
Eight Place	Germany

April 28–May 10, 1992

Prague/Bratislava, Czechoslovakia

GOLD MEDAL	Sweden
SILVER MEDAL	Finland
BRONZE MEDAL	Czechoslovakia
Fourth Place	Switzerland
Fifth Place	Russia
Sixth Place	Germany
Seventh Place	United States
Eighth Place	Canada
Ninth Place	Italy
Tenth Place	Norway
Eleventh Place	France
Twelfth Place	Poland

April 18–May 2, 1993

Munich, Germany

GOLD MEDAL	Russia
SILVER MEDAL	Sweden
BRONZE MEDAL	Czech Republic
Fourth Place	Canada

Fifth Place	Germany
Sixth Place	United States
Seventh Place	Finland
Eighth Place	Italy
Ninth Place	Austria
Tenth Place	France
Eleventh Place	Norway
Twelfth Place	Switzerland

April 25–May 8, 1994

Bolzano, Italy

GOLD MEDAL	Canada
SILVER MEDAL	Finland
BRONZE MEDAL	Sweden
Fourth Place	United States
Fifth Place	Russia
Sixth Place	Italy
Seventh Place	Czech Republic
Eighth Place	Austria
Ninth Place	Germany
Tenth Place	France
Eleventh Place	Norway
Twelfth Place	Great Britain

April 23–May 7, 1995

Stockholm/Gavle, Sweden

GOLD MEDAL	Finland
SILVER MEDAL	Sweden
BRONZE MEDAL	Canada
Fourth Place	Czech Republic
Fifth Place	Russia
Sixth Place	United States
Seventh Place	Italy

Eighth Place	France
Ninth Place	Germany
Tenth Place	Norway
Eleventh Place	Austria
Twelfth Place	Switzerland

April 21–May 5, 1996

Vienna, Austria

GOLD MEDAL	Czech Republic
SILVER MEDAL	Canada
BRONZE MEDAL	United States
Fourth Place	Russia
Fifth Place	Finland
Sixth Place	Sweden
Seventh Place	Italy
Eighth Place	Germany
Ninth Place	Norway
Tenth Place	Slovakia
Eleventh Place	France
Twelfth Place	Austria

April 26–May 14, 1997

Helsinki/Tampere/Turku, Finland

GOLD MEDAL	Canada
SILVER MEDAL	Sweden
BRONZE MEDAL	Czech Republic
Fourth Place	Russia
Fifth Place	Finland
Sixth Place	United States
Seventh Place	Latvia
Eighth Place	Italy
Ninth Place	Slovakia

Tenth Place	France
Eleventh Place	Germany
Twelfth Place	Norway

May 1–17, 1998

Zurich, Switzerland

GOLD MEDAL	Sweden
SILVER MEDAL	Finland
BRONZE MEDAL	Czech Republic
Fourth Place	Switzerland
Fifth Place	Russia
Sixth Place	Canada
Seventh Place	Slovakia
Eighth Place	Belarus
Ninth Place	Latvia
Tenth Place	Italy
Eleventh Place	Germany
Twelfth Place	United States

May 1–16, 1999

Oslo/Hamar/Lillehammer, Norway

GOLD MEDAL	Czech Republic
SILVER MEDAL	Finland
BRONZE MEDAL	Sweden
Fourth Place	Canada
Fifth Place	Russia
Sixth Place	United States
Seventh Place	Slovakia
Eighth Place	Switzerland
Ninth Place	Belarus
Tenth Place	Austria
Eleventh Place	Latvia

Twelfth Place	Norway
Thirteenth Place	Italy
Fourteenth Place	Ukraine
Fifteenth Place	France
Sixteenth Place	Japan

April 29–May 14, 2000

St. Petersburg, Russia

GOLD MEDAL	Czech Republic
SILVER MEDAL	Slovakia
BRONZE MEDAL	Finland
Fourth Place	Canada
Fifth Place	United States
Sixth Place	Switzerland
Seventh Place	Sweden
Eighth Place	Latvia
Ninth Place	Belarus
Tenth Place	Norway
Eleventh Place	Russia
Twelfth Place	Italy
Thirteenth Place	Austria
Fourteenth Place	Ukraine
Fifteenth Place	France
Sixteenth Place	Japan

April 28–May 13, 2001

Hanover/Cologne/Nuremberg, Germany

GOLD MEDAL	Czech Republic
SILVER MEDAL	Finland
BRONZE MEDAL	Sweden
Fourth Place	United States
Fifth Place	Canada

Sixth Place	Russia
Seventh Place	Slovakia
Eighth Place	Germany
Ninth Place	Switzerland
Tenth Place	Ukraine
Eleventh Place	Austria
Twelfth Place	Italy
Thirteenth Place	Latvia
Fourteenth Place	Belarus
Fifteenth Place	Norway
Sixteenth Place	Japan

April 26–May 11, 2002

Gothenburg/Karlstad/Jonkoping, Sweden

GOLD MEDAL	Slovakia
SILVER MEDAL	Russia
BRONZE MEDAL	Sweden
Fourth Place	Finland
Fifth Place	Czech Republic
Sixth Place	Canada
Seventh Place	United States
Eighth Place	Germany
Ninth Place	Ukraine
Tenth Place	Switzerland
Eleventh Place	Latvia
Tweflth Place	Austria
Thirteenth Place	Slovenia
Fourteenth Place	Poland
Fifteenth Place	Italy
Sixteenth Place	Japan

April 27–May 11, 2003

Helsinki/Tampere/Turku, Finland

GOLD MEDAL	Canada
SILVER MEDAL	Sweden
BRONZE MEDAL	Slovakia
Fourth Place	Czech Republic
Fifth Place	Finland
Sixth Place	Germany
Seventh Place	Russia
Eighth Place	Switzerland
Ninth Place	Latvia
Tenth Place	Austria
Eleventh Place	Denmark
Twelfth Place	Ukraine
Thirteenth Place	United States
Fourteenth Place	Belarus
Fifteenth Place	Slovenia
Sixteenth Place	Japan

April 24–May 9, 2004

Prague/Ostrava, Czech Republic

GOLD MEDAL	Canada
SILVER MEDAL	Sweden
BRONZE MEDAL	United States
Fourth Place	Slovakia
Fifth Place	Czech Republic
Sixth Place	Finland
Seventh Place	Latvia
Eighth Place	Switzerland
Ninth Place	Germany
Tenth Place	Russia
Eleventh Place	Austria

Twelfth Place	Denmark
Thirteenth Place	Kazakhstan
Fourteenth Place	Ukraine
Fifteenth Place	Japan
Sixteenth Place	France

April 30–May 15, 2005

Vienna/Innsbruck, Austria

GOLD MEDAL	Czech Republic
SILVER MEDAL	Canada
BRONZE MEDAL	Russia
Fourth Place	Sweden
Fifth Place	Slovakia
Sixth Place	United States
Seventh Place	Finland
Eighth Place	Switzerland
Ninth Place	Latvia
Tenth Place	Belarus
Eleventh Place	Ukraine
Twelfth Place	Kazakhstan
Thirteenth Place	Slovenia
Fourteenth Place	Denmark
Fifteenth Place	Germany
Sixteenth Place	Austria

May 5–May 21, 2006

Riga,Latvia

GOLD MEDAL	Sweden
SILVER MEDAL	Czech Republic
BRONZE MEDAL	Finland
Fourth Place	Canada
Fifth Place	Russia

Sixth Place	Belarus
Seventh Place	United States
Eighth Place	Slovakia
Ninth Place	Switzerland
Tenth Place	Latvia
Eleventh Place	Norway
Twelfth Place	Ukraine
Thirteenth Place	Denmark
Fourteenth Place	Italy
Fifteenth Place	Kazakhstan
Sixteenth Place	Slovenia

WORLD JUNIOR CHAMPIONSHIPS, 1977–2007

ALL MEDAL WINNERS BY CUMULATIVE STANDINGS (1977–2007)

Country	Gold	Silver	Bronze	Total
Canada	13	6	4	23
Soviet Union	9	3	2	14
Finland	2	4	6	12
Sweden	1	6	4	11
Czechoslovakia	0	5	6	11
Russia	3	5	3	11
United States	1	1	3	5
Czech Republic	2	0	1	3
Slovakia	0	0	1	1
Switzerland	0	0	1	1

1977 WORLD JUNIOR CHAMPIONSHIPS
CZECHOSLOVAKIA, DECEMBER 22, 1976–JANUARY 2, 1977

FINAL PLACINGS

GOLD MEDAL	Soviet Union
SILVER MEDAL	Canada
BRONZE MEDAL	Czechoslovakia
Fourth Place	Finland
Fifth Place	Sweden
Sixth Place	West Germany
Seventh Place	United States
Eighth Place	Poland*

* relegated to 'B' pool for 1978

ALL-STAR TEAM

Goal	Alexander Tyznych (Soviet Union)
Defence	Risto Siltanen (Finland)
	Lubos Oslizlo (Czechoslovakia)
Forward	Dale McCourt (Canada)
	Bengt-Ake Gustafsson (Sweden)
	Igor Romasin (Soviet Union)

DIRECTORATE AWARDS

BEST GOALIE	Jan Hrabak (Czechoslovakia)
BEST DEFENCEMAN	Viacheslav Fetisov (Soviet Union)
BEST FORWARD	Dale McCourt (Canada)

1978 WORLD JUNIOR CHAMPIONSHIPS

CANADA, DECEMBER 22, 1977–JANUARY 3, 1978

FINAL PLACINGS

GOLD MEDAL	Soviet Union
SILVER MEDAL	Sweden
BRONZE MEDAL	Canada
Fourth Place	Czechoslovakia
Fifth Place	United States
Sixth Place	Finland
Seventh Place	West Germany
Eighth Place	Switzerland*

* promoted from 'B' pool in 1977; relegated to 'B' pool for 1979

ALL-STAR TEAM

Goal	Alexander Tyznych (Soviet Union)
Defence	Risto Siltanen (Finland)
	Viacheslav Fetisov (Soviet Union)
Forward	Wayne Gretzky (Canada)
	Mats Naslund (Sweden)
	Anton Stastny (Czechoslovakia)

DIRECTORATE AWARDS

BEST GOALIE	Alexander Tyznych (Soviet Union)
BEST DEFENCEMAN	Viacheslav Fetisov (Soviet Union)
BEST FORWARD	Wayne Gretzky (Canada)

1979 WORLD JUNIOR CHAMPIONSHIPS

SWEDEN, DECEMBER 27, 1978–JANUARY 3, 1979

FINAL PLACINGS

GOLD MEDAL	Soviet Union
SILVER MEDAL	Sweden
BRONZE MEDAL	Czechoslovakia
Fourth Place	Finland
Fifth Place	Canada
Sixth Place	United States
Seventh Place	West Germany
Eighth Place	Norway*

* promoted from 'B' pool in 1978; relegated to 'B' pool for 1980

ALL-STAR TEAM

Goal	Pelle Lindbergh (Sweden)
Defence	Ivan Cerny (Czechoslovakia)
	Alexei Kasatonov (Soviet Union)
Forward	Anatoli Tarasov (Soviet Union)
	Thomas Steen (Sweden)
	Vladimir Krutov (Soviet Union)

DIRECTORATE AWARDS

BEST GOALIE	Pelle Lindbergh (Sweden)
BEST DEFENCEMAN	Alexei Kasatonov (Soviet Union)
BEST FORWARD	Vladimir Krutov (Soviet Union)

1980 WORLD JUNIOR CHAMPIONSHIPS

FINLAND, DECEMBER 27, 1979–JANUARY 2, 1980

FINAL PLACINGS

GOLD MEDAL	Soviet Union
SILVER MEDAL	Finland
BRONZE MEDAL	Sweden
Fourth Place	Czechoslovakia
Fifth Place	Canada
Sixth Place	West Germany
Seventh Place	United States
Eighth Place	Switzerland*

* promoted from 'B' pool in 1979; relegated to 'B' pool for 1981

ALL-STAR TEAM

Goal	Jari Paavola (Finland)
Defence	Reijo Ruotsalainen (Finland)
	Tomas Jonsson (Sweden)
Forward	Hakan Loob (Sweden)
	Igor Larionov (Soviet Union)
	Vladimir Krutov (Soviet Union)

DIRECTORATE AWARDS

BEST GOALIE	Jari Paavola (Finland)
BEST DEFENCEMAN	Reijo Ruotsalainen (Finland)
BEST FORWARD	Vladimir Krutov (Soviet Union)

1981 WORLD JUNIOR CHAMPIONSHIPS

WEST GERMANY, DECEMBER 27, 1980–JANUARY 2, 1981

FINAL PLACINGS

GOLD MEDAL	Sweden
SILVER MEDAL	Finland
BRONZE MEDAL	Soviet Union
Fourth Place	Czechoslovakia
Fifth Place	West Germany
Sixth Place	United States
Seventh Place	Canada
Eighth Place	Austria*

* promoted from 'B' pool in 1980; relegated to 'B' pool for 1982

ALL-STAR TEAM

Goal   Lars Eriksson (Sweden)

Defence   Miloslav Horava (Czechoslovakia)
            Hakan Nordin (Sweden)

Forward   Ari Lahteenmaki (Finland)
            Patrik Sundstrom (Sweden)
            Jan Erixon (Sweden)

DIRECTORATE AWARDS

BEST GOALIE   Lars Eriksson (Sweden)
BEST DEFENCEMAN   Miloslav Horava (Czechoslovakia)
BEST FORWARD   Patrik Sundstrom (Sweden)

1982 WORLD JUNIOR CHAMPIONSHIPS

UNITED STATES, DECEMBER 22, 1981–JANUARY 2, 1982
(some games played in Canada)

FINAL PLACINGS

GOLD MEDAL   Canada
SILVER MEDAL   Czechoslovakia
BRONZE MEDAL   Finland
Fourth Place   Soviet Union
Fifth Place   Sweden
Sixth Place   United States
Seventh Place   West Germany
Eighth Place   Switzerland*

* promoted from 'B' pool in 1981; relegated to 'B' pool for 1983

ALL-STAR TEAM

Goal	Mike Moffat (Canada)
Defence	Gord Kluzak (Canada)
	Ilya Biakin (Soviet Union)
Forward	Mike Moller (Canada)
	Petri Skriko (Finland)
	Vladimir Ruzicka (Czechoslovakia)

DIRECTORATE AWARDS

BEST GOALIE	Mike Moffat (Canada)
BEST DEFENCEMAN	Gord Kluzak (Canada)
BEST FORWARD	Petri Skriko (Finland)

1983 WORLD JUNIOR CHAMPIONSHIPS

SOVIET UNION, DECEMBER 26, 1982–JANUARY 4, 1983

FINAL PLACINGS

GOLD MEDAL	Soviet Union
SILVER MEDAL	Czechoslovakia
BRONZE MEDAL	Canada
Fourth Place	Sweden
Fifth Place	United States
Sixth Place	Finland
Seventh Place	West Germany
Eighth Place	Norway*

* promoted from 'B' pool in 1982; relegated to 'B' pool for 1984

ALL-STAR TEAM

Goal	Matti Rautiainen (Finland)
Defence	Ilya Biakin (Soviet Union)
	Simo Saarinen (Finland)
Forward	Tomas Sandstrom (Sweden)
	Vladimir Ruzicka (Czechoslovakia)
	German Volgin (Soviet Union)

DIRECTORATE AWARDS

BEST GOALIE	Dominik Hasek (Czechoslovakia)
BEST DEFENCEMAN	Ilya Biakin (Soviet Union)
BEST FORWARD	Tomas Sandstrom (Sweden)

1984 WORLD JUNIOR CHAMPIONSHIPS

SWEDEN, DECEMBER 25, 1983–JANUARY 3, 1984

FINAL PLACINGS

GOLD MEDAL	Soviet Union
SILVER MEDAL	Finland
BRONZE MEDAL	Czechoslovakia
Fourth Place	Canada
Fifth Place	Sweden
Sixth Place	United States
Seventh Place	West Germany
Eighth Place	Switzerland*

* promoted from 'B' pool in 1983; relegated to 'B' pool for 1985

ALL-STAR TEAM

Goal   Evgeny Belosheikin (Soviet Union)

Defence   Alexei Gusarov (Soviet Union)
            Frantisek Musil (Czechoslovakia)

Forward   Petr Rosol (Czechoslovakia)
            Raimo Helminen (Finland)
            Nikolai Borschevsky (Soviet Union)

DIRECTORATE AWARDS

BEST GOALIE   Alan Perry (United States)
BEST DEFENCEMAN   Alexei Gusarov (Soviet Union)
BEST FORWARD   Raimo Helminen (Finland)

1985 WORLD JUNIOR CHAMPIONSHIPS

FINLAND, DECEMBER 23, 1984–JANUARY 1, 1985

FINAL PLACINGS

GOLD MEDAL   Canada
SILVER MEDAL   Czechoslovakia
BRONZE MEDAL   Soviet Union
Fourth Place   Finland
Fifth Place   Sweden
Sixth Place   United States
Seventh Place   West Germany
Eighth Place   Poland*

* promoted from 'B' pool in 1984; relegated to 'B' pool for 1986

ALL-STAR TEAM

Goal	Timo Lehkonen (Finland)
Defence	Bobby Dollas (Canada)
	Mikhail Tatarinov (Soviet Union)
Forward	Mikko Makela (Finland)
	Michal Pivonka (Czechoslovakia)
	Esa Tikkanen (Finland)

DIRECTORATE AWARDS

BEST GOALIE	Craig Billington (Canada)
BEST DEFENCEMAN	Vesa Salo (Finland)
BEST FORWARD	Michal Pivonka (Czechoslovakia)

1986 WORLD JUNIOR CHAMPIONSHIPS

CANADA, DECEMBER 26, 1985–JANUARY 4, 1986

FINAL PLACINGS

GOLD MEDAL	Soviet Union
SILVER MEDAL	Canada
BRONZE MEDAL	United States
Fourth Place	Czechoslovakia
Fifth Place	Sweden
Sixth Place	Finland
Seventh Place	Switzerland*
Eighth Place	West Germany**

* promoted from 'B' pool in 1985
** relegated to 'B' pool for 1987

ALL-STAR TEAM

Goal	Evgeny Belosheikin (Soviet Union)
Defence	Sylvain Cote (Canada)
	Mikhail Tatarinov (Soviet Union)
Forward	Shayne Corson (Canada)
	Igor Viazmikin (Soviet Union)
	Michal Pivonka (Czechoslovakia)

DIRECTORATE AWARDS

BEST GOALIE	Evgeny Belosheikin (Soviet Union)
BEST DEFENCEMAN	Mikhail Tatarinov (Soviet Union)
BEST FORWARD	Jim Sandlak (Canada)

1987 WORLD JUNIOR CHAMPIONSHIPS

CZECHOSLOVAKIA, DECEMBER 26, 1986–JANUARY 4, 1987

FINAL PLACINGS

GOLD MEDAL	Finland
SILVER MEDAL	Czechoslovakia
BRONZE MEDAL	Sweden
Fourth Place	United States
Fifth Place	Poland*
Sixth PLace	Switzerland**

Canada and the Soviet Union were disqualified

* promoted from 'B' pool in 1986
** relegated to 'B' pool for 1988

ALL-STAR TEAM

Goal   Sam Lindstahl (Sweden)

Defence   Jiri Latal (Czechoslovakia)
            Brian Leetch (United States)

Forward   Ulf Dahlen (Sweden)
            Juraj Jurik (Czechoslovakia)
            Scott Young (United States)

DIRECTORATE AWARDS

BEST GOALIE   Markus Ketterer (Finland)
BEST DEFENCEMAN   Calle Johansson (Sweden)
BEST FORWARD   Robert Kron (Czechoslovakia)

1988 WORLD JUNIOR CHAMPIONSHIPS

RUSSIA, DECEMBER 26, 1987–JANUARY 4, 1988

FINAL PLACINGS

GOLD MEDAL   Canada
SILVER MEDAL   Soviet Union
BRONZE MEDAL   Finland
Fourth Place   Czechosloavkia
Fifth Place   Sweden
Sixth Place   United States
Seventh Place   West Germany*
Eighth Place   Poland**

* promoted from 'B' pool in 1987
** relegated to 'B' pool for 1989

ALL-STAR TEAM

Goal	Jimmy Waite (Canada)
Defence	Greg Hawgood (Canada)
	Teppo Numminen (Finland)
Forward	Theoren Fleury (Canada)
	Alexander Mogilny (Soviet Union)
	Petr Hrbek (Czechoslovakia)

DIRECTORATE AWARDS

BEST GOALIE	Jimmy Waite (Canada)
BEST DEFENCEMAN	Teppo Numminen (Finland)
BEST FORWARD	Alexander Mogilny (Soviet Union)

1989 WORLD JUNIOR CHAMPIONSHIPS

UNITED STATES, DECEMBER 26, 1988–JANUARY 4, 1989

FINAL PLACINGS

GOLD MEDAL	Soviet Union
SILVER MEDAL	Sweden
BRONZE MEDAL	Czechoslovakia
Fourth Place	Canada
Fifth Place	United States
Sixth Place	Finland
Seventh Place	Norway*
Eighth Place	West Germany**

* promoted from 'B' pool in 1988
** relegated to 'B' pool for 1990

ALL-STAR TEAM

Goal   Alexei Ivashkin (Soviet Union)

Defence   Rickard Persson (Sweden)
            Milan Tichy (Czechoslovakia)

Forward   Niklas Eriksson (Sweden)
            Pavel Bure (Soviet Union)
            Jeremy Roenick (United States)

DIRECTORATE AWARDS

BEST GOALIE   Alexei Ivashkin (Soviet Union)
BEST DEFENCEMAN   Rickard Persson (Sweden)
BEST FORWARD   Pavel Bure (Soviet Union)

1990 WORLD JUNIOR CHAMPIONSHIPS

FINLAND, DECEMBER 26, 1989–JANUARY 4, 1990

FINAL PLACINGS

GOLD MEDAL   Canada
SILVER MEDAL   Soviet Union
BRONZE MEDAL   Czechoslovakia
Fourth Place   Finland
Fifth Place   Sweden
Sixth Place   Norway
Seventh Place   United States
Eighth Place   Poland*

* promoted from 'B' pool in 1989; relegated to 'B' pool for 1991

ALL-STAR TEAM

Goal	Stephane Fiset (Canada)
Defence	Alexander Godynyuk (Soviet Union)
	Jiri Slegr (Czechoslovakia)
Forward	Dave Chyzowski (Canada)
	Jaromir Jagr (Czechoslovakia)
	Robert Reichel (Czechoslovakia)

DIRECTORATE AWARDS

BEST GOALIE	Stephane Fiset (Canada)
BEST DEFENCEMAN	Alexander Godynyuk (Soviet Union)
BEST FORWARD	Robert Reichel (Czechoslovakia)

1991 WORLD JUNIOR CHAMPIONSHIPS

CANADA, DECEMBER 26, 1990–JANUARY 4, 1991

FINAL PLACINGS

GOLD MEDAL	Canada
SILVER MEDAL	Soviet Union
BRONZE MEDAL	Czechoslovakia
Fourth Place	United States
Fifth Place	Finland
Sixth Place	Sweden
Seventh Place	Switzerland*
Eighth Place	Norway**

* promoted from 'B' pool in 1990
** relegated to 'B' pool for 1992

ALL-STAR TEAM
Goal   Pauli Jaks (Switzerland)

Defence   Dmitri Yushkevich (Soviet Union)
            Scott Lachance (United States)

Forward   Mike Craig (Canada)
            Eric Lindros (Canada)
            Martin Rucinsky (Czechoslovakia)

DIRECTORATE AWARDS
BEST GOALIE   Pauli Jaks (Switzerland)
BEST DEFENCEMAN   Jiri Slegr (Czechoslovakia)
BEST FORWARD   Eric Lindros (Canada)

1992 WORLD JUNIOR CHAMPIONSHIPS
GERMANY, DECEMBER 26, 1991–JANUARY 4, 1992

FINAL PLACINGS
GOLD MEDAL   Commonwealth of Independent States
SILVER MEDAL   Sweden
BRONZE MEDAL   United States
Fourth Place   Finland
Fifth Place   Czechoslovakia
Sixth Place   Canada
Seventh Place   Germany*
Eighth Place   Switzerland**

* promoted from 'B' pool in 1991
** relegated to 'B' pool for 1993

ALL-STAR TEAM

Goal	Mike Dunham (United States)
Defence	Scott Niedermayer (Canada)
	Janne Gronvall (Finland)
Forward	Alexei Kovalev (CIS)
	Michael Nylander (Sweden)
	Peter Ferraro (United States)

DIRECTORATE AWARDS

BEST GOALIE	Mike Dunham (United States)
BEST DEFENCEMAN	Darius Kasparaitis (CIS)
BEST FORWARD	Michael Nylander (Sweden)

1993 WORLD JUNIOR CHAMPIONSHIPS

SWEDEN, DECEMBER 26, 1992–JANUARY 4, 1993

FINAL PLACINGS

GOLD MEDAL	Canada
SILVER MEDAL	Sweden
BRONZE MEDAL	Czech Republic
Fourth Place	United States
Fifth Place	Finland
Sixth Place	Russia
Seventh Place	Germany
Eighth place	Japan*

* promoted from 'B' pool in 1992; relegated to 'B' pool for 1994

ALL-STAR TEAM

Goal	Manny Legace (Canada)
Defence	Brent Tully (Canada)
	Kenny Jonsson (Sweden)
Forward	Paul Kariya (Canada)
	Markus Naslund (Sweden)
	Peter Forsberg (Sweden)

DIRECTORATE AWARDS

BEST GOALIE	Manny Legace (Canada)
BEST DEFENCEMAN	Janne Gronvall (Finland)
BEST FORWARD	Peter Forsberg (Sweden)

1994 WORLD JUNIOR CHAMPIONSHIPS

CZECH REPUBLIC, DECEMBER 26, 1993–JANUARY 4, 1994

FINAL PLACINGS

GOLD MEDAL	Canada
SILVER MEDAL	Sweden
BRONZE MEDAL	Russia
Fourth Place	Finland
Fifth Place	Czech Republic
Sixth Place	United States
Seventh Place	Germany
Eighth Place	Switzerland*

* promoted from 'B' pool in 1993; relegated to 'B' pool for 1995

ALL-STAR TEAM

Goal	Evgeny Riabchikov (Russia)
Defence	Kenny Jonsson (Sweden)
	Kimmo Timonen (Finland)
Forward	Niklas Sundstrom (Sweden)
	Valeri Bure (Russia)
	David Vyborny (Czech Republic)

DIRECTORATE AWARDS

BEST GOALIE	Jamie Storr (Canada)
BEST DEFENCEMAN	Kenny Jonsson (Sweden)
BEST FORWARD	Niklas Sundstrom (Sweden)

1995 WORLD JUNIOR CHAMPIONSHIPS

CANADA, DECEMBER 26, 1994–JANUARY 4, 1995

FINAL PLACINGS

GOLD MEDAL	Canada
SILVER MEDAL	Russia
BRONZE MEDAL	Sweden
Fourth Place	Finland
Fifth Place	United States
Sixth Place	Czech Republic
Seventh Place	Germany
Eighth Place	Ukraine*

* promoted from 'B' pool in 1994

Note: no team was relegated to 'B' pool from this year's tournament because
in 1996 the 'A' pool expanded to ten teams and a new round-robin format

ALL-STAR TEAM

Goal   Igor Karpenko (Ukraine)

Defence   Bryan McCabe (Canada)
           Anders Eriksson (Sweden)

Forward   Jason Allison (Canada)
           Eric Daze (Canada)
           Marty Murray (Canada)

DIRECTORATE AWARDS

BEST GOALIE   Evgeny Tarasov (Russia)
BEST DEFENCEMAN   Bryan McCabe (Canada)
BEST FORWARD   Marty Murray (Canada)

1996 WORLD JUNIOR CHAMPIONSHIPS

UNITED STATES, DECEMBER 26, 1995–JANUARY 4, 1996

FINAL PLACINGS

GOLD MEDAL   Canada
SILVER MEDAL   Sweden
BRONZE MEDAL   Russia
Fourth Place   Czech Republic
Fifth Place   United States
Sixth Place   Finland
Seventh Place   Slovakia*
Eighth Place   Germany
Ninth Place   Switzerland*
Tenth Place   Ukraine**

* promoted from 'B' pool in 1995
** relegated to 'B' pool for 1997

ALL-STAR TEAM

Goal   Jose Theodore (Canada)

Defence   Nolan Baumgartner (Canada)
           Mattias Ohlund (Sweden)

Forward   Jarome Iginla (Canada)
           Johan Davidsson (Sweden)
           Alexei Morozov (Russia)

DIRECTORATE AWARDS
BEST GOALIE   Jose Theodore (Canada)
BEST DEFENCEMAN   Mattias Ohlund (Sweden)
BEST FORWARD   Jarome Iginla (Canada)

1997 WORLD JUNIOR CHAMPIONSHIPS

SWITZERLAND, DECEMBER 26, 1996–JANUARY 4, 1997

FINAL PLACINGS
GOLD MEDAL   Canada
SILVER MEDAL   United States
BRONZE MEDAL   Russia
Fourth Place   Czech Republic
Fifth Place   Finland
Sixth Place   Slovakia
Seventh Place   Switzerland
Eighth Place   Sweden
Ninth Place   Germany
Tenth Place   Poland*

* promoted from 'B' pool in 1996; relegated to 'B' pool for 1998

ALL-STAR TEAM

Goal	Brian Boucher (United States)
Defence	Chris Phillips (Canada)
	Mark Streit (Switzerland)
Forward	Christian Dube (Canada)
	Sergei Samsonov (Russia)
	Michael York (United States)

DIRECTORATE AWARDS

BEST GOALIE	Marc Denis (Canada)
BEST DEFENCEMAN	Joseph Corvo (United States)
BEST FORWARD	Alexei Morozov (Russia)

1998 WORLD JUNIOR CHAMPIONSHIPS

FINLAND, DECEMBER 25, 1997–JANUARY 3, 1998

FINAL PLACINGS

GOLD MEDAL	Finland
SILVER MEDAL	Russia
BRONZE MEDAL	Switzerland
Fourth Place	Czech Republic
Fifth Place	United States
Sixth Place	Sweden
Seventh Place	Kazakhstan*
Eighth Place	Canada
Ninth Place	Slovakia
Tenth Place	Germany**

* promoted from 'B' pool in 1997
** relegated to 'B' pool for 1999

ALL-STAR TEAM

Goal	David Aebischer (Switzerland)
Defence	Pierre Hedin (Sweden)
	Andrei Markov (Russia)
Forward	Olli Jokinen (Finland)
	Eero Somervuori (Finland)
	Maxim Balmochnykh (Russia)

DIRECTORATE AWARDS

BEST GOALIE	David Aebischer (Switzerland)
BEST DEFENCEMAN	Pavel Skrbek (Czech Republic)
BEST FORWARD	Olli Jokinen (Finland)

1999 WORLD JUNIOR CHAMPIONSHIPS

CANADA, DECEMBER 26, 1998–JANUARY 5, 1999

FINAL PLACINGS

GOLD MEDAL	Russia
SILVER MEDAL	Canada
BRONZE MEDAL	Slovakia
Fourth Place	Sweden
Fifth Place	Finland
Sixth Place	Kazakhstan
Seventh Place	Czech Republic
Eighth Place	United States
Ninth Place	Switzerland
Tenth Place	Belarus*

* promoted from 'B' pool in 1998; relegated to 'B' pool for 2000

ALL-STAR TEAM

Goal	Roberto Luongo (Canada)
Defence	Vitali Vishnevsky (Russia)
	Brian Campbell (Canada)
Forward	Daniel Tkachuk (Canada)
	Brian Gionta (United States)
	Maxim Balmochnykh (Russia)

DIRECTORATE AWARDS

BEST GOALIE	Roberto Luongo (Canada)
BEST DEFENCEMAN	Maxim Afinigenov (Russia)
BEST FORWARD	Vitali Vishnevski (Russia)

2000 WORLD JUNIOR CHAMPIONSHIPS

SWEDEN, DECEMBER 25, 1999–JANUARY 4, 2000

FINAL PLACINGS

GOLD MEDAL	Czech Republic
SILVER MEDAL	Russia
BRONZE MEDAL	Canada
Fourth Place	United States
Fifth Place	Sweden
Sixth Place	Switzerland
Seventh Place	Finland
Eighth Place	Kazakhstan
Ninth Place	Slovakia
Tenth Place	Ukraine*

* promoted from 'B' pool in 1999; demoted to 'B' pool for 2001

ALL-STAR TEAM

Goal	Rick DiPietro (United States)
Defence	Mathieu Biron (Canada)
	Alexander Rjasantsev (Russia)
Forward	Milan Kraft (Czech Republic)
	Alexei Tereschenko (Russia)
	Evgeny Muratov (Russia)

DIRECTORATE AWARDS

BEST GOALIE	Rick DiPietro (United States)
BEST DEFENCEMAN	Alexander Rjasantsev (Russia)
BEST FORWARD	Milan Kraft (Czech Republic)

2001 WORLD JUNIOR CHAMPIONSHIPS

RUSSIA, DECEMBER 26, 2000–JANUARY 5, 2001

FINAL PLACINGS

GOLD MEDAL	Czech Republic
SILVER MEDAL	Finland
BRONZE MEDAL	Canada
Fourth Place	Sweden
Fifth Place	United States
Sixth Place	Switzerland
Seventh Place	Russia
Eighth Place	Slovakia
Ninth Place	Belarus*
Tenth Place	Kazakhstan**

* promoted from 'B' pool in 2000
** demoted to 'B' pool for 2002

ALL-STAR TEAM

Goal	Ari Ahonen (Finland)
Defence	Rostislav Klesla (Czech Republic)
	Tuukka Mantyla (Finland)
Forward	Jason Spezza (Canada)
	Jani Rita (Finland)
	Pavel Brendl (Czech Republic)

DIRECTORATE AWARDS

BEST GOALIE	Tomas Duba (Czech Republic)
BEST DEFENCEMAN	Rostislav Klesla (Czech Republic)
BEST FORWARD	Pavel Brendl (Czech Republic)

2002 WORLD JUNIOR CHAMPIONSHIPS

CZECH REPUBLIC, DECEMBER 25, 2001–JUANUARY 4, 2002

FINAL PLACINGS

GOLD MEDAL	Russia
SILVER MEDAL	Canada
BRONZE MEDAL	Finland
Fourth Place	Switzerland
Fifth Place	United States
Sixth Place	Sweden
Seventh Place	Czech Republic
Eighth Place	Slovakia
Ninth Place	Belarus
Tenth Place	France*

* promoted from 2001; demoted for 2003

ALL-STAR TEAM

Goal	Pascal Leclaire (Canada)
Defence	Jay Bouwmeester (Canada)
	Igor Knyazev (Russia)
Forward	Mike Cammalleri (Canada)
	Marek Svatos (Canada)
	Stanislav Chistov (Russia)

DIRECTORATE AWARDS

BEST GOALIE	Kari Lehtonen (Finland)
BEST DEFENCEMAN	Igor Knyazev (Russia)
BEST FORWARD	Mike Cammalleri (Canada)

2003 WORLD JUNIOR CHAMPIONSHIPS

CANADA, DECEMBER 26, 2002–JANUARY 5, 2003

FINAL PLACINGS

GOLD MEDAL	Russia
SILVER MEDAL	Canada
BRONZE MEDAL	Finland
Fourth Place	United States
Fifth Place	Slovakia
Sixth Place	Czech Republic
Seventh Place	Switzerland
Eighth Place	Sweden
Ninth Place	Germany*
Tenth Place	Belarus**

* promoted from 2002
** demoted for 2004

ALL-STAR TEAM

Goal	Marc-Andre Fleury (Canada)
Defence	Carlo Colaiacovo (Canada)
	Joni Pitkanen (Finland)
Forward	Scottie Upshall (Canada)
	Igor Grigorenko (Russia)
	Yuri Trubachev (Russia)

DIRECTORATE AWARDS

BEST GOALIE	Marc-Andre Fleury (Canada)
BEST DEFENCEMAN	Joni Pitkanen (Finland)
BEST FORWARD	Igor Grigorenko (Russia)

2004 WORLD JUNIOR CHAMPIONSHIPS

FINLAND, DECEMBER 26, 2003–JANUARY 6, 2004

FINAL PLACINGS

GOLD MEDAL	United States
SILVER MEDAL	Canada
BRONZE MEDAL	Finland
Fourth Place	Czech Republic
Fifth Place	Russia
Sixth Place	Slovakia
Seventh Place	Sweden
Eighth Place	Switzerland
Ninth Place	Austria*
Tenth Place	Ukraine**

* promoted from 2003
** demoted for 2005

ALL-STAR TEAM

Goal	Al Montoya (United States)
Defence	Dion Phaneuf (Canada)
	Sami Lepisto (Finland)
Forward	Jeff Carter (Canada)
	Valtteri Filppula (Finland)
	Zach Parise (United States)

DIRECTORATE AWARDS

BEST GOALIE	Al Montoya (United States)
BEST DEFENCEMAN	Sami Lepisto (Finland)
BEST FORWARD	Zach Parise (United States)

2005 WORLD JUNIOR CHAMPIONSHIP

UNITED STATES, December 25, 2004–January 4, 2005

FINAL PLACINGS

GOLD MEDAL	Canada
SILVER MEDAL	Russia
BRONZE MEDAL	Czech Republic
Fourth Place	United States
Fifth Place	Finland
Sixth Place	Sweden
Seventh Place	Slovakia
Eighth Place	Switzerland
Ninth Place	Germany*
Tenth Place	Belarus*

* promoted from 2004; demoted for 2006

ALL-STAR TEAM

Goal   Marek Schwarz (Czech Republic)

Defence   Dion Phaneuf (Canada)
            Gary Suter (United States)

Forward   Patrice Bergeron (Canada)
            Jeff Carter (Canada)
            Alexander Ovechkin (Russia)

DIRECTORATE AWARDS

BEST GOALIE	Marek Schwarz (Czech Republic)
BEST DEFENCEMAN	Dion Phaneuf (Canada)
BEST FORWARD	Alexander Ovechkin (Russia)

2006 WORLD JUNIOR CHAMPIONSHIP

CANADA, December 26, 2005–January 5, 2006

FINAL PLACINGS

GOLD MEDAL	Canada
SILVER MEDAL	Russia
BRONZE MEDAL	Finland
Fourth Place	United States
Fifth Place	Sweden
Sixth Place	Czech Republic
Seventh Place	Switzerland
Eighth Place	Slovakia
Ninth Place	Latvia*
Tenth Place	Norway*

* promoted from 2005; demoted for 2007

ALL-STAR TEAM

Goal	Tuukka Rask (Finland)
Defence	Luc Bourdon (Canada) Jack Johnson (United States)
Forward	Steve Downie (Canada) Evgeni Malkin (Russia) Lauri Tukonen (Finland)

DIRECTORATE AWARDS

BEST GOALIE	Tuukka Rask (Finland)
BEST DEFENCEMAN	Marc Staal (Canada)
BEST FORWARD	Evgeni Malkin (Russia)

2007 WORLD JUNIOR CHAMPIONSHIP

SWEDEN, December 26, 2006–January 5, 2007

FINAL PLACINGS

GOLD MEDAL	Canada
SILVER MEDAL	Russia
BRONZE MEDAL	United States
Fourth Place	Sweden
Fifth Place	Czech Republic
Sixth Place	Finland
Seventh Place	Switzerland
Eighth Place	Slovakia
Ninth Place	Germany
Tenth Place	Belarus

ALL-STAR TEAM
Goal	Carey Price (Canada)
Defence	Kristopher Letang (Canada)
	Erik Johnson (United States)
Forward	Jonathan Toews (Canada)
	Alexei Cherepanov (Russia)
	Pat Kane (United States)

DIRECTORATE AWARDS
BEST GOALIE	Carey Price (Canada)
BEST DEFENCEMAN	Erik Johnson (United States)
BEST FORWARD	Alexi Cherepanov (Russia)
TOURNAMENT MVP	Carey Price (Canada)

WORLD WOMEN'S CHAMPIONSHIPS RESULTS, 1990–2007

1990 World Women's Championships

CANADA, March 19–25, 1990

FINAL PLACINGS

GOLD MEDAL	Canada
SILVER MEDAL	United States
BRONZE MEDAL	Finland
Fourth Place	Sweden
Fifth Place	Switzerland
Sixth Place	Norway
Seventh Place	Germany
Eighth Place	Japan

1992 World Women's Championships

FINLAND, April 20–26, 1992

FINAL PLACINGS

GOLD MEDAL	Canada
SILVER MEDAL	United States
BRONZE MEDAL	Finland
Fourth Place	Sweden
Fifth Place	China
Sixth Place	Norway
Seventh Place	Denmark
Eighth Place	Switzerland

DIRECTORATE AWARDS

BEST GOALIE	Annica Ahlen (Sweden)
BEST DEFENCEMAN	Geraldine Heaney (Canada)
BEST FORWARD	Cammi Granato (United States)

1994 World Women's Championships

UNITED STATES, April 11–17, 1994

FINAL PLACINGS

GOLD MEDAL	Canada
SILVER MEDAL	United States
BRONZE MEDAL	Finland
Fourth Place	China
Fifth Place	Sweden
Sixth Place	Norway
Seventh Place	Switzerland
Eighth Place	Germany

DIRECTORATE AWARDS

BEST GOALIE	Erin Whitten (United States)
BEST DEFENCEMAN	Geraldine Heaney (Canada)
BEST FORWARD	Riikka Nieminen (Finland)

1997 World Women's Championships

CANADA, March 31–April 6, 1997

FINAL PLACINGS

GOLD MEDAL	Canada
SILVER MEDAL	United States
BRONZE MEDAL	Finland
Fourth Place	China
Fifth Place	Sweden
Sixth Place	Russia

| Seventh Place | Switzerland |
| Eighth Place | Norway |

DIRECTORATE AWARDS
None awarded

1999 World Women's Championships

FINLAND, March 8–14, 1999

FINAL PLACINGS

GOLD MEDAL	Canada
SILVER MEDAL	United States
BRONZE MEDAL	Finland
Fourth Place	Sweden
Fifth Place	China
Sixth Place	Russia
Seventh Place	Germany
Eighth Place	Switzerland

DIRECTORATE AWARDS

BEST GOALIE	Sami Jo Small (Canada)
BEST DEFENCEMAN	Kirsi Hanninen (Finland)
BEST FORWARD	Jenny Schmidgall (United States)

2000 World Women's Championships

CANADA, April 3–9, 2000

FINAL PLACINGS

GOLD MEDAL	Canada
SILVER MEDAL	United States
BRONZE MEDAL	Finland
Fourth Place	Sweden
Fifth Place	Russia
Sixth Place	China

| Seventh Place | Germany |
| Eighth Place | Japan |

DIRECTORATE AWARDS

BEST GOALIE	Sami Jo Small (Canada)
BEST DEFENCEMAN	Angela Ruggiero (United States)
BEST FORWARD	Katja Riipi (Finland)

2001 World Women's Championships

UNITED STATES, April 2–8, 2001

FINAL PLACINGS

GOLD MEDAL	Canada
SILVER MEDAL	United States
BRONZE MEDAL	Russia
Fourth Place	Finland
Fifth Place	Sweden
Sixth Place	Germany
Seventh Place	China
Eighth Place	Kazakhstan

DIRECTORATE AWARDS

BEST GOALIE	Kim St. Pierre (Canada)
BEST DEFENCEMAN	Karyn Bye (United States)
BEST FORWARD	Jennifer Botterill (Canada)
MVP	Jennifer Botterill (Canada)

2003 World Women's Championships

CHINA, April 3–9, 2003

CANCELLED DUE TO SARS OUTBREAK

2004 World Women's Championships

CANADA, March 30–April 6, 2004

FINAL PLACINGS

GOLD MEDAL	Canada
SILVER MEDAL	United States
BRONZE MEDAL	Finland
Fourth Place	Sweden
Fifth Place	Russia
Sixth Place	Germany
Seventh Place	China
Eighth Place	Switzerland
Ninth Place	Japan

DIRECTORATE AWARDS

BEST GOALIE	Kim St. Pierre (Canada)
BEST DEFENCEMAN	Angela Ruggiero (United States)
BEST FORWARD	Jayna Hefford (Canada)
MVP	Jennifer Botterill (Canada)

ALL-STAR TEAM

Goal	Pam Dreyer (United States)
Defence	Gunilla Andersson (Sweden), Angela Ruggiero (United States)
Forward	Jayna Hefford (Canada), Jennifer Botterill (Canada), Natalie Darwitz (United States)

2005 World Women's Championships

SWEDEN, April 2–9, 2005

FINAL PLACINGS

GOLD MEDAL	United States
SILVER MEDAL	Canada
BRONZE MEDAL	Sweden

Fourth Place	Finland
Fifth Place	Germany
Sixth Place	China
Seventh Place	Kazakhstan
Eighth Place	Russia

DIRECTORATE AWARDS

BEST GOALIE	Chanda Gunn (United States)
BEST DEFENCEMAN	Angela Ruggiero (United States)
BEST FORWARD	Jayna Hefford (Canada)
MVP	Krissy Wendell (United States)

ALL-STAR TEAM

Goalie	Natalya Turnova (Kazakhstan)
Defence	Cheryl Pounder (Canada), Angela Ruggiero (United States)
Forward	Hayley Wickenheiser (Canada), Maria Rooth (Sweden), Krissy Wendell (United States)

NATIONAL WOMEN'S HOCKEY LEAGUE

ALL-TIME STANDINGS

1999–2000
Eastern Division

	GP	W	L	T	GF	GA	P
Sainte Julie Pantheres	35	20	8	7	109	68	47
Montreal Wingstar	35	18	7	10	116	62	46
Ottawa Raiders	35	9	20	6	61	109	24
Laval Le Mistral	35	7	23	5	78	177	19

Western Division

	GP	W	L	T	GF	GA	P
Beatrice Aeros	40	35	3	2	217	37	72
Brampton Thunder	40	29	5	6	208	64	64
Mississauga Chiefs	40	21	13	6	133	79	48
Clearnet Lightning	40	4	33	3	44	249	11
Scarborough Sting	40	3	34	3	49	170	9

CHAMPIONSHIP FINALS
March 18   Sainte Julie Pantheres 2/Beatrice Aeros 2
March 19   Beatrice Aeros 1/Sainte Julie Pantheres 0
Beatrice wins championship 3–1 in points

2000–01
Eastern Division

	GP	W	L	T	GF	GA	P
Montreal Wingstar	40	30	6	4	163	63	64
Sainte Julie Pantheres	40	22	15	3	168	102	47
Ottawa Raiders	40	11	25	4	78	150	26
Laval Le Mistral	40	5	33	2	68	261	12

Western Division

Beatrice Aeros	40	35	2	3	222	46	73
Brampton Thunder	40	30	7	3	223	82	63
Mississauga Ice Bears	40	21	16	3	107	97	45
Toronto Sting	40	8	29	3	82	168	19
Clearnet Lightning	40	5	34	1	77	219	11
Vancouver Griffins	18	14	4	0	91	43	28

CHAMPIONSHIP FINALS

Beatrice Aeros 2/Sainte Julie Pantheres 2
Beatrice Aeros 8/Sainte Julie Pantheres 1
Beatrice wins championship 3–1 in points

2001–2002

Eastern Division

	GP	W	L	T	GF	GA	P
Ottawa Raiders	30	14	10	6	71	72	34
Montreal Wingstar	30	11	14	5	66	78	27
Le Cheyenne de la Metropol	30	11	15	4	73	85	26

Western Division

	G	W	L	T	OTL	GF	GA	PTS
Beatrice Aeros	30	23	2	5		149	39	51
Mississauga Ice Bears	30	12	10	8		82	81	32
Brampton Thunder	30	8	14	8		73	97	24
Telus Lightning	30	4	18	8		59	120	16

Pacific Division

Vancouver Griffins	31	27	4	0		84	14	54

CHAMPIONSHIP FINALS

Beatrice Aeros 3/Brampton Thunder 2 (OT)

2002–03
Eastern Division

	GP	W	L	T	OTL	GF	GA	P
Montreal Wingstar	36	18	15	3	0	83	81	39
Ottawa Raiders	36	13	20	1	2	96	122	29
Quebec Avalanche	36	10	20	5	1	87	120	26

Central Division

	GP	W	L	T	OTL	GF	GA	P
Beatrice Aeros	36	32	3	1	0	201	54	65
Brampton Thunder	36	27	9	0	0	152	71	54
Mississauga Ice Bears	36	19	13	3	1	122	111	42
Telus Lightning	36	0	34	1	1	54	236	2

Western Division

	GP	W	L	T	OTL	GF	GA	P
Calgary X-Treme	24	23	1	0	0	144	37	46
Vancouver Griffins	24	10	13	0	1	82	92	21
Edmonton Chimos	24	3	20	0	1	35	132	7

CHAMPIONSHIP FINALS
Calgary X-Treme 3/Beatrice Aeros 0

2003–04
Eastern Division

	G	W	L	T	OTL	GF	GA	PTS
Montreal Axion	36	20	10	5	1	113	84	46
Ottawa Raiders	36	9	23	4	0	85	144	22
Quebec Avalanche	36	4	28	2	2	65	163	12

Central Division

	G	W	L	T	OTL	GF	GA	PTS
Toronto Aeros	36	33	2	1	0	197	42	67
Brampton Thunder	36	28	6	2	0	190	72	58
Oakville Ice	36	17	17	2	0	118	99	36
Telus Lightning	36	8	28	0	0	66	224	16

Western Division

Calgary X-Treme	12	11	1	0	0	64	9	22
Edmonton Chimos	12	1	11	0	0	9	64	2

CHAMPIONSHIP FINALS

Calgary X-Treme 5/Brampton Thunder 4 (OT/SO)

2004–05

Eastern Division

	G	W	L	T	OTL	GF	GA	PTS
Montreal Axion	36	24	9	2	1	140	85	51
Ottawa Raiders	36	14	19	2	1	101	128	31
Quebec Avalanche	36	5	25	4	2	53	132	16

Central Division

	G	W	L	T	OTL	GF	GA	PTS
Brampton Thunder	36	30	3	2	1	165	70	63
Toronto Aeros	36	24	6	4	2	142	68	54
Oakville Ice	36	13	15	6	2	97	99	34
Telus Lightning	36	4	28	4	0	72	189	12

CHAMPIONSHIP FINALS

Toronto Aeros 5/Montreal Axion 4 (OT)

2005–06

Eastern Division

	G	W	L	T	OTL	GF	GA	PTS
Ottawa Raiders	36	21	8	4	3	122	77	49
Montreal Axion	36	14	17	3	2	100	122	33
Quebec Avalanche	36	4	28	2	2	58	135	12

Central Division

	G	W	L	T	OTL	GF	GA	PTS
Durham Lightning	36	23	6	5	2	107	74	53
Brampton Thunder	36	19	12	5	0	113	97	43
Oakville Ice	36	20	14	1	1	118	100	42
Toronto Aeros	36	13	17	4	2	114	127	32

CHAMPIONSHIP FINALS
April 15   Montreal 1/Brampton 0

2006–07

	G	W	L	T	OTL	GF	GA	PTS
Etobicoke Dolphins	20	15	1	2	2	87	66	64
Mississauga Aeros	21	15	5	0	1	107	51	31
Brampton Thunder	16	8	8	0	0	71	66	16
Oakville Ice	17	6	8	1	2	40	53	15
Montreal Axion	13	6	6	0	0	66	56	13
Quebec Avalanche	12	2	8	2	0	41	91	6
Ottawa Raiders	11	2	8	0	0	25	54	5

CHAMPIONSHIP FINALS
April 14   Brampton 4/Montreal 0

note: at the conclusion of the season, the NWHL suspended operations for the
   2007-08 year